Kiss Kiss Bang! Bang!

The Unofficial *James Bond* Film Companion

Alan Barnes & Marcus Hearn

The Overlook Press
Woodstock · New York

First published in the United States in 1998 by
The Overlook Press, Peter Mayer Publishers, Inc.
Lewis Hollow Road,
Woodstock, New York 12498

Library of Congress Cataloging-in-Publications Data

Barnes, Alan.
Kiss, kiss, bang, bang: the secret history of James Bond / Alan Barnes and Marcus Hearn.
p. cm.
Includes bibliographical references and index.
1. James Bond films–History and Criticism. I. Hearn, Marcus. II. Title.
PN1995.9.J3B37   1998   791.43'651–dc21   98-10937

ISBN 087951-874-X

FIRST EDITION

9 8 7 6 5 4 3 2 1

Printed and bound in Great Britain by
Butler & Tanner Ltd, Frome and London

Prologue: Everything or nothing

Initially, few shared Ian Fleming's conviction that James Bond could make a credible transition from the printed page.

Fleming courted many offers during the Fifties, but few were suggested by those with the temerity – or good fortune – to close a deal. Impressed by a proof copy of *Live and Let Die*, in January 1953 Sir Alexander Korda approached Fleming about adapting Bond for the cinema. Greatly enthused, Fleming framed his next novel, *Moonraker*, with a cinematic eye. Unfortunately, Korda failed to follow through.

In May 1954, Russian-born actor/director/producer Gregory Ratoff purchased a six-month option to film *Casino Royale*. He took the property to CBS Television in the United States, and the network broadcast a creaking adaptation of the story on Thursday 21 October 1954. The live production featured Barry Nelson as American agent 'Jimmy' Bond and Peter Lorre as Le Chiffre. American trade paper *Variety* reviewed the show in its 27 October issue: 'Last week's cloak-and-daggery ... drew laughs along the course by running with all legs off the ground.' Fleming could take solace from the $1,000 he received from CBS.

In March 1955 Ratoff purchased the full rights to *Casino Royale* from Fleming for $6,000. Fleming treated himself to a Ford Thunderbird with the money. The following year, Fleming wrote a screenplay for *Moonraker* when an indecisive Rank were toying with the idea of filming the novel. Nothing came of it.

In 1958, Fleming's friend Ivar Bryce introduced him to a young Irish film-maker called Kevin McClory. Bryce had financed *The Boy and the Bridge*, a modest directorial debut for McClory, who also co-wrote and produced the picture. 'Fleming saw a rough cut and liked it,' recalled McClory in 1996. 'At the time he was frustrated that the Bond novels had not yet been made into films.'

From 1959 to 1960 McClory, Fleming and Jack Whittingham, together with Ivar Bryce and another of Fleming's friends Ernest Cuneo, pooled their talents to prepare a number of James Bond treatments on the broad understanding that McClory would direct the resulting picture. The relationship between McClory and Fleming was occasionally strained: 'He was upper class and Eton-educated, and I was an uneducated Irishman, despite my film experience; we clashed a lot.'

The 1 October 1959 edition of British trade paper *Kinematograph Weekly* reported what seemed to be a concrete development from the collaboration. It was reported that McClory had begun pre-production on an underwater adventure with the working title *James Bond of the Secret Service*. 'It will be shot in colour and in a wide-screen process – either Todd-AO or Technirama,' claimed the magazine. 'Manoeuvring such large cameras under water is a technical problem in itself and technicians were exploring the snags in Uxbridge baths last week, while other experts were testing suitable diving spots off the south coast, where the water is clear, the bottom is sandy and the currents are not too strong ... Believing that a producer must stay with his team, McClory is taking lessons in the use of aqualung equipment.'

A proposed shooting date of February 1960 came and went. McClory found it impossible to find the finance he needed to take the film to the Bahamas and the project was left to languish. Fleming recycled a number of the ideas and situations that had been devised during discussions with McClory and Whittingham (notably the Special Executive for Terrorism Revenge and Extortion organisation: SPECTRE) for his next 007 novel *Thunderball*. In 1961, Whittingham read the serialisation of *Thunderball* in *Life* magazine and, upon identifying a number of familiar elements, contacted McClory. There ensued a lengthy legal action over alleged copyright infringement. The terms of its resolution in 1963 would have a profound effect.

A more immediately fruitful proposition was already taking shape. Harry Saltzman was born in New Brunswick, Canada, in 1915, and subsequently made his home in New York. Saltzman displayed an entrepreneurial spirit from an early age, and enjoyed a meteoric rise in showbusiness: at various points he managed a Parisian travelling circus, became a television producer, bought into the Royal Court Theatre and co-founded influential film production company Woodfall. Saltzman and Ian Fleming shared a mutual London solicitor, Brian Lewis, who helped organise a meeting between the two men late in 1960. Saltzman purchased an option, but found it difficult to stimulate any interest in 007. His agreed six months had almost expired when, in May 1961, writer Wolf Mankowitz suggested he meet a man with a mutual aim: producer Albert Broccoli.

Albert 'Cubby' Broccoli, born in New York in 1909, had been a coffin manufacturer and cosmetics salesman before finding work as a tea boy at Twentieth Century-Fox. Under the patronage of Howard Hughes, Broccoli became assistant director on *The Outlaw* (1943) and, after the war, worked at the influential Famous Artists Agency run by Charles Feldman. Together with Irving Allen, Broccoli founded British production company Warwick Films and went on to make 20 largely undistinguished, albeit largely profitable, films between 1952 and 1960. The first of these, *The Red Beret,* was directed by Terence Young and co-scripted by Richard Maibaum – both key figures in the later establishment of the Bond films. Maibaum, like Broccoli, was born in New York in 1909, and boasted considerable Broadway and Hollywood experience. He first read the Bond novels in 1958 when Broccoli asked him to consider scripting a proposed

Warwick adaptation.

Warwick disintegrated in 1960, the same year that Saltzman split from his Woodfall co-directors John Osborne and Tony Richardson. Although initially wary, Broccoli and Saltzman agreed to become 50/50 partners in an attempt to secure backing for a Bond film in the little time remaining on Saltzman's option. They soon formalised their relationship: Saltzman's Canadian citizenship allowed them to set up their new company Danjaq (the title was an amalgam of their wives' names: Dana Broccoli and Jacqueline Saltzman) in Switzerland. They christened their British-based operation Eon Productions. The name stood for Everything Or Nothing.

Talks with Columbia broke down when the distributor refused to pledge more than $400,000 towards any prospective production. Broccoli next approached Arthur Krim, the chairman of United Artists. Krim, in turn, suggested that Broccoli contact fellow UA executive David Picker, and a meeting was arranged. Broccoli and Saltzman flew to UA's headquarters at 729 Seventh Avenue, New York. On 20 June 1961, UA's board of directors assembled to hear the pitch. Within 40 minutes, Krim shook hands with Broccoli and Saltzman on a six-picture deal. Unprecedented success, and indelible influence, were closer than either men could have imagined.

Introduction

'Everyone wants to be a superman, to make love to anything that walks, and call on the army, navy and air force if he gets into trouble. With a Bond movie, the guy in the audience pays his 3s 6d and buys a dream.'
James Bond film producer Harry Saltzman

It seems a staggering coincidence that the first James Bond film, *Dr. No*, was unleashed upon the British public in the very same week as both The Beatles' debut 45 *Love Me Do* and snoot-cocking television revue *That Was the Week That Was*. All three have come to be recognised as watersheds in their respective media; all three would be retrospectively championed as somehow anti-establishment; all three are held to have heralded the beginning of a new epoch, to have encapsulated the shiny new freedoms of the Sixties. If we must pinpoint the

dawning of the modern age, then 5 October 1962 seems as good a date as any. Strange that James Bond, secret agent, is now so inextricably linked to Sixties style, for Bond was a product of the briefly flowering 'new Elizabethan age' before. Ian Fleming's first Bond novel, *Casino Royale*, appeared in 1953, the year of a young Queen's coronation; the last of the 12, *The Man With the Golden Gun*, was published posthumously in 1965, the year of Churchill's funeral, an event 'self-consciously recognised as being a requiem for Britain as a great power' [1]. It is an irony bordering on the perverse that Bond, James Bond – a conservative, reactionary sadist forged in the golden typewriter of another – should become an icon of classlessness, sophistication and voguish, easy sex.

As a literary figure, James Bond died with his creator, a creator who saw fit to pen his monster's own Times obituary [2]. But another James Bond is still very much alive – a smirking, punning rogue male who has outlived Kruschev and Kennedy, an ever-ready libido on legs with a Walther PPK perma-cocked and hot for action. Perhaps James Bond is the only fictional character of the 20th century to have acquired the aura of myth. This, we argue, owes everything to his incarnation on the cinema screen, and little to the novels of Fleming; like Sherlock Holmes, he might be identified by his silhouette alone anywhere in the developed world (even by his preferences and habits), but ask for a recap of, say, his specific adventures on the printed page and one will more often than not meet only blank looks.

This, then, is a book about the James Bond films – and unashamedly so, for Fleming is, perhaps sadly, tangential to the figure appearing at multiplexes this winter in *Tomorrow Never Dies*, the latest in 35 years of screen escapades. Bond is our property now – he fits in the dreams and nightmares of our post-atomic age every bit as snugly as he donned the mantle of crusading Cold Warrior, as his gadgets bestowed upon us all the democracy of mass production, as his travelogue adventures opened up a world suddenly available via cheap air flight. We seek to reclaim Bond from the humourless Fleming pedants who view Bond as fixed, immutable, an unalterable period antiquity. Bond has become 'a moving sign of the times' [3], and there are pleasures aplenty to be found in his ongoing reincarnation, from louche Sixties mannequin via clubbable Seventies Cinzano Man through to the post-

post-modern (representation of today. We value all these James Bonds equally, not simply those which appear to take us, as viewers, seriously.

To this end, our history of the development of James Bond as pop icon is augmented by dossiers which aspire to give an even-handed assessment of each and every film in turn. We assess from scratch their individual merits, broken down into categories, intending to give each film a percentage score reflecting its success as a James Bond film (not, we stress, as a rounded work of inverted-commas 'art'). We don't propose to definitively settle that great last-orders argument, 'So, who was the best James Bond?' [4], but we do hope to nominate the greatest ever James Bond film.

The Bond films are nothing if not formula pictures; we have chosen ten key elements of that formula to base each film's assessment on. Each element is given a mark out of ten. They are: **Teaser** (the Bond films are renowned for their OTT pre-credits sequences, often mini-movies in themselves); **Titles** (likewise, their heavily symbolic, eroticised title sequences are much noted); **Bonkers plot** (we look for out-of-the-ordinary, epic ideas, and discuss their overall coherence); **Locations** (the so-called 'Fleming Sweep' in passport stamps); **Gadgets** (we note those devices given Bond by Q, like the gifts granted Greek heroes by their gods); **Girls** (we look for fantasy figures with character, not fantastic figures alone); **Villains** (those great oppositional others, the anti-Bonds, nemeses worthy of Our Man); **Fights, chases, explosions** (we seek all-out fuck-me spectacle, not solely vicarious thrills); **Dialogue and double entendres**; and **Bond** (what we learn of him, what he is, how our icon is expressed). To acknowledge both those elements which don't fit happily into these strict categories, and reflect the notion that any one film may be greater or lesser than the sum of its parts, up to ten plus/minus points may then be added/subtracted from each film's overall score, giving a final (fixed) percentage.

Neither of us was alive on 5 October 1962, but we've since bought the videos, the John Barry soundtrack LPs, the Corgi Lotus Esprits and DB5s. We bought the dream, and we buy it still.

Alan Barnes and Marcus Hearn
London, September 1997

[1] David Cannadine in *Encounter*, 1979 [CHECK].
[2] in *You Only Live Twice*, Jonathan Cape, 1964.
[3] Tony Bennett and Janet Woollacott, Bond and Beyond, Macmillan Education, 1987.
[4] Connery, obviously.

Albert Broccoli, pictured in August 1984 during production of A View To A Kill

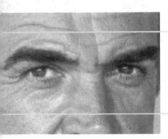

An Elizabethan gangster: *Dr. No*

1962: on a small Caribbean island, a despotic ideologue with Communist sympathies holds the West to ransom via a terrifying plot involving space-age rockets. The parallels between the Cuban missile crisis (which commenced on 22 October) and the events of the first Eon-produced James Bond picture, *Dr. No* (released exactly two weeks earlier), were, of course, quite coincidental – but nevertheless indicated the degree to which Bond's screen career would continue to tap the *Zeitgeist*.

Dr. No's origins, both as novel and film, lay in *James Gunn – Secret Agent*, an unproduced 28-page teleplay prepared by Ian Fleming in the summer of 1956 for would-be film impresario Henry Morgenthau III, a New Yorker whose association with a member of the Jamaican government had begat a desire to see the island develop a film and television industry. Morgenthau hooked up with Jamaican emigré Fleming, who pitched him *Gunn*, a thinly veiled version of Bond given American descent, in a bid to attract US television executives to the project. The half-hour film would have pitted Commander Gunn against Doctor No, a Sino-German spy in the Fu Manchu mould who sought to destabilise a Western rocket station in the Caribbean; Gunn would be assisted by Pearl, a half-Oriental swimming champion. Fleming suggested a local calypso for the theme tune that would introduce both the pilot and its follow-on series. It wasn't to be. Morgenthau's ambitious vehicle had reportedly foundered by the end of the year.

Fleming cannibalised James Gunn (aka Commander Jamaica) wholesale for the Bond novel he began early in 1957. *Dr No* would, quite literally, resurrect the character he'd left for dead, *Final Problem*-style, at the conclusion of the preceding *From Russia With Love*. Shortly after its 1958 publication, a small independent sniffed around the film rights, but was waylaid by the giant CBS corporation, whose president Hubell Robinson expressed a desire to pursue Bond as a 13-part TV series. Fleming exhumed the James Gunn script, duly Bondified, for Robinson's consideration; this, too, would sink after no small effort on Fleming's part. But Bond – and *Dr No* – had attracted attention elsewhere . . .

The arrival of the James Bond film series proper merited little more than an inch of copy in the trade press of 1961. 'Television comedian Arthur Haynes has been signed by producer Harry Saltzman to make a comedy called *The Good Samaritan*,' reported the 20 July issue of *Kinematograph Weekly*. 'If it comes off it'll be Haynes' first picture. Early October is envisaged as the starting date . . .' Haynes' big screen ambitions would, however, be delayed: 'In the meantime,' the report

Ian Fleming (right) originally disapproved of Sean Connery's casting as 007, but warmed to the actor, and his characterisation, throughout the filming of Dr. No, From Russia with Love and Goldfinger. Here the two meet at Pinewood Studios early in 1962

continued, 'Saltzman's project with Albert Broccoli to film the Ian Fleming spy-thriller books is maturing nicely. They have clinched a deal with United Artists for 100 per cent financial backing and distribution of seven stories [sic] which will be filmed here and on foreign locations.'

Saltman and Broccoli had already commissioned Richard Maibaum to adapt *Thunderball* as the first film of the UA deal. It wasn't until Maibaum's screenplay was complete that the ongoing legal rumblings over the properrty prompted the producers to opt for *Dr. No* instead. The 5 October edition of *Kinematograph Weekly* announced that filming on the first James Bond movie would not take place until early 1962. 'Reason: no James Bond has

yet materialised. After a national newspaper had run a contest to find a new face to play the character created by thriller writer Ian Fleming, six finalists were chosen out of more than 1,000 entries.' The six were screen-tested at Twickenham Studios, one man emerging as the most promising: London model Peter Anthony. 'He's often seen these days in tobacco adverts,' claimed *Kinematograph Weekly*, 'laying flat on his back, a straw hat pushed over his eyes, smoking a cigarette.' Anthony was ultimately rejected, but consoled with the offer of a role in the first film.

Meanwhile, Peter Hunt was editing RAF comedy *On the Fiddle* for Polish producer Benjamin Fisz, an associate of Harry Saltzman. 'We were all having dinner at the

Polish club in London when Harry came in and joined us with his wife and various people and announced that he was going to make a James Bond film and that they had been testing people. It was Ben Fisz who turned to me and said "What about that Sean Connery – don't you think he might make a good James Bond?"' Hunt loaned Saltzman two reels from *On the Fiddle*, in which Connery played racketeering recruit Pedlar Pascoe. In America, Albert Broccoli had already noted Connery's performance as Irishman Michael McBride in the Walt Disney musical *Darby O'Gill and the Little People* (1959).

Thomas Sean Connery was born on 25 August 1930, in the Fountainbridge district of Edinburgh. The first of two sons born to Joseph and Euphamia, he endured relative poverty. 'In those days it was never a question of one's ambitions,' he recalled. 'It was the struggle of going day to day that counted.' Leaving school without qualifications, Connery became a full-time milkman in 1943, and joined the Navy four years later. (While serving, he gained two tattoos on his right forearm: 'Mum and Dad' and 'Scotland Forever'.) Medically discharged in 1949, Connery took up a series of labouring jobs before his entry to the 1952 'Mr Universe' contest indirectly led to a role in a touring production of *South Pacific*. When the tour ended 18 months later, Connery moved to London and pursued his ambition to become an actor with minor roles in repertory theatre and extra work in television series such as *Dixon of Dock Green*. The BBC's production of Rod Serling's play *Requiem for a Heavyweight* offered Connery his greatest opportunity to date when star Jack Palance pulled out shortly before rehearsals began. Acting on the suggestion of leading lady Jacqueline Hill, director Alvin Rakoff cast Connery

as boxer Mountain McClintock; *Requiem for a Heavyweight,* performed and broadcast on Sunday 31 March 1957, brought him to the attention of Twentieth Century-Fox, who put him under contract. Although Fox ultimately did little for Connery's career, acclaimed television roles continued to come his way. Notable productions included *Anna Christie* (1957), *The Square Ring* (1959) and *Anna Karenina* (1961). Connery's film career in the late Fifties was less distinguished; his first film, *No Road Back* (1953), cast him as a criminal gang-member in a small role typical of the less cerebral characters he would be offered away from his television work. In the following year's *Hell Drivers* he would play a tough truck driver, and in the same year's *Time Lock* he wouldn't even receive an on-screen credit for his role as '2nd Welder'. *Action of the Tiger*, also released in 1957, was helmed by future Bond director Terence Young. Connery's growing reputation as a television actor was reflected in his higher billing following *Another Time, Another Place*, a 1957-produced film in which Lana Turner requested Connery as her co-star. *Tarzan's Greatest Adventure* (1959), *The Frightened City* (1961) and *On the Fiddle* (1961) saw him gradually rise to the top of the credit roller. A cameo as Private Flanagan in *The Longest Day* saw Connery briefly relegated to unaccredited artiste, but he was amongst distinguished company.

The weeks following *The Longest Day*'s 25 September premiere were crucial to Connery. In October, he was invited to attend the first of several interviews at Eon's South Audley Street office in Mayfair, London. Despite resistance from United Artists (Broccoli cabled Saltzman with 'New York did not care for Connery. Stop. Feels we can do better. Stop') Connery was offered a multi-picture contract later that month. The casting of James Bond 007 was first announced by *The Daily Cinema* on 3 November 1961. Eon had already dismissed later Bulldog Drummond star Richard Johnson and future Saint Roger Moore; Patrick McGoohan had reportedly been offered the role, but had baulked at the licentious and violent behaviour indulged in by the character. Albert Broccoli had originally favoured Cary Grant (who had been best man at his wedding to Dana in 1959) for the role of Bond, but was won over by the macho Connery's body language. 'I wanted a ballsy guy,' he later said. 'Put a bit of veneer over that tough Scottish hide and you've got Fleming's Bond instead of all the mincing poofs we had applying for the job.' Saltzman, however, had a clearer rationale for Connery's casting: 'I liked the way he moved,' he told the BBC's Alan Whicker in 1967. 'There's only one other actor who moves as well as he does, and that's Albert Finney. They move like cats... for a big man to be light on his feet is most unusual.' The Finney comparison is illuminating, as is another remark in the same interview. 'The Bonds came out at the right time,' he claimed. 'The kitchen sink realistic pictures were just about over.' Having produced Finney in *Saturday Night and Sunday Morning* (and had a hand in the feature version of *Look Back in Anger*), Saltzman was in a position to observe at first hand the sudden rise to prominence of the Angry Young Man as popular icon, the new face of a certain brash modernity and suddenly-monied meritocracy – anathema to Fleming's clubbable, rakish, officer élite Commander Bond. Connery's Bond would continue from where these classless, rootless (anti-) heroes left off: Joe Lampton with a Walther PPK, Arthur Seaton wrapped up in the Union Jack, the never-quite-attainable dream of a million Billy Liars

stuck on provincial platforms watching the Julie Christies and Honey Ryders pass them by.

In *The Sunday Express* on 31 December 1961, Susan Barnes quizzed Connery on his forthcoming role. 'Like some other people in the northern countries James Bond is very much for breaking the rules,' said the actor, armed with a vodka and a cigarette. 'He enjoys freedom that the normal person doesn't get. He likes to eat. He likes to drink. He likes his girls. He is rather cruel, sadistic . . . I have no compunction at all admitting that I like to eat. I like to drink. I like girls.' Following a lengthy discourse over violence towards women and body language, a perturbed Ms Barnes beat a 'rapid retreat' from the St John's Wood bachelor pad.

'It was a bit of a joke around town that I was chosen for Bond,' revealed Connery in 1974. 'The character is not really me, after all. I talked a lot to the author of the Bond novels, Ian Fleming, and to the director, Terence Young, about the physical aspect, and also about my accent. I'd always had a terrible fight to get work in Britain on account of my Edinburgh accent . . . I had worked with Terence Young before, on location in Spain for *Action of the Tiger* [1957], which was a pretty rotten film, but we got along well.'

Terence Young had been selected to direct *Dr. No* only after Bryan Forbes, Guy Green and Guy Hamilton had passed on the opportunity. Born in Shanghai in 1915, Young had served in the Irish Guards Armoured Division during the war, and pursued a career as a director of relatively undistinguished British films from the late Forties onwards. Among these was *The Red Beret* (1953), a Warwick production co-written by Richard Maibaum (a scene in which begat the hat-tossing sequence which, as a way of signifying the hero's arrival in Moneypenny's office, would become a Bond *leitmotif*). Other than a past association with Albert Broccoli, Young also boasted a knowledge of, and enthusiasm for, Ian Fleming's work in his favour. Indeed, Young's wartime experience and refined taste would earn him a reputation as Bond personified over the coming years. One of Young's first tasks was to spruce up Connery's image in line with the elegantly coutured gentleman spy of the novels: 'I went to all his fittings for his clothes and I took him to my shirt-makers in Paris and also in London. And I must say, I think Sean was much better dressed in my three pictures than in any others.' Despite Eon's earlier offer, Peter Anthony failed to appear in *Dr. No*. Sean Connery, however, earned his place in cinema history when James Bond was finally unveiled through a haze of cigarette smoke at a casino roulette wheel. It was, as Terence Young later observed, 'One hell of a good introduction.'

By year end, 1961, Saltzman and Broccoli had both their director and now, at last, a star. All that remained to be finalised was the script, still being reworked as *Dr. No* prepared to go into full production. 'I [originally] wrote *Dr. No* and [Richard] Maibaum doctored it,' remembered Wolf Mankowitz, 'but I fell out with the boys [Saltzman and Broccoli] and removed my credit. I had a deal to do the rest of the things, but I didn't want to go on working with them and they paid me out on the whole thing – after a bit of argy-bargy – and that was the end of that. I was offered a percentage of Eon if I would go on acting as principal writer and script editor of any other Bond films . . . but working on with them just seemed entrapment.' Dated 12 December, Richard Maibaum

and Wolf Mankowitz's 145-page fourth draft screenplay affords a tantalising insight into the film as it might have been. In adapting the novel, the screenwriters elect to massively compress its timescale; some six weeks elapse during the course of Fleming's original, but here the story spans just four days and nights. To introduce Bond, Maibaum and Mankowitz concoct the now-famous nightclub sequence featuring Sylvia Trench ('Trenchard' in this draft). The precise details of Bond's revelation are intact at this early stage: at the *chemin-de-fer* table, Bond 'has his back to the camera' and remains unrevealed until he lights a cigarette after delivering the line, 'Bond . . . James Bond.' According to this script, again as per Fleming, Bond has 'Dark, rather cruel good looks and a faint scar down one cheek . . .'

The first Bond/M scene is much as the original, the only key difference being that Fleming would have M only vaguely concerned about the disappearance of Strangways, believing that he and secretary Trueblood have eloped. The screenwriters instead have M give away the entire thrust of Doctor No's secret plan – the 'toppling' of American rockets – in his briefing of Bond; the novel doesn't reveal this until some four-fifths of the way through! (One wonders why, given that the filmic No is already causing the spacecraft to go AWOL, there is no effort made to depict such dramatic scenes at the outset.) CIA man Felix Leiter – a semi-regular character from *Casino Royale* – is not present in Fleming's *Dr No*; his drafting into the film is presumably intended as a sop to the American distributor. The bogus chauffeur who whisks Bond away from the airport is an invention of the screenwriters. The character of Professor Dent is another Maibaum/Mankowitz addition, too; he bears the lion's share of the villainy until

No himself appears in the film's third act.

Doctor No's base is glimpsed early on, where the shaken Professor Dent visits his employer. Unlike the final version, where the unseen No's voice threatens Dent in a sterile, high-vaulted chamber, here Dent is actually in the room with No: 'All we see of Dr. No is the edge of his desk . . .'

Following Bond's nocturnal encounter with a strategically placed tarantula – a five-inch poisonous tropical centipede in Fleming – the draft screenplay then cuts back to M's office, where Moneypenny brings M Bond's cable requesting a geiger counter. This is the only scene in the draft missing entirely from the final film. Honey Rider is no longer Fleming's broken-nosed Venus; the screenwriters give her a personal grudge to bear against No, whom she now believes to be responsible for the death of her father, a marine biologist.

Doctor No himself differs markedly between all three interpretations – novel, draft and finished film. In this draft, he is given pointed 'steel claws' – a legacy of his 'experiments in radiation' – more akin to Fleming's 'hooks' than the metallic gauntlets he sports in the film. Maibaum and Mankowitz's early No is unrelentingly vicious. After Bond taunts No by comparing him to Hitler-cum-Al Capone, No 'strikes downwards and obliquely right across Bond's chest and belly with the hook. The blood seeps through the material.' Bond – who is held down in a chair by No's guards at this point – raises his head and says quietly, 'Forgive the coarseness, Dr. No' – whereupon he 'spits full in Dr. No's face as the hook comes down and the guards club him simultaneously.' (As an appendix to this scene, the authors have noted: 'It is realised that this is not orthodox

Bondsmanship, but is included as the only really defiant gesture he can make under the circumstances . . . and he does apologise in advance.')

Fleming's novel climaxes with Bond forced to endure an 'assault course on death' for No's amusement; after crawling through umpteen tiny shafts – including one stuffed with tarantulas – he falls from a cliff, battles with a giant squid, and finally finishes No off by manouevring him beneath a colossal heap of bird dung with the aid of a crane. (Fleming had first become intrigued by 'guano' during a March 1956 visit to Inagua in the Bahamas.) Perhaps unsurprisingly, the screenwriters retain only a short scene of Bond in the lethal ducting, whereupon he escapes to wreck No's efforts to 'topple' another rocket by setting his nuclear reactor to critical. No dies in the reactor after a fistfight with Bond (and this, given No's pointed appendages, is considered differently in the draft, where 'Dr No is tearing and slashing with his claws. Bond's suit and headpiece are now in tatters and fall away, finally disclosing him'). Bond discovers Honey back in the furnished bedroom to which they were earlier assigned, 'sweeps Honey up into his arms' and carries her through to the boat: a very conventional ending, made a little less pat during filming. A later lost scene would give Honey her own ordeal . . .

'It is realised that this is not orthodox Bondsmanship'

Just days prior to the commencement of principal photography, Broccoli locked Young in a suite in the Dorchester with assistant Johanna Harwood, instructing them to give Maibaum's draft one final, last-minute polish. The script delivered on 8 January 1962 contained three versions of scene 135, the fundamental sequence in which Bond kills Dent. As written, Bond would cold-bloodedly murder the Professor after the latter had used up all his bullets ('His eyes are hard'). Probably fearing the censors of the Motion Picture Association of America (MPAA) – whose revised Production Code of 1956 insisted that 'crime shall never be presented in such a way as to throw sympathy with the crime as against law and justice . . . Revenge in modern times shall not be justified' – two alternatives were supplied. In one, Dent manages to loose off a single bullet at Bond, which 'smacks into the wall behind' – but, simultaneously, Bond fires 'that much faster, and just that more accurately.' In the other, Bond fires just as Dent is reaching for his gun. (It's uncertain, but likely that all three versions were shot; in the event, the intended original would remain extant – and is one of the most powerful scenes in the entire series. The MPAA's absurdly restrictive Code – founded around the relativistic and nonsensical principle that 'No picture shall be produced which will lower the moral standards of those who see it' – was in tatters by 1968. In his own small way, Bond maybe helped hasten its demise.)

The cameras finally rolled on *Dr. No* on Tuesday 16 January 1962. Location shooting in Jamaica came first, and casting for the actors used in these scenes was given priority. While censorship rules would never have allowed for as brazen an entrance as that described in the novel, Terence Young knew his leading lady would still have to possess an alluring figure. While in the office of Twentieth Century-Fox magnate Darryl F Zanuck, a picture of a woman with just such a figure caught his eye. The stunning actress, clinging to a wet shirt, was Swiss-born 25-year-old Ursula Andress. Zanuck assured

Young that he didn't intend to use her for anything and let him take the photograph back to London. 'I gave [the photograph] to Cubby and Harry and they liked it,' remembered Young. 'You couldn't not like it – she looked marvellous. We had lots of other pictures there. Harry and Cubby shared a big desk – every morning I used to go by their office on the way to my office and put Ursula's picture on the top.' In late 1961, some four weeks after Young first suggested Andress, Broccoli called Columbia's casting guru Max Arno and asked his opinion. Young remembered that Arno was clearly impressed: 'She came to see him and Max said "Look, I can't tell you if she can act or not, but my God she looks great." So Cubby said "That's it."' A deal was struck with Andress' agent – her air fare from Los Angeles to New York was paid and she was given an additional $1,000. 'I was to meet her at the airport,' said Young, 'and I had a ticket to take her to Jamaica and her return ticket to LA. I took one look at her and said 'Where's your luggage?' and we took her to Jamaica.' Andress flew to Jamaica with her husband John Derek, joining the shoot towards the end of January. 'I tell you, it is a mystery,' she'd later say of the role which made her a cinema icon. 'All I did was wear this bikini in *Dr. No*, not even a small one, and Whoosh! Overnight I have made it. For that film I got 10,000 dollars; suddenly I was worth 50,000.' Any nagging doubts about Andress' pronounced Swiss accent were alleviated when her lines were overdubbed by actress Monica Van der Syl in post-production.

Zena Marshall, playing the exotic and traitorous Miss Taro, was the Nairobi-born daughter of a coffee-planter. Educated in Holland, France, Belgium and at a convent school in Ascot, Marshall had toured with ENSA before making her film debut in *Caesar and Cleopatra* (1945).

Young and his crew arrived in Jamaica on Sunday 14 January, later filming at Kingston, Oncaros, Montego Bay and Palisadoes Airport itself. Many locals were recruited along the way: Delores Keator was given the role of Strangways' (now renamed) secretary Mary Prescott simply because she owned the house the crew shot in. Likewise, both the construction worker who witnesses the fatal dive taken by the thugs who pursue Bond to Miss Taro's and the Chief of Police were local amateurs. The recruitment of local talent was not restricted to actors – costumes were created by Tessa Welborn, who was related to a bartender seen at Puss-Feller's establishment.

The most reknowned scene in *Dr. No*, Bond witnessing Honey's Venus-like emergence from the waves, was filmed at Laughing Water, down-beach from Ina Fleming's home 'Goldeneye'. Indeed, Fleming, along with friends Noel Coward, poet Stephen Spender and journalist Peter Quennell, stumbled across the crew on the day the scene was shot. Apparently unperturbed at the indignity of hastily falling to the ground to stay out of shot, the three men stayed with the crew until evening. After dinner, Coward spent some time with Connery, advising him on matters ranging from acting to dealing with the press.

On 17 February, Fleming visited the crew on location at Falmouth, this time accompanied by his wife, Ann, Quennell and Spender. In a letter to Evelyn Waugh, Ann described how they went 'to lunch on location with the film company producing *Dr. No*: they were shooting a beach scene, the hero and heroine cowering behind a ridge of sand to escape death from a machine gun mounted on a deep-sea fishing craft borrowed from a neighbouring hotel and manned by communist negroes. The sand ridge was planted with French letters full of explosive – by magic mechanism they blew up the sand in little puffs. The machine gun gave mild pops, but I was assured it will be improved on the sound track; all this endeavour was wasted because unluckily a detachment of the American Navy entered the bay in speed launches and buggered it all up . . .'

'I can't tell you if she can act or not, but my God she looks great'

An incomplete patchwork of location filming came to an end on 21 February, inclement weather preventing Young from capturing everything he wanted. While some of the supplemental shots he filmed afterwards are very succcessful (such as the scenes where Bond, Quarrel and Rider are pursued in the swamp), the changing colour of Bond's car dashboard (red in close-up and black in medium shot) reveal the shortcomings of the staggered schedule.

While production designer Ken Adam, unwittingly styling a pop-art approach that would define the Bond style for years to come, laboured on the sets at Pinewood Studios, casting continued. Back in London, Young and Broccoli both received calls from 35-year-old Canadian actress Lois Maxwell (formerly 'Hooker'), whose husband had recently suffered a double coronary on her son's second birthday. Concerned about her family's finances, she was calling directors and producers she had previously worked with. Terence Young, who had earlier refused her a different role on the grounds that she looked like she 'smelt of soap', offered her

Bernard Lee (centre), one of Britain's busiest character actors, in Basil Dearden's 1961 thriller **The Secret Partner**. In 1962 Lee joined the cast of **Dr. No** as 'M'

appearances in pictures such as *Carry On Admiral* (not a Peter Rogers/Gerald Thomas production), and Hammer horror *The Revenge of Frankenstein*.

Bernard Lee was cast as Bond's superior, 'M', on 25 February, just one day before studio filming commenced. London-born Lee first trod the boards aged six, when he appeared on stage with his father at the Oxford Music Hall. Briefly employed as a fruit salesman in Southampton before being enrolled at the Royal Academy of Dramatic Arts, he'd made his stage debut proper in 1926. He'd netted hundreds of stage and screen credits following his first cinematic outing in 1934. 'Bernard Lee got the job because everyone else was away,' claimed Young. In the first studio scene to be shot, Peter Burton made his one and only appearance as armourer Major Boothroyd (the character was renamed 'Q' in subsequent films). When he chose another project over appearing in *From Russia With Love*, the part was given to Desmond LLewellyn, who made the role his own.

either Miss Moneypenny or Sylvia Trench. Neurotic about the scene where Trench greets Bond wearing only one of his shirts, Maxwell chose Miss Moneypenny. She was offered £100 per day, guaranteed only two days' work, and told to supply her own clothes.

The role of Sylvia Trench went to Eunice Gayson (35-24-36), a former Rank starlet who had achieved some degree of press notoriety after marrying writer/producer Leigh Vance live on US television on 1 July 1953 (her payment for the stunt, sponsored by an American piecrust manufacturer, had been £700 in wedding gifts). Controversially, she'd very publically torn up her restrictive Rank contract three years later, and made subsequent

Careful consideration was given to the actor selected for Bond's chief adversary, Doctor No. Richard Maibaum's second draft of the screenplay had ousted the chimpanzee/spider monkey suggested by Wolf Mankowitz, leaving the way clear for Canadian Joseph Wiseman, who was cast by Harry Saltzman in December 1961. (Fleming famously suggested Jamaican neighbour Noel Coward for the role.) Born in 1918, Wiseman had made his stage debut in New York in 1936, graduating to the cinema screen 14 years later in *With These Hands*. It was his role as a drug fiend in William Wyler's *Detective Story* the following year which singled him out as a putative No. The cruel Doctor's submarine quarters house a Goya painting entitled *The Duke of Wellington*. Bond does a double-take because the original had, famously, been stolen shortly prior to shooting. The in-joke had been suggested by Johanna Harwood.

Shooting wrapped on Friday 30 March 1962. During the cast and crew's celebrations, the daring Ursula Andress made a big impression. 'At the party she danced with all the crew,' remembered Lois Maxwell, 'and she was the first grown woman I had ever known who didn't wear a bra. As she danced, those wonderful breasts were just swaying. I remember thinking how marvellous it must be to be that uninhibited and I wanted to throw my bra off, but I didn't have the courage.'

Composer Monty Norman had previously written the short-lived stage musical *Belle* for Albert Broccoli. Undeterred by the production's poor reception, late in 1961 Broccoli commissioned Norman to score *Dr. No*. Norman accompanied Terence Young's crew in Jamaica during January, seeking inspiration for his calypso-flavoured soundtrack. Scoring was well under way before it was suggested that the film should carry a distinctive theme tune. 'I'd played around with all sorts of ideas but none of them I was happy with, nor indeed were they, for that matter,' recalls Norman. 'Somebody suggested "Underneath the Mango Tree" [the song Bond overhears Honey singing when he first spies her on the beach] as the theme, and I thought "No . . . it's a nice little thing, but it certainly wouldn't be the theme for a James Bond film."' Norman found inspiration in a song originally composed for a musical version of *A House for Mr Biswas*, the 1961 satrical novel by Trinidadian author VS Naipaul. The musical had never been produced, so Norman used the discarded song's strident

hook as the basis for his 'James Bond Theme'. Controversy surrounds what followed; Norman's authorship of the song is beyond dispute (he once successfully litigated against a magazine that had claimed he'd bought the tune from an old Jamaican for £100), but the contribution made by arranger John Barry cannot be overlooked. Trumpeter Barry had formed his first professional band, John Barry and the Seven, in 1957; television spots on seminal youth programmes *6.5 Special*, *Oh Boy!* and *Drumbeat*, and a recording contract with EMI/Parlophone, soon followed. In 1960, the renamed John Barry Seven recruited lead guitarist Vic Flick and recorded the score for Adam Faith vehicle *Beat Girl* (aka *Wild for Kicks*). Barry's *Beat Girl* soundtrack became the first British film score committed to vinyl when released as a long playing record the same year.

In 1962, Barry was called by Noel Rodgers, United Artists' head of music, and asked to overhaul Monty Norman's tune. 'The James Bond Theme', performed by The John Barry Seven and The John Barry Orchestra, highlights Flick's twangy guitar in an awesome reworking of Norman's original. It has been suggested that Barry's Bond theme is redolent of his earlier work – echoes of the expansive brass can perhaps be heard in 'Bees Knees' (sic: a track recorded and released in 1959 by The John Barry Seven and Bob Miller and the Miller Men) while the string arrangement has its roots in the strangely familiar *Black Stockings* (recorded and released in 1960 by The John Barry Seven). Whatever the inspiration, the result was one of the most distinctive signatures in cinema history. John Barry's contribution would become an integral part of Eon's James Bond films thereon. (No less iconic was the work of titles designer Maurice

15

Binder, whose 'gun barrel' view of Bond – similar to a design by Saul Bass for Hitchcock's *Vertigo* four years previous – at the outset of the film's Pop-inspired title sequence would be reprised throughout the series.)

Late in July 1962, Terence Young hosted a discreet preview of *Dr. No* in a private room in London's Travellers' Club. Guests included both Ian and Ann Fleming, plus 'the Duke and Duchess of Bedford, Lord and Lady Bessborough, John Sutro and Peter Quennell'. In a letter to Evelyn Waugh, Ann remembered: 'it was an abominable occasion. . . we arrived very late at the private cinema. . . found the film 'quite gripping'. I wish I had, for our fortune depends on it. There were howls of laughter when the tarantula walks up James Bond's body; it was a close-up of a spider on a piece of anatomy too small to be an arm'.

'The British cinema will never be the same again'

Fleming himself was dismayed by the film. Following a Leicester Square preview screening, his proof reader/research assistant Peter Garnham remembered: 'He strode out as the end credits rolled, said not a word, hailed a taxi, and sat silently as we were driven back to the pub across from his office. He got out, paid the cab, walked into the pub and ordered a couple of drinks, took a swig, and finally addressed me: "Dreadful. Simply dreadful." We never mentioned the movies after that.' In public, Fleming was rather more generous: 'Those who've read the book are likely to be disappointed,' he told *Time* in October 1962, 'but those who haven't will find it a wonderful movie. Audiences laugh in all the right places.'

Dr. No was first shown to the press at the London Pavilion on 2 October; it opened at the same cinema on 5 October and went on general release three days later. The critics were distinctly hostile. Nina Hibbin, writing in the left-wing *Daily Worker* on 6 October, asserted: 'it is vicious hokum, skilfully designed to appeal to the filmgoer's basest feelings . . . Set in the West Indies, it has sinister racialist implications. All the bad men except one are Negroes or Chinese.' '*Dr. No* ('A' certificate): no, no,' quipped *The Spectator*'s I Cameron on 12 October. 'Too inept to be as pernicious as it might have been. Costly gloss flawed by insidious economy on girls. Superannuated Rank starlet tries to act sexy. Grotesque.' Connery's Bond was not well-received – 'the dark hood looks of Scottish Actor Sean Connery . . . do not suggest Fleming's tasteful pagan so much as a used-up gigolo', sniffed *Time*, rudely – and even those who approved were noticeably guarded: according to *Scene*'s Derek Hill on 5 October, Bond was 'played with exactly the right mixture of strong-arm fascist and telly commercial salesman by Sean Connery', but he went on to claim that, 'The skill with which the men behind *Dr. No* present the adventures of their monstrous hero . . . tends to disguise the fact that our applause is invited for jingoism, thuggishness and blind obedience.'

Most remarkable of all, *Films and Filming*'s Richard Whitehall felt compelled to pen an extraordinary diatribe against the film; the cinematic Bond, he asserted, was the end of civilisation as we know it. 'There hasn't been a film like *Dr. No* since . . . when? The Mickey Spillane thrillers of the middle Fifties? *Dr. No* is the headiest box-office concoction of sex and sadism ever brewed in a British studio, strictly bath-tub hooch but a brutally potent intoxicant for all that. Just as Mike Hammer was the softening-up for James Bond, so James Bond is the softening up for... what? A fascist cinema uncorrupted by moral scruples? The riot of a completely anarchist cinema? *Dr. No* could be the breakthrough to something... but what? At one point Bond nonchalantly fires half a dozen shots into the back of a helpless opponent – the British cinema will never be the same again.

'As a considerable work of artifice (and it is pre-eminently that, every detail calculated to a nicety), *Dr. No* slipped by the censor with one cut (reducing the number of blows in a beating-up sequence) and an "A" certificate.' Whitehall's invective continues, despairing of John Trevelyan, then Secretary of the British Board of Film Censors: 'Oh, Trevelyan, art though sleeping in Soho? This is one of the X'iest films imaginable, a monstrously overblown sex fantasy of nightmarish proportions. Morally the film is indefensible with its lovingly detailed excesses, the contemporary equivalent of watching Christians being fed to lions, and yet its lascivious dedication to violence is a genuine hypnotic . . . Bursting at the seams with violence – the perfect film for a sado-masochist society – *Dr. No* lacks the unrestrained nastiness of that other British mutation, *Peeping Tom*; it never gives itself time to stop and gloat over its perversions (an extraordinary little scene in which a girl photographer is tortured). There's never been a British film like *Dr. No* since . . . what?'

Fascinatingly, the gentlemen of the press appear to have been fortunate enough to witness a scene cut from the film for its public release. It seems that Honey's ordeal at the behest of No – being staked out to be eaten by giant crabs (a scene reported in the novel) – was indeed filmed. The scene was something of a highlight for the *Daily Express*' Leonard Mosley, who described it thus on 5 October: 'The beautiful blonde has been shackled to the ground and a couple of Oriental villains are grinning lasciviously over her as poison spiders [sic] crawl over her limbs... it is the most splendidly absurd moment I have seen in films since the days of the old Pearl White serials.' The scene was also mentioned by Alexander Walker in his *Evening Standard* review of 4 October. By 12 October, *The Spectator* had picked up on the scene's excisement from the release print: 'In the book we are told that Honey... is staked out to be eaten by land-crabs, and this episode was mentioned in one or two notices of the film. Only in the version I saw it was never stated at all. True, she was chained in a dungeon with the water rising through a sluice, but we were not told she was going to be eaten. This was either deleted by the censor or furnished by the critics. I should like to know which.' However, Ann Fleming, recalling the film's private screening, had remarked: 'The heroine could not be eaten by crabs, for though they imported huge land crabs from Guernsey they died the minute they were placed on the heroine's body.' As the film stands, Honey is discovered by Bond staked out in a dungeon; water runs through a sluice, but the offending crustaceans are nowhere to be seen. 'I couldn't make it work,' lamented editor Peter Hunt many years later.

Even three years after its release, *Dr. No* could still excite controversy. On 18 May 1965, London's *Evening Standard* noted its condemnation by none other than the Vatican: 'The first James Bond film, *Dr. No*, has been described as "a dangerous mixture of violence, vulgarity, sadism and sex" in an article in the Vatican City newspaper, *Osservatore Romano*', remarked the piece. 'The article yesterday, entitled "The James Bond Case", said: "All was incarnated in a hero specially designed to attract the sympathies of the public, with the danger of one who is above the law because he has the double zero licence to kill and to do everything normally forbidden. But we had the ingenuousness [sic] to hope that the film would not have met with such a wide success." Producer [sic] Terence Young, writer Ian Fleming and actor Sean Connery had found "an easy commercial formula in 007. Their consistency is deplorable but explicable," it said.'

Dubious, United Artists didn't release *Dr. No* in America until 8 May 1963, but UK returns alone recouped its $1 million production outlay and assured a sequel. Principal photography on *From Russia With Love* had commenced in Istanbul on 1 April; Bond's screen career had begun in earnest.

File *Dr. No*

Teaser None. **0**

Titles The James Bond films begin, bizarrely, with a burst of sound from a *musique concrète* xylophone (or so it seems). A pinhole, iris, or gun barrel opens up to reveal a suited silhouette striding in profile. It turns, lithe, fires a gun ... A sequence of coloured dots begin to flash in an apparently random sequence – then, quite suddenly, the flavour turns all Caribbean. Sashaying torsos, both male and female, give way to three blind men shuffling across to screen right ... Iconic and utterly strange. **9**

Bonkers plot From his heavily staffed underground base, and using atomic energy, a crippled criminal scientist is 'toppling' American space rockets on behalf of the shady SPECTRE organisation. (We are never told precisely to what end he pursues this distinctly ostentatious form of terrorism.) **7**

Locations London; in and around Kingston, Jamaica; Crab Key. Pretty. **3**

Gadgets The bad guys have them all: bogus driver Jones has a cyanide cigarette, and No's henchmen scare off trespassers with a less-than-discreet flamethrowing tank disguised as a dragon. **2**

Girls Sylvia Trench, who enjoys playing around inside Bond's shirt; Miss Moneypenny; snap-happy harpy 'Freelance'; eavesdropping Government House mole Miss Taro; sea-shell seller Honey Ryder, both rape victim and murderess. Bond scores thrice. **8**

Villains Doctor No, who doesn't appear on screen until 24 minutes before the end – but does create an enduring template for all subsequent Bond baddies, both in his dialogue ('I do not like failure', 'Clumsy effort, Mister Bond. You disappoint me') and in his habit for hurriedly explaining to Bond the plot as the film nears its climax ('I only gratify your curiosity because you're the one man I've met capable of appreciating what I've done ...'). His bizarre assortment of henchmen include: the three 20-20-sighted 'blind mice'; photographer 'Freelance'; the lemming-like Jones; the wretched Dent, who looks to be on the verge of tears when given a dressing-down by his elsewhere employer; Miss Taro; fussy Sisters Lily and Rose. And although No's association with SPECTRE would suggest his operation to be apolitical, one can clearly see several Chinese in Red Army uniform at his base (particularly when Dent is led into the high-vaulted chamber). **9**

Fights, chases, explosions A few minor scuffles only: Bond's one-sided tussle with Jones, a nearly punch-up with Quarrel and Puss-Feller, some wrangling with both No and his guards. Two car chases (the villains go over a cliff in the second). At least No's base explodes in the final reel. **3**

Dialogue and double entendres Two screamingly funny one-liners: the first, when Bond drives up to Government House with Jones' corpse propped up in the back seat ('Sergeant, make sure he doesn't get away'); the second, Bond's wry assessment of the accident which befalls the assassins in their hearse ('I think they were on their way to a funeral'). No gets a few wonderful lines, too:'East, West … points of the compass'. Unforgettable, as Bond confronts Dent:'That's a Smith and Wesson … and you've had your six.' **7**

Bond Delivers that first line with a cigarette clenched between his teeth. Gives Sylvia his card, and tells her to come calling – an outrageous display of licentiousness for 1962. Cuts in over ladies waiting for a taxi at the airport. A cold and possibly psychopathological killer, too; not only does he shoot an extra bullet into Dent's back after he's killed him, he shows no remorse whatsoever when he knifes a lone guard in the lake at Crab Key ('Why?' wails Honey.'Cause I had to,' he replies. No, he didn't). Checks his watch discreetly while snogging Miss Taro. Plays patience while waiting for Dent. Strangely, he's presented as an intercontinental bobby: his examination of the Strangways house is exactly that of a detective, as is his subsequent investigation. He even tells Leiter 'It's my beat', and both Honey and No see him as a jet-set Plod; the former asks if Bond is going to arrest the Doctor, and the latter calls Bond 'a stupid policeman whose luck has run out'. Wears an iffy *chapeau* early on, but the collarless Nehru jacket he wears to dinner *chez* No is just the thing. He's fantastic. No wonder that hotel receptionist eyes him up. **10**

Plus/minus points Doctor No has succeeded in devising a unique method for purging oneself of pesky radioactive contamination: he scrubs it off with a broom. And just why does he affix a wheel to his atomic reactor which sends it critical when one increases the clearly marked 'DANGER LEVEL'? Is it entirely necessary? Never mind, he's thought to set up 'ABANDON AREA' signs for just such an eventuality. **-4**

55% It's easy to underestimate *Dr. No*, the template for everything to come: a Bond/M scene in London, a jet to an exotic locale, three girls (two good, one bad), a loyal local to show Bond around before getting killed, a variety of interesting attempts made on Bond's life, an inscrutable villain with a hidden HQ soon to be devoured by pyrotechnics … For all that, it feels like two films: the first

a colourful detective story in the *Our Man in Havana* mould, the second a naive and sometimes rather poor science fiction flick. Although it's handsomely made, it's Connery that holds this thing together. And he does it magnificently …

CAST
Sean Connery James Bond
Ursula Andress Honey Ryder   **Joseph Wiseman** Dr. No
Jack Lord Felix Leiter   **Bernard Lee** M   **Antony Dawson** Professor Dent
Zena Marshall Miss Taro   **John Kitzmuller** Quarrel   **Eunice Gayson** Sylvia
Lois Maxwell Miss Moneypenny   **Peter Burton** Major Boothroyd
Yvonne Shima Sister Lily   **Michel Mok** Sister Rose   **Marguerite Le Wars** Photographer
William Foster-Davis Superintendent   **Dolores Keator** Mary   **Reginald Carter** Jones
Louis Blaazer Pleydell-Smith   **Colonel Burton** General Potter
Lester Prendergast Puss-Feller   **Tim Moxton** Strangways

SELECTED CREDITS
Directed by **Terence Young**   Produced by **Harry Saltzman, Albert R Broccoli**
Director of Photography **Ted Moore BSC**   Editor **Peter Hunt**
Music composed by **Monty Norman**, conducted by **Eric Rodgers**,
orchestrated by **Burt Rhodes**
James Bond theme played by **John Barry & Orchestra**
Screenplay by **Richard Maibaum, Johanna Harwood, Berkely Mather**
Based on the novel by **Ian Fleming**
Production Designer **Ken Adam**   Assistant Director **Clive Reed**
Camera Operator **John Winbolt**   Special Effects **Frank George**
Costumes **Tessa Welborn**   Main Title designed by **Maurice Binder**
Animation **Trevor Bond**

Sadism for the family: *From Russia With Love*

1963: *Dr. No*'s sequel was being realised to a grand design. 'It's a much bigger picture. Just look at this set.' Co-producer Harry Saltzman was pointing to a mocked-up Pinewood ballroom where the final of a chess championship would occur early on in *From Russia With Love*. 'We use 160 extras in this scene,' he told the man from *Cinema* magazine. 'The set cost £60,000 to construct. And it's all for one-and-a-half minutes of film ... without Bond.'

'We think it's silly to cut corners,' chipped in his fellow producer, Albert Broccoli. 'We know from the success of *Dr. No* that Bond films are important. Important because this is the type of entertainment that people prefer. This is what people want to see. Bond is a unique hero,' he continued, wondering aloud – and not for the first time – just why a certain fictional character seemed to have caught the mood of the times. 'There's none of this rubbish about I won't pull my gun until three seconds after he's pulled his . . . We try to keep the character of Bond as a hard, sometimes cruel man in the films. You might even call it 'sadism for the family'.

An endorsement from President John F Kennedy, who had placed Fleming's *From Russia With Love* among his ten favourite novels in March 1961, had stoked American paperback sales and suggested the story as an obvious follow-up to *Dr. No*. Fleming's plot remained largely extant, but the novel's depth of characterisation – particularly as regards assassin Grant, repulsive Rosa Klebb and Tatiana, the bait used to reel Bond in – would be pointedly unplumbed in the screenplay. Bond would survive his

ultimate encounter with Klebb's poisoned toecaps, as opposed to the novel's original intent, but the single largest shift in emphasis would be in the loyalties of the villains at the story's heart – something which would be later noted by critic Richard Roud of *The Guardian*: 'Those who have read the book will wonder at my calling the divine Klebb former head of the Russian Secret Service; I was surprised, too. For whatever reasons (Foreign Office? post-test-ban-euphoria? distribution in the uncommitted countries?) the straight fight between us and the Russians has been changed in the film to a battle between us and "SPECTRE", the international crime syndicate . . .'

The film's cast was assembled over the first few months of 1963. Retained as Bond, Sean Connery had married actress Diane Cilento in Gibraltar on 29 November. Saltzman and Broccoli had originally wanted Elga Andersson for the role of Tatiana Romanova, but Daniela Bianchi ultimately won out over Ingrid Bergman's daughter, Pia Lindstrom. Reports differ, but it seems Bianchi was possibly a Miss Rome, and definitely a runner-up in the Miss Universe contest of 1960; she would

1 April 1963 – on the first day of filming From Russia with Love, *Sean Connery snuggles up to his Italian co-star Daniela Bianchi at Pinewood Studios*

be dubbed by actress Barbara Jefford, according to the *Daily Herald* of 9 October 1963. SPECTRE head Blofeld, credited to '?', would be played by *Dr. No*'s Anthony Dawson, but voiced by Eric Pohlmann.

'Miscasting of the year,' remarked *Esquire*, 'is Lotte Lenya as a sadistic officer in the Russian secret police: receiving wounds is her forte, nor giving them; her eyes are hopelessly kind and long-suffering, no matter what riding whips she brandishes.' Loathsome as squat bulldyke Rosa Klebb, Lenya, born Karoline Blamauer in Vienna on 18 October 1898, had been, variously, an actress, a circus performer, a singer and a ballet dancer; she'd played Shakespeare on the Berlin stage at 22. She'd married the composer Kurt Weill, and had appeared in the 1930 film version of Weill's *Die Dreigroschenoper* (*The Threepenny Opera*, aka *The Beggars Opera*). She had left Germany in 1933, settling in Paris for four

years before making her New York debut in *The Eternal Road* at the Manhattan Opera House. Her most recent film appearance prior to *From Russia With Love* had been in *The Roman Spring of Mrs Stone* (1961).

Eunice Gayson returned to play Sylvia Trench for the second and last time; her character had probably been intended to make up a running gag throughout the series – forever denied a moment's peace with the off-, then on-duty, superspy – but it wasn't to be. Gayson endured a rocky ride in the years to come; after a five-year West End run in *The Sound of Music*, she was to find herself underemployed post-1969 – and made a less-than-welcome return to press notoriety in 1974, when she was accused of shoplifting. Happily, daughter Kate Jackson would make a tiny appearance in 1995's *GoldenEye*. Mother

Bond promised to make love to Tatiana 'day and night', but Sean Connery and Daniela Bianchi were allowed a break to meet the press on 9 April. Dissatisfied with the actress' legs, director Terence Young substituted a model for the scene where Bond and Kerim Bey spy on Tatiana's pins with a discreet periscope. Perhaps significantly, she wears black stockings in this photocall

Terence Young's 1950 war film *They Were Not Divided*. He would find lasting fame as the increasingly exasperated Q, repeatedly berating a nonchalant Bond and becoming the longest-serving actor in the entire Eon-produced series. His briefing in *From Russia With Love*, however, was more in keeping with the film's grittier outlook than with the avuncular persona he would develop from *Goldfinger* onwards. '*Russia* is more realistic than the others,' believed co-scriptwriter Richard Maibaum. 'We hadn't gone so far yet into the fantastical – it was entirely believable. Real people in real situations.'

Taking his cue from *Last Year in Marienbad* (1961) Terence Young shot an atmospheric teaser sequence in which Bond was stalked by Red Grant (a blond Robert Shaw) through a tall-hedged garden. When Grant murders 'Bond', a rubber mask torn from 007's face reveals the victim to be a disguised SPECTRE operative – fodder for the latest training mission. A night-time shoot in the garden of Pinewood's main administrative block on 12 April had to be remounted when an examination of the rushes betrayed too close a resemblance between the unmasked extra and Connery himself. Fearing the point would be lost on his audience, Young reshot the unmasking using an actor with a moustache.

Dr. No's budget had been more than doubled to $2.2 million here, allowing for just such a luxury, and the extravagance of lengthy location shooting while filming continued at Pinewood. On Saturday 20 April, cast and crew flew to Turkey and filming commenced in Saint Sophia on Monday 22nd. Ian Fleming, who had earlier visited Istanbul on an assignment for *The Sunday Times*, went along for the ride. He had an enthusiastic admirer in

and daughter were pictured together in the *Daily Mail* at the time ('Having a Bond girl for a mother was always huge fun . . . my male friends have always queued up to meet her – even as young boys . . .').

Shooting began at Pinewood Studios on 1 April 1963 with Bond's arrival in M's office (the set had been retained by Eon, optimistic following production of *Dr. No*). Desmond LLewellyn, delivering the first of many crash courses in Q branch's latest gadgets, had previously appeared in

Terence Young, with whom he stayed: 'I always thought that was the best of all the Ian Fleming books,' said Young. 'I think it's the only one that's really foolproof as a story. All the others, when you analyse them, are really like the plots of those old Republic pictures. I think it had far and away the best cast of any Bond picture.' A small change to the story as described in the novel was the scene in which Bond assassinates SPECTRE agent Krilencu when he emerges from a panel inside a billboard advertisement for the Marilyn Monroe film *Niagara*. The scene remained, but the billboard for *Niagara* was replaced by an advertisement for the recently completed Saltzman/Broccoli slapstick *Call Me Bwana*. (The film, which was co-written by Johanna Harwood, opened in April 1963 and starred Bob Hope and Anita Ekberg; it is in the inside of Ekberg's 'lovely mouth' where Krilencu meets his doom.)

Editor Peter Hunt worked in close collaboration with his director, shooting insert material to add suspense to the teaser sequence, creatively cutting footage of Blofeld's disappointgly passive 'fighting' fish and trimming a number of sequences of Daniela Bianchi walking when her gait was considered ungainly. For the scene in which Bond and Kerim Bey spy Tatiana's legs through a periscope intruding into the Russian embassy, a model substituted Bianchi.

During May, it became clear that Pedro Armendariz, who was playing Bond's ally Kerim Bey, had become increasingly uncomfortable. A pronounced limp had first alerted Young to the fact something was wrong, and the actor soon admitted he was suffering from cancer – by this advanced stage, only morphine was keeping his pain in check. Armendariz had been recommended to Young by director John Ford, who, knowing that Armendariz was dying, had helped him secure work on the Bond picture so that his wife might ultimately benefit from his salary. As Armendariz faded away, Young hurriedly rescheduled the remaining studio work at Pinewood in an attempt to get the actor's scenes in the can as quickly as possible on the unit's return to England. Armendariz's final scene, set in the gypsy encampment constructed at the Paddock at Pinewood, was completed in the second week of June. Armendariz could no longer walk, and a double substituted for shots of the actor filmed from behind. (When Armendariz's work was complete, Terence Young hosted a party in his honour on Sunday 9 June. Armendariz and Ian Fleming, who had struck up a friendship during filming in Istanbul, reportedly spent much time discussing the actor's late friend Ernest Hemingway, who had committed suicide when faced with debilitating terminal illness. On 18 June, while hospitalised in Los Angeles, Pedro Armendariz took his own life.)

The gypsy encampment sequence, at which Bond and Kerim Bey are spectators, is best remembered for the vicious catfight performed by actress Martine Beswick and former Miss Israel Aliza Gur. Beswick, born in 1941, had been brought to England at the age of 12; her mother had enrolled her in a Richmond drama school. Back in Jamaica, she took up modelling, and appeared in several promotional films for the local tourist board, which drew her to the attention of agents MCA, who took her on their books upon her return to England in 1961 – and duly put her up for a part in *Dr. No* (Miss Taro, perhaps). 'I met the director Terence Young,' she told *The Dark Side* magazine. 'I got on well with him socially, and he kept on saying,

"I'm going to use you." So when *From Russia With Love* came up, it was mine...' The tussle was choreographed at Pinewood for three whole weeks: 'We were supposed to do the scene on location in Turkey. Much to my disgust, they decided to shoot the scene on the backlot. Everyone went to Turkey except us . . .' The scene would net Beswick a number of other feisty film roles, before she was called back to the Eon harem in 1965.

Editor Peter Hunt remembers that the fight attracted close scrutiny from the British Board of Film Censors: 'At one point I remember [secretary John Trevelyan] telling me he could see the girls' pubic hair. I said to him "I've been watching it frame by frame on a Moviola, and I can't!"' Ian Fleming expressed disappointment that the scene was less explicit than the fight described in the novel, wherein one girl bit the other's breast. 'How the hell did you expect I was going to get away with that?' asked an incredulous Terence Young in response. *From Russia With Love* would ultimately be granted an A certificate following minimum editing of the catfight. 'I took a few frames out here and there,' remembers Hunt. 'It didn't make any difference really.'

By the beginning of July, Young had taken his unit to Scotland to shoot the location sequences for the film's protracted chase climax. The helicopter swoops (something of a debt to *North By Northwest*) were filmed in Kilmichall. During filming, a camera operator was struck by a rotary blade and had to have his foot amputated. Young had earlier attempted to shoot the motor boat footage in Turkey, only to have his plans scuppered by poor weather. Preparing to start again off the coast of Crinan, Young nearly drowned when his boat capsized; he was briefly hospitalised

and given stitches in his leg for the wounds he received struggling to get to the surface. A jittery Harry Saltzman approached David Lean to step in and continue, but Albert Broccoli insisted Young should complete the film himself. Ultimately, the director lost little time and soon limped back to location.

Principal photography wrapped on 23 August 1963, but there was still work to be done. Terence Young had yet to shoot the back-projected footage of Venice to accompany Bond and Tatiana's romantic gondola smooch (Young's wife would make a cameo appearance as a tourist in a red dress standing on a bridge). As the delivery date to United Artists loomed, Eon were under pressure to complete the film quickly – it was decided there was no time to prepare an animated title sequence of the kind that Maurice Binder and Trevor Bond had developed for *Dr. No*. Instead, Canadian Robert Brownjohn directed an evocative set of titles that ultimately had a greater influence on the future style of the series; credits were projected through prisms onto the shimmying flesh of a belly dancer. Cinematographer Frank Tidy, who worked with Brownjohn on the sequence, recalled that the idea was born when Mrs Brownjohn had accidentally walked in front of her husband's slide projector. An in-joke saw fellow cinematographer Ted Moore suffer the indignity of having his credit illuminated across the girl's rear.

An exclusive version of the film was specially prepared by Peter Hunt for the initial screening to solemn United Artists' executives. Almost half an hour into the picture, upon Bond's demonstration of the 'safe' opening procedure of Q's deadly briefcase, Hunt cut to the explosion of Doctor No's base from the climax of the previous film. Although the American executives were fleetingly perturbed, Terence Young was reportedly highly amused and kept Hunt's unique 'editor's cut' for his own future screenings.

Like its predecessor, *From Russia With Love* opened with an instrumental signature tune. During the picture, however, and again over the closing credits, former bus driver Terry Parsons (aka Matt Monro) crooned the first of the series' many vocal themes; Lionel Bart's lyrics carefully avoided any references that may have given away any of the film's plot points. John Barry replaced Monty Norman as incidental composer, and even got to accompany the crew to Turkey: 'I had a hilarious time in Istanbul when they did *From Russia With Love*,' he remembers. 'Me and a guy called Earl Rogers went into this bar, there was nobody in there except us and he leant on this bar and the whole thing just collapsed! I mean we're talking about a bar 50 feet long and this brass rail was holding it together. It'd been there for probably 60 years and the whole thing just fell apart onto the floor. The barman looked up and kind of chuckled and that was it. We stayed there for another two hours drinking . . . Istanbul's a very, very strange place.' Back in England, Barry and his orchestra recorded 007, an 'alternative' Bond signature with an urgent crescendo; it would later reappear in Barry's scores for *Thunderball*, *Diamonds Are Forever* and *Moonraker*.

The film's press show, at the Leicester Square Odeon on 8 October, proved to be, by all accounts, a riotous affair. Fleet Street's finest had fallen for Bond in a big way. 'The applause crashed out like hand grenades for every feat of matchless courage and stunning bedroom virility that

Our Man pulls off', noted Alexander Walker of London's *Evening Standard*. The frenzy peaked during the trainbound scrap between Bond and Grant, according to *Financial Times* correspondent David Robinson: 'At the end of the sequence the screen sound was quite obliterated by a mass exhalation of indrawn breath from the auditorium', he noted. Scowling while the boys had their fun, however, was *Spectator* killjoy Isabel Quigly. 'It's terribly lowering to sit unamused while everyone around you is yelping with glee,' she whined ten days later. 'Bond, from the press show, is man of the year. There were shouts of joy when a kitten was fed to a live fish . . . and later, when he [Bond] set a whole sea alight by tossing petrol drums among the pursuing boats, and you saw the men jumping about with their clothes aflame, but unable to put them out in the blazing water, it grew hysterical . . .'

'The applause crashed out like hand grenades'

The lads, nevertheless, curbed their evident excitement when they came to file their copy. According to Thomas Wiseman of the *Sunday Express*: 'We tend to get the movie heroes we deserve, and I suppose nowadays that means James Bond. He is very much a figment of our times, the arch exponent of pop fascism ("licensed to kill"), the patriot-libertine, always ready to seduce a pretty spy for his country . . .

'The new James Bond film, like its predecessor, is an expensive penny-dreadful, enjoyably absurd, calculatingly sadistic (it contains a totally irrelevant, no-holds-barred fight between two briefly attired gipsy girls) and very bizarre.'

Likewise, *Daily Mail* writer Cecil Wilson

Heathrow Airport, Saturday 20 April. With hire car details at the ready, Sean Connery and Daniela Bianchi board their flight to Istanbul

stopped just short of endorsing the film – 'Terence Young directs this orgy of strip cartoon blood and thunder with the zest of a lounge-suited Western' – as did the aforementioned Alexander Walker: 'Agent 007 is still a tailor's delight and a maiden's prayer. But I begin to wish for likeable Mr. Connery's sake that they will equip the character with a sense of humour in time for the film version of *Goldfinger*.' *The Observer*'s Penelope Gilliatt was nearer the mark, rising above the anti-Bond snobs thus: 'The Bond films are brilliantly skilful. Among other things, they seem to have cottoned on to a kind of brutal flippancy that is a voice of the age, the voice of sick jokes about the Bomb and gruesomes about Belsen. Sociologists worry about the seductiveness of the lies in the films, but what audiences surely respond to more is the mockery in the lies. People understand perfectly well that the Bond films are telling them a string of whoppers; this is what makes them laugh.'

That's not to say that negative readings weren't very much in evidence. Philip Oakes in the *Sunday Telegraph*, for example: 'James Bond has already been the subject of much sociological huffing and

puffing, and the moral heat generated by his critics must be enough by now to warm a small city. Much of the indignation strikes me as bogus, but what I find extraordinary is that quasi-pornography (which seems to me a fairly clinical description of the Bond dossier) can now be presented as run-of-the-mill entertainment . . .

'It is a movie made entirely for kicks. Guns go off; girls get undressed; people have sex; people die. Happening succeeds happening, but nothing and no one is of any real significance. At no time is character explored, or motive examined . . . There is no hint of regret for life taken, or life wasted. Love is reduced to a bedroom workout. Sensation becomes a series of exchanges between a variety of blunt instruments.'

The Daily Worker's Nina Hibbin couldn't even bring herself to muster up even a thin veneer of reason. Under the headline, 'No, James Bond is not 'fun' – he's just sick!', she wrote: 'As for James Bond himself (Sean Connery) – well, there's a hero for you, with one hand holding a gun and the other fondling a girl, dividing his time equally between assassination and fornication! It's fashionable these days to suggest that the James Bond approach is only a bit of fun, and musn't be taken too seriously. Fun? That only makes it worse! What sort of people are we becoming if we can accept such perversion as a giggle?'

Peter G Baker, in the highbrow *Films and Filming*, drew his readers' attention to the film's certification (as his magazine had regarding *Dr. No*): 'I dislike the hypocrisy in British cinema today,' he wrote in the December issue. 'A few weeks ago John Davis, the chairman of Odeon, on which circuit *From Russia With Love* is generally released, complained that producers are making too many X certificate pictures because cinemas need more pictures that are 'family entertainment'. Now as *From Russia With Love* has an A certificate I may be forgiven if I assume that Mr Davis regards it as family entertainment. (I don't know what vice – or virtue? – has to be filmed for the British Board of Film Censors to give such pictures an X.) If Odeon cinemas really think the new Bond film is nice clean fun for all the family, then Britain has some pretty kinky families . . . or soon will have.'

BBFC secretary John Trevelyan was later queried on just such a point in the same magazine: 'When you have a British film, like, say, *From Russia With Love*, do you not think that if the film had been French it would have been awarded an X certificate rather than an A?' he was asked. 'Oh, no,' replied Trevelyan. 'This kind of really good "hokum" picture is seldom made in France, if ever. If you take *From Russia With Love* seriously, you've probably got to give it a double-X.' 'So,' pressed the interviewer, 'providing all kinds of abnormality and perversion are not taken seriously, the Board will award its A and not X certificate?' Answered Trevelyan: 'We've had this in lots of other pictures, you can't just put it down to that.'

'Crowds had been gathered at the theatre since mid-day,' claimed *Kinematograph Weekly*, reporting on *From Russia With Love*'s opening at the Leicester Square Odeon on 10 October. 'By early afternoon it was obvious the opening day house record was going to be beaten – it was just a question of by how much.

'By the time the last house was due to start the queues around the theatre had grown to fantastic proportions. The arrival of the film's stars, Sean Connery and Daniela Bianchi, together with Diane Cilento, Trevor Howard, the Duke and Duchess of Bedford, among other celebrities, added glamour to the occasion . . .' Saltzman and Broccoli were present, too; on its first day, the film beat the theatre's opening record by £481. The trend would continue. 'It's truly sensational. Nothing like it has been experienced before in the trade', claimed *Kinematograph Weekly* on 24 October. '*From Russia With Love* is breaking all records – I repeat, all records – in the simultaneous runs in the four Rank cinemas in central London.' The first week's takings – £14,528 at the Leicester Square Odeon , £6,874 at the New Victoria, £6,328 at the Kensington Odeon, and £5,077 in four days at the Marble Arch Odeon – were astounding enough, but the magazine noted that 'records in admissions, as well as takings, are being registered'.

'A movie made entirely for kicks . . .'

Nor was such success confined to the capital. Pre-release runs in 27 key provincial cinemas were equally remarkable: £7,976 in a week at the Birmingham Odeon, for example. 'Everyone is gasping about the figures', remarked the same magazine one week later. (Even Soviet premier Brezhnev would fall under the film's spell, watching *From Russia With Love* no less than three times after obtaining a print from the British embassy!)

The film was released in the US much later, on 27 May 1964, and double-billed with *War Is Hell*. There, its star would have cause to reflect upon the monster Eon had created. 'Sean and I went to America

Bond's Bentley whisks Sylvia Trench to a romantic riverside picnic, in this scene filmed at Hurley, Berkshire, on 26 July. The Bentley made a comeback in Casino Royale, but actress Eunice Gayson was playing Trench for the last time

just after *From Russia With Love* in 1963,' remembered Terence Young, 'and we sneaked out of the side entrance of the airport. And there must have been 700 or 800 people out there. There was an old lady there who came through the ring of cops, wanting an autograph, and I said, "Sean, sign the bloody thing." So Sean signed it and gave it to her, and she looked horrified. "No, no," she said, "I wanted James Bond." She looked at Sean and Sean kind of crumpled. It suddenly occurred to him that he was no longer a human being, he was a sex symbol.'

The closing caption of *From Russia With Love* ran thus: 'The End. Not quite the end. James Bond will return in the next Ian Fleming thriller. . .'

The title then disclosed was apt enough. Eon, it seems, had struck gold.

File: *From Russia With Love*

Teaser Black-clad assassin Grant stalks Bond through a moonlit garden – and garottes him. 'Bond' collapses, dead – but turns out to be an actor in a Sean Connery mask. It's all been a 'training exercise' conducted by SPECTRE ... **7**

Titles A belly dancer does her 'thing' to the cheesy buzz of a peepshow Hammond organ – and then proceeds to make amusing silhouette animals with her hands. Captions projected, perhaps artistically, over bits of her body. **5**

Bonkers plot Agents of SPECTRE use Bond to steal a valuable Lektor decoding device from the Russians, tendering both machine and apparently defecting Marxist Tatiana Romanova as bait. 'This is so obviously a trap,' explains chess Grand Master Kronsteen, the plan's deviser. 'My reading of the British mentality is that they always treat a trap as a challenge.' Handy, that. **6**

Locations SPECTRE's base, wherever that may be. Istanbul. London. Across Europe on the Orient Express. Venice. Bond confined to one continent. **5**

Gadgets Grant's watch contains a lethal cheesewire. Bond owns a prototype pager and has a hefty bakelite phone in his car. A tape recorder concealed in an innocuous box camera. The magical Lektor itself. Rosa Klebb's poisonous shoes. Best of all, Q branch turn up a black leather case which conceals twenty rounds of ammunition, a flat throwing knife, an .22-calibre AR7 folding sniper's rifle with infra-red sights, 50 gold sovereigns and a tin of talcum powder which contains a cartridge of tear gas. We want one for Christmas. **9**

Girls A buxom masseuse oiling Grant. Sylvia Trench. Miss Moneypenny (smoking). Ex-ballet dancer Tatiana

Romanova, whom we — and Bond — glimpse stark naked (bar a cute collar) as she slips into the bed of Bond's bridal suite. Kerim's slinky mistress. A belly dancer at the gypsy encampment, overwhelming Our Man with her — ahem — abdominal dexterity. Two gypsy girls, Vida and Zora, who indulge in a no-holds-barred catfight at the camp (later, Bond is told to select the victor. He's still 'choosing' come morning; indeed, he appears to spend 24 hours at it). Plus Anita Ekberg and her 'lovely mouth', of course. **8**

Villains Although his features remain unseen, here SPECTRE overlord Blofeld makes his first appearance. Aryan 'homicidal paranoiac' Grant, whose only other given name is 'Donald'. Arch-plotter Kronsteen. Scruffy Soviet killer Krilencu, plus rabble. The repugnant be-knuckle-dustered Rosa Klebb. **9**

Fights, chases, explosions Short on action scenes for the most part — the attack on the gypsy encampment and Bond's single-handed storming of the Russian Consulate during daylight hours excepted — *From Russia With Love* more than compensates with its set piece showdown between Grant and 007 in the cramped confines of a cabin in the Orient Express — surely among the hardest-hitting (no pun intended) of fistfights ever committed to film. The helicopter and boat sequences in the final reel seem a little cursory, but at least the latter results in a number of satisfyingly cathartic bangs. **7**

Dialogue and double entendres Disappointing, bar a couple of noteworthy Bond asides — 'From this angle, things are shaping up nicely,' as he observes Tatiana's legs through a periscope, plus his glib summation of Klebb's eventual fate ('She's had her kicks'). Actually, Klebb herself proves far more prone to making suggestive remarks — witness the distinctly Sapphic subtext to her initial encounter with Tatiana ('You're fine looking girl' [sic]), wherein our Rosa gropes Tatiana's knee, strokes her hair and leers all over the hapless lovely. **4**

Bond Urbane, wry and a little too relaxed throughout the earlier sections, our Englishman Abroad transforms effortlessly into the Most Dangerous Man in the World during the journey on the Orient Express, particularly after the death of Kerim Bey (a fabulous foil for our hero throughout). He's hard as nails during his interrogation of

---

CAST

Sean Connery James Bond
Daniela Bianchi Tatiana   Pedro Armendariz Kerim Bey
Lotte Lenya Rosa Klebb   Robert Shaw Grant   Bernard Lee 'M'
Eunice Gayson Sylvia   Walter Gotell Morzeny   Francis de Wolff Vavra
George Pastell Train Conductor   Nadja Regin Kerim's Girl
Lois Maxwell Miss Moneypenny   Aliza Gur Vida   Martine Beswick Zora
Vladek Sheybal Kronsteen   ? Ernst Blofeld   Leila Belly Dancer
Hasan Ceylan Foreign Agent   Fred Haggerty Krilencu
Neville Jason Kerim's Chauffeur   Peter Bayliss Benz   Nushet Ataer Mehmet
Peter Brayham Rhoda   Desmond Llewellyn Boothroyd
Jan Williams Masseuse   Peter Madden McAdams

Stunt work arranged by **Peter Perkins**. "From Russia With Love" sung by **Matt Monro**

SELECTED CREDITS

Directed by **Terence Young**
Produced by **Harry Saltzman, Albert R. Broccoli**
Director of photography **Ted Moore BSC**   Editor **Peter Hunt**
Art director **Syd Cain**   Assistant director **David Anderson**
Camera operator **Johnny Winbolt**
Special effects by **John Stears**, assisted by **Frank George**
Costume designer **Jocelyn Rickards**
Titles designed by **Robert Brownjohn**, assisted by **Trevor Bond**
Screenplay by **Richard Maibaum**   Adapted by **Joanna Harwood**
Title song written by **Lionel Bart**
Orchestral music composed and conducted by **John Barry**

Tatiana, too (that slap must have hurt). Docked a point for a very dodgy titfer, however. **8**

Plus/minus points The all-too-short sequence wherein Klebb tours SPECTRE's training camp and testing-grounds — machine-guns, crossbows, karate artistes, flamethrowers, gladiatorial refugees from *Spartacus* and kung fu ahoy! — pre-empts numerous later Q branch scenes, and tops them all. There's a fabulous bit where M, Moneypenny and assorted chiefs of staff play back a recording of Bond and Tatiana's conversation. 'James, James,' says Tatiana, 'Tell me ze truth. Am I as exciting as all zose western girls?' 'Well,' replies Bond, 'once, when I was with M in Tokyo, we had an interesting experience ...' M leaps to switch the machine off. And glows. **+8**

76% This slick and confident espionage thriller has much to commend it, but, despite a colourful array of supporting characters — some more comic-strip than others — doesn't really take off until its final third.

A kind of joke Superman: *Goldfinger*

1964: and, during a break in the shooting of the third James Bond film, Sean Connery tucked into a lunch of smoked salmon and roast Aylesbury duckling. His companion, the *Daily Mail's* Barry Norman, noted that Connery dined 'in the careless manner of one who can afford to eat such snacks every day of his life'. Pinewood Studios was hosting the most expensive Bond yet. Connery's increased salary and the film's expanded budget were monies wisely invested: *Goldfinger* would bring the 007 franchise unprecedented international success, and raise Connery's asking price into the six-figure bracket. 'He is going to make me rich,' said Connery of Bond, 'depending on how the tax works out. Rich enough to retire I suppose.' However, following this, the coming-of-age of the James Bond formula, retirement would be out of the question.

Terence Young had initiated pre-production on *Goldfinger*, in 1963, but the director's chair was vacated before shooting even began. When denied a percentage of *Goldfinger's* profits, Young instead turned his attention to Paramount's *The Amorous Adventures of Moll Flanders*. He was replaced by Guy Hamilton, who, having already turned down *Dr. No*, wasn't about to look Eon's gift horse in teh mouth twice. Hamilton was an experienced film-maker who had begun his career as a clapper boy at the Victorine Studio in Nice in 1939. After serving in the Navy during the war, he worked alongside Carol Reed as an assistant director, making his debut proper with *The Ringer*, an above-average Edgar Wallace thriller, in 1952. He directed and co-wrote *The Colditz Story*, his most

notable pre-*Goldfinger effort*, in 1954. Like Young, Hamilton's quintessentially English style and manner would have a profound effect on the Bond series, but he is also widely credited for accentuating the knowing humour that found a new prominence in *Goldfinger*. Hamilton would return to direct *Diamonds Are Forever*, *Live and Let Die* and *The Man With the Golden Gun*.

Following Young's departure from the production, scriptwriter Richard Maibaum found a new collaborator in Paul Dehn. A former intelligence officer in the Second World War, Dehn had shared an Academy Award in 1952 (with James Bernard) for the storyline of his very first film, *Seven Days to Noon* (1950). Dehn was later given a British Academy Award for scripting

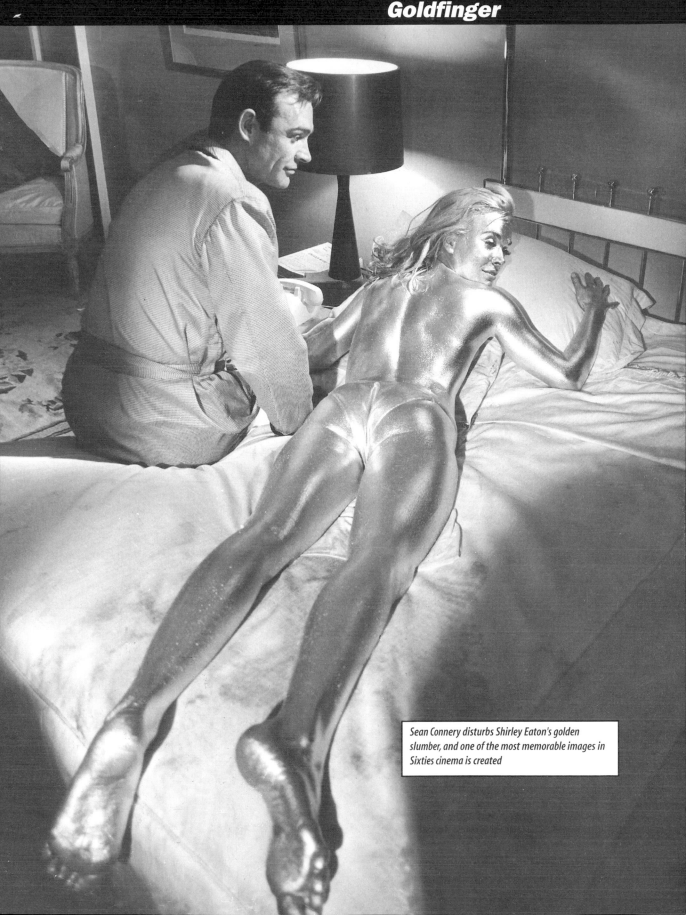

Sean Connery disturbs Shirley Eaton's golden slumber, and one of the most memorable images in Sixties cinema is created

Orders to Kill (1958). Best known as the *News Chronicle*'s film critic in the early Sixties, he would soon devote his time to screenwriting. 'I'm not too bad at adapting or improving somebody else's original,' he modestly claimed in November 1964, 'but the original has to be there to start with.' His illustrious career continued post-*Goldfinger*: highlights would include credits on *The Spy Who Came In From the Cold* (1965), *The Taming of the Shrew* (1967) and four *Planet of the Apes* sequels in the Seventies. His final film, *Murder on the Orient Express*, co-starred Sean Connery and was released in 1974, two years before Dehn's death.

The screenplay retains much of Fleming's original, but the Maibaum and Dehn restructuring is instructive. The teaser scene is derived from the briefest of references to a recent mission in Mexico City – 'Bond broke into [the] warehouse one night and left a thermite bomb. He then went and sat in a café a mile away and watched the flames' – and Bond's subsequent encounter with a *capungo*

(Mexican for 'assassin', apparently). Bond's happenstance meeting with Goldfinger in Miami – via Du Pont, who first appears in *Casino Royale* – is reconfigured as a task set by M from the outset, giving the narrative a greater drive and direction. Critically, the event which kicks the film into first gear – Jill Masterson's gilt-edged demise – isn't revealed until two-thirds of the way through the novel, and then reported to Bond at second-hand. A long sequence in which Goldfinger dines Bond at his Kentish mansion following their game of golf is omitted entirely; it reveals little bar Odd-job's predeliction for cat flesh (and later, cannibalism). The screenwriters have Odd-job's bowler remove Tilly from their narrative with near-indecent haste, preferring to build up Pussy Galore instead. Fleming's Tilly, like Bond, is retained as a secretary to assist Goldfinger in his plan to break into Fort Knox. In the film, Tilly doesn't live to meet Pussy, to whom Fleming would have her unrequitedly attracted ('Tilly Masterson was one of those girls whose hormones had got mixed up'). Perhaps Maibaum and Dehn's only misjudgment comes in

Honor Blackman became the first Avengers *star to appear in a James Bond film; Diana Rigg, Joanna Lumley and Patrick Macnee would follow in her footsteps*

eliminating Goldfinger's companion using Bond as an unwilling accomplice, for it means that for most of the film's middle third Bond is locked up in a cell. Fleming's Pussy, meanwhile, is the leader of a posse of criminally minded lesbian acrobats – the Cement Mixers – and is one of the gang lords whom Goldfinger assembles to help supply troops for his raid on the Fort. She can neither fly nor fight judo, and is needed simply to supply aggressive women to pose as nurses in a bogus Red Cross convoy.

The film's masterstroke, however, is to alter Goldfinger's intention from merely breaking into the repository at Fort Knox and stealing the bullion therein – but to irradiate it, thus taking it out of circulation. (The notion is probably an extrapolation from Fleming's ludicrous notion that the Fort's doors can be blown open with a 'clean', fall-out free, atomic warhead.) This allows the finale to take place within Fort Knox itself – in the novel, Goldfinger doesn't get much past the gates before the military blow Operation Grand Slam wide open in the space of just over two rather cursory pages. Bond's final showdown with Goldfinger, aboard a hi-jacked BOAC jet, takes place two days later in Fleming, but is otherwise little changed. One slightly disturbing aspect of the screenplay is its senseless use of the Chinese as the villains 'behind' Goldfinger (Russia's SMERSH aid Auric in the novel). Indeed, it makes the Mob leaders assembled by the villain oddly redundant – they have merely arranged the smuggling of weapons and troops into the States, whereas Fleming's Goldfinger needs them to supply him outright. The only seriously discordant note struck by the film, this token use of communist villains smacks of American brow-beating and, sadly, anti-Oriental triumphalism (then again, perhaps it was done solely to wind up Nina Hibbin of *The Daily Worker*.)

Although Maibaum and Dehn were the only writers accorded credits on *Goldfinger*'s opening titles, another familiar name had also made a contribution. Despite turning down Eon's potentially lucrative offer during the production of *Dr. No*, Wolf Mankowitz remained on good terms with its producers. 'One day, I went to see Harry and Cubby about something else, and they were sitting there pondering and pondering. I said, "What's the problem?" And they said, "We gotta get rid of this body, and nobody can come up with a good new way of getting rid of it . . ." Well, I'd been looking at that day's *Times*, and there was a full-page article about the Mafia disposing of bodies by sticking them in the boots of cars and getting the cars trashed in one of those things. I said to them, "Look, I'll give you an idea – but it'll cost you £500 in cash, which you'll have to pay me before I leave here." They said okay, so I said, "Well, this is it. They put the body in an old car, and they put the car into a crusher. A big machine comes down and . . . bang, smash, wallop: there's a square of dirt, with a little blood coming out of it – any good?" "Fantastic – great!" they said, and that was the scene. And it's a very famous scene. There were lots of other things like that which gave me loose cash in my pocket.'

The butch lesbianism of Pussy Galore had been merely alluded to in the screenplay, but during pre-production even the character's name was brought into question; United Artists at one point favoured 'Kitty' Galore as an acceptable alternative. Ultimately, Eon's publicist Tom Carlile ensured that the character's name was 'leaked' to the press, thus precluding any attempts at imposing a more conservative compromise before the film's release.

After *From Russia With Love*, Sean Connery had starred alongside Gina Lollobrigida in *Woman of Straw* for director Basil Dearden. Albert Broccoli next exercised a little influence to help secure Connery a starring role in Alfred Hitchcock's *Marnie*. Connery was booked to begin principal photography on *Goldfinger* as soon as he completed work for Hitch. Although reportedly unhappy at the prospect of a third Bond film, Connery was contracted and, as he conceded in 1963, there were worse characters he could be playing: 'I'm reasonably content. I've got the power of the greatest governments in the world behind me. I eat and drink nothing but the best, and I also get the loveliest ladies in the world. What could be better?' Editor Peter Hunt was convinced that Connery was the series' greatest asset: '[He] really was a very sexy man. There are very few film stars who had that sort of quality . . . they virtually could walk into a room and fuck anybody.'

Goldfinger's accomplice, Pussy Galore – a lesbian whose sexuality and allegiance are both influenced by Bond during the course of the story – was a role perhaps more demanding than that of *Dr. No*'s Honey or *From Russia*'s Tatiana. Honor Blackman, the co-star (with Patrick Macnee) of ABC Television's thriller series *The Avengers*, was duly poached, despite bearing scant resemblance to the raven-haired redneck described by Fleming. For her portrayal of sassy *Avengers* heroine Mrs Catherine Gale, a widowed judo expert with a natty line in leather, Blackman was awarded the title ITV Personality of 1963 by the Variety Club. Her defection from television to film was, however, no less than a continuation

of a prolific career that began in the late Forties. A popular lead in potboilers from such British studios as Rank and Hammer, Blackman nevertheless occasionally appeared in notable productions such as *So Long at the Fair* (1954) and *A Night to Remember* (1958), her blonde hair and buxom femininity ensuring her pin-up status even when, as an *Avengers* star, she was pushing 40. Blackman handed ABC her notice on 19 September 1963, although news of her *Goldfinger* casting was suppressed until early January 1964. In February 1964, it was made public that she would be quitting *The Avengers*. Her final episode ('Lobster Quadrille', recorded on 21 March 1964 and transmitted one day later) concluded with her character telling Patrick Macnee's Steed that she was taking a break: 'I'm not going to be pussy-footing along those shores,' says Cathy, to which Steed replies: 'No pussy-footing? I must have been misinformed!' (In the episode 'Too Many Christmas Trees', transmitted on Christmas Day 1965, Steed receives a card from Mrs Gale – posted from Fort Knox!) *The Avengers* provided Blackman with a sound training for the rigours of *Goldfinger* – being tumbled by Connery in the hayloft set at Pinewood was relative luxury compared to the beatings she would regularly receive on concrete floors during episodes of *The Avengers*.

In December 1963 Viennese character actor Theodore Bikel tested for the role of Goldfinger. Bikel, who first came to prominence with his appearance in *The African Queen* (1951), was passed over, but his faltering description of the laser about to slice 007 still exists in his screen test footage. (The laser, incidentally, was the first portrayed on film and stands as another example of the way Maibaum and Dehn altered the events of Fleming's novel – in the book, Bond is tied to a table and threatened with a revolving buzz-saw.) The role of Auric Goldfinger ultimately went to Carl Gerhart Frobe, an actor Broccoli had recommended to Guy Hamilton after recalling his compelling performance as a child molester in the 1958 film *Es Geschah Am Hellichten Tag* (*It Happened in Broad Daylight*). A star in Germany, Gert Frobe was a relative unknown outside his homeland. Prior to *Goldfinger*, he had made small appearances in the Edgar Wallace thriller *Backfire* (1961) and *The Longest Day* (1962) – after *Goldfinger*, major roles in international films would continue to come his way until the late Seventies. One of the most prominent was in Broccoli's own production of Ian Fleming's *Chitty Chitty Bang Bang* (1968).

Goldfinger's mute heavy 'Odd-job' was brought to life by 284-pound wrestler and former Olympic weightlifter Harold Sakata, better known to wrestling fans as 'Tosh Togo' (the stage name was presented in brackets on the film's end titles). Odd-job's lethal steel bowler hat contributed to the character's impact; he remains perhaps the best-remembered henchman of the entire Bond series. Sakata later exploited his character's fame in an amusing American television commercial for Vicks' 'Formula 44' cough mixture, in which a tickly throat leads Sakata's Odd-job-style character to demolish his neighbourhood in a hand-chopping frenzy.

Despite being granted less than five minutes' screen time, Shirley Eaton earned a lifetime of notoriety in the role of Goldfinger's moll Jill Masterson. 'To be murdered by being covered naked in gold paint meant the fans of the Bond films have never forgotten me,' she claims. Eaton's successful career had already included three of the earliest *Carry On*s (*Sergeant*, *Nurse* and *Constable*) and

Doctor At Large (1957). Leading roles in four films released in 1961 – *Dentist on the Job*, *Nearly a Nasty Accident*, *A Weekend With Lulu* and *What a Carve Up* – confirmed her status as the queen of British comedy. *Goldfinger*, she hoped, would bring her wider recognition, but although she would famously appear on the cover of *Life* magazine, her career ultimately benefited little.

Bolstered by the sort of confidence only a $3.5million budget could bring, Guy Hamilton commenced preliminary photography before casting and set construction were complete. On 15 January 1964, Hamilton accompanied cinematographer Ted Moore and production designer Ken Adam (whose duties on Kubrick's *Dr Strangelove* had prevented him participating in *From Russia With Love*) from New York to Miami to shoot the aerial photography of the Fountainbleau Hotel, seen in the opening moments of the film proper. The only actors this 'second unit' had to shoot between 20 and 24 January were Polish/Canadian Cec Linder and Austin Willis. Originally hired to play Mr Simmons (Goldfinger's duped gin opponent) and Felix Leiter respectively, a last-minute decision was taken to switch the actors' roles; Linder became Felix Leiter. Hamilton's hope that the Miami location photography would match the later Pinewood shoot was over-optimistic. The result is a collage of mis-matching shots and unconvincing back projection that gives this otherwise slick film something of a faltering start. 'It was a very unfocused beginning,' believes editor Peter Hunt. 'In order to make it work I had to do a lot of inserts of the cards and change the construction of [Goldfinger] listening to the fall guy in his room. The sequence didn't work [but] there was not time to reshoot it.' At Pinewood and in nearby Black Park, Hamilton shot the overcranked sequences where Bond and Tilly Masterson are chased in the Aston Martin DB5 by Auric Enterprises' guards; Connery and Tania Mallet (a friend of Harry Saltzman's) had yet to arrive at Pinewood so stuntman Bob Simmons and Phyllis Cornell stood in. Two Aston Martins, including the development prototype DP216I, were used in the film (at that time, the firm could produce only 11 vehicles a year); one was left intact while the other was 'customised' by special effects supervisor John Stears and his team. Stears followed plans outlined by an enthusiastic Ken Adam: 'I was a sports car freak in those days so I got rid of a lot of my inhibitions when it came to redesigning the Aston Martin.' In January 1964, Stears' own enthusiasm suffered when the time came to implement such 'added extras' as a sunroof to accommodate the ejector seat. 'I can still remember making a hole in this lovely Aston Martin, my pride and joy!' Other amendments included a radar device, a pop-up bullet-proof screen, a pair of Browning machine guns, tyre

'When Cubby and Harry saw the rushes they went bananas'

slashers, an oil spray and extending overriders. Two gadgets – a sliding weapons tray beneath the front seat and chambers intended to release clusters of nails – were added, but never seen in the finished film. Another gimmick, the revolving number plates, was prompted by the frustrated Guy Hamilton, whose Bentley had recently been slapped with a parking ticket. The ejector seat was suggested by his 12-year-old son. The car would grip the public's imagination like no other before it: the toy manufacturer Corgi

would sell two million replicas. Aston Martin's Newport Pagnell plant later produced a one-off miniature (top speed 6mph), collected by the Queen on Prince Andrew's behalf.

When the traumatic shoot for *Marnie* came to an end, Sean Connery arrived at Pinewood. Principal photography on *Goldfinger* commenced on 9 March with the pre-credits sequence: Bond's explosive disruption of a South American heroin smuggling operation. From the moment a frogsuited Bond emerged from water and discarded the dummy duck attached to his head it was clear that the film would usher in a new era. 'To tell a complete story in four minutes and, above all, set the mood of the picture . . . [is] a real challenge,' insists Guy Hamilton. The carefully balanced lightheartedness is compounded when, his sabotage complete, Bond unzips his wetsuit to reveal a perfectly pressed white tuxedo underneath. Carnation at the ready, Bond samples the pleasures of the El Scorpio Café. Hamilton: 'The sequence [also had to] satisfy Harry Saltzman's passion for gadgets and Cubby's generous quota of pretty ladies.' Luckily, Nadja Regin (who had played 'Kerim's Girl' in *From Russia With Love*) was on hand as Bonita, the dancer Bond is seducing while a thug creeps up behind him. Bond sees his assailant reflected in Bonita's eye (an optical effect courtesy of Cliff Culley) and one of the most memorable fights in the Bond series ensues. Stuntman Alf Joint, who played the *capungo*, recalled that he was cast when the cat burglar earmarked for the part was arrested the day before shooting! 'I got the part because I had high cheekbones and I could be made up to look like a Mexican more than anybody else.'

Towards the end of March, work continued on E Stage with Gert Frobe's first scene: Goldfinger's attempted castration of Bond using an industrial laser. When Hamilton discovered that it was impossible to photograph the pencil-thin beam of light satisfactorily, Culley was again called upon to overlay an optical effect. The laser's advancing flame was supplied by effects technicians crouching beneath the table; Connery would shoot nervous glances at John Stears as the heat of an oxyacetylene torch approached.

During shooting a more serious problem first became apparent – Gert Frobe's thick German accent had rendered his dialogue unintelligible. He had learned his lines parrot-fashion, and found difficulty in investing them with any meaning. 'When Cubby and Harry saw the rushes they went bananas,' recalled Hamilton. Frobe was urged to relax his lip movements to improve the pace of his delivery. In the finished film he is dubbed by actor Michael Collins throughout.

Last-minute script changes to the scene where Bond discovers his Bentley has been replaced by a souped-up Aston Martin would distinguish 007's latest encounter with Q as a defining moment. Guy Hamilton asked Desmond LLewellyn to redefine Q as intolerant of Bond's cavalier attitude towards his gadgetry. The bickering between the two characters was so effective that it was retained for each of Q's subsequent appearances. As originally scripted, Q's briefing ended short of describing the DB5's ejector seat. 'Cubby appeared on the set and asked me to continue the scene with Q demonstrating or pointing out every single feature,' recalled Guy Hamilton. 'I thought this was crass, because it would spoil all surprise for the audience.' Hamilton nevertheless rewrote LLewellyn's lines on the spot, secretly hoping that the extra dialogue

could be discarded at editing stage. 'I learned a great lesson,' he later conceded, admitting that advance warning of the car's ejector seat was wise. 'Cubby was absolutely right: "Tell them what you're going to do and then do it." Audience reaction proved him right, and I've always been grateful to him.'

During April, the interior of Miami's Fountainbleau Hotel was recreated on D Stage, and attempts were made to match the location footage shot in January. Shirley Eaton remains justifiably proud of her contribution during this time: 'When I shot my last scene in *Goldfinger* with Sean Connery – the Famous Scene – I had been in the make-up room since 7am. For one-and-a-half hours a lovely French make-up man had painted my body with a thick layer of millions of gold-leaf particles, while I stood there in a tiny G-string. He left a small area around my tummy button free from paint so that my body could breathe. Left on for too many hours it can prove fatal. As I walked on to the set the technicians whistled and smiled, and one of them said, "You look great, Shirley" Little did I know when I had finished my one week of shooting on *Goldfinger* that it would become an all-time 007 classic.' Her modesty preserved only by a pair of gold-coloured knickers and conical caps covering her nipples, Eaton posed once for the film cameras and once for the gentlemen of the press on 21 April. A doctor was kept on standby throughout.

While Connery and Eaton filmed the scenes where they observe Goldfinger's card game from a distance, they were visited by Ian Fleming. In 1964 a heavy chest cold weakened Fleming's already failing heart. It would prove to be his final visit to the set of a Bond picture. As far as can be established, it seems that a

Pussy Galore's carefully choreographed tudssle with Bond (here doubled by Bob Simmons) is staged for the benefit of Fleet Street photographers on 2 June

pay dispute between Connery and Eon came to a head at some point during shooting on the Fountainbleau scenes. The slight back injury suffered by Connery when filming the scene in which Odd-job knocks Bond out with a karate chop necessitated an early bath for the actor, who was forced to return home. It is said that by the time of his return to work he had received a salary increase and five per cent of profits from all Bond films subsequent to *From Russia With Love*. (The agreement, struck with Broccoli and Saltzman's Danjaq company, was the subject of a $225 million lawsuit brought by Connery in 1984.)

During May, Hamilton took his crew to Buckinghamshire's Stoke Poges golf club, one of the nearest courses to Pinewood. It is on the fairway that 007 drops the gold bar (in reality aluminium alloy coated with golden enamel) that whets Goldfinger's appetite. A scene added to the novel as little more than an afterthought on Fleming's part would become one of the film's highlights. A double performed Gert Frobe's necessary swings, but Connery coped admirably, having already benefited from some elementary lessons at a nearby golf school. Terence Young had first introduced Connery to the game while shooting *Dr. No* in Jamaica, but the nine days spent at Stoke Poges catalysed the actor's initial interest into a lifelong love of the game that continues unabated. In 1997, a Bond unit returned to Stoke Poges with Pierce Brosnan and Teri Hatcher to shoot scenes for *Tomorrow Never Dies*.

Among the final studio scenes were the battle sequences set inside Fort Knox itself. Denied access to the building, Ken Adam let his imagination run riot in creating what Albert Broccoli imagined to be 'a cathedral of gold.' Ignoring the conventions of bullion storage (gold is never stacked more than two feet high) Adam created a glittering vault that served as a suitably opulent backdrop to Bond's climactic struggle with Odd-job. When Goldfinger's henchman finally perished while retrieving his hat from an electrified gate, Harold Sakata was badly burned by the searing heat generated by the flying sparks – he hung on simply because Guy Hamilton, unaware of the difficulty the actor was in, hadn't thought to curtail the scene. The Fort Knox exterior, originally envisaged as a location in Portugal, was constructed on the Pinewood backlot. (Adam had been granted permission to inspect the outside of the building, following a little string-pulling by Robert Kennedy.)

Nineteen weeks of principal photography ended with location shooting at Andermatt in Switzerland between 7 and 11 July 1964, after which Connery joined Diane Cilento in Rome for a much-needed holiday. Meanwhile, post-production work continued. Margaret Nolan (who auditioned for the role of Jill Masterson but ultimately played Bond's masseuse Dink) was the golden girl posing in Robert Brownjohn's opening credits: scenes from *Goldfinger*, *From Russia With Love* and *Dr. No* were projected onto her body.

As *Goldfinger*'s release date loomed, Guy Hamilton, Ted Moore and Albert Broccoli flew to Louisville, Kentucky, to shoot the aerial photography required for the raid on Fort Knox. Broccoli's stepson Michael G Wilson, then in his first year at law school, was roped in as an assistant director (he also acted as an extra in the scene where Pussy Galore's Flying Circus prepares to take off). Pussy's Flying Circus of Piper Cubs buzzed the real Fort Knox

from the nearby Goodman Airfield, breaking the establishment's minimum height restriction of 5,000 feet by 'dusting' the nearby military base from a height of just 500. The soldiers in question collapsed under the influence of the 'gas' on cue from Guy Hamilton, who blew a whistle from a hovering helicopter. The troops each received $20 and a beer for their trouble.

One of the very final changes to *Goldfinger* took place when photography was complete. As originally shot, Leiter saved Bond's life by switching off the Fort Knox atomic bomb as the countdown reached 003. Harry Saltzman was unable to resist the temptation of asking editor Peter Hunt to alter the scene with an insert shot showing the countdown stalling at 007. Release scripts were doctored accordingly and the joke made it into the finished print. Unfortunately, so did Bond's quip: 'Three more ticks and Mr Goldfinger would have hit the jackpot.'

The film's score was the most accomplished yet from John Barry. 'It was a question of finding the style,' he recalled for *The Face* magazine in 1987. '*From Russia With Love* consolidated after *Dr. No*. I'm not just talking from a musical point of view. I'm talking about directorial and stylistic points of view. *Goldfinger* came together. They knew what they'd got. It had a freshness and an energy. It was the true birth.

'*Goldfinger* was the craziest song ever. Weird song. We couldn't have written that song as a song. I remember I went to Tony Newley to write the lyric. He said, "What the hell do I do with it?" I said, 'It's Mack the Knife.' It just worked. . . Shirley Bassey didn't know what the song was about, but she sang it with such extraordinary conviction that she convinced the rest of the world that it meant something.' Anthony Newley's original vocal version of the theme tune was rejected, and remained unheard until its inclusion on EMI's limited edition *The Best of James Bond* double album in 1992. Shirley Bassey's powerful rendition charted at number 21 in the British hit parade of autumn 1964; John Barry's soundtrack LP reached number 8 in America's Billboard chart – the highest placing yet for a Bond album.

Goldfinger's world premiere took place at the Leicester Square Odeon on Thursday 17 September 1964. The event, sponsored by *The Sun* in aid of the 'Old Ben' Newsvendor Benevolent Institution, caused hysterical scenes. 'Real-life drama, in the action-packed James Bond style, hit Leicester Square last Thursday night, when over 5,000 fans fought the police outside the Odeon Theatre,' reported the *Kinematograph Weekly* of 24 September. 'In the near riots, the massive glass door of the theatre was shattered and police reinforcements had to be sent for. Wildest moment of all was when Honor Blackman appeared, dazzling in white and gold and wearing a fabulous diamond and gold finger, valued at £10,000. Only swift police action saved her from being swept from her feet.' With Connery unable to attend (he was in Spain, shooting *The Hill*) Blackman stole the limelight. 'It was, I think, the most glamorous night of my life,' she recalled. Other guests included the Broccolis and Saltzmans, Mr and Mrs Frobe, Shirley Eaton, Nadja Regin and Shirley Bassey. Even the film print attracted attention on its arrival – inside golden cans transported by a Security Express armoured car. The following week, Beatlemania-style crowds followed Blackman on her publicity tour of Rank 'Premiere Showcase' cinemas in Bromley, Finsbury Park, Hammersmith, Ilford,

Streatham and Watford. The 1 October edition of *Kinematograph Weekly* chronicled the mayhem, describing how almost 1,200 fans crowded around the Streatham Odeon in anticipation of her visit. 'Honor – a dazzle of gold lamé under the spotlights – just about made it to the entrance past 'House Full' signs.' In Bromley, dozens of policemen reportedly cleared her way through a barrier of queues and sightseers. Blackman continued to promote the film by appearing at cinemas in Leicester, Birmingham, Sheffield, Leeds, Manchester, Newcastle and Glasgow in October.

Although the crowds welcomed the film's leading lady, *Goldfinger* barely needed the publicity. The Leicester Square Odeon reported takings of £17,327 in the first week alone, breaking *From Russia With Love*'s all-time box-office record by £2,799. Elsewhere in the West End, the New Victoria took £9,004 in its first week, beating the house record by £1,129. At the eight suburban 'Premiere Showcases' (the six visited by Blackman plus those at Kingston and Purley) records were broken in each one, with a total of £48,982 grossed in seven days. *Kinematograph Weekly*'s 15 October edition reported that *Goldfinger*'s success was continuing, and had been complemented by 'staggering figures' for a re-release of *Dr. No* playing at the Leicester Square Theatre.

'There was no difficulty in picking out the top release of 1964,' summised editor Bill Altria in the 17 December edition. '*Goldfinger* stands out as No.1. Chosen to initiate the "Premiere Showcase" pattern of release, it was a fabulous, record-breaking success and is expected to gross £1 milion in the UK. It is a triumph for United Artists and Harry Saltzman and Cubby

Broccoli who have achieved the hat-trick with three Ian Fleming James Bond thrillers – first, *Dr. No*, the runner-up in the 1962 box-office stakes; then *From Russia With Love*, the top release in 1963; and now *Goldfinger*, the best in 1964.'

In the United States, *Goldfinger* premiered at New York's DeMille Theater on 21 December 1964. Going on to play in 64 cinemas across 41 cities, it soon earned the distinction of being the fastest-grossing film yet made. American and Canadian takings for the first 14 weeks totalled a staggering $10,374,807.

'*Goldfinger* is one vast, gigantic confidence trick to blind the masses to what is going on underneath,' warned *The Daily Worker*, but no-one was listening. *Kinematograph Weekly* was amongst the first publications to smell a winner when it advised the trade that 'This film has everything required for instant and prolonged success. It cannot fail to hit the jackpot.

'It was not easy to go one better than *From Russia With Love*,' the review continued, 'but it has been done. Bond's insouciant adventures are even larger than the largest life and the death dealt out so liberally throughout is as deadly as can be. The incredible, almost impossible plot is carried along from one smashing incident to another and the ability of the more astonishing incidents to provoke admiring laughter as well as chills is a tribute to screenwriting, direction and the stars.'

Monthly Film Bulletin was similarly impressed: 'So Bond is off again; and, as with *From Russia With Love*, a pre-credits sequence of breathless speed and impudence tips a colossal wink at the audience. After these first five minutes of outrageous violence, callous fun and bland

self-mockery, the tone is so firmly set that the film could get away with almost anything . . . Ken Adam's sets, notably the operations room at the Kentucky ranch and the glittering vaults of Fort Knox, are masterpieces of technological fantasy. Only characters as extreme as Gert Frobe's bloated, tweedy Goldfinger, and Harold Sakata's entirely imperturbable Odd-job could live up to them, and even Honor Blackman's Pussy, in spite of the judo and the wardrobe, seems a trifle diminished. Characters in *Goldfinger* have to make an immediate impact: they will probably be dead before they get a second chance.

'It was, I think, the most glamorous night of my life'

'In all his adventures, sexual and lethal, Bond is a kind of joke superman, as preposterously resilient as one of those cartoon cats. It may be Paul Dehn's collaboration on the script which here gives new finesse to the jokes; or it may simply be a growing confidence on the part of everyone concerned, and most notably of Sean Connery himself. *Goldfinger* really is a dazzling object lesson in the principle that nothing succeeds like excess.'

Sadly, the man who initiated the Bond phenomenon was absent from the celebrations. At 1am on 12 August 1964, Ian Fleming finally lost his battle with heart disease and died, aged 56. He didn't live to see *Goldfinger*, cinematic proof that, although he had been the inspiration, Eon had earned its greatest success with a style that was all its own. 'Everything in *Goldfinger* worked,' concluded Richard Maibaum, a chief architect of that certain something. 'It just worked.' In more ways than one, James Bond had left his creator behind.

File: *Goldfinger*

Teaser Using both a toothpaste-tube style gelignite dispenser and a fake duck atop his head, Bond blows up a Latin American drugs plant essential to the political ambitions of one Mr Ramirez. Back at his hotel, a fiery flamenco type attempts to lure him into the path of an assassin's bullet, but Bond puts paid to the killer with the aid of a bath, an open-bar electric fire and the greatest mock-eulogy of them all ('Shocking. Positively shocking'). The first teaser to truly function as a mini-movie, and easily the best. **10**

Titles Scenes from film projected over parts of the body of a girl painted gold. An Aston Martin's numberplate rotates where her mouth should be; a golf ball runs the length of her arm. Less one point for the hairs on her leg. **9**

Bonkers plot With the blessing of Red China and the assistance of the Mob, a barking mad dealer in gold bullion attempts to irradiate the United States' entire gold reserves by detonating a cobalt and iodine atomic bomb inside Fort Knox, thus increasing his own market value exponentially. **10**

Locations A Latino banana republic; Miami Beach, Florida; London; the Kent countryside; somewhere north of Geneva, Switzerland; 35,000 feet above Newfoundland; Baltimore; Bluegrass Field, Kentucky; and finally Fort Knox. Globe-trotting, but a little unexotic. **7**

Gadgets A gas-spraying parking meter; magnetic transmitting/homing devices in both small and large sizes; Odd-job's bowler probably counts. Goldfinger's presumably patented 'Auric Spectrometer', which detects the presence of nerve gas. The snooker table at Auric Stud, which flips over to reveal a wargaming board with Fort Knox at its centre, shows Goldfinger's stunted and childish nature only too well (it's the business, incidentally). Plus, of course, one of only two vehicles to have acquired the status of pop culture icon (the other being Adam West's Batmobile) – Q Branch's Aston Martin DB5, with modifications. Comes complete with: bulletproof windscreens on both its sides and rear; rotating numberplates, 'naturally' (valid all countries, according to Q, but it clearly only rotates thrice); a

radar tracking screen, a smokescreen, a sprayable oil slick, front-wing machine guns and rotating blades concealed beneath its hubcaps. (The fabled ejector seat is something of a mystery: why can only the passenger seat be expelled? Surely it'd be equally, if not more, useful for the driver's side to be similarly augmented? Perhaps Q doesn't want to risk the car ending up in enemy hands.) Begat the best Corgi toy ever, too. **10**

Girls Bonita, a raven-haired *femme fatale* having a scrub in the teaser; eminently slappable masseuse Dink, who runs along smartly when told to; a 'very sweet' chambermaid; spray-painted Goldfinger co-conspirator Jill Masterson; Miss Moneypenny, whose 'customary byplay' with 007 includes not only tossing his hat onto the stand, but threatening to cook him up an angel cake; sniper Tilly Masterson (aka Tilly Soames), who causes Bond to 'discipline' himself; nose-wrinkling pilot, judo expert and 'woman of many parts' Pussy Galore – 'strictly the outdoor type', she is 'immune' to his charm, and plans to get back to nature in 'a little island in the Bahamas' come her retirement; Mai Lei, Auric's personal lamé-clad air hostess; Sydney, Pussy's black co-pilot; and finally, the five blonde babes who make up Pussy's Flying Circus (the forerunners, surely, of *Captain Scarlet*'s Angels). Bond scores twice for sure (Jill and Pussy) but both Bonita and Dink are pretty safe bets. **10**

Villains Briton Auric Goldfinger, whose name 'sounds like a French nail varnish'. He's a legitimate bullion dealer who 'likes to win' and is worth £20 million, with deposits in Zurich, Amsterdam and Curacao. Has own golf club in Kent, a stud farm in Kentucky, a factory in Switzerland and a sometimes gold-plated Rolls Royce with the numberplate AU1 (how vulgar; how *arriviste*). Has formed 'business partnership' of sorts with Mr Ling and his Chinese associates – Bond is recognised by one of his Chinese opposite numbers, 'who is also licenced to kill' – and has devoted 15 years of his life to Operation Grand Slam. Other baddies include mute Korean Odd-job, whose attachment to his bowler hat leads to his death, assorted mobsters, the unseen Mr Ramirez and his nasty *capungo*, plus a Sten gun-toting little old lady. **10**

Fights, chases, explosions Surprisingly few outside the teaser. There's a cursory car chase in and around the Auric

Enterprises plant, a shoot-out at Fort Knox and Bond's extremely hard-hitting showdown with Odd-job, but that's about it. Is this is the least violent Bond film of all? **2**

Dialogue and double entendres Bond and Jill are post-coital when a radio newscaster announces, 'At the White House this afternoon, the President said he was entirely satisfied .' 'That makes two of us,' says Bond, switching off the set. Goldfinger's *raison d'être* (paraphrased directly from Fleming): 'Man has climbed Mount Everest, gone to the bottom of the ocean. He has fired rockets at the moon, split the atom. Achieved miracles in every field of human endeavour – except crime!' Plus two immortal exchanges ('You expect me to talk?'/'No Mr Bond, I expect you to die!', and 'My name is Pussy Galore.'/'I musht [sic] be dreaming . . .'). **10**

Bond A million style points for unzipping his scuba gear to reveal an immaculate white tux, plus carnation, in the teaser – and dock them all for that disastrous all-in-one pastel blue terry towelling romper suit seen in the Miami Beach scenes. He doesn't think much of a certain popular beat combo from England: drinking Dom Perignon '53 above room temperature is, we learn, 'as bad as listening to The Beatles without earmuffs'. He's a brandy bore, too, and takes his mint julep with 'sour mash, not too sweet'. Uses a Penfold Hearts golf ball, once had a hunting case just like Tilly's, and thinks that ice skating is a 'lovely sport'. Successfully talks his way out of being castrated by laser beam, although it has to be said that it's the first time in any of the films that he looks seriously worried about anything – which rather gives the lie to Pussy's claim that he likes close shaves. Spends an inordinate amount of time locked up throughout. **7**

Plus/minus points Plus points for a couple of continuity references to both *Dr. No* and *From Russia With Love* (via Felix and mention of a certain black attaché case), plus word of one 008. Minus points for what might be surmised as two early examples of tacky product placement: Felix's stop-off for a box of finger-lickin' good Kentucky Fried Chicken, and the screenplay's otherwise inexplicable substitution of a Slazenger 1 for the novel's Dunlop 65 as Goldfinger's golf ball of choice. **0**

85% The acme of stylish action cinema, effortlessly cool and endlessly rewarding. Its opulence is all-consuming, as is the richness of its *mise-en-scène* – what else might take in nerve gas, laser beams, private jets and smuggled armies, golf clubs and stud farms, a platoon of pulchritudinous pilots? – and yet all these elements are tangential to the plot, passing glances almost lost in the kinetic hyperactivity of the whole.

CAST

Sean Connery James Bond
Honor Blackman Pussy Galore   Gert Frobe Auric Goldfinger
Shirley Eaton Jill Masterson   Tania Mallet Tilly Masterson
Harold Sakata (Tosh Togo) Odd-job   Bernard Lee 'M'   Martin Benson Solo
Cec Linder Felix Leiter   Austin Willis Simmons   Lois Maxwell Moneypenny
Bill Nagy Midnight   Michael Mellinger Kisch   Peter Cranwell Johnny
Nadja Regin Bonita   Richard Vernon Smithers   Burt Kwouk Mr Ling
Desmond LLewelyn 'Q'   Mai Ling Mai Lei   Varley Thomas Swiss gatekeeper
Margaret Nolan Dink   John McLaren Brigadier   Robert Macleod Atomic scientist
Victor Brooks Blacking   Alf Joint Capungo
Gerry Duggan Hawker and Denis Cowles Brunskill   Hal Galili Strap
Lenny Rabin Henchman   Raymond Young Sierra

SELECTED CREDITS

Produced by **Harry Saltzman, Albert R. Broccoli**
Directed by **Guy Hamilton**
Production designed by **Ken Adam**
Director of photography **Ted Moore B.S.C.**   Editor **Peter Hunt**
Art director **Peter Murton**   Production manager **L.C. Rudkin**
Assistant director **Frank Ernst**   Camera operator **John Winbolt**
Make-up **Paul Rabiger, Basil Newall**   Action sequences by **Bob Simmons**
Wardrobe mistress **Eileen Sullivan**   Wardrobe master **John Hilling**
Special effects **John Stears**, assisted by **Frank George**
Technical advisor **Charles Russhon**   Titles designed by **Robert Brownjohn**
Screenplay by **Richard Maibaum, Paul Dehn**
Title song sung by **Shirley Bassey**
Music composed and conducted by **John Barry**
Title song lyrics by **Leslie Bricusse, Anthony Newley**

Swimming, slugging and necking: *Thunderball*

1963: weak through heart disease and the strain incurred by a lengthy hearing, Ian Fleming foreshortened his lengthy litigation with Kevin McClory and Jack Whittingham by agreeing to a settlement out of court. On Tuesday 26 November, high court judge Mr Justice Ungoed-Thomas heard the resolution of the copyright action brought against Fleming, publishers Jonathan Cape and financier John Bryce. McClory would share an additional credit on all subsequent printings of *Thunderball* and, crucially, screen rights to the story. 'I consider it a total victory, and I'm very happy,' McClory told journalists. 'I'm glad this expensive misunderstanding is all over,' said a weary Fleming. But the *Thunderball* saga still had a long way to go.

On 8 January 1964 *The Daily Mail* reported that McClory's long-held ambition to bring *Thunderball* to the screen had gathered momentum. Reporter Gerard Kemp's description of Eon's rival product made it seem mundane in comparison: 'Albert Broccoli and Harry Saltzman are following their two earlier Bond thrillers with *Goldfinger*, in which Bond plays a desperate life-or-death golf match. Kevin McClory is making *Thunderball*, in which a madman steals an H-bomb and holds the world to ransom.'

McClory had begun the new year in Rome, auditioning girls for his new film. In a telephone conversation with Kemp, he claimed there were three actors earmarked for the role of Bond (both Sean Connery's contract with Eon and commitment to *Goldfinger* precluded his involvement). Laurence Harvey, star of both dour kitchen-sink drama *Room at the Top* (1959) and Cold War thriller *The Manchurian Candidate* (1962), was one of the names on the list; McClory refused to name the others. 'All I will say is that the man chosen will not be an American actor,' he said. 'But you can take it from me that my Bond will be a big "animal type" actor.' (He would later reveal that his favoured star was Richard Burton.) As 1964 progressed, McClory advanced his plans to make *Thunderball* the debut production of his newly formed Branwell Film Productions, rewriting the Whittingham's screenplay and scouting locations in the Bahamas. By September, however, McClory had abandoned the idea of competing with Eon and approached Harry Saltzman and Albert Broccoli with the proposition of making *Thunderball* a co-production. An agreement (reportedly earmarking 20 per cent of the film's profits for McClory) was struck, and the end credits of *Goldfinger* hastily amended – the finished print proclaimed that James Bond would return in *Thunderball* and not *On Her Majesty's*

April 1965: near Clifton Pier in the Bahamas, Connery and Auger take to the water

Secret Service, as originally intended.

'*Thunderball* is to be the next James Bond film and it will be produced by Kevin McClory in association with Cubby Broccoli and Harry Saltzman,' reported the 1 October edition of *Kinematograph Weekly*. 'To star Sean Connery as 007, the film is scheduled for production in February next year with many scenes to be shot in the actual Bahamas Islands location of the story.'

McClory had, it seems, abandoned any hope he may have retained to direct the film. 'Cubby and Kevin McClory came out to ask me to do *Thunderball*,' recalled Guy Hamilton. 'I was drained of ideas. I was very fond of Bond, but felt that I had nothing to contribute until I'd recharged batteries.' Similarly, Paul Dehn declined to resume his association with Eon. Ultimately, Richard Maibaum's 1961 screenplay was dusted off, revised and given a polish by British television writer John Hopkins, a veteran of shows such as *Sunday-Night Theatre* and seminal police drama *Z Cars* (his later film work includes *The Virgin Soldiers* and Sherlock Holmes meets Jack the Ripper thriller *Murder By Decree*). Terence Young was contracted to direct. By the end of 1964, the phenomenal success of *Goldfinger* had sufficiently swelled the coffers of Eon and United Artists to allow for *Thunderball*'s $5.6 million budget. While the Maibaum/Hopkins screenplay was developed, casting began.

The role of Domino, mistress of SPECTRE's Emil Largo and ultimate ally to Bond, was hotly contested; over 150 girls would audition. Albert Broccoli had been impressed by Julie Christie's performance in *Billy Liar* (1963) and invited her to an interview. On her arrival at his office, however, he would be disappointed by her casual appearance and relatively modest bust. Broccoli also pursued Raquel Welch after seeing her on the cover of *Life* magazine in October 1964. Welch was contracted, only to be sidelined into *Fantastic Voyage* following lobbying by Twentieth Century-Fox's Richard Zanuck. Faye Dunaway came close to signing, but allowed her agent to persuade her into appearing in dotty caper movie *The Happening* (1967) instead. Lesser known actresses who donned distinctive black swimsuits for screen tests included French Hammer horror heroine Yvonne Monlaur, former Miss Italy Maria Grazia Buccella, Marisa Menzies and Gloria Paul. The role eventually went to 23-year-old Claudine Auger, who had won the title Miss France when just 15 years old. Miss Auger had studied English while working as an au pair in Mill Hill, London, and, in 1961, married French film director Pierre Gaspard-Hut. Her casting necessitated a switch in Domino's nationality – the Italian Domino Palazzi became Dominique Derval to accommodate her accent. (There would ultimately be no need for this – her unacceptably deep voice would be dubbed in post-production.)

Villain Emilio Largo was played by Adolfo Celi. Born in 1922, Celi would also appear in the French/Italian spy thriller spoof *L'Homme De Rio* (*That Man From Rio*) in 1964. A prolific and popular leading man in European films, he would later gain notoriety for playing Pope Alexander VI in the BBC television series *The Borgias*.

Although unsuccessful in her bid to play Domino, Luciana Paluzzi won the role of Irish SPECTRE assassin Fiona Kelly, a character named by Richard Maibaum. Fiona's nationality was fixed with a surname change to Volpe to reflect Paluzzi's casting. Paluzzi had made her screen debut playing a country girl in *Three Coins In the Fountain* (1954) and went on to briefly become a Rank contract artiste. Prior to *Thunderball*, one of her most prominent British roles had been the female lead (opposite Stanley Baker) in the 1958 film *Sea Fury*. She told the autumn 1965 issue of *Girls International*: 'Appearing in a Bond film is like doing four or five years' work in one. Not only are you given the greatest exposure possible in a single film today, but there is a special kind of magic associated with the whole Bond legend.'

Felix Leiter was played by Rik Van Nutter, the husband of actress Anita Ekberg (who had starred alongside Bob Hope in *Call Me Bwana*). Despite being dubbed throughout *Thunderball*, Nutter was confidently expected to reprise the role of Leiter in future Bond films. It was not to be. The voluptuous Molly Peters, who was contracted to play the saucy health farm masseuse Patricia Fearing, had worked as an extra in Terence Young's previous film, *The Amorous Adventures of Moll Flanders* (1965). She next appeared in *Joey Boy* (1965), a wartime comedy directed by Frank Launder and starring Harry H Corbett. Following *Thunderball*, a wrangle with the modelling agency to which she was contracted hampered her attempts to

pursue an acting career. Other notables in the cast included Kiwi actor Guy Doleman, who played hapless SPECTRE agent Count Lippe. In 1965, the year of *Thunderball*'s release, Doleman could also be seen as Major Ross in producer Harry Saltzman's *The Ipcress File*.

Interviewed by *The Daily Mail*'s Roderick Mann in February 1965, Sean Connery seemed eager to start work. '*Thunderball* is the best story of them all really. There are wonderful underwater sequences in the Bahamas and the premise is wildly exciting. I think it could be even better than the last one, but I can't see the cycle going on past that. Though I am signed to do two more – *OHMSS* and one other. But who knows? America seems to lap them up.

'My only grumble about the Bond films is that they don't tax one as an actor. All one really needs is the constitution of a rugby player to get through 18 weeks of swimming, slugging and necking . . . I'd like to see someone else tackle Bond, I must say – though I think they'd be crazy to do it. There was talk of Richard Burton doing one, and I said he must be out of his mind. It would be like putting his head on a chopping block. Whatever he did he couldn't make the films more successful than they are. Even if Sam Spiegel and David Lean made one, there's no guarantee it would do any better.' On 16 February, two days after the interview was published, Connery flew to Paris to begin principal photography on *Thunderball*. (While in the capital, he took the opportunity to attend his first premiere of *Goldfinger*. He may have had cause to regret the decision when his DB5 was invaded by a frenzied female fan while he was driving down the Champs-Elysées.)

Terence Young began filming the pre-credit

sequence at the Chateau D'Anet, outside Paris. As originally scripted by Richard Maibaum, Bond would have sought his quarry in a 'fan-tan' strip club in Hong Kong – an alluring dancer would have been Bond's cross-dressed quarry. Maibaum and Hopkins' shooting script (a revision dated 19 January 1965) shifted the action to the funeral of one Colonel Jacques Boitier. While accompanied by Mademoiselle La Porte (Maryse Guy Mitsouko, whose voice was dubbed by Catherine Clemence) Bond begins to suspect that Mr Boitier's veiled widow (Rose Alba) is not all she seems. Bond notices Mrs Boitier open a car door by herself, and becomes immediately suspicious. (Mrs Boitier's behaviour might be incongruous to Bond, but the fact it betrays her true identity as a man must have seemed anachronistic to an audience who, in Pussy Galore, had been presented with a female to whom opening car doors must have been a doddle.) Jacques Boitier is alive and well, and dressed as his mourning wife. When the overcranked punch-up began, Rose Alba exited to be replaced by ubiquitous stunt man Bob Simmons in drag. For key moments during the fight, Connery was doubled by Harold Sanderson.

On 19 February, one of the most striking images in the entire picture was filmed: Bond's escape from the roof of the Chateau strapped to a Bell Textron jet pack. The only two pilots qualified to fly the jet pack were brought to France specially. One of them, Bill Suitor, doubled for Connery during the short flight. When Terence Young asked Suitor to make the flight without a crash helmet he refused – as a result Connery was filmed hastily strapping on head gear in front of a back projection of the Chateau rooftop. Connery resumed duties as Bond to bundle the jet pack into the boot of the DB5

Enjoying the view in the Bahamas, Sean Connery and Claudine Auger pose for the press

before using one of the car's gadgets to drench his pursuing assailants. The pre-credits sequence was to have ended with a crane-shot of the DB5 speeding away, but in the summer the sequence was cut to end with the drenching when Maurice Binder's underwater title sequence suggested the opportunity for a perfect *segue*.

For the next four weeks, cast and crew based themselves at Pinewood Studios while preparations were made for their arrival in the Bahamas. The Shrublands health farm, which 007 visits at the beginning of the film, was the venue for Bond's latest sexual conquest – the beautiful Patricia Fearing, as played by Molly Peters. 'I was very nervous since I'd never actually been on a sound stage before,' she recalled. 'In another corner of the studio I saw a very tall handsome man and I remember Terence Young said to me

47

"Darling, of course you know Sean, don't you?" and I'd never met Sean in my life. I was quite overawed by this.'

The DB5 chase that resulted in Count Lippe's disintegration was filmed at Silverstone race track in Northamptonshire. The rocket-firing BSA motorbike carrying the leather-clad Fiona was tracked by Terence Young's crew at over 100mph. Bob Simmons, driving Lippe's car, ignited wads of petrol-soaked felt on cue via a dashboard switch. Amid fears over Simmons' safety, Young filmed the car's crash and subsequent explosion, although the stunt man seemed to have vanished. Young was relieved to find Simmons re-emerge from behind him – the stunt man had been lucky to escape with his life.

In Nassau, Kevin McClory's years of preparation paid off when he directed production designer Ken Adam to the best areas. 'At the time no-one had ever built a set underwater,' recalls senior draughtsman Peter Lamont. 'Ken breezed into the office one day and said "We're going to do *Thunderball*. You'd better learn to swim."' Adam's greatest challenge on *Thunderball* was not designing expansive sets of the type that dominated *Goldfinger*, but dreaming up nautical hardware. 'I had to design a lot of underwater craft and so on . . . I thought nobody could ever realise these designs and they weren't practical. We found this expert on mini-submarines in Miami – Jordan Klein – and he said "No, no, we can build that." That gave me a great deal of confidence because I found on subsequent Bonds that whatever I designed somebody in the world was able to realise these designs and make it practical.'

The flagship of Adam's fleet was Largo's yacht, the two-part *Disco Volante* (Italian

for 'flying saucer'). $500,000 was allocated to buying the ship (*The Flying Fish*, a hydrofoil Adam purchased in Puerto Rico in December 1964) and converting it for its spectacular transformation during the film's closing scenes. 'All my naval advisors thought it wouldn't work because the catamaran part of it was attached to the hydrofoil with two one-inch slipboards – that was the only thing that held those two hulls together. Once the slipboards were pulled out the hydrofoil just sped away.'

In Miami, where the engineering work was carried out, Jordan Klein and his team slept in shifts so their work would meet shooting deadlines. On 22 March 1965, cast and crew flew to Nassau to commence location (and underwater) filming.

Jamaican-born Martine Beswick was hired to play Bond's ally Paula Kaplan. 'I'd been in England so long my skin had gone pale,' she remembers. 'When they shipped us out to Nassau, they put me on a call sheet to go to work every day – the work was simply getting an even suntan! We were living the life of Riley – we were hot, hot, hot. Everyone came to visit while we were filming, tourists as well as friends. The richest of the rich came to play on Paradise Island. It was a riot. We had lunches on tablecloths under coconut trees. It was the same thing off screen as it was on.' In amateur footage taken during the shooting in Nassau, a dapper Terence Young can indeed be seen handing champagne to cast and crew members aboard Eon's yacht.

Mainland filming on Nassau included the memorable pursuit of Bond through a local parade. The parade, or 'Junkanoo', is traditionally held on 26 December; Young arranged an out-of-season celebration using a combination of locals and extras.

Camera crews descended 50 feet under water to film the scenes showing SPECTRE frogmen stealing the atomic bombs from the grounded Vulcan bomber. (The 'bombs' manufactured by Jordan Klein for the film are of an authentic design; Peter Lamont had surreptitiously photographed the real thing on an air base using a secret camera.)

Filming in Largo's shark-infested pool caused Connery understandable concern. Ken Adam had discovered a private villa, and ordered 15 sharks to be delivered to one of its pools. Connery promptly ordered some protection, so Adam submerged a corridor of flexiglass that the sharks would theoretically stay behind. (Terence Young apparently assured Connery that sharks couldn't jump.) Unfortunately, Adam neglected to tell Connery that he had mistakenly failed to order sufficient flexiglass to partition the pool entirely. '[A] shark went straight down the corridor and went out through the four-foot gap,' remembered Adam. 'I got out of the water,' said Connery, recalling the sheer terror that is all too evident on screen. 'I think I was dry when I touched the side. I don't know whose fault it was, but it didn't happen again.' The shark seen pursuing Bond to the edge of the pool as he gets out was actually a dead predator, towed on a line behind Connery. Stunt supervisor John Stears was standing in the middle of the pool preparing the apparently dead animal when it suddenly awoke, and started snapping at the other sharks. While Stears screamed 'Get me out of here!' a bloody frenzy ensued, which Young duly filmed.

Although the danger to humans was apparently slight (sharks rarely attack unless they detect blood in the water) stunt man Bill Cummings, playing failed Largo

flunkey Quist, demanded £250 of danger money before he agreed to being dropped into the pool. Terence Young had concerns of his own: 'My wife refused to go to bed with me for two weeks afterwards,' he remembered. 'She said "You stink of shark and rotten fish – go and sleep somewhere else!"'

'The biggest explosion ever in a motion picture'

Sixty divers participated in the climactic battle filmed in the shallow water off Clifton Pier. The lengthy sequences were largely choreographed by Ricou Browning, an underwater photography specialist who, in 1954, had donned a rubber suit to play *The Creature From the Black Lagoon*. Browning rehearsed the divers out of the water, on board a rented barge, and communicated with them underwater through a system of hand signals Lemar Boren was also crucial to the success of the underwater sequences. Boren had originally been contacted by Albert Broccoli in 1961, when *Thunderball* was anticipated to be the first James Bond film, and was able to bring years of experience with Ivan Tors Studios (who produced such television series as *Flipper* and *Sea Hunt*) to his ground-breaking Panavision photography of the battle. Connery took no risks with the tiger, bull and lemon sharks that weaved in and out of the action, and was doubled by Frank Cousins in most scenes.

Jordan Klein (who had been an underwater stills photographer on *The Creature From the Black Lagoon*) worked alongside John Stears, who in turn received some help from Eon's unofficial military liaison, Lieutenant-Colonel Charles Russhon. The retired air force officer had previously pulled strings in Turkey (for *From Russia With Love*) and at Fort Knox (for *Goldfinger*), but *Thunderball* would witness his most spectacular contribution yet to the Bond films. He procured underwater hardware from the US Navy and helped secure the 'Skyhook' rescue gadgetry that scoops up Bond and Domino at the end of the film. When Stears was looking for a way to explode the *Disco Volante*, Russhon helped supply experimental rocket fuel which was only delivered the night before filming. 'It really was "suck it and see",' says Stears. 'I hit the TX and I just couldn't believe what happened – the thing just disappeared in front of our eyes. I didn't know where the boat had gone to – I thought we'd just vapourised it. I looked up and there was a little black pinpoint in the sky. I said, "I don't want to worry you guys, but the boat is coming back down on top of us and there's nowhere to go." A very nasty mess . . . When we got back to Nassau all the windows were out in Bay Street – that was 30 miles away! It must have been the biggest explosion ever in a motion picture.' (Russhon, incidentally, received extra recognition for his Bond contributions towards the end of *Goldfinger* – a sign on an aircraft hangar reads 'Welcome General Russhon'. In *Thunderball*, he actually appears as an air force officer present at the '00' briefing in London near the beginning of the film.)

Stears' contribution would be rewarded with an Oscar for special visual effects. Stears and Norman Wanstall (who received an Academy award for *Goldfinger*'s sound effects) remain the only two recipients of Oscars for any category in any James Bond film.

In 1965, even the relatively conservative *Kinematograph Weekly* claimed that 'Sean Connery is James Bond; it is, indeed, becoming very hard to separate the real from the fictional.' Towards the end of the Nassau shoot, Connery's frustration with his invasive alter ego was again becoming apparent. *Thunderball* had coincided with a difficult time in the actor's private life: on 17 March 1965 *The Daily Express* claimed he had begun a trial separation from Diane Cilento, his wife of two-and-a-half years. Connery refused to co-operate with the journalists who hounded him throughout filming, granting only one interview during the entire shoot. He told *Playboy* magazine: 'I find that fame tends to turn one from an actor and a human being into a piece of merchandise, a public institution. Well, I don't intend to undergo that metamorphosis.'

The release of *Thunderball* would be trailed by Wolper Productions' The *Incredible World of James Bond*, transmitted by American network NBC on 26 November. The documentary, sponsored by Pepsico and produced/directed by Jack Haley Jr, included exclusive behind-the-scenes coverage of *Thunderball*'s production. Connery declined Wolper's offer to participate, even after Pepsico's Joan Crawford tried to talk him round. 'They offered me a lot of money and a percentage of the profits to take part in it,' he recalled in 1967. 'But they were going to do it as if Bond were a real person and came from Edinburgh, my home town. And they'd taken whole scenes from the Bond films and weren't paying the actors in them any extra money. So I turned it down.'

In May 1965, principal photography concluded at Pinewood Studios with the staging of the final fist-fight aboard the bridge of the *Disco Volante*. A partial replica of the boat had been built in the studio, and careful attempts were made to match the footage from Nassau. Terence Young would later complain that shooting the real thing had been easier.

As Peter Hunt embarked on a long and arduous editing job, Maurice Binder began work on the title sequence (a dispute over design had kept Binder's name off the credits of the previous two Bond pictures). The gun barrel opening sequence (which Binder remembered devising just 20 minutes before his first meeting with Saltzman and Broccoli) had to be remounted for filming in the Panavision widescreen process. As before, the sequence was realised using pinhole photography of the inside of a real gun barrel – this time, however, it was Sean Connery and not Bob Simmons (who appeared in silhouette on the first three Bond films) who strode into view and turned to shoot.

Binder's racy title sequence was shot in the tank at Pinewood during July, using two girls who had previously swum in nightclub tanks. They reluctantly stripped naked, and were photographed in black and white on a white background. (Binder later added a deep blue as an optical effect.) The provocative title sequence would prove unacceptable to prudish Spanish censors, who cut certain shots. Binder's title sequence was first synchronised with *Thunderball*'s original theme tune, 'Mr Kiss Kiss Bang Bang'. The song was inspired by a phrase coined by an Italian journalist in 1962 (he was writing about a publicity tour of Turin, Bologna, Milan and Rome undertaken by Sean Connery to publicise *Dr. No*). The phrase had found real popularity in Japan, and loaned itself to the title of the John Barry/Leslie Bricusse track. (During

shooting, a Nassau nightclub visited by 007 and Fiona had been renamed 'Kiss Kiss Club' especially.) The song was first recorded by Shirley Bassey, then Dionne Warwick, only to be dropped from the opening credits just weeks before release. Apparently nervous about a theme tune that didn't mention the film's title, Saltzman and Broccoli asked John Barry for a last-minute replacement. Working with lyricist Don Black, he came up with *Thunderball*, which was recorded by Tom Jones shortly before the film's premiere. The strain of hitting the song's final note actually caused Jones to faint in the studio. 'Thankfully, he didn't have to sing it more than once,' recalls Black. 'He got it right the first time. When he sings it live now he takes it down a bit.' The recording schedule was so tight that *Thunderball*'s original soundtrack album, issued prior to the film's release, was dominated by music from the first half of the film – at the time of the album's release, Barry had yet to finish scoring the rest.

Thunderball's world premiere took place in New York on 21 December 1965. In late November, Manhattan's Paramount Theater had erected a special booth that looped the film's trailer for the benefit of curious members of the public. For the premiere itself, the Bell Textron jet pack was launched from the Paramount's marquee to the ground below; soon after, both its pilot and United Artists publicists were arrested for staging the stunt without a licence. None of the attendant publicity hurt box office takings, and the Paramount became one of many American cinemas to stay open 24 hours a day to cope with demand.

Thunderball's British gala premieres took place simultaneously at Piccadilly Circus' Pavilion and Coventry Street's Rialto cinemas on 29 December. At the Pavilion, Claudine Auger and Luciana Paluzzi were joined by *Goldfinger*'s Honor Blackman and Tania Mallet. A hundred yards away, guests at the Rialto gala included Molly Peters, Martine Beswick, Adolfo Celi and Guy Doleman. At a supper party held at the Royal Garden Hotel following the twin shows, it was announced that the premieres had raised a total of £60,000 for the Newspaper Press Fund. Neither Connery nor Saltzman appeared at any of the evening's events. Broccoli, grieving for his recently deceased mother, was also absent.

Few were surprised when *Thunderball* smashed the Pavilion's house record, taking £8,120 in its first four days. At the smaller Rialto, takings were an incredible £3,724 in the same period. Amid stiff competition from *The Sound of Music* and *The Battle of the Bulge*, *Thunderball*'s business continued to significantly outstrip even that of *Goldfinger*. In Rank's nine 'Premiere Showcase' cinemas *Thunderball* was first shown at midnight matinees on 1 January 1966. Each show played to capacity; when the Odeons at Bromley and Streatham were fully booked, they even sold tickets to customers who willingly stood for the duration of the performance. Figures proudly presented by Eric Pleskow, United Artists' vice-president in charge of foreign distribution, told a story of phenomenal global success for the first three days of the film's release: in Paris, *Thunderball* grossed over $95,000 in three days; Rome $79,000; Milan $25,000 and Stockholm $20,000. In Japan, the Bond frenzy reached new heights – four cinemas in the Osaka region registered takings of $61,379 in just two days. In Tokyo, a new record was set at the Hibiya Theatre where *Thunderball* grossed a staggering $110,000 in nine days. United Artists estimated that *Thunderball*'s worldwide gross would recover the film's

negative cost within just three months. 'The initial figures from overseas, exceeding the sky-high takings of *Goldfinger*, certainly point to this prospect,' concurred *Kinematograph Weekly* editor Bill Altria in the 6 January 1966 issue. 'What a lot of bank interest charges this is going to save.'

'Crammed with pop value . . .'

On Thursday 10 February, a charity premiere took place at the Savoy in Dublin. Luciana Paluzzi, Molly Peters and Albert Broccoli arrived to a welcoming committee of harpoon-wielding frogmen (and women). After the screening, Kevin McClory hosted a party in the Terrace Suite at the Gresham Hotel. In London, the unstoppable *Thunderball*'s competition by now included a profitable re-release of *Goldfinger* at the Haymarket Odeon and American spy spoofs *Our Man Flint* and *One Spy Too Many*. There was plenty of room at the top.

On 30 December 1965, *Kinematograph Weekly* was in no doubt that *Thunderball* represented a 'Jackpot certainty' for cinema managers everywhere. 'The explanation of SPECTRE's ransom plan takes a little time, but once the plot is clear it gallops from one lethal situation to another, dallying amusingly between them in the company of (with Bond) a succession of lovely girls, some good, some bad. The whole improbable concoction is put over with shattering speed and an irresistible sense of humour; you can't help laughing while you enjoy the dangers and admire the dazzling use of Caribbean colour on the very large screen.' *Variety*'s 'Whit' was similarly impressed: 'There's visible evidence that the reported

$5,500,000 budget was no mere publicity figure; it's posh all the way, crammed with pop value, as company moves from France and England to the Bahamas . . . One of highlight sequences is the underwater battle between US Aquatroops, whom Bond calls upon after he locates the hidden bombs, and the heavies, both using spear guns for spectacular effect . . .'

On 17 June 1965, the London *Evening Standard* reported that American television network CBS had approached Saltzman and Broccoli for their stake in the the 007 franchise. Some $30 million (£10 million) had been offered for Eon's rights in all James Bond films, past, present and future. A 'source close to' Saltzman and Broccoli claimed that negotiations for all Bond stories bar *Casino Royale* had taken place, before talks broke down in May over 'tax problems and division of rights.'

Saltzman and Broccoli were wise to safeguard their film empire: in 1965 the first three Bond films were earning £8 10d every 30 seconds – £1,000 an hour, day and night. American admissions to *Thunderball* would total 74.8 million – a figure that no James Bond film before or after could even challenge. The film's worldwide gross would hit $141.2 million. Eon was never more successful. In Holland, *Thunderball* was released under an apposite new title: *Calm Down, Mr Bond*.

File: *Thunderball*

Teaser The funeral of one 'JB' – Colonel Jacques Boitier, a Gallic grotesque responsible for the deaths of two Bond associates. (The name is actually pronounced 'Beauvard' on screen, but the credits have it otherwise. Very odd.) Suspicious, Our Man waits for Boitier's veiled widow at a nearby chateau and socks 'her' on the jaw, revealing the Colonel himself. Cue punch-up. Bond throttles the bad guy

with a poker, escaping Boitier's goons with the assistance of a jet-powered back-pack, a doe-eyed French popsy and *Goldfinger*'s Aston Martin. **8**

Titles The first of the heavily symbolic cod-Freudian sequences for which Maurice Binder would become notorious. An underwater sex fantasy in which silhouetted women are hunted down and shot at by a frogman carrying an absurdly literal harpoon gun; at one point, a projectile is even fired between the legs of a departing nymphet. I think, to paraphrase a later scene, we get the point. **10**

Bonkers plot SPECTRE steal a Vulcan bomber carrying two atomic bombs (serial numbers 456 and 457) from the Brits and attempt to extort £100 million for their return. But Bond's mission is not to prevent the warheads being detonated; the Government has agreed to pay up. No, Bond has to locate the bombs so as to prevent Great Britain from losing face. Hardly a thrilling premise, eh? **4**

Locations France; a health farm close to a NATO base, England; Paris; in and around (but mostly beneath the seas of) Nassau; London. The film's events unfold late one May. **6**

Gadgets Bond's sci-fi jet pack ('No well-dressed man should be without one'); Largo's electronic cigarette case; various underwater vehicles employed by Largo's scuba-clad goons; a tape recorder concealed inside a hollowed-out book; a Geiger counter worn on the wrist; an underwater camera; a miniature flare pistol; a minuscule mouth-held canister containing four minutes' oxygen; and an ingestible homing device. Fiona has a side-armed motorbike, and the Aston Martin makes a reappearance. **8**

Girls Or 'Ravishing redheads! Bronzed brunettes! Honey blondes! The Bond women – 007 style!' as the trailer has it. (No wonder this is, apparently, the 'biggest Bond of all!') Teaser tease Mademoiselle La Porte ('Is there anything else our French station can do for you, Mister Bond?' 'Later, perhaps . . .'); Miss Moneypenny, whom Bond threatens with a spanking; physiotherapist/masseuse/radiographer Pat, whose at-first-successful efforts to cool Bond's ardour ('Behave yourself!') melt in the health farm's sauna (Bond's 'price' for not informing her boss of his 'accident' on the traction table. What a charmer); Bad

Girl Fiona Volpe, a crack shot with a taste for speed on two wheels or four — and who, in undoubtedly the most explicit, wild sex scene in the series so far, informs Bond that 'this bed feels like a cage'; Paula, Bond's first ever field assistant, who proves loyal to the point of suicide; and Good Girl Dominique, aka 'Domino', who 'swims like a man' (and who appears to indulge in sub-aqua sex with Bond). There's an exotic firewalker on display at the Kiss Kiss Club, too, as well as a posh English girl who mistakes Fiona for Bond's wife. Three more notches on the Bond bedstead (Pat, Fiona, Domino). **9**

Villains SPECTRE, otherwise known as the 'purely philanthropic' International Brotherhood for the Assistance of Stateless Persons; members include Boitier, SPECTRE's Number Six, plus blackmailer Seven, assassin Ten, drug pusher Eleven, found-out and fried embezzler Nine, and Five, a consultant to the Great Train Robbery (did Slipper of the Yard know about this?). We meet Blofeld once more; again, his features are concealed. Number Two is big game fish collector Emilio Largo; responsible for the NATO project, SPECTRE's 'most ambitious' plan to date, he's not above a little

asphyxiation nor hot and cold torture (applied 'slowly and scientifically', natch). Unusually for a Bond villain, he's happy to immerse himself in the thick of the fighting. Associates include broiled Tong/SPECTRE agent Count Lippe, who gets fired by Fiona at Blofeld's request; Domino's brother, Angelo Palazzi — who, after two years' plastic surgery in the pursuit of Largo's plot to steal the Vulcan, has the brassneck to demand his fee be upped at the eleventh hour (and pays for it, too); taciturn henchmen Yanni and Vargas (the latter being an unreconstructed sadist who 'doesn't drink, smoke, or make love'); cringing Quist, who ends up as shark food; vamp Fiona. Big players behind them, sure, but Largo and chums are strictly small-time hoods. **4**

Fights, chases, explosions A good old-fashioned brawl, with furniture, between Boitier and Bond (the former in drag, which is always a plus). Lippe's car is blown to smithereens courtesy of Fiona's rockets. Endless slo-mo underwater grappling, complete with much severing of air lines and subsequent overdone stuntman writhing. Shockingly, there's a moment when Bond impales one of Largo's frogmen in the eye with his harpoon; we see it penetrating his face mask. (This is not comic-strip James

In June 1965, sequences showing 007's inspection of the submerged Vulcan bomber were recreated at Pinewood Studios, and later matched to footage shot in the Bahamas. The Pinewood tank held 500,000 gallons of water and was 16 feet deep

Bond fun. This is nasty.) Largo's *Disco Volante* gets blown up twice – its cocoon by warships, its sleek body by collision with rocks – and the knockabout in its cabin immediately beforehand is gratifyingly brutal. Unlike in *Goldfinger*, where the hordes of US infantry summoned up in the climax are germane to its location, the armies of frogmen who parachute in to save the day defy credulity. This trend will, sadly, continue as each film attempts to outdo its precursor … **4**

Dialogue and double entendres Pat to Bond: 'Haven't you had enough exercise for one evening?' Bond to Pat: 'Funny you should mention that …' But it's Fiona and Bond's double act which elicits all the best lines. Fiona, speeding a night with Bond in the passenger seat: 'Some men don't like to be driven.' Bond: 'No, some men don't like to be taken for a ride …' Held at gunpoint by Fiona's goons following the 'bed like a cage' incident, Bond announces that: 'What I did this evening was for King and country. You don't think it gave me any pleasure, do you?' Whereupon Fiona loses the plot: 'I forgot your ego, Mister Bond. James Bond, who only has to make love to a woman and she starts to hear 'eavenly choirs singing. She repents, then immediately returns to the side of right and virtue. But not this one. What a blow it must have been – you, having a failure.' Smirks Bond, *sotto voce*: 'Well, you can't win them all …' Had this exchange featured in *GoldenEye* 29 years later, it'd have been called reflexive, post-modern. Here, it's smart. **8**

Bond is at his most feline while slinking like a burglar through the health clinic at night; the nonchalant slam of his elbow against the fire alarm is a nice touch. Has 'sharp little eyes', according to Domino. Consumes conch chowder ('an aphrodisiac'), Beluga caviare and Dom Perignon '55. Keeps his gun under his pillow. Has one defining moment after barging into Fiona's bath. 'Since you're here, wouldn't you give me something to put on?' she asks. He hands her a pair of sandals. Then sits back to watch. **8**

Plus/minus points Bond's escape from Largo's shark pool is a real highlight, as is the wonderfully staged (and scored) death of Fiona ('Do you mind if my friend sits this one out? She's just dead …'). The notion of the British Government having Big Ben strike seven times at six o'clock to signal its acceptance of SPECTRE's terms is brilliant – but why don't we see it happen? Bond's arrival

---

CAST

Sean Connery James Bond
Claudine Auger Domino   Adolfo Celi Largo
Luciana Paluzzi Fiona   Rik Van Nutter Felix Leiter   Guy Doleman Count Lippe
Molly Peters Patricia   Martine Beswick Paula   Bernard Lee 'M'
Desmond LLewelyn 'Q'   Lois Maxwell Moneypenny
Roland Culver Foreign Secretary   Earl Cameron Pinder   Paul Stassino Palazzi
Rose Alba Madame Boitier   Philip Locke Vargas   George Pravda Kutze
Michael Brennan Janni   Leonard Sachs Group Captain
Edward Underdown Air Vice Marshal   Reginald Beckwith Kenniston
Harold Sanderson Hydrofoil Captain and Bill Cummings Quist*
Maryse Guy Mitsouko Mademoiselle La Porte*   Bob Simmons Jacques Boitier*

SELECTED CREDITS

Director of Photography Ted Moore BSC   Supervising Editor Peter Hunt
Art Director Peter Murton   Production Supervisor David Middlemas
Special Effects John Stears   Assistant Director Gus Agosti
Location Manager Frank Ernst   Camera Operator John Winbolt
Make-up Paul Rabiger, Basil Newall   Action Sequences by Bob Simmons
Underwater Sequences Director Ricou Browning   Editor Ernest Hosler
Wardrobe Designer Anthony Mendleson   Wardrobe Mistress Eileen Sullivan
Wardrobe Master John Brady   Hairdresser Eileen Warwick
Sean Connery's Suits Anthony Sinclair   Main Title Designed by Maurice Binder
Music Composed and Conducted by John Barry   Song 'Thunderball' Lyrics by Don Black
Sung by Tom Jones   Screenplay by Richard Maibaum and John Hopkins
Based on an original screenplay by Jack Whittingham
Based on the original story by Kevin McClory, Jack Whittingham and Ian Fleming.
Produced by Kevin McClory
Directed by Terence Young

*unaccredited

---

in Nassau – and thus, the whole of the plot – hinges upon the lamest, limpest possible clue (a picture of Domino). The underwater scenes go on forever – one can surmise that in 1966 these were indeed truly novel, but seem staid, run-of-the-mill and poorly edited 30-something years on. The Bond series does, at least, get its second ever casino scene. Sadly, it's not a patch on the first. **-7**

62% Despite the fabulous Fiona, whose few scenes elevate the picture to a higher plane, the ho-hum *Thunderball* is the first Bond to be significantly less than the sum of its parts. Terence Young directs this underinvolving and overlong exercise like a turgid travelogue, failing to evoke any of *Goldfinger*'s zippy Pop bluster. A big step back.

Sheer, unadulterated hell: *Casino Royale*

1966: the film described by flamboyant producer Charles K Feldman as 'the wildest Bond picture ever made' had spiralled out of control. A reporter from *The Sun* located star Ursula Andress at Shepperton Studios early in March. 'I'm in a daze,' she said. 'I don't know what I'm supposed to say. I don't know what I'm supposed not to say. I don't know which script, which director, which producer, which scene. It's a confusion.' Such was the drama surrounding the film's convoluted development, the secrecy shrouding its protracted shooting schedule, and the mutual bafflement of those nominally in charge, it is difficult to establish an accurate chronology of events leading up to the release of the notorious *Casino Royale*.

That *Casino Royale*, the first of Ian Fleming's 007 novels, did not obviously lend itself to a cinematic treatment was of little concern to distributor Columbia. By 1965, it was the only Bond story that had escaped Eon and, as such, was a valuable commodity in a market craving new escapades for the world-famous spy.

The film rights to *Casino Royale* were now in the hands of Charles K Feldman, who represented the widow of Gregory Ratoff. Feldman (real name Charles Gould) was the long-standing president of the Famous Artists talent agency that had once counted Albert Broccoli among its employees. As a producer, Feldman's career began with *Pittsburgh* in 1942 and included such notable films as *A Streetcar Named Desire* (1951), *The Seven Year Itch* (1955) and *Walk on the Wild Side* (1962). The screwball *What's New, Pussycat?*, which Feldman produced for United Artists, had proved one of the most lucrative films of

1965 and starred Peter O'Toole, Peter Sellers, Woody Allen and Ursula Andress. All would reappear in *Casino Royale*.

Columbia had been snapping at Saltzman and Broccoli's heels in summer 1965, when it made an ultimately unsuccessful attempt to purchase Eon's increasingly valuable stake in the Bond franchise. When negotiations collapsed in May, the distributor offered Feldman the backing to produce *Casino Royale*. Feldman, who had already failed to interest Broccoli in entering into a new partnership to produce the picture, seized the opportunity.

The screenplay appears to have originated with Ben Hecht, whose estimated 70 screen credits include *Gone With the Wind* (1939), *Spellbound* (1945) and *Notorious* (1946). Hecht died in 1964, before completing his third draft of *Casino Royale*. Feldman offered numerous talents the chance to pick up the reins: Billy Wilder, whose

Little Jimmy Bond (Woody Allen) is revealed as the evil mastermind behind a dastardly plot to rid the world of anyone taller than 4'6". Allen loathed **Casino Royale**, and came to regret his participation in the picture

distinguished CV included both directing and sharing the producer's credit on *The Seven Year Itch*, contributed material, and *Catch 22* author Joseph Heller spent two weeks on dialogue that was ultimately abandoned. Terry Southern, who had collaborated with Stanley Kubrick on *Dr Strangelove or, How I Learned to Stop Worrying and Love the Bomb* (1963), would later pitch in. A chief scriptwriter emerged in Wolf Mankowitz, who had been instrumental in establishing Eon's Bond series and had contributed to a number of its screenplays – notably *Dr. No* and *Goldfinger*. In November 1965, Mankowitz revealed that the writing credit would go to himself 'and friends'. Ultimately, credited 'friends' would include only John Law and Michael Sayers, but material from unaccredited authors of early drafts, directors John Huston and Val Guest, and stars Peter Sellers and Woody Allen, would also be used. (Guest even remembers Feldman presenting him with a screenplay by Richard Maibaum, unlikely as that may seem.)

The nature of the finished product, and Feldman's huge success with *What's New, Pussycat?*, might suggest that *Casino Royale* was conceived as a spoof from the outset. However, it seems the film only became a send-up when it proved impossible to sign Sean Connery to play 007. Presumably unaware of Connery's ongoing commitment to Eon, Feldman approached him in 1965. 'Charlie Feldman rang me up and asked if I'd be interested,' Connery recalled. 'I said "Only for a million dollars," and he said the budget wouldn't run to that. Some time later I ran into him in a London night club. By that time the film had already cost millions and he was up to his neck in it. "You know something," he told me, "at a million dollars for you I'd have got off lightly."'

Resigned to the fact that, without Connery, his only option was to spoof the Bond films, Feldman next turned to Peter Sellers, whose manic psychiatrist in *Pussycat* had proved a highlight of the film. Sellers also turned him down, dismissing 007 as a 'big oaf'. Determined to secure Sellers, Feldman instructed Wolf Mankowitz to write the actor a new role. The script was rewritten once more, Mankowitz's new plot effectively eliminating James Bond and allowing for a new protagonist:

57

croupier Nigel Force. Sellers agreed to both the role and the £750,000 offered by Feldman.

In early summer 1965, Feldman approached David Niven to star as Sir James Bond – the retired gentleman superspy who recruits Force to impersonate the 'real' James Bond. 'I said that I had to see the script first,' Niven remembered. '[Feldman] took me home, stood over me while I read it, and when I had finished took it away and three minutes later I heard the clang of the safe door shutting.' Niven agreed to play Sir James, a linking character presiding over a quartet of stories, each highlighting a different James Bond. The film would have culminated in an extravagant showdown between Bond and his nemesis Le Chiffre at Casino Royale itself.

September 1965 reports that Shirley MacLaine had been contracted to star alongside Niven would soon prove premature, protracted negotiations with MacLaine, which included having Mankowitz rewrite the script to her specifications, would come to a sudden end. By November, Feldman was forced to admit that MacLaine's contractual commitment to Universal precluded her appearance in Columbia's Casino Royale. Trevor Howard, whose name was also linked to the film in early press reports, would similarly fall by the wayside. As the projected shooting date of 8 December loomed, Sellers and Niven had committed to the picture, along with Terence Cooper, a 33-year-old unknown earmarked for the role of 'Bond'. Amid confusion over who was going to star in the film, and indeed, which characters they would be playing, Feldman announced that his confidence in the script (at this stage a collaboration between Mankowitz and Irish writer

Michael Sayers) was such that it could be realised 'without stars as such'.

Columbia, having authorised an enormous $6 million budget, spent November and December deciding whether to base Casino Royale in the UK, and thus benefit from Eady money made available by the government. (The Cinematograph Film Act of 1927 had decreed that a percentage of films screened in the UK should be of UK origin, as a way of safeguarding the struggling British film industry from the commercial threat posed by more popular American product. The Eady levy, a tax drawn from ticket sales, provided certain financial benefits to UK film producers.) At the end of December, the ratio of British/American talent was adjusted, and plans to shoot in Spain, Germany and France were abandoned as Casino Royale was booked into Shepperton Studios. Feldman, who had been dividing his time between New York and London, finally relocated to offices in Grosvenor House.

Sellers asked Feldman to meet with Scottish television director Joe McGrath. The two had worked together before: Sellers had played poet William McGonagall in a McGrath-directed edition of arts series Tempo, and guested in an edition of McGrath's Not Only . . . But Also shortly after his first major heart attack in 1964. Sellers biographer Roger Lewis has suggested that the appointment of McGrath as Casino Royale director was indicative of the star's ill-fated attempt to 'recreate the happy anarchy of his early days on TV'.

The role of Vesper Lynd, the double agent Sir James Bond hires to seduce Nigel Force, went to to Dr. No's Ursula Andress. Since her breakthrough appearance as Honey, Andress had fortified her reputation as one of the most desirable sex symbols of the decade in such films as *Fun In Acapulco* (1963) and *She* (1965). In *Casino Royale* she would face stiff competition from Joanna Pettet (who replaced MacLaine as Mata Bond, Sir James and Mata Hari's love child), Barbara Bouchet (as Miss Moneypenny's daughter, Miss Moneypenny) and Jacqueline Bisset (as Miss Goodthighs).

A shooting schedule intended to last between 24 and 26 weeks finally commenced at Shepperton on Wednesday 11 January 1966. On Sellers' first day as Evelyn Tremble (his character had been renamed and promoted from mere croupier to world-class baccarat expert) he was presented with a gift of a white Rolls-Royce by the appreciative Feldman, who was still flush from *Pussycat*'s impressive box-office.

Shortly after filming began, it was decided to overhaul the shooting script. 'Charlie, Peter and I felt it needed to be funnier,' remembers McGrath. 'John Law [a co-writer of the award-winning series *It's a Small World* with Michael Bentine] was brought in on a daily basis to polish dialogue. He was on set for most of the time.

'After about three weeks, Feldman showed some rushes and some assembled stuff to Columbia and got more money out of them because they liked it so much. Then he started bringing in other writers and art directors, saying that we could build sets at other studios and save money. This annoyed everyone. I said "Wait a minute, can we just get on with this sequence – for the next sequence we can move to another studio if you want to, but let's get on with this."'
It was during this first phase of filming that Feldman introduced Terry Southern,

who spent between three and four weeks working on the screenplay. Sellers was proud of his own input – '[I] will be getting an author's screen credit,' he later mistakenly boasted.

Sellers began to cause headaches: reportedly, he ordered one set torn down before it had even been used because, the night before, he had suffered a nightmare in which his mother had visited Shepperton and told him she didn't like it. 'Peter was having trouble with [his wife] Britt Ekland,' says McGrath. 'She had gone back to Sweden and Peter was telephoning her, and nipping across to see her at the weekends. Peter was late on a few occasions, and Feldman was getting very annoyed. He told [associate producer] John Dark to get Peter to arrive on time. John couldn't do this – Peter just wouldn't pay any attention to him. Feldman then telephoned me and said "You're the director   tell him to get there on time." I refused, saying "No, I'm the director. When Peter's here I'll direct him. When he's not here we'll do something else. You're paying him, Charlie – you get him there on time." Peter got to hear about this and asked to talk to me in his caravan. He said: "Why are you on their side, and what the hell's going on?" I told him I wasn't on anybody's side, and he said: "You should be on my side." The problem was that they saw me as a friend of Peter's, and they were asking me, as his friend, to get him there on time. I wasn't going to do that. I told him: "If you want to behave like a naughty boy . . . get on with it." Then he tried to hit me. When [Spike] Milligan heard about it he said to me: "You'll be friends for life now. You really have to face up to Peter. That's why Peter and I are friends – we've gone through that stage too."'
Filming broke down during the baccarat table confrontation between Tremble (as

James Bond) and Le Chiffre (played by Orson Welles) at Casino Royale. Little work had been done on the scene when a sarcastic comment from Welles concerning Sellers' continued late arrival on set triggered Sellers' simmering resentment. It became a jealous rage when Sellers' friend, Princess Margaret, made a bee-line for Welles during a studio visit. From that point on, Sellers refused to speak to Welles, and insisted that a stand-in spoke his lines so he needn't be present during Tremble's scenes with Le Chiffre. McGrath relented, only to be accused later by Sellers that he had sided with Welles against him. Sellers then had actor John Bluthal fired (Bluthal was due to play numerous parts in the finished film, but ultimately appeared only as the Casino doorman and an MI5 man) because he believed him to be in league with McGrath.

'Eventually he disappeared,' recalls McGrath, 'went off chasing Britt. No-one one knew where he was, or would tell Feldman where he was. We couldn't do anything. It destroyed the film. When Peter disappeared Charlie put this second plan into operation and started building at Pinewood and so on. I walked off the picture. Peter phoned me later and said: "Please come back! Charlie will give you a Rolls-Royce if you come back. He gave me one!" Then Feldman rang me and asked me to come back, offering me this Rolls-Royce. Two years later I was in Los Angeles when this white Rolls-Royce pulled up. The man inside asked me "Are you Joe McGrath?" and when I said yes he said: "I'm Jerry Bresler. I'm driving the car Charlie Feldman was going to give you if you'd come back to the movie."'

Feldman enlisted Jerry Bresler, Famous Artists' head of production, as co-producer after McGrath's departure. Bresler's previous credits included *Main*

Street After Dark (1944), *The Vikings* (1958) and, most recently, Sam Peckinpah's *Major Dundee* (1965). Richard Lester was asked to take over the picture, but refused on the grounds that he was friends with both McGrath and Sellers. After a week, McGrath was replaced by Robert Parrish, whose career as a director dated back to 1929's *Drums Along the Mohawk*. (In 1967 Parrish would team Sellers with Britt Ekland for *The Bobo*, a film that would prove almost as traumatic.)

In the last week of February 1966, the scenes with Sellers and Welles were somehow completed under Parrish's supervision. (To complicate matters further, during late February two days' filming had been lost when Andress sustained an eye injury while feeding deer in Hampton Court.)

With the departure of McGrath and the arrival of Parrish, Feldman formulated a bizarre new approach that would, once again, radically alter *Casino Royale*'s direction. Sellers' involvement with *Casino Royale* redefined the film as a comedy. His tantrums would instigate a virtual free-for-all. Feldman announced that Parrish would simply be the first of a number of additional directors invited to helm different parts of the picture. 'Although our screenplay basically follows the book,' Feldman told the 2 March edition of *Variety*, 'the story breaks into various sequences and we've been trying to find the ideal director to match the mood of each …This is the age of specialisation. Our concept for this film includes not only multiple stars, such as Peter Sellers, Ursula Andress and Orson Welles among others, but also multiple directors.'

On 8 March, Hollywood veteran John Huston signed a contract to direct, write

At Casino Royale, a tense Vesper Lynd (Ursula Andress) observes the baccarat confrontation between '007' (Peter Sellers) and Le Chiffre (Orson Welles). When the erratic Sellers refused to continue working with Welles, careful editing disguised the fact that stand-ins were substituted on alternate days

and appear in David Niven's principal segment of the story. In return for the agreed 25 minutes' footage, he requested that Feldman pay him enough to clear his gambling debts. Shortly afterwards, Val Guest, and later Ken Hughes, were also contracted to shoot segments of a screenplay that had been thrown into disarray by Sellers' behaviour. Guest was an experienced and efficient director who had achieved great things at Hammer Film Productions in the Fifties before winning a British Academy Award for his acclaimed thriller *The Day the Earth Caught Fire* (1961). A deciding factor in Guest's appointment may have been his 1965 espionage spoof *Where the Spies Are*, starring David Niven as Dr Jason Love. 'I went on [*Casino Royale*] under contract for eight weeks,' Guest told *Scarlet Street* magazine, 'and I was still under contract nine months later! Charlie Feldman was a madman. There were days when you could hug him, and then other days when you could throttle him! An extraordinary man, who would change his mind overnight – during the night, mostly – and call you at all hours.'

Guest was assigned to direct footage starring *What's New, Pussycat?*'s Woody

Allen as Sir James' nephew, Little Jimmy Bond. 'Woody and I sat down and wrote it togther,' remembered Guest. 'Then we took it over to Charlie Feldman, who would go through it and send it back with all the gags cut out, having left all the build-ups! Woody would be in tears; Woody'd say, "How can a guy do this?" I'd say, "Look, don't worry about it. Let him think he's cutting something. We can put 'em back when we shoot" – which is exactly what we did.' Letters from Allen to his friend Richard O'Brien reprinted in Eric Lax's *Woody Allen: A Biography*, highlight the actor's dissatisfaction: '*Casino* is a madhouse. I haven't begun filming yet but saw the sets for my scenes. They are the height of bad pop art expensive vulgarity . . . my part changes every day as new stars fall in . . . I think the film stinks as does my role . . .' Allen's frustration should not be underestimated – he had already insisted that his name shouldn't appear amongst those credited for the screenplay.

Huston later broke the news to Guest that

a third director, Ken Hughes, had also been hired. Hughes' varied career had included Warwick's *The Trials of Oscar Wilde* (1960) and would soon take in Albert Broccoli's *Chitty Chitty Bang Bang* (1968). Hughes' contribution would be Mata Bond's surreal excursion to Berlin. Striking cinematography from future director Nicholas Roeg would lend these scenes an extra psychadelic *frisson*.

'The height of bad pop art expensive vulgarity'

On 8 March, *The Sun* carried a report from the set. 'No, I'm not in a position to mention any of our ideas,' Jerry Bresler told reporter David Nathan. 'No, I can't tell you who plays Bond. Yes, this is a Bond picture. But once you give that [information away] you're dead. If I give it to you anybody can make it. No, Peter Sellers isn't James Bond.' Nathan found a more willing interviewee in the disgruntled Sellers, who gladly blew most of the plot: 'The last part isn't finalised yet, but I go into this lavatory to make contact on my telephone wristwatch and a small dwarf comes in and pulls the chain. I'm last seen disappearing down the lavatory well. No-one has actually seen the other half of the script, the part that David Niven's in . . . If you are asking me if I would make the gamble after all those other spy parodies, I would probably not. But as far as the part goes it is interesting – this 'Bond for a day' idea.'

On 10 March, an increasingly bemused *Kinematograph Weekly* noted that the budget for *Casino Royale* had now hit $8 million.

Sellers brought his association with Robert Parrish's segment of *Casino Royale* to an abrupt end early in April. His contract

with Feldman had expired before he had completed his scenes. 'I was approached by the producer and asked if I would be prepared to continue and make what they called "a gesture",' Sellers told the 15 April edition of the *Evening Standard*. 'I told them "all right, but we've got to get on with it." We were just about to begin one week's extra work when they decided not to continue [with the section]. It's all very strange, and I simply don't know what will happen. . . It's a gigantic puzzle, the whole film.'

A distraught Parrish had a curt response to the *Standard*'s enquiry over the fate of the picture: 'I'm sitting here at a viewing machine trying to figure things out.'

Following Parrish's departure, second unit director Richard Talmadge shot around the absent Sellers. The 70-year-old Talmadge had been a stuntman in Twenties Hollywood, doubling for such stars as Douglas Fairbanks and Harold Lloyd. His career suffered following the introduction of talkies, and he specialised in directing action sequences (including those in *What's New, Pussycat?*) thereon. The introduction of the Keystone Cops during *Casino Royale*'s chaotic climax was at Talmadge's suggestion – he had appeared as a double in their films.

Casino Royale's demand for floor space shunted John Huston's segment into Pinewood Studios. Huston began shooting *The David Niven Story* (a working title apparently intended to dissuade the inquisitive from straying near his closed set) from his own script at the end of April. 'It's all very silly,' Huston told *The Guardian*, 'although my part is comparatively logical – only the threshold to madness.' Huston starred in his own segment as a bewigged M. Following a bizarre accident in which M is apparently blown up, Bond visits M's widow at a Highland estate. To play M's bogus widow, Lady Fiona, Huston cast Deborah Kerr, whom he had previously directed in *Heaven Knows, Mr Allison* (1957) and *The Night of the Iguana* (1964). Kerr recalled that Charles Feldman offered her an extra payment for each day over the original ten she was contracted for. Eight weeks later, she had earned enough from *Casino Royale* to purchase a new luxury – dubbed 'The Charles K Feldman Memorial Swimming Pool' – for her Swiss home.

By May, there was little anyone could do to stem the bad word-of-mouth surrounding the production. 'The Niven Story' title, it turns out, is just a cover,' surmised *Time* magazine. 'What is really shooting is Ian Fleming's first 007 book, *Casino Royale*. And from the looks of what's happening, shooting may be too good for it.'

With Huston, Guest and Hughes filming concurrently, Feldman's health began to suffer as he struggled to stay on top of the triple-headed monster the film had become. '[Columbia] keep saying "Stop it – no more people,"' he told *Time* in May. 'But I tell them, "It's a circus. I can't stop it now."'

Wolf Mankowitz put the brakes on his involvement with a strongly worded letter dated 9 June. He later explained his dissatisfaction to the *Daily Mail*'s Barry Norman: 'First there was just one Bond (now Sir James) who struck such terror into the hearts of the opposition that thereafter the British Secret Service called all its agents James Bond to confuse everyone. I saw the story as a kind of Trials of Hercules. Each task Bond faced

needed a different talent so someone with that talent was recruited and called James Bond to deal with it. This way everyone who sees the picture will find at least one Bond with whom he can identify.

'When I started on it it was a serious business, Charlie [Feldman] had even toyed with the idea of having Sean Connery as Bond, but decided he wasn't suitable for the part. When I finished, the whole thing was a comedy. Actually, I think it's a new concept in films, the movie version of a four-ring circus.' Mankowitz left behind a screenplay that even featured a dog called James Bond.

The projected wrap-date of mid-June came and went. By July, Eon's *You Only Live Twice* had moved into Pinewood, and *Casino Royale* had moved out. By the end of the month, Ken Hughes was shooting at Shepperton and Val Guest was filming additional David Niven sequences at MGM Borehamwood Studios. In Mankowitz's absence, Guest was charged with the unenviable task of papering over the gaping cracks in the storyline: 'It was an impossible job,' he remembers. 'I ended up working on the film to the extent that Charlie said, "You've done so much on this, I'm going to give you a credit of your own – Co-ordinating Director: Val Guest." I said, "If you do that, I'll sue you." Because people were going to say, "This is co-ordinated?"' A compromise was agreed whereby Guest received an 'additional sequences' credit.

The climactic fight at Casino Royale, which supervisor Talmadge dubbed 'Custer's Last Stand', took six weeks to film. The resulting 14 minutes' screen time featured 200 extras participating in 70 simultaneous fights. Guest stars Jean-Paul

Charles Feldman, on a rare visit to one of the three studios employed for **Casino Royale**. 'He was a very elegant man,' remembers co-director Joe McGrath, 'and he could get a table in any restaurant. I was impressed.'

Belmondo and George Raft were thrown in for good measure.

Principal photography finally came to an end early in November 1966 and the work of McGrath, Parrish, Huston, Guest, Hughes and Talmadge – six directors who had little or no contact with each other during the 11-month shoot – was finally compiled. *Variety* would estimate Columbia's final bill at around $12 million. The cost to Charles Feldman had almost been greater – he had suffered a heart attack during production, the blame for which he reportedly pinned on Sellers.

The film's most satisfying legacy is its engaging soundtrack, composed by Burt Bacharach. Formerly Marlene Dietrich's musical arranger, Bacharach came to international prominence collaborating with lyricist Hal David on a string of hits beginning with 1958's *The Story Of My Life*. Highlights of their film work included the title songs for *What's New, Pussycat?* and *Alfie* (1966); they'd go on to claim Oscars for *Butch Cassidy and the Sundance Kid* (1969) and its memorable *Raindrops Keep Falling On My Head*. Bacharach's shrill title song, which surely ranks among the finest in any Bond film, was performed by Herb Alpert and the

Tijuana Brass, and featured on their fourth chart-topping album *Sounds Like …* (In 1966 Alpert sold an incredible 13.7 million albums, and at one point had four LPs in Billboard's top ten. He would go on to produce the title track for the 1983 *Thunderball* adaptation *Never Say Never Again*.) Better remembered, however, is the song that Bacharach and David composed to accompany Vesper Lynd's dream-like seduction of Evelyn Tremble. Bacharach's inspiration for 'The Look of Love' came, as he recalled, while he repeatedly ran footage of the beguiling Ursula Andress at home. Given a sultry vocal by Dusty Springfield, the song was ensured classic status. Nominated for an Oscar in 1967, 'The Look of Love' lost out to 'Talk to the Animals' from *Dr Doolittle*.

During post-production, Feldman, Bresler and co-elected to leave Andress' own voice on the soundtrack, thus affording viewers the opportunity to hear the Swiss-inflected accent Saltzman and Broccoli had deemed unacceptable five years before. Themselves busy with preparations for *You Only Live Twice*, Saltzman and Broccoli made little public comment during the run-up to *Casino Royale*'s release. At a Pinewood press conference for *You Only Live Twice* on 4 November, several reporters took the opportunity to ask the Eon chiefs if they felt anxious about the competition. Clyde Gilmour of the *Telegram Showcase* relished Broccoli's 'fine blend of scorn and tolerant amusement' when the producer anticipated *Casino Royale* as 'a sort of enlarged *Pussycat*, just a harmless spoof'. 'Wait till you see the picture,' maintained a stiff-upper-lipped Jerry Bresler. 'It's impossible to describe in advance.'

In a manner befitting its chaotic shooting schedule, *Casino Royale* overshot Columbia's optimistic Christmas release date by some months. At the press preview, held on Thursday 13 April 1967, the *Financial Times*' Tom Milne smelled a rat. 'Coyly revealed to the press . . . at a time when most wicked critics have normally put their columns to bed, *Casino Royale* is 142 minutes of sheer, unadulterated hell.' The film's royal charity premiere, attended by Princess Alexandra, was held at the Leicester Square Odeon that same evening. History doesn't record Her Royal Highness' opinion of the incomprehensible film that greeted her, but Fleet Street was certainly not about to let anyone off the hook.

'Nobody concentrates on the story for more than a second,' claimed Penelope Gilliatt in *The Observer* on 16 April. 'Every scene is ambushed by some preening gag or egomaniacal bit of business . . . It was rash of the picture, I should have thought, to spend such a lot of its time elaborately bitching the rival Sean Connery Bond series, which have a lot more popular sense, grasp of movies and circus flair . . . When it penetrates even this bemused film's skull that all action and no motive are suffocating under the weight of the awful guest list, then it is only time for another hair-raising piece of producer's folly. Let's interest them with a flying saucer in Trafalgar Square; let's have a parachute drop of Cowboys and Indians; oh, yes, I know; let's have somebody *famous*.'

Ernest Betts in *The People* was no less savage: 'A two-hour burlesque of all the James Bonds you've seen; not a single scene makes sense.'

In *The Saturday Review* of 20 April, Arthur Knight highlighted a fundamental flaw: 'In this broad parody of earlier James Bond epics, even Ian Fleming would

have got lost in the plot's insane convolutions . . . As more than one critic has observed, it is rather difficult to parody something that is already a parody.'

It is a measure of the heights Bondmania reached in 1967 that even *Casino Royale*, which came nowhere near equalling the best of the 'unofficial' Bond spoofs in circulation at the time, grossed $17.2 million in worldwide film rentals (the distributor's share of box-office returns). Although significantly less profitable than Eon's least successful Bond film to date (*Dr. No*, which garnered total rentals of $22 million) *Casino Royale* earned more than enough to recoup its massive negative cost. Of greater concern to Eon was the way this relatively successful spoof was perceived to have damaged the box-office performance of *You Only Live Twice*, which opened just two months later.

In retrospect, it seems *Casino Royale* arrived too late to fully capitalise on the boom in spy films it sought to better. The careers of David Niven and Woody Allen (whose 1966 spoof *What's Up, Tiger Lily?* was much more amusing) were damaged little. Peter Sellers had yet to begin the most commercially successful phase of his career, but inspired a loyalty that guaranteed continual employment. (He would be reunited with Joe McGrath for *The Magic Christian* in 1969 and *The Great McGonagall* in 1974. The latter film also featured John Bluthal.)

Casino Royale's long-term performance was of little consequence to Charles Feldman, who produced but one further film – *The Honey Pot* – before his death from stomach cancer on 25 May 1968. He was 63. Joe McGrath's last meeting with the producer was a poignant one: 'I saw

Charlie in Los Angeles just before died. He told me "I think that film drove me crazy. I didn't know what had been shot and what hadn't been shot . . . I just lost control.'"

The film rights to *Casino Royale* are now reportedly divided between Columbia and MGM/UA. The property's tarnished reputation and tangled status has, it would seem, precluded any attempts to bring a new interpretation of Fleming's original Bond story to the screen.

File: *Casino Royale*

Teaser In a Parisian *pissoir*, a French police inspector with a Scots accent shows his 'credentials' to a Mister Bond. No true teaser this, being a flash-forward. Very poor. One sole point for the 'Les Beatles' graffiti. **1**

Titles Spaces within elaborate animated letters disclose tiny vignettes from the film; trumpets in the letters move in time to the sounds of Herb Alpert and the Tijuana Brass. Elegant and endearing. No nudes. **6**

Bonkers plot As briefly as possible . . . In cosy retirement, Sir James Bond is visited by M and representatives of the CIA, the KGB and the French Secret Service; one common enemy is liquidating their agents. Bond is only persuaded to lead an investigation when M has his house and gardens blown to smithereens – which does for M in the process. Bond goes to Castle McTarry in Scotland to hand over M's toupée to his widow, Lady Fiona – unaware that the enemy organisation SMERSH has stuffed the castle with gorgeous women overseen by a bogus Fiona, Agent Mimi; they plan to besmirch Sir James' celibate image. Mimi, however, falls in love with Bond and the plot is undone; she tells him that she receives her instructions from a Berlin organisation known as International Mothers' Help. Bond is attacked by another female assassin on the road to London, only narrowly escaping death; he orders Miss Moneypenny to seek out a man who can resist the advances of the world's most beautiful women – an 'anti-female spy device'. One Agent Cooper is selected; Bond orders that both he and all remaining agents are given the codename 'James Bond, 007' in a bid

to confuse the enemy. For no clear reason, Sir James visits occasional spy Vesper Lynd and has her train Evelyn Tremble, an expert in baccarat, as a spy. Sir James next visits his daughter, Mata Bond, in a foreign temple and persuades her to infiltrate International Mothers' Help – which is derived from an espionage school founded by her mother, Mata Hari. There, Mata attends an auction attended by officers of four armies; Le Chiffre, a SMERSH agent, is selling compromising pictures of various army officers in a bid to pay back SMERSH his gambling debts. Mata destroys the pictures. At the exclusive Casino Royale in France, Tremble, acting on Vesper's instructions, challenges Le Chiffre to a 50 million franc game of baccarat; he wins. Le Chiffre has Tremble tortured and (presumably) killed, perhaps with the aid of Vesper (who may or may not be a double agent). Bankrupt, Le Chiffre is himself executed by agents of SMERSH. Meanwhile, a SMERSH flying saucer kidnaps Mata in Trafalgar Square; Mimi tells Sir James that she has been taken to the Casino. There, Sir James discovers the underground base of SMERSH head Doctor Noah – who is revealed to be none other than his nephew, a cringing inadequate named Jimmy Bond. Jimmy plans to(a) release a bacillus into the air which will make all women beautiful and destroy all men over four foot six, and (b) substitute all world leaders with robot doubles that he has constructed. One of Sir James' 007s, the Detainer, forces Jimmy to swallow a pill which transforms him into an atomic bomb. Agents from all over the world converge on the Casino; Jimmy explodes, taking the Casino and all the James Bonds with him. The Bonds go to heaven, and Jimmy to hell. Yes, Bond plots are supposed to be a little deranged; this, however, ought to be fitted into a straitjacket and locked up tight for the good of society. **0**

Locations Paris; the English countryside; the Scottish Highlands; London; Latin America; India (probably); Berlin, both East and West; the Casino Royale, France; somewhere within the mind of Evelyn Tremble, if that qualifies. An amazing itinerary. **8**

Gadgets Scorned by Sir James, who coruscates both Connery-Bond and his peers thus: 'Him and his wretched gadgets . . . You, Ransome, with your trick carnation that spits cyanide . . . you, Smernov, with an armoury concealed in your grotesque boots. Listen to them tinkle

...You, Le Grand, with different deadly poison in each of your fly buttons. And you, M, with your flame-throwing fountain pens. You're joke shop spies, gentlemen.' He's equally dismissive of 'an Aston Martin with lethal accessories'. Sir James' enemies employ, variously, radio transmitters in buttons, exploding robot grouse, driverless milk floats with protruding rods, exploding telephone kiosks, infra-red spectacles, mental torture devices, machine guns concealed in bagpipes, a flying saucer, android doubles of world leaders, mad germ warfare and something that 'looks like an aspirin, tastes like an aspirin, but it isn't an aspirin' – a tiny pill which sets off a chain reaction in the body of the ingestee, transforming him or her into an atomic bomb. Nor are the Brits slouches in the field – within Q branch (which, it's suggested, is beneath Harrods) they've developed underwater archery, bowler hat guns, a pen which releases a stream of poison gas into the eye of its user, and a two-way television and radio wristwatch ('it's an American idea, they got it from one of their comic strips'). Best of all is the gadget we don't see; upon meeting Vesper, Sir James remarks, 'The whole world believes you were eaten by a shark, Miss Lynd.' 'That was no shark,' she counters. 'That was my personal submarine ...' Thingumajig heaven. **10**

Girls A seemingly endless parade. Mimi has 11 ersatz daughters, all aged between 16 and 19 – including Heather, Meg and bath-bound Buttercup (Daddy's 'little thermometer'). SMERSH employ bobbed blonde 'Jack' to kill M on the road to London; its control room is staffed with lovelies, too. In London, Sir James meets slinky Miss Moneypenny, daughter of the original – 'After you left the Service, she took the vows' – and it's Moneypenny who assembles 'a few dozen girls' for Anti-Female Spy Device Cooper to try out, including Lorelei (who wears Honey Ryder's bikini), and the mysterious Detainer, 'the new secret weapon'. Vesper – a commodities dealer and resting (Red) spy – is a little disappointing (she does, however, have a body-ejecting chute fitted in her kitchen). Despite having a voice like Joan Sims, Mata Bond, 'the celestial virgin of the sacred altar', proves her worth. In a Parisian carwash, Evelyn meets a gang of kinky PVC-clad scrubbers – and, in his hotel, the poisonous but oh-so-well named Miss Goodthighs (drugged, he has a fantasy involving both Vesper and an

unidentified blonde – and witnesses a bizarre 'beauty contest' as part of his torture at the hands of Le Chiffre). Doctor Noah's HQ is staffed exclusively by gun-toting guards in gold lamé (p'raps he's already detonated his bacillus there). Oh, and naked Jill Masterson clones behind the walls at the Casino. Is that enough? **10**

Villains See most of the above, plus: the colourless Frau Hoffner, Mata Hari's teacher, and lecherous battery-operated dwarf Polo; Le Chiffre, a tricksome gambler and blackmailer who studied illusion under 'an ancient vegetarian in the mountain vastnesses of Tibet', plus his manic auction master; various Scots pipers and members of the Household Cavalry; world leaders – including Mao Tse-Tung and Fidel Castro – who've been substituted by robot doubles; and little Jimmy Bond – 'Doctor Noah' himself – whose Napoleon complex is the cause of it all. The gadgets are huge fun, the girls effortlessly gorgeous – but are any of this lot even remotely menacing? Not really, no. **2**

Fights, chases, explosions Slapstick. Very good slapstick, but slapstick nonetheless. **2**

Dialogue and double entendres Where to begin? Little Jimmy, facing a firing squad: 'You can't shoot me. I have a very low threshold of death. My doctor says I can't have bullets enter my body at any time.' The Anti-Female Spy Device tells Moneypenny his name: 'Cooper, big eyes, but you can call me Coop.' 'Sounds like something for keeping birds.' 'That's me ...' Mata to Polo, upon entering her mother's boudoir: 'What an enormous bed!' 'The German army was very large in those days ...' The Detainer, strapped down, to Jimmy: 'Do you treat all the girls you desire this way?' 'Yes, I undress them and tie them up ... Yes, I learned that in the boy scouts.' Nor is the script limited solely to one-liners (see below ...) **8**

Bonds There's only one who really counts, of course (although Agent Cooper does manage a fair approximation of the real thing). Sir James – 'the greatest spy in history ... the true, one and only, original James Bond' – drinks 'Jasmine tea, lapsang souchong', plays Debussy 'from sunset until it's too dark to read the music, stands on his head a lot, eats royal jelly, lets his intestines down and washes them by hand' – and retired after

Sir James Bond (David Niven) and Miss Moneypenny (Barbara Bouchet) infiltrate the psychedelic headquarters of the fiendish Dr Noah

betraying the only woman he ever loved. 'In my day,' he says, 'spying was an alternative to war, and the spy was a member of a select and immaculate priesthood – vocationally devoted, sublimely disinterested. Hardly a description of that sexual acrobat who leaves a trail of beautiful dead women like blown roses behind him. That bounder to whom you gave my name and number …' He's no idle fantasy figure – this is Bond as a King Arthur, a Saint George. And judging by the evidence, it's a perfectly fair interpretation. **7**

Plus/minus points *Casino Royale* is enveloped in beautiful, kitschy production design – particularly inside SMERSH's mad HQ, Mata Bond's temple and the Berlin school. The latter sequence takes visual cues from both *The Cabinet of Doctor Caligari* and *Battleship Potemkin* – which almost makes up for the snatch of 'Born Free' at Sir James' estate (note how the 'official' Bond series later begins to drop in such references, too). Burt Bacharach's score is inspirational. Bar perhaps Peter Sellers' – and definitely Ursula Andress' – there's not a single performance herein which is anything less than sublime. But do any of these distinguished parts help cement the whole, make it cohesive, make it a rounded work? However amusing the set pieces, the whole just doesn't add up. **0**

54% Not necessarily as bad as its reputation might suggest – it's a comedy, and for the most part succeeds as such, whatever humourless Fleming purists claim (and it contains a great deal more of Fleming's novel than, say, Eon's version of *Moonraker*, right down to the carpet beater stuffed behind the chair in the 'mental torture' scenes) – but *Casino Royale* was never going to be anything other than a grand folly. It's bitty, disparate, and outstays its welcome by a good half-hour. But it's a product of its time, and we're glad it exists. (We're equally glad it could never happen again.)

CAST

Peter Sellers Evelyn Tremble (James Bond – 007)
Ursula Andress Vesper Lynd (007)   David Niven Sir James Bond
Orson Welles Le Chiffre   Joanna Pettet Mata Bond
Daliah Lavi The Detainer (007)   Woody Allen Jimmy Bond (Dr. Noah)
Deborah Kerr Agent Mimi (alias Lady Fiona)   William Holden Ransome
Charles Boyer Le Grand   John Huston McTarry (M)   Kurt Kasznar Smernov
George Raft Himself   Jean-Paul Belmondo French Legionnaire
Terence Cooper Cooper (James Bond – 007)   Barbara Bouchet Moneypenny
Angela Scoular Buttercup   Gabriella Licudi Eliza   Tracey Crisp Heather
Elaine Taylor Peg   Jacky Bisset Miss Goodthighs   Alexandra Bastedo Meg
Anna Quayle Frau Hoffner   Derek Nimmo Hadley   Ronnie Corbett Polo
Colin Gordon Casino director   Bernard Cribbins Taxi driver   Tracy Reed Fang leader
John Bluthal Casino doorman and M.I.5 man   Geoffrey Bayldon 'Q'
John Wells 'Q's assistant   Duncan Macrae Inspector Mathis   Graham Stark Cashier
Chic Murray Chic   Jonathan Routh John   Richard Wattis British army officer
Burt Kwouk Chinese army officer   Vladek Sheybal Le Chiffre's representative
Percy Herbert 1st piper   Penny Riley Control girl
Jeanne Roland Captain of the guards   John Le Mesurier Chauffeur*
Peter O'Toole Piper*

SELECTED CREDITS

Director of photography **Jack Hildyard B.S.C.**
Additional photography **John Wilcox B.S.C., Nicolas Roeg B.S.C.**
Production designer **Michael Stringer**   Costume designer **Julie Harris**
Film editor **Bill Lenny**   Titles and montage effects **Richard Williams**
Associate producer **John Dark**
Art directors **John Howell, Ivor Beddoes, Lionel Couch**
Assistant directors **Roy Baird, John Stoneman, Carl Mannin**
Second unit directors **Richard Talmadge, Anthony Squire**
Choreography **Tutte Lemkow**   Set dresser **Terence Morgan**   Casting **Maude Spector**
Costumes for Ursula Andress and Joanna Pettet by **Bermans, London**
From Paris: furs for Ursula Andress **Chombert**   Guard girl dresses **Paco Rabanne**
Casino dresses **Guy Laroche**   Chief make up artist **Neville Smallwood**
Chief hairdresser **Joan Smallwood**   Wardrobe supervisor **Betty Adamson**
Special effects **Cliff Richardson, Roy Whybrow**
Special matte work **Les Bowie**   Technical adviser **David Berglas**
Music composed and conducted by **Burt Bacharach**
Main title theme played by **Herb Alpert and the Tijuana Brass**
Lyrics by **Hal David**   *The Look of Love* sung by **Dusty Springfield**
Screenplay **Wolf Mankowitz, John Law, Michael Sayers**
Suggested by the novel *Casino Royale* by **Ian Fleming**
Produced by **Charles K Feldman** and **Jerry Bresler**
Directed by **John Huston, Kenneth Hughes, Val Guest, Robert Parrish,
Joseph McGrath**
Additional sequences **Val Guest**

*unaccredited

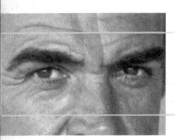

Juvenile, insane ideas: *You Only Live Twice*

1966: on a sun-dappled lawn in Buckinghamshire, BBC journalist Alan Whicker was in conversation with Harry Saltzman, probably one of the two most noted film producers of his generation. 'I'm told he's not the easiest star to handle now . . .' suggested Whicker, bidding for an intimation of upset between producer and James Bond actor Sean Connery. 'No stars are easy to handle, but he's all right,' replied a laid-back Saltzman. 'We have our differences, but the pictures get made . . .' Shortly after, Whicker faced Connery on a studio set for *You Only Live Twice*, Eon Productions' fifth Bond venture. 'How has being James Bond affected your life?' he asked. The most famous man in the world, a very picture of the phrase 'still waters run deep', bemoaned his lack of privacy at home in Acton: 'You get some real headcases that come round and have the most absurd requests like, "It would be marvellous to come and have tea" or, "Could I sign on your wall?" – juvenile, insane ideas. I have no publicity agent, I have no personal manager . . . consequently, one goes into the barbers and reads absolute shit, you know, written about one that some tinhead has put up . . .' But those pushy fans and pressmen would be as nothing compared to the ordeal that awaited him in the East – one that contributed to his decision to quit Bondage.

Ian Fleming's *You Only Live Twice* employs a curiously elegiac and leisurely narrative which draws Bond on a quest to slay one Guntram Shatterhand, a 'death collector' who has set up a suicide centre at a remote castle in Japan. Following on from the traumatic climax to *On Her Majesty's Secret Service* – in which Bond's wife, Tracy, had been suddenly murdered – the book splits into two halves, the first being a protracted essay on Japanese culture, the second being Bond's mission proper. The book culminates with Bond missing presumed dead, his memory lost to him after executing 'Shatterhand', who turns out to be no less than SPECTRE head Blofeld. Clearly, big changes would have to be made to Fleming's tale if its cinema adaptation were to live up to Eon's slam-bang efforts to date.

The screenwriter initially selected to work on the project was Harold Jack Bloom, an American who'd co-written pictures as varied as MGM western *The Naked Spur* (1953), Douglas Sirk melodrama *Magnificent Obsession* (1954) and *Last of the Pharaohs* (1955). In February 1966, Bloom joined producers Saltzman and Broccoli, chosen director Lewis Gilbert, designer Ken Adam, production supervisor David Middlemas, lighting cameraman Freddie Young and consultant Charles Russhon in Tokyo, where they were to begin assembling the elements that would comprise *You Only Live Twice*. The film was to be shot in the most alien territory the company had yet breached. The Eon team's Japanese recce took them to Kyoto, Yokohama and Hokkaido; in addition to searching out suitable locations, they made, according to *Kinematograph Weekly*, 'a comprehensive survey of Japanese studio facilities and equipment available for the planned 12-week schedule of filming'. The producers then journeyed on to Hong Kong and Macao, where they looked over further possible sites.

The signing of both Gilbert and Young in such key roles marked a considerable coup for Eon, keen to give its fifth Bond an edge over not only *Casino Royale* but the other Bond imitators clogging up the box office. Gilbert, who'd reportedly shied away from Eon's initial offer, had enjoyed over 20 years' largely distinguished work in the British film industry; his swinging London tragi-comedy *Alfie*, a massive international hit, had recently propelled Michael Caine to pre-eminence. Lines below this on his CV included pictures as varied as *Cosh Boy* (1952), *Albert RN* (1953), *Reach For the Sky* (1956), *The Admirable Crichton* (1957) and *Carve Her Name With Pride* (1958). No less fêted was the 64-year-old Young; a second Oscar, for *Doctor Zhivago*, had joined that for *Lawrence of*

Monday 26 September – at Pinewood Studios, Connery recreates 007's pampering for the benefit of visiting photographers. Tetsuo Tamba claps his hands in the background. The home helps were Mai Ling (left), Yee Wah Yang (centre) and Jeanne Roland (right). Conveniently, the girls were relatively local: Ling and Roland lived in London, Yang lived in Shepperton

Arabia on his mantelpiece just beforehand.

It had presumably been intended that the film would at least retain the novel's key feature – Shatterhand's seaside castle, plus the surrounding anti-Eden in which Blofeld grows the lethal flora which attract so many lemming-minded Japanese. The story goes that the recce failed to suggest any suitable ancient fortresses; the feudal Japanese, it seems, had built no castles on their coastlines lest they be blown away in typhoons. Crossing over a national park on the island of Kyushu by helicopter, a number of volcanic craters, one containing a lake, were sighted; either Broccoli or Adam devised the notion that Blofeld might conceal himself therein.

Bloom would be retired from the project in favour of Briton Roald Dahl, but later told Dahl's biographer that the film's storyline

In Himeji, former American Marine Corps Major Don Draeger trained Connery in the ancient martial art of jujitsu

Whereas Fleming would have Bond inured into assassinating Shatterhand – whose sole offence is the very existence of his 'garden of death' – at the behest of the Japanese Secret Service, the Bloom/Dahl storyline dismisses this in favour of a fanciful set-up wherein SPECTRE act as *agents provacateurs* in a bid to bring about World War Three (the novel does contain a very minor subplot concerning nuclear weapons, but the film retains none of its detail). Only three Fleming characters remain extant, but only Japanese Secret Service head Tiger Tanaka remains largely unadjusted; Henderson, named 'Dikko' no longer, is now an upper-class Briton, not a vulgar Australian, and 'Kissy' (named such only in the film's credits) loses both surname 'Suzuki' and her former film star status. Scenes at the ninja training school survive in bowdlerised form, and there's a reference to the Japanese *on* code of honour – a major Fleming fascination. The piranhas in Blofeld's garden now surround his luxurious living quarters. Bond's Japanese makeover is retained, too, as are the Ama fishing people; cheekily, the newspaper obituary for Bond – which comprises the novel's penultimate chapter – is glimpsed right at the very beginning of the film!

In a feature for *Playboy* magazine, Dahl famously claimed that he'd been instructed to write three women into the picture: 'Girl number one is pro-Bond . . . she is bumped off by the enemy, preferably in Bond's arms . . . Girl number two is anti-Bond. She works for the enemy . . . This girl should also be bumped off . . . Girl number three is violently pro-Bond . . . she must on no account be killed. Nor must she permit Bond to take any lecherous liberties with her until the very end of the story . . .' Although clearly a tongue-in-cheek account, it's worth noting that the

was largely his invention. Dahl had only a smattering of screenwriting experience – gathered through a flirtation with Disney (who'd developed his RAF-inspired fantasy *Gremlin Lore* for production in the Forties), working on an early version of John Huston's *Moby Dick*, and penning an unproduced First World War caper for Robert Altman titled *Oh Death Where Is Thy Sting-a-ling-a-ling*. Dahl's wife, actress Patricia Neal, had recently suffered two strokes, and it has been suggested that his commission was partly out of sympathy for her. (Dahl and Ian Fleming had met many times through mutual friend Ivar Bryce, too.) Whatever its provenance, the screenplay for *You Only Live Twice* would be both ambitious and audacious in equal measure.

formula can be applied almost exactly to *Thunderball*'s Pat, Fiona and Domino – although Pat, of course, survived. Dahl and Gilbert worked closely on the script, which would incorporate contemporary commentary in reflecting both the so-called 'space race' between the US and the USSR – on 3 June 1965, USAF Major Edward H White II had performed the first ever space walk as part of the Gemini 4 mission – and, in the evil Osato Corporation, Western fears regarding the resurgent Japan's 'economic miracle' (Fleming's Japan comes across as a rural, semi-feudal state).

A second recce in May was used to hold auditions for the Japanese actors required to work on the film. Toho Studios contract starlets Akiko Wakabayashi and Mie Hama (both 35-23-35) had previously appeared together in Toho monster movie *King Kong Versus Godzilla* (1962); both had appeared in over 60 films. Contemporary press material noted that Wakabayashi had become known for playing 'policewomen, secret agents and spies'. Oddly, however, she and Hama were first cast as Kissy and Tanaka agent 'Suki' respectively. Hama's problems with the English language led to her being given the less dialogue-intensive role of Kissy instead. 'Suki' was duly renamed 'Aki' after Wakabayashi's own first name.

Claiming to be able to memorise dialogue through self-hypnosis, Tetsuro Tamba – playing Japan's shady M, Tiger Tanaka – was cast following his major role in Gilbert and Young's earlier collaboration, *The Seventh Dawn* (1964). Teru Shimada, the 59-year-old cast as businessman Osato, was a Japanese *emigré* who had appeared in some hundred Hollywood films, more often than not as an extra; he'd had featured roles in pictures such as *The Bridges at Toko-Ri* (1954), *Run Silent, Run Deep* (1958) and *Batman* (1966), and was apparently odd-jobbing as a janitor at Paramount Studios when spotted by Broccoli and Gilbert. Shimada was screen tested in London – where the team were struggling to find a suitable Helga Brandt, Dahl's cruel, Teutonic 'girl number two' …

Throughout both pre-production and much of principal photography, the Eon team were shadowed by a BBC camera crew who were putting together an edition of *Whicker's World*, a long-running series of jet-set profiles presented by journalist Alan Whicker, then a byword for 'urbane'. Produced and directed by Fred Burnley, the revealing 'Bond wants a woman they said… but three would be better!' was broadcast by BBC2 on Saturday 25 March 1967. One of the vignettes captured by the BBC team was the audition and screen testing of the hopefuls aiming to play Helga – 'luscious Bond birds converging upon London from across the world', as Whicker later put it in *Radio Times*. Between 50 and 60 German and Swiss girls read for Helga, but only one-fifth of these were granted a screen test with Gilbert, who took Bond's role in the 'handsome brute' torture/seduction scene. 'We are trying to do something different with the Bond girl,' Gilbert told Whicker. 'This time, we'd like to find somebody who can act.' Gilbert's eventual Helga was 29-year-old Wiesbaden-born Karin Dor, who'd made her film debut at 16. Mostly noted for exploitation pictures, she'd featured in *The Face of Fu Manchu* (1965), the first in the Harry Allan Towers-produced series starring Christopher Lee, whom she'd play opposite in the rather less savoury *Die Schlangengrube und das Pendel*, aka *The Blood Demon* (1967). She'd go on to appear in Hitchcock espionage thriller *Topaz* (1969).

Bernard Lee and Lois Maxwell reprised their roles as M and Moneypenny, but their relationship with Connery would briefly turn frosty. The then-insatiable Bond-inspired vogue for spy films would reach its zenith/nadir with the 1967 producton *Operation Kid Brother*, a bizarre Italian effort starring Neil Connery, £3-a-day plasterer sibling to Sean. Lee and Maxwell would be drafted into exploitation producer Dario Sabatello's folly alongside a host of other Bond artistes. 'It was a dreadful movie, but we needed the money,' said Maxwell later. 'Sean was livid that we were in it and wouldn't speak to us.'

In this little-seen film, Neil played 'Doctor Connery', plastic surgeon-cum-hypnotist brother to top British secret agent 'zero-zero' . . . something, who is otherwise engaged on a mission. Connery is persuaded by his brother's superior, Commander Cunningham (Lee), to assist in an investigation into the nefarious activities of THANATOS, a SPECTRE-like organisation encompassing yacht-owner Thair Beta (Adolfo Celi, *Thunderball*'s Largo, seen clad in red PVC inside Beta's ultimately-exploded underground base), Alpha (Anthony Dawson, *Dr. No*'s Dent) and Maya, deadly leader of the 'Wild Pussy Club' (Daniela Bianchi, *From Russia With Love*'s Tatiana). In his bid to foil THANATOS' plan – which involves an 'atomic nucleus', a plot to seize world gold reserves, and probably-lesbian Rosa Klebb-alike 'Lotte' – Connery is aided by Cunningham's super-efficient, machine gun-toting secretary 'Miss Maxwell'. Directed by one Alberto De Martino and replete with a loungecore score co-written by Ennio Morricone and comprised largely of cheesy variations on its theme song, 'OK Connery', sung by 'Khristy', *Operation*

Kid Brother was eventually released in Britain in May 1968. 'If Sabatello had discovered a man with two heads and the hind quarters of a horse, dislodged him from his environment, put him in a glass dome at the ICA building and charged 5s admission, the world would have adjudged him cruel. [Neil] Connery now has just this exposure . . .' remarked *Londoner*, roundly condemning 'This little vampire of a film'. (Lee, Maxwell and Neil were eventually forgiven by Sean; Neil guest-starred in 1969's *The Body Stealers*, a British SF knock-off which, though barely possible, was actually even worse.)

Whicker's crew were present at Pinewood on 4 July to cover the first day's work on *You Only Live Twice* – the shooting of the 'death of Bond' teaser sequence. The first few weeks' studio work included the sequences set in Osato's penthouse, the aforementioned 'handsome brute' scene, and Bond's encounter with the very, er, aesthetic Henderson, played by Charles Gray. His film career to date spanning both *Tommy the Toreador* (1959) and *The Entertainer* (1960) – the ridiculous and the sublime – Gray, then 39, would take a higher-profile Bond role just four years later. And while Gilbert's principal unit prepared to shift to the Far East, work on the immense, be-girdered infrastructure of the volcano interior continued. Ken Adam, showing Whicker a scale model, claimed that the cost would be 'as much, if not more, than the whole of *Dr. No*' – £350,000, ten percent of the film's £3.5 million budget.

The Bond films were huge in Japan – often screened back-to-back in triple bills – and the novelty of an international film star's presence would excite hysteria during the six weeks' location filming for *You Only Live Twice*. Connery's arrival at Tokyo's airport on 27 July was heralded by a fanfare from an all-girl brass band. Waiting for him was a throng of fans and an immense body of pressmen and photographers, who soon ran the actor to ground at the Hilton Hotel.

There, the *Whicker's World* crew captured a tense Broccoli puffing on a cigar and surrounded by journalists, all of whom were desperate to get to Connery. Via an interpreter, Broccoli explained away the recalcitrant star's whereabouts: 'He had to go back up to his room because he didn't even have the privacy of having a little lunch. Now, he's an actor. He's here to do a job. He's not just a publicity idol for them. Now, he's here and he has not been given the privilege and respect of Japan for a certain amount of privacy. Today he is supposed to rest, under my orders. If they promise to leave him alone the rest of the afternoon, perhaps I can persuade him to let them take some pictures . . .'

A later press conference failed to dampen Japanese excitement. Although Connery initially appeared to be in good humour – asked about the release of *Casino Royale*, he replied: 'I hope it makes a lot of money, 'cause it cost a lot of money' – the event was soured by aggressive questioning of Connery's crumpled, jet-lagged appearance. Worse, Connery went on to state that 'Japanese women are just not sexy', reportedly offending Japanese national pride.

Several days' location work at the southern seaport of Kagoshima followed, Connery's footsteps ever dogged by snappers and scandalmongers. Soon, it would become clear that the actor would be unlikely to submit himself to the demands of a Bond shoot again. In the light of Connery's apparent resignation, Broccoli told Whicker: 'Sean can't move at all here. It's

'You should have seen your brother's face, doctor, when he heard of it!' Cunningham (Bernard Lee), Miss Maxwell (Lois Maxwell) and Doctor Connery (Neil Connery) in the literally incredible Operation Kid Brother

terribly uncomfortable for him . . . It won't be the last Bond under any circumstances – with all due respect to Sean, who I think has been certainly the best man to play this part. We will, in our own way, try to continue the Bond series for the audience because it's too important and if Sean doesn't want to do it we can't force him to...'

The unit then moved to the southern village of Akime, where a quarter of the 400 inhabitants would appear as extras in the film's Ama fishing village scenes (although the team would have a hard time persuading the modest local girls to remove their beach gowns and be filmed wearing bikinis). Police checkpoints were set up on the roads leading into Akime to discourage sightseers, but the press corps remained as tenacious as ever. The eight-day schedule at Akime included sea-bound shots outside the cave mouth which leads inside the SPECTRE volcano; while on the water, the crew were chased by a motor launch packed full of pressmen and photographers. Here, Broccoli was made righteously irate by the publication of a story in the local press which had

75

intimated that the company would be unlikely to settle bills racked up on location.

Stealing the honours as gadget of the year was 'Little Nellie', a flat-packed autogiro delivered to Bond by Q, in one of Desmond LLewellyn's rare location visits. Harry Saltzman had noticed the device in the pages of a magazine, and enlisted its owner, Wing Commander Ken Wallis, to the production. Little Nellie was souped up to Eon specifications by effects supervisor John Stears, and unveiled as a veritable flying DB5. Wallis doubled for Connery in the aerial tussle with SPECTRE helicopters, supervised by second unit director Peter Hunt while Lewis Gilbert was busy elsewhere in Japan. Hunt's cinematographer, Johnny Jordan, photographed the carefully choreographed action from one of the Alouette helicopters that buzzed the autogiro and its Hillier assailants. On 22 September, shortly after filming had begun, one of the Hilliers flew too close to Jordan's Alouette – the Hillier's rotor blades clipped away the Alouette's underside skis and practically severed Jordan's dangling leg. When the Alouette crashed, Jordan was rushed to a hospital in the nearby village of Ebino, where surgeons struggled to save his leg. Their success was only temporary; in London, three months later, the limb was amputated. Jordan's accident foreshortened the shoot; little more than establishing shots of the helicopters were in the can. The actual dogfight was filmed when Hunt and replacement cinematograpaher Tony Brown filmed additional aerial sequences over near-identical scenery at Torremolinos, Spain, nearly three months later.

Lewis Gilbert and a despondent Peter Hunt returned to Pinewood in late September to resume studio photography. Joining the cast for this phase of filming was Czechoslovakian actor Jan Werich, signed to appear as the first actor to reveal the face of Ernst Stavro Blofeld. Werich had completed few scenes when, on 11 November, he was reportedly taken ill and forced to retire from the production. A last-minute replacement was found in Donald Pleasence, whose reputation as one of the decade's most distinctive character actors had been forged in such films as *Dr Crippen*, *The Great Escape* (both 1963), *Cul-De-Sac* and *Fantastic Voyage* (both 1966). Pleasence's relatively brief appearance in *You Only Live Twice* would nevertheless leave an indelible mark on his career. His snarling Blofeld was arrived at only after a week of experimentation with the character at Pinewood; Pleasence reportedly tried Blofeld with a hump, a limp, a beard and a lame hand. Ultimately, a deep facial scar (courtesy of the make-up department) suggested much of the character's villainy. During filming he claimed: 'I finally took the old French matron's advice to the young girl before she goes on a date: look in the mirror and take something off.' The *Evening Standard's* Alexander Walker would later describe Pleasence's head as recalling 'an egg cracked in the boiling'.

Werich had been taken ill just days after shooting had commenced on Ken Adam's immense volcano set. Construction had begun at Pinewood on 11 May, and utilised 200 miles of tubular steel; over 700 tons of structural steel; 200 tons of plasterwork; half a million tubular couplings (weighing more than the combined tonnage of 1,100 family cars); 8,000 railway sleepers for the monorail (at a cost of 16/9 each) and more than 250,000 square yards of canvas. The result of 379 conceptual drawings, the awe-inspiring rocket base was physically realised by 250 plasterers, riggers, painters and carpenters working seven days a week. 'The nightmare,' said Adam, 'is suddenly realising every now and again that you have designed something that has never been done before in films and which is bigger than anything that has gone before. You wake up at night wondering whether the thing will work. You can surround yourself with construction engineers, but that doesn't help. They may be qualified to build the Empire State Building or the London Hilton – buildings which are a part of their trade and follow construction patterns – but we have built something for which there are no terms of reference.'

Three separate crews filmed inside the volcano and its attendant sets throughout November and December, only slightly delayed by the need to backtrack over Werich's scenes with Pleasence. (The actor recalled having to react to an absent Connery when appearing in footage replacing that originally shot with Werich.) At the end of November, Hunt took his second unit to Finmere in Scotland to shoot the arrival of Helga's plane. From there, Hunt and his crew went to Gibraltar to film the sea burial of Bond's coffin and finally to Spain to complete the work curtailed by Johnny Jordan's accident. Although primary and second unit photography was over by Christmas 1966, the demanding special effects photography had yet begun. Between January and March 1967, John Stears supervised the relatively ambitious model work illustrating the space capsule piracy that the plot hinged upon.

During post-production two elements essential in the classic Eon mix fell into place when John Barry composed his most evocative Bond score yet and Peter Hunt relented to Saltzman and Broccoli's request

that he prepare the final cut of the picture (thus relieving contracted editor Thelma Connell of the responsibility).

For the world premiere of *You Only Live Twice* on Monday 12 June 1967, a billboard proclaiming 'Sean Connery IS James Bond' adorned the Leicester Square Odeon, as if to forestall any confusion with the multi-Bond farrago that had opened at the same cinema two months before. The Queen, attending her first Bond premiere, was introduced to Sean Connery, attending his first British Bond premiere since *From Russia With Love*. Her Royal Highness asked Connery if he felt he was typecast. From beneath a thick Mexican-style moustache he replied: 'Well, ma'am, I think so.' When asked for confirmation that he was giving up playing 007, Connery gave what the *Daily Mail* described as 'an unqualified yes.'

You Only Live Twice's first week at the Odeon was the cinema's most profitable to date. Even by its fourth week, during which the Odeon sold £15,149 worth of tickets, *You Only Live Twice* was still breaking records. In America, the film opened on 13 June with a four-cinema premiere in New York. It went on to gross over $19 million in the US, coming second only to *The Dirty Dozen* as highest earning picture of the year.

You Only Live Twice's total worldwide gross of $111,600,000, against an estimated negative cost of $9.5 million, distinguished the film as a huge hit, if not the phenomenon that *Thunderball* had been in 1965. Although the film earned $30 million less than *Thunderball*, its US admissions – at 36.2 million – were less than half of those achieved by its Eon predecessor. 'I imagine the next one, *On Her Majesty's Secret Service*, will be made on a relatively small budget,' said

At the end of October, as the immense volcano set neared completion, the press were invited to view Ken Adam's most astonishing achievement yet. From left to right: Lois Maxwell (wearing Miss Moneypenny's naval uniform), Akiko Wakabayashi, Sean Connery, Karin Dor and Mie Hama

Connery in July 1967. 'You Only Live Twice reached the peak, I think.' The near unanimous praise that greeted the release of Goldfinger, then

'The machines have taken over at last'

Thunderball, was replaced with a polarised mix of opinion in the reviews for You Only Live Twice. The Times' John Russell Taylor described 'this new episode in the legitimate Bond succession' as 'a distinct return to form,' but fellow critics were less impressed. 'Rather less enjoyable because the formula has become so completely mechanical (and Bond himself so predictably indestructible) without any compensation in other directions', moaned Monthly Film Bulletin, berating Bond's

'expressionless competence' and going on to claim that 'the machines don't give the humans a look in. Even Donald Pleasence, scar-faced, sneering and fondling a supercilious cat as the chief villain, seems diminished.'

The Sunday Times' Dilys Powell noted that 'Ken Adam has outdone himself. The elegant, industrial offices, Blofeld's sub-volcanic headquarters with the monorail and the camouflaged sliding roof and the rocket-launching pad – everybody concerned in the erection of the huge sets has done wonders. The marriage of real locations and the manufactured backgrounds is an achievement; technically, You Only Live Twice is overpowering. So overpowering, in fact, that it threatens to extinguish the players, and I don't mean merely the scores of extras who are drowned, strangled, shot, stabbed and blown up . . . The machines have taken over at last.'

'Can it go on indefinitely?' asked Variety's 'Mosk', expressing his concern that the Bond bubble was about to burst – financially, if not artistically. 'Whether You Only Live Twice will surpass Thunderball's domestic rental take of $26,000,000 is perhaps open to question, since the market has lately been flooded with the likes of Matt Helm and Derek Flint . . . Sean Connery plays 007 with his usual finesse, although he does look a bit older and more tired (as who wouldn't be?) . . .'

'The Bond formula has now been run into the ground and only requires a headstone,' claimed Alexander Walker in the Evening Standard. 'But the hallmarks of a Saltzman-Broccoli production, aided by Lewis Gilbert's smooth direction and Peter Hunt's snappy editing may ensure another box-office hit. By the way, they shouldn't worry too much if Sean Connery keeps his promise to himself and calls a halt to playing 007 – I'm sure Ken Adam could now run up a robot Bond to replace him.' Connery's traumatic experience in the Far East had strengthened his resolve to avoid signing a new contract for further Bond pictures. 'It was completely swamping,' he recalled in the March 1974 edition of *Films and Filming*. 'When we went to Japan. . . and then to Bangkok and Hong Kong, there were people crowded into the hotel lobbies and on the street corners, just waiting to look at me. It became a terrible pressure, like living in a goldfish bowl .. . That was part of the reason why I wanted to be finished with Bond. Also I had become completely identified with it, and it became very wearing and boring.'

In 1966, Whicker had suggested to Broccoli that finding a new 007 would be an almighty headache. 'Everything is a headache making a picture,' replied the mogul, 'but you have to be determined to find a way to do this . . . This won't stop us from making another Bond, 'cause an audience out there wanna see it. We'll present what we have for their approval.' Following the release of Eon's sixth Bond, the audience's judgement would prove damning.

File: *You Only Live Twice*

Teaser US space rocket Jupiter 16 is swallowed up by an unidentified flying object, severing a spacewalking astronaut's safety line as it does so. (The music and sound cut here is hugely affecting, too; in space, no-one can hear you scream.) Jump to a belligerent crisis summit between the Eagle and the Bear – presided over, of course, by the naturally cool-headed Brits. The Americans have fingered the Soviets for the incident; interference with any further launch will be interpreted as an act of war. The UK have a man following a lead in Hong Kong; however, Bond is also called up. But, apparently betrayed by an Oriental lover, Bond is gunned to death in bed . . . A thrilling prologue to the main action, yes – but far from being the 'mini-movie' we've come to expect. **6**

Titles Shadowed geisha girls bearing elaborate fans mounted over shots of erupting volcanoes. Elegant, if curiously static. The final shot – a time-lapse photography dawn over Hong Kong – melts effortlessly back into the film proper, and is sublime. **8**

Bonkers plot Hidden away beneath a Japanese volcano, SPECTRE kidnap American and Russian space capsules, playing on the two superpowers' mutual distrust in anticipation of the inevitable outbreak of atomic war. When the US and USSR have wiped one another out, SPECTRE's Blofeld will rule the world (in association, presumably, with certain Japanese, who are footing the £100 million SPECTRE bill). Mad science, outer space, nuclear rockets and a bid for global domination – an easy . . . **10**

Locations Outer space (although Bond doesn't actually get there); Hong Kong; somewhere under the South China Sea; Tokyo; in and above rural Japan; more outer space; and the island of Matsu, somewhere between Kobe and Shanghai. **7**

Gadgets Bond is carrying a safe-cracking device when he arrives, unexpectedly, at the Osato building (are we to assume, then, that he carries it with him at all times, just in case? The same happens much later, when he produces the suction cups for his hands and knees which help him break into SPECTRE's base. This is lazy preparation). Osato's desktop X-ray. Tanaka's absurd sky-high giant magnet. The viewscreen in Aki's car. Q, in flappy Gurkha pants, unveils 'toy helicopter' Little Nellie, clearly an attempt to do to the air what the Aston Martin did to the road (with two machine guns, two rocket launchers, heat-seeking air-to-air missiles, flame guns, smoke ejectors, aerial mines and a cine camera, she's probably the single most gadget-intensive vehicle in the series). The Japanese Secret Service's rather obvious rocket technology, including that fatal last cigarette, implies that the East is encouragingly behind the Brits in the gadgets field. And let's not forget the rockets, SPECTRE's base itself . . . an orgy of toytime fun. **10**

At Pinewood on 6 December, Donald Pleasence brushes up on lines originally intended for Jan Werich. Karin Dor keeps an eye on SPECTRE's malevolent moggie

who makes the connection that leads Bond to SPECTRE's base. **7**

Villains Bond finally meets Blofeld and – with his staccato snarl of 'Goodbye, Mister Bond!' – he doesn't disappoint. Blofeld's stooges – Osato and his heavies – are, however, a bit of a let-down (Helga excepted – even though she's a straight rehash of *Thunderball*'s Fiona, just as Blofeld bodyguard Hans is *From Russia With Love*'s Grant summarily recast). But what Blofeld's employees lack in quality, they do make up in absurd quantity (*viz* the climax). What does SPECTRE's wage bill come to? And is it liable for employee death and injury? I think we should be told ... **6**

Fights, chases, explosions A terrific set-to – featuring a couch, an idol and a samurai sword – between Bond and a mountainous Osato heavy. A perfunctory but effective car chase through the fag-end of suburban Tokyo. The fight on the Kobe docks rooftop is magnificent – the camera cranes out from Bond as he kicks and punches his way past tens of assailants – and its effect is magnified still further by John Barry's soaring score. Helga's plane explodes pleasingly, as do the 'four big shots' who make 'improper advances' on Little Nellie. The lethal practice sessions at the ninja training school imply a disturbingly high turnover of recruits. Finally, a mammoth free-for-all (which actually outdoes the excess of *Casino Royale*), featuring grenades, machine guns, swords and ninja stars (that being this film's Really Nasty Moment). Oh, and then Blofeld presses the self-destruct, his base blows up and the volcano erupts. By now, the madness has reached such a peak that the latter point isn't even mentioned. **10**

Dialogue and double entendres A deathless exchange of single entendres between the two HK policemen who uncover Bond's bedridden 'corpse' ('At least he died on the job'/'He'd have wanted it this way'). Bond on the bath girls:'I like the plumbing.' When Tiger tells Bond that 'in Japan men always come first, women second,' our incorrigible misogynist murmurs,'I might just retire to here ...' Connery's understated delivery of the word 'really' when Helga Brandt informs Bond that 'Mr Osato believes in a healthy chest' is a sure sign of a master at work. Bond's wry 'Oh the things I do for England ...' as he unzips Helga's dress, despite being an off-cut from *Thunderball*, is simply

Girls Hong Kong consort Ling who, besides tasting 'different' and promising Bond 'very best duck', has been procured by Moneypenny; Moneypenny herself, who, very smart in naval uniform, gets outside London for the first time in the Eon series (and connives to have Bond say 'I love you', too); artful secret agent Aki, who enjoys very much 'serving under' Bond; Tanaka's 'very sexyful' bath girls; face-slapping secretary-cum-torturer-cum-pilot Miss Helga Brandt, SPECTRE's Number Eleven (*Thunderball*'s drug-pushing Eleven is, presumably, no more); outrageously, nurses in bikinis in the plastic surgery scene; bride Kissy, who proves herself useful only in that it's she without peer. And *You Only Live Twice* does establish what will become notorious as a clichéd Bond villain line: Helga's death in the piranha pool is pre-empted by Blofeld's 'This organisation does not tolerate failure ...' First time round, it's positively Grand Guignol. **10**

Bond is late for his own funeral. Received a First in Oriental languages at Cambridge. Drinks Russian vodka and sake (but only at the correct temperature, mind). Tiger Tanaka remarks that his 'honourable mother' taught him long ago 'never to get in a car with a strange girl', and goes on to observe astutely that Bond 'will get into anything with any girl ...' Bond seems positively keen to marry Aki – but reacts coldly, matter-of-factly to her death (not that this stops him from trying it on with Kissy a very short time later). As per *Thunderball*, he keeps a gun by his bedside. His petulant strop – pushing aside a bowl of oysters and saying, 'Well, I won't need these' – when told that he and bride Kissy will have separate beds, is utterly right. **10**

Plus/minus points Who's the bloke watching Bond's burial at sea through binoculars? The scene is directed as though it's a major plot point, but it's never referred to again. Osato's 'ah so' in his penthouse scene pushes past satire and into an uglier arena (*pace Goldfinger*). Whose camera is taking the pictures of the helicopter picking up the sedan which we see in Aki's car? There are some really poor back-projected sunsets, too, and the chit-chat we overhear between the US astronauts and their Russian equivalents just before Bond breaks them out of their cell is excruciatingly bad ('In our country, we say "cosmonaut.. ."' 'We kid you not). But ... the Kobe docks rooftop tussle is, quite simply, superb; it implies not only that mainstream action cinema is an artform, but establishes its aesthetic, too. Likewise the set-piece death of Aki; these two scenes alone far outweigh our niggles. **10**

94% Spectacular in a sense now forgotten. The mix done right, as per *Goldfinger*, but four key areas – direction, production design, the script and the score – are all ever so much sharper, glossier, wilder. Throughout its considerable but effortlessly sustained length, *You Only Live Twice* teeters constantly on the brink of excess and inanity – and never once crosses that elusive line. Magnificent.

CAST

Sean Connery James Bond
Akiko Wakabayashi Aki　**Mie Hama** Kissy　**Tetsuro Tamba** Tiger Tanaka
Teru Shimada Mr. Osato　**Karin Dor** Helga Brandt　**Donald Pleasence** Blofeld
Bernard Lee 'M'　**Lois Maxwell** Miss Moneypenny　**Desmond LLewelyn** 'Q'
Charles Gray Henderson　**Tsai Chin** Chinese Girl (Hong Kong)
Peter Fanene Maivia Car Driver　**Burt Kwouk** SPECTRE 3　**Michael Chow** SPECTRE 4
Ronald Rich Blofeld's Bodyguard　**Jeanne Roland** Bond's Masseuse
David Toguri Assassin (Bedroom)　**John Stone** Submarine Captain
Norman Jones, Paul Carson Astronauts (1st American Spacecraft)
Laurence Herder, Richard Graydon Astronauts (Russian Spacecraft)
Bill Mitchell, George Roubicek Astronauts (2nd American Spacecraft)
Anthony Chin SPECTRE guard　**Robert Hutton** President's Aide*
Alexander Knox American President*
Anthony Ainley, Patrick Jordan military policemen*
Mai Ling, Yasuko Nagazumi, Yee-Wah Yang bath girls*

SELECTED CREDITS

Second unit director and supervising editor **Peter Hunt**
Art director **Harry Pottle**　Production supervisor **David Middlemas**
Special effects **John Stears**　Action sequences by **Bob Simmons**
Assistant director **William P. Cartlidge**　Location manager **Robert Watts**
Camera operator **Ernie Day**　Make-up **Basil Newall** & **Paul Rabiger**
Wardrobe Mistress **Eileen Sullivan**　Hairstylist **Eileen Warwick**
Set dresser **David ffolkes**　Editor **Thelma Connell***
Technical adviser **Kikumaru Okuda***
Main title designed by **Maurice Binder**
Music composed conducted and arranged by **John Barry**
Title song lyrics by **Leslie Bricusse**　Title song sung by **Nancy Sinatra**
Additional story material by **Harold Jack Bloom**　Screenplay **Roald Dahl**
Production designed by **Ken Adam**
Director of photography **Freddie Young B.S.C.**
Produced by **Harry Saltzman** and **Albert R. Broccoli**
Directed by **Lewis Gilbert**

*unaccredited

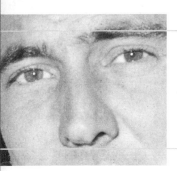

Better than winning the pools: *On Her Majesty's Secret Service*

1967: when it dawned that Sean Connery had no intention of renewing his licence to kill, Harry Saltzman and Albert Broccoli resigned themselves to casting a new leading man. In July, as *You Only Live Twice* packed cinemas around the world, Saltzman told The *Daily Mail*'s Barry Norman: 'The guy who gets this part will take off ... Cubby and I made Sean a millionaire. I don't think any actor has got as rich as he has in recent years. Believe me, playing Bond is better than winning the pools.' Saltzman went on to suggest that television star Roger Moore would make a great James Bond, 'but we couldn't use him. He's too well known as The Saint. So it'll have to be an unknown, and finding good, undiscovered actors of 30 is not too easy.'

The search began in earnest in October 1967, when actors' agencies and provincial repertory companies were trawled for suitable talent. In April 1968, a shortlist of around 100 actors were called to appear in screen tests, with the intention of then submitting footage for the approval of distributor United Artists. Amongst the hopefuls tested at Pinewood were Robert Campbell, Timothy Dalton, Hans de Vries, George Lazenby, John Richardson and Anthony Rogers. Notable amongst the group was Lazenby, a 28-year-old Australian model, then best known for his athletic portrayal of the 'Big Fry man' in a series of television commercials advertising Fry's Chocolate Creams. (Before talking his way into an interview with Harry Saltzman, Lazenby had his hair styled like Connery's at the same Mayfair barber's shop frequented by Albert Broccoli. The

producer had already noticed the model, and made a mental note of his potential suitability for the role of Bond.)

Thirty-two-year-old John Richardson was a former Fox contract artist who had been seconded to Hammer to star alongside Ursula Andress in 1965's *She*. His lover at the time was Hammer starlet Martine Beswick, who had come to prominence in *From Russia With Love* and *Thunderball*. Timothy Dalton, a 22-year-old actor, was on the verge of great things and would be considered for the role several times subsequently. Elsewhere in this motley crew was Hans de Vries, who, the previous year, had been wrapped top to toe in silver for a minor role in the *Doctor Who* serial 'The Tomb of the Cybermen'. (Although never formally tested, BBC newsreader Peter Snow was apparently summoned to meet Broccoli around this time too. He was dismissed, being considered too tall.)

Both director Peter Hunt, promoted on a long-standing promise from Saltzman and Broccoli, and stunt supervisor George Leech presided over the audition pieces, which pitted the would-be 007 against wrestler Yuri Borienko on a specially constructed set. Impressed with Lazenby's physique – Lazenby accidentally broke Borienko's nose during one punch-up – Hunt moved him to the top of his list.

OHMSS demanded much of its leading lady. The Contessa Teresa de Vincenzo is a complex, initially suicidal, blonde in Fleming's novel, and she becomes Bond's wife towards the end of the story (which, unlike *You Only Lives Twice*, remains virtually unchanged in the screenplay). Saltzman's first choice was Brigitte Bardot, but tentative negotiations with the sex kitten were cut short when, during her third meeting with Peter Hunt, she announced that he had just been contracted to co-star in Edward Dmytryk's Western *Shalako* opposite Sean Connery. 'Harry and I looked at one another and that was the end of that,' recalled Hunt. Saltzman next approached Catherine Deneuve, but she turned him down before a meeting with Hunt could even be arranged.

When Honor Blackman quit *The Avengers* to resume her film career with *Goldfinger*, her replacement proved even more popular. As Steed's new sidekick Mrs Emma Peel, Diana Rigg karate-chopped her way through *The Avengers*' transition onto film, into an American network transmission slot and, ultimately, colour. Rigg hung up her catsuit after filming her farewell episode, 'The Forget Me-Knot', on 19 January 1968, enthusiastically accepted

Monday 7 October 1968 – George Lazenby celebrates receiving his licence to kill with a Scotch at the Dorchester. Lazenby was a model by profession, and had never heard of a screen test until he was invited to attend one

Hunt's offer to consider the role of Tracy, and was invited to a 'getting to know you' dinner with her prospective director and co-star. Aware that her experience would prove a useful counterbalance to the novice Lazenby, Hunt was delighted when she agreed to audition.

While Saltzman, Broccoli and Hunt sought their new Bond, Richard Maibaum returned to the fold to adapt the novel widely regarded as one of Ian Fleming's finest. Maibaum was mindful that a new actor would be stepping into Connery's shoes. 'We had this plastic surgery idea,' he recalled. 'Bond had to have plastic surgery because he was being recognised by all his country's enemies. But we thought that was awful and threw it out. Finally, I came up with that line when the girl leaves him flat after he rescues her. Bond said, "This never happened to the other fellow." Because it was funny, the audience liked it. It said, '"Look, you know it's not the same James Bond, so we're not going to kid you or do anything corny to excuse it."' Hunt later enlisted novelist Simon Raven to refine some of Maibaum's dialogue. (Raven's acclaimed book *Doctors Wear Scarlet* was optioned in 1968, and produced the following year as *Incense for the Damned*.) During filming, Hunt would have considerable input into the screenplay himself which benefited from the expertise of consultants from London's College of Arms, the heraldic and genealogical experts Fleming had consulted when preparing the novel. JCG George, principal secretary to the *York Herald*, explained the college's input to the film in an interview with *The Guardian*: 'What did we do? Dialogue polish. And could a chap have borne arms in 1066? No he couldn't; earliest would have been 1127. As you can imagine, being a part of the Royal Household, we didn't want any howlers like that.' College scholars also designed the briefly seen Sable Basilisk letterheads and Blofeld's coat of arms. The College itself would appear in the film, both as a location exterior and as an authentic-looking, mocked-up interior at Pinewood.

Test footage of George Lazenby and Diana Rigg was flown to United Artists in New York on 7 July; Eon had already enrolled Lazenby on an intensive course of acting lessons and brushed up his elocution. As press speculation mounted over the casting of the next James Bond film, the *Daily Mirror* revealed leaked information that Saltzman and Broccoli had accompanied Lazenby's footage with a 'top recommendation'. United Artists didn't share Eon's faith in Lazenby. On 23 September, UA president David Picker flew to London to begin negotiations that he hoped would see Sean Connery relent to the lure of another Bond film. Since completing *You Only Live Twice*, Connery had directed the acclaimed (though little seen) television documentary *The Bowler and the Bunnet*, which concerned the devastating effect of industrial unrest upon Scotland's Clydeside shipyards. He was in a position to pick and choose his work (one project he turned down was Terence Young's *Monte Carlo Mob*) and, by his own admission, refused to accept any assignment 'just for money'. He stood his ground, and the despondent Picker flew back to New York. Shortly afterwards, United Artists sent confirmation to Eon that its choices for the two leads in *OHMSS* had been approved. Paid a retainer of £150 a week, Lazenby was instructed to lie low on the Riviera until Eon had primed the press for his return to London. His widely anticipated appointment as the new 007 was announced in *The Daily Mail* on 3 October. *The Daily Express*' Victor Davis had already conducted enough espionage to present an intriguing biography of the latest James Bond: 'My Paris spy reports that the Bond producers are buying up the advertising material intended for future publication for which George has modelled. They don't want 007 promoting deodorants. They've also had him medically examined for a multi-million dollar insurance policy . . .
 George has ceased working for a Mayfair model agency and acquired a theatrical agent and membership of Equity, the actors' union . . .'

He was a car salesman in a Park Lane showroom when photographer Chard Jenkins discovered him. Jenkins recalled: 'English male models were at that time pale and rather effeminate. George was rugged, tanned, with a face that looked lived-in, and very extrovert in that masculine, Aussie way.' The ebullient Lazenby certainly lived up to his image, telling *L'Express* magazine that he was looking forward to playing Bond 'for the bread and the birds'.

There was noticeably more decorum when the new 007 was formally introduced to the press during a reception held at the Dorchester Hotel on Monday 7 October. Harry Saltzman, who had helped such actors as Albert Finney, Michael Caine and Sean Connery to stardom, proclaimed 'He's my best looking boy yet.' On Sunday 13 October, the Hilton Hotel Roof Restaurant played host to another press call, this time to introduce the rest of the cast. Lazenby posed for photographs alongside Diana Rigg (who, reporters had discovered, would be receiving over £50,000 to appear in the film – more than twice Lazenby's salary), American star Telly Savalas (whose bald pate made him a natural successor to Donald Pleasence in the role of Blofeld) and German actress Ilse Steppat, who had been contracted to play Blofeld's henchwoman Irma Bunt. Amidst the clinking Champagne glasses and the popping flashguns, Harry Saltzman, Albert Broccoli and Peter Hunt kept a lower profile, their thoughts preoccupied with the imminent location photography. *OHMSS* was due to begin shooting in Switzerland just eight days later.

Connery's prediction that *OHMSS* would be produced for a lower budget than *You Only Live Twice* proved correct. Aside from the obvious savings made by signing an unknown leading man, Eon had chosen to dispense with Ken Adam's extravagant sets and seek an existing architectural showstopper. Saltzman had originally suggested shooting Blofeld's lair inside the fortified Maginot Line, and accompanied

Hunt on a guided tour of the underground complex in France. Hunt was unenthusiastic, however, and eventually found what he wanted following a tip-off from the film's Swiss production manager, Hubert Froelich. In 1961, some 9,748 feet above sea level, atop one of the peaks of the Schiltorn, the Swiss Schilthornbahn company had commenced construction on the world's highest circular restaurant and it was still far from finished. Hunt's team seized upon the site, which stood at the end of an existing cable car railway originating in the small village of Murren, but suffered a setback when the Swiss government refused them planning permission to carry out the alterations production designer Syd Cain desired. Saltzman and Broccoli offered to foot the bill for a genuine interior refit (which included adding a mechanism to revolve the inside of the building) and to pay for a real helicopter pad to be built on the restaurant's roof. Attracted by the idea of being able to use the restaurant, which stood alongside the Eiger, as a mountain rescue centre, the Swiss government agreed and work began in spring 1968. The final cost, which took in the 500 tons of concrete that went into the helicopter pad, came to $60,000. Tailoring the mountain-top structure to the demands of filming not only proved relatively economical, but reduced the dependance on replicated interiors at Pinewood Studios. Although extensively modernised in 1989, the restaurant still exists, and still bears the on-screen title it carries in the film: Piz Gloria. A 120-strong crew descended on Murren (population 250) and immediately faced a number of unforeseen problems. Outside the restaurant, the rarified air made any exertion hazardous; inside, cinematographer Michael Reed discovered that the glass encircling the building caused the crew to be reflected in it

85

wherever he placed his camera. Five thousand feet below Piz Gloria, a nervous Saltzman surveyed the snowscapes. 'If that lot melts,' he told the *Daily Express'* Sue Freeman on 20 October, 'it's going to cost me a fortune waiting about for more.'

Filming began inside Piz Gloria on Monday 21 October, and Lazenby was plunged into the first in a long series of location photo-calls and interviews. The actresses playing Blofeld's 'angels of death' vied with the breathtaking scenery for the attentions of the world's press. Some of them – such as Angela Scoular, who had appeared as one of M's numerous 'daughters' in *Casino Royale* – were familiar faces. Others – such as Jenny Hanley, Julie Ege and Anoushka Hempel – would be snapped up by Hammer to achieve minor stardom in the Seventies. One – young Joanna Lumley – remains one of British television's biggest stars. Lazenby found the experience overwhelming almost from the beginning. Despite being warned by Saltzman about the manipulative nature of the press men hounding him, he felt ill-equipped for the pressure he was facing. 'I had no idea of the kind of exposure to expect,' he claims. 'They wanted me to be Bond morning, afternoon and night. Then they kicked up when I asked for a car and a place to sit down.' Most frustratingly, however, Lazenby felt he wasn't receiving the guidance he needed from Hunt, who had his hands full with the technical challenges posed by the unusual environment. He took much of his inspiration from Fleming's novel, largely shunning the advice of his acting coach. In what little spare time he had, Lazenby would visit Murren to relax and hang out with female admirers.

Outside Piz Gloria, George Leech doubled

for Lazenby in the scenes in which 007 clings to the thick, metal cable suspending the mountainside railway cars. The grease on the cable caused Leech to lose his grip and, as his body twisted around his remaining gripping hand, he dislocated his arm and fell onto the boxes prepared for just such an eventuality. Stuntmen Chris Webb and Dickie Greydon completed the shots. Saltzman's greatest fear – a mild winter – happened; a thaw hampered filming. Murren was abandoned altogether in mid-December, and Peter Hunt took his cast and crew back to England. A second unit returned to Switzerland early in January, while studio photography continued at Pinewood. The cable car wheelhouse scenes – intended to lead to the cable suspension sequences already shot on location – were filmed on a set built to effects supervisor John Stears' specifications. After Lazenby had nimbly negotiated Stears' giant (wooden) cogs, he was filmed hanging from the metal cable by a more securely suspended Alec Mills, who at one point travelled towards his subject at 15 miles per hour. (Although it seems greater on screen, both men were in fact hanging just 12 feet above mattresses that cushioned Lazenby's fall when he lost his grip.) One of the greatest challenges facing Stears was keeping the metal cable taut under the combined weight of Lazenby, Mills and his camera. To obtain zero sag, Stears had to tense the cable to a weight of approximately three tons.

Studio shooting continued throughout January, and Lazenby's behaviour began to cause concern. 'I understand that he was a bit flash with the other actors,' says George Leech, recalling Lazenby's over-confidence. 'He was working with such experienced actors – Diana Rigg, Gabriele Ferzetti [playing Tracy's father, Draco], George Baker [playing the real Sir Hilary

Oblivious to the Eiger behind him, Lazenby is surrounded by Blofeld's 'Angels of Death': (at the back) Helena Ronney (left) and Zara; in front from the left are Anoushka Hempel, Julie Ege, Joanna Lumley, Catherine von Schell and Mona Chung. This picture was taken on Monday 21 October, the day principal photography began

Joanna Lumley and George Lazenby find time for a quiet smoke at Piz Gloria. Lumley recalls that the two actors relaxed in different ways during their lengthy stay in Switzerland: she collected wild flowers and knitted a blanket for her young son; Lazenby learned to play 'Hey Jude' on his guitar

Bray] – and he finishes up telling them what to do.'

Of greater concern to Broccoli was the fact that, by January 1969, Lazenby had been shooting for nearly three months without ever having signed a contract. UA had tried to commit Lazenby to a seven-year deal, but had only succeeded in getting him to sign a letter of intent. Intimidated by the sheer size of the contract he had been presented, Lazenby had passed it to a friend to read. While this friend, a real estate lawyer, waded through the paperwork, the star stalled the producers.

Such was the close scrutiny accorded *OHMSS* that the press soon became aware of Lazenby's reputation on set. Most notorious of all the stories circulated about the actor was that of his reported 'feud' with Diana Rigg. The stories were fuelled by a lunchtime incident at the Pinewood commissary. On remembering that she was soon to shoot the hayloft scene in which Bond proposed to Tracy, a playful Rigg decided to apologise for having ordered squid in wine and garlic. She shouted across to Lazenby: 'Hey George, I'm having garlic for lunch, I hope you are!' Reporters blew the incident out of all proportion, intimating that the stars' relationship was poor. Lazenby stringently denies this was the case, but Lois Maxwell later claimed in *Bondage* magazine that the situation was more complicated than it seemed: 'George Lazenby told me . . . That he and Diana were emotionally involved, but he kept on chasing other women as well and she didn't like that at all, so by the time they got to Portugal [in April] they weren't speaking to each other . . . Of course, the London press got this and said they hated each other and there was a sort of battle – Diana would say something to one reporter and he would say something to another reporter and churn up the whole mess. But, according to George Lazenby, when the film was finished, he went off to the coast of Naples with a couple of pals to relax in the sun and swim, and Diana joined him about a week later . . . I quite liked George. I mean, I didn't think he was much of an actor, but his escapades amused me immensely. The way he would chase women was just a hoot.'

By February, a slipping schedule had prompted Peter Hunt to invite John Glen to join the production as second unit director. 'All of that film was obviously filled with such intense action because of George Lazenby's inexperience,' believes Glen. 'We couldn't rely on George the actor; he had to be surrounded by lots of action so that people didn't dwell too much on a line.' Some of the most memorable action sequences were Glen's responsibility. Hunt had first met Glen at London Films in 1947, and the two editors had worked together intermittently over the following years. Glen had most recently edited the 1968 sexploitation curio *Baby Love* when Hunt renewed their acquaintance back in Murren.

Hunt had originally envisaged shooting the climactic bobsleigh chase between Bond and Blofeld at the Cresta Run in St Moritz. The very public nature of the run rendered it impractical for use as a film location, so bobsleigh champion Franz Capose was commissioned to construct a two-mile run near Murren, on the site of a hazardous run that had closed in 1937. The new run proved an expensive addition to Eon's overheads, and Hunt needed a quick return on the investment. John Glen: 'The best time of year to shoot this particular sequence [was] February, and they thought it would take a month to shoot. But the other unit which was doing scenes on the

Diana Rigg and George Lazenby in Murren, December 1968. The two stars' relationship would be the subject of increasing speculation and rumour as shooting progressed

ice had gotten themselves really bogged down, so Peter called me in.' Glen met Cubby Broccoli for the first time at Murren, when the producer commissioned him to shoot the bob run sequence. To Glen's alarm, Broccoli insisted on personally road testing the track before filming began. Glen imported ice from Berne, some 80 miles away, to compensate

89

for the melting blocks that lined the run. 'The logistics were horrific,' he recalls. 'The costs were tremendous.' Carefully camouflaged cameramen shot bobsleigh champion Heinz Lau (doubling for Lazenby) and Olympic skier Robert Zimmerman (doubling for Savalas) as they sped past each corner. Aerial photography was undertaken by Johnny Jordan, now wearing an artificial leg following his *You Only Live Twice* accident. Jordan and his camera hung from a tailor-made circular rig, suspended from a helicopter piloted by John Crewdson. Film-maker and former Olympic downhill racer Willy Bogner Jr followed the bobsleighs with a hand-held camera.

The relatively mild weather made the ice dangerous for the grappling stunt doubles. A near-fatal accident saw Heinz Lau's bobsleigh career off the run midway round a particularly brittle and slippery bend, throwing its occupant back on the track. While Zimmerman struggled to prevent his own bobsleigh from hitting the skidding Lau, he suffered a collision that resulted in facial injuries and a number of stiches inside his mouth. The accident, captured by the pursuing Bogner, can be seen in the finished film. Bogner also shot much of the footage projected behind Lazenby and Savalas in sequences later filmed at Pinewood.

While Glen supervised the bobsleigh chase, Anthony Squires supervised the stock car pile-up at Lauterbrunnen, two miles away from Murren. From there, the second unit went to the village of Grindelwald to shoot Bond's ice rink encounter with Tracy. (An experienced skater doubled for Diana Rigg in all bar close-ups.)

Although he was forbidden from skiing by Eon's insurers, Lazenby was keen to perform his own stunts whenever he was allowed. 'Every time I was in contact with George he was he was as sweet as a nut,' recalls stuntman Alf Joint. 'I never heard him say a thing wrong. He was always chatting to the girls and helping them out in shots.'

For Bond and Tracy's ill-fated escape from the barn, the two actors were doubled by expert skiers and filmed by Bogner, who was adept enough to shoot the high-speed chase while skiing backwards. The use of flares by the skiers pursuing the couple was instigated by Glen, who shot the spectacular scenes over five nights near the village of Winteregg. For the gruesome moment when one of Blofeld's skiers is thrown into a snowplough, a dead goat was minced inside the machine to turn the expelled torrent of snow literally blood red.

Ever committed to realism, Hunt had asked the Swiss army to plant explosive charges in summer 1968, in the hope that by spring 1969 enough snow would have fallen to create an impressive avalanche at the flick of a detonating switch. Remote-controlled cameras and dummies of Bond and Tracy had been prepared when, during filming of the bobsleigh sequences, the avalanche of snow inconveniently fell of its own accord. Glen attempted to engineer his own avalanche using a snowplough, and later detonated the Swiss army's explosives, to little resultant effect. The sequence seen in the film comprised library footage, shots of a huge avalanche engineered by Glen in a nearby valley in May, and the after-effects of the first, natural, avalanche. Glen was ahead of his time by deciding to lend the impressive sequences extra impact by recording them in stereo, thus distinguishing *OHMSS* as the first Bond film to benefit from the effect. (New speakers would be specially installed at the Leicester Square Odeon so patrons could fully appreciate the innovation.)

Lazenby had still not signed his UA contract, causing Saltzman and Broccoli mounting concern. He was therefore offered a new incentive to sign on the dotted line: 'Harry, not Cubby, was offering me money under the counter to sign the goddam contract, and then United Artists offered me any picture that they owned, [which] we could do in between each Bond movie.' Lazenby had fallen under the influence of film producer and Radio Caroline boss Ronan O'Reilly, who advised him not to sign. 'He convinced me the Bonds were over, finished. The hippy generation was in . . . films like *Easy Rider* and all those that were coming out were going to take over.'

Confused, Lazenby approached Peter Hunt, who diplomatically avoided coming between Lazenby and his producers. As UA piled pressure on to Eon, Saltzman and Broccoli pressed Lazenby for a decision. Midway through shooting the star dropped a bombshell – *OHMSS* would be his first and last James Bond film. 'He had very bad advice,' lamented Peter Hunt.

Lazenby and Rigg stayed in Switzerland for pick-up shots and close-up inserts for various scenes (notably the avalanche, bobsleigh, stock car and ice rink scenes) before returning to England to shoot less exotic location material.

Bond's visit to M's house was shot in the second week of April. Thames Lawn, a house in Marlow, was chosen as a suitable location following a recommendation from set decorator Peter Lamont, who lived nearby. Situated just ten miles away

from Pinewood, it was ideal. Hammond, M's butler, was played by John Gay, an old school friend of Hunt's. By April, the main unit was in northern Portugal; Bond's wedding to Tracy was filmed at the Palacio Hotel in the small town of Estoril. Series regulars Bernard Lee, Lois Maxwell and Desmond Llewelyn were recruited to help wave the happy couple off on their honeymoon. Guincho beach, near Estoril, played host to the elegantly choreographed pre-credits punch-up. Draco's birthday party was filmed at the De Vinho estate in Zambujal.

'The most moving scene in any Bond picture . . .'

The traumatic ending of the film – Tracy's murder at the hands of hit-and-run assassin Irma Bunt – is perhaps the most moving scene in any Bond picture. Hunt worked hard to manipulate Lazenby into achieving the right tone as Bond cradled his dead bride in his arms. The first take, in which Lazenby mustered tears, was ultimately rejected in favour of a more restrained performance.

OHMSS wrapped on 23 June 1969, almost two months over schedule thanks to problems caused by Switzerland's warm winter. John Glen began editing Hunt's footage, initially producing a rough cut that ran to two hours 50 minutes. A further 30 minutes were cut – including a long sequence in which Bond, discovering that his conversation with Sir Hilary Bray has been bugged, pursues Sir Hilary's traitorous assistant through the streets of London. Nevertheless, *OHMSS* remains the longest Bond film yet made.

John Barry's score comprised perhaps his very finest James Bond music, with strident orchestral arrangements now complemented by subtle synthesiser texturing. As if in an attempt to recreate the fresh start of *Dr. No*, Barry composed an instrumental theme to accompany Maurice Binder's opening credits, which featured a clock face showing the hands of time spinning backwards. Some of Binder's most innovative and stylish work was contained within titles that maintained series continuity by highlighting memorable scenes from Connery Bond films within the falling sands of an hourglass.

Barry realised his ambition to get Louis Armstrong to record the film's romantic theme, 'We Have All the Time in the World'. Satchmo, who had been hospitalised for around a year when he received Barry's request, was delighted by the commission, even though he was too ill to play the trumpet. This haunting number, written by Barry and lyricist Hal David, was already familiar to audiences on the film's release – the single had topped the British charts in spring 1968, shortly after it was recorded. It remains one of Barry's favourite tracks: 'I love that song, and it's Hal David's favourite song, funnily enough. The pleasure of it was working with Louis Armstrong. He was very ill, but when he sang we all just broke up. I'm very emotionally attached to that song and the whole thing with Armstrong. It was the last record he made.' At the time, Lazenby lobbied to have American jazz/rock outfit Blood, Sweat and Tears contribute to the soundtrack, but he now concedes that Armstrong's poignant love song is one of the film's highlights.

On Her Majesty's Secret Service received its premiere at the Leicester Square Odeon on Thursday 18 December 1969. Lazenby accompanied Diana Rigg, and strained his already fragile relationship with Saltzman and Broccoli by wearing shoulder-length hair and a thick beard. Acclaim for the film, if not Lazenby, had been widespread: 'I must say that it's quite a jolly frolic in the familiar money-spinning fashion,' admitted Derek Malcolm in *The Guardian* of 16 December. 'Not a penny spared on production values, smart direction from Peter Hunt, and a shrewd eye kept throughout on the well-worn mixture of sex, violence, thrills and laughs.' The *Evening Standard*'s Alexander Walker was one of few critics to give Lazenby the benefit of the doubt: 'Lazenby's voice is more suave than sexy-sinister. But he could pass for the other fellow's twin on the shady side of the casino. In battle tactics there's nothing to let you know which has the better stuntman stand-in. And Lazenby definitely wins in fighting his way alone into a skin-fit shirt . . . One load Lazenby doesn't have to carry is the electronic gadgetry. He depends on what God, not IBM, gave him, except for an automatic safecracker that slaves away on the enemy's combination while Bond reads the fold-out section of *Playboy*. (That puts the machine in its place.) 'The result is a film with far more human action than in most recent Bonds. And a lot more zip and pow, not to mention zowie, inside the action . . . The film's glaring error is to end four times before it actually does, a sure sign of film-makers so surfeited with good scenes they want to cram them all in – and in the end take our appetite away. But Bond is definitely all set for the Seventies.'

Overshadowing nearly every other review, however, were some savage assessments of Lazenby's performance. 'Mr Lazenby . . . looks like a Willerby Brothers clothes peg and acts as if he's just come out of Burton's short on credit,' said Derek Malcolm. 'It is reported that he would just as soon go back to lorry driving, and indeed I share his sentiments exactly . . .'

'I don't agree with the press,' retaliated Albert Broccoli in the *Sunday Times*. 'They should have given him an A for Effort. It's true he's not Olivier, but Olivier could not play Bond in any circumstances. In fairness to George, he must have something Olivier doesn't have. There will be a lot of tear stains on the bank deposit slips.' Broccoli was non-committal when answering the question on every critic's lips – would Lazenby star in the next film, *Diamonds Are Forever*? 'It's a question of relationships,' he replied. 'I find it incredible that a plum role can't be respected. We chose George because in his physique and looks and his walk he was the best of the candidates. He had the masculinity. Looking at the film, to put it in an old Spanish phrase, one could wish he had less *cojones* and more charm.'

By no means the commercial disaster many have since construed it to be, *On Her Majesty's Secret Service*'s UK takings of £750,000 made it as the most successful picture on British general release in 1970. The film nevertheless took longer than hoped to recoup its estimated $6 million production cost. A worldwide gross of $64.6 million, just over half the amount generated by *You Only Live Twice*, continued Eon's downward trend. US admission figures of 16 million told a similarly worrying story. In the world's most important market, the audience for new 007 product had halved. At the end of a decade that saw the James Bond films scale their greatest commercial and artistic heights (in *Thunderball* and *You Only Live Twice*, respectively) and plumb their lowest depths (*Casino Royale*) the future of the cinema's greatest fictional hero hung in the balance. With or without Lazenby, who,

despite contemporary criticism ably portrayed a more than credible Bond, a rethink was required. Still under the influence of the tumultuous shifts in attitudes and sensibilities that would characterise the era, Lazenby had all but left the character behind by the beginning of the new decade. As the last definitive slice of Sixties Bond chic, *On Her Majesty's Secret Service* truly represented the end of an era.

File: *On Her Majesty's Secret Service*

Teaser A painful joke at the expense of the audience. While hunting Blofeld in Europe, Bond, his features obscured, gets cut up by a careless woman driver. 'Hmm,' he mutters, butchly overdubbed. He observes the girl stop her car and run towards a beach. This is, apparently, enough reason for him to rev his car onto the sand and yank her out of the surf (and here we see his face fully for the first time). Whereupon three heavies appear; Bond gives them a good pasting. The girl drives off, leaving Bond her shoes. 'This never happened to the other feller,' Bond tells the viewer. Ravishingly photographed, yes, but lumpenly executed; for cheek alone, then … **7**

Titles A *tour de force*. Writhing nymphets are sidelined to favour silhouetted Britannias, a cocktail glass, an hourglass and a man dangling on the hands of a giant clock running backwards (*pace* Harold Lloyd, *The Thirty-nine Steps*). Images from all five Eon films previous scroll up inside the hourglass and the cocktail glass; the sand and the liquid in both drains away meaningfully. We call it Art with a capital A. **10**

Bonkers plot With the unwitting aid of at least 12 international beauties, his so-called 'angels of death', Blofeld – now masquerading as a benevolent allergy specialist – threatens to release a life-destroying sterility virus across the globe. Meanwhile Bond, who's been on Blofeld's trail for two years, falls in love with a gangster's daughter – and marries her. And if that isn't mad enough for you, we don't know what is. **10**

Locations London; Portugal; Geneva; above, beneath and on the slopes of Alpine Switzerland. Milks its main setting for all its exotic worth – a bobsleigh track! An avalanche! And, er, a cowshed! – which merits at least a very reasonable **7**

Gadgets Oh dear. Q branch can offer only 'radioactive lint' and a none-too-portable safecracker-cum-photocopier this time round (at his wedding, Bond unsubtly emasculates Q when he quips: 'this time I've got the gadgets – and I know how to use them . . .'). Still, at least Bond's mini oxygen canister (*Thunderball*) and Grant's wristwatch with cheesewire (*From Russia With Love*) put in a reappearance (and did he pilfer the latter from Grant's corpse?). Blofeld's 'angels' carry compacts which conceal a radio receiver, but that hardly compensates. No vehicles with absurd extras, either. Whoops. A meagre **3**

Girls Poor little rich girl Tracy, who spurns her entitlement to be known as Teresa, Contessa di Vicenzo, lest she be mistaken for a saint (fat chance). Greedy living, we learn, has burned the heart out of her, hence her death wish – granted, with due irony, in the finale (all the time in the world? No. She's on borrowed time from the moment Bond saves her from suicide). A good skater, but dangerous with a car, a broken bottle, or at a baccarat table. Stroppy and spoiled; what does Bond see in her? Roll on Olympe, Draco's adoring cherie – and, of course, Blofeld's angels, a united nations of babes (just when you think this film can't get any better, Joanna Lumley turns up). Bond scores – with Tracy, with chicken-loathing, Lancashire lass Ruby Bartlett, and exotic Nancy (and the last two within half an hour of each other!) He makes a date with the Chinese representative, too. But, at long last, it's Moneypenny – 'Britain's last line of defence,' as Bond puts it – who steals the show (see later) **9**

Villains Blofeld, who may or may not have undergone plastic surgery since *You Only Live Twice* (we're told only that he's snipped off his earlobes in his vain pursuit of the title 'Count de Bleuchamp'. Perhaps he had a Donald Pleasence mask on when we saw him last). More urbane and physical than before – and a lot less European – but he does reveal sides to his character previously unseen: the class snobbery which M remarks upon ('a very curious thing') and the vanity which Tracy flatters to force him off

his guard (she compares him to the 'Master of the World', after lines by the 19th-century playwright James Elroy Flecker). His irritation with his employees is fun – when one of his skiers ends up in a tree in pursuit of Bond, he snarls 'Idiot!' Main henchperson is Fraulein Irma Bunt, a Rosa Klebb lookalike with 'ears like an elephant' who, unsurprisingly, acts as a living bromide. **9**

Fights, chases, explosions These are easily the hardest-hitting of all Bond's film fights. We begin with a set-to on the shoreline which calls for the imaginative use of flick-knives, an anchor, and an oar – and we graduate to a full-scale assault on Piz Gloria with Sten guns, grenades and even a flamethrower. Every punch is overdubbed hard – a hefty, bone-splintering crack being called upon most often – and, especially in the short section just outside Draco's office, directed like a ballet; the camera reduces Bond and his assailants to flying hands and feet, fetishising the mechanics of unarmed combat in a fashion not dissimilar to Hong Kong chopsocky. It isn't until the stock car sequence that we get the first bang, followed soon after by a rather humdrum demolition of Piz Gloria itself – but the several snowbound pursuit scenes are all spectacular enough to compensate for the lack of action in the film's middle third. **9**

Dialogue and double entendres The ersatz Sir Hilary directs a fabulous insult at the repulsive Irma when he tells her that 'bunt' is a nautical term meaning the 'baggy and swollen parts of a sail'. The dinner scene between the 12 angels and 'Hilly' mines a *Tom Jones*-esque seam of metaphor – witness the way in which the Jamaican girl wolfs that banana! – but Bond's acquired knowledge of 'golden balls' in heraldry prompts only tiresome titters (ditto Bond's reaction to Ruby's discreet manipulation of his inner thigh: 'Just a slight stiffness coming on'). We reach a nadir when Blofeld's men, chasing Bond across the slopes, receive the instruction 'We'll head him off at the precipice!' Much better is the glorious moment when Draco knocks Tracy unconscious to prevent her going back inside the wired-up Piz Gloria to search for Bond: 'Spare the rod and spoil the child,' he tells an associate. **7**

Bond is descended from both a baronet of Peckham and a 14th-century knight. Dom Perignon '57 and five-star Hennessey brandy are his mouthwashes of choice; after the fight in Tracy's suite, he pauses to take a finger of caviare. Visual references to earlier exploits abound; besides the gadgets mentioned earlier, we see Honey's knife (presumably confiscated by guards in *Dr. No*) – and the golf clubs he carries out of Tracy's hotel evoke *Goldfinger* in spades. 'Steals' a *Playboy* centrefold from Gumbold's office. Wears nothing under Sir Hilary's kilt. Is terrified by a man in a polar bear suit. Spurns Draco's one million gold dowry. So, is this new feller any good? A little soft around the edges, sure – he tosses Moneypenny his hat one last time on his wedding day. He means it to act like a bride's bouquet, but he's a man you'd not want to get on the wrong side of in a fight. **9**

Plus/minus points The London scenes, in which Moneypenny hands M a request for two weeks' leave rather than Bond's dictated resignation are at once funny, moving and warm ('What would I do without you?' ask both Bond and M separately of Moneypenny, once she's settled their *contretemps*). Ruby gets a split-second's sheer pathos (but you have to listen out for it); just as she's being hypnotised by Blofeld, the gawky girl from Morecambe Bay wonders aloud of Bond, 'You do love me just a little, don't you?' The soundtrack's probably John Barry's finest – the rising swell where Bond first sees the 'angels' is especially fine. 'We Have All the Time in the World' is, of course, a standard. Even the sound effects are magnificent (the hits mentioned earlier, the 'space noises' heard as Bond first descends into Blofeld's labs). Best of all is the buttock-clenchingly suspenseful sequence where Bond breaks into Gumbold's office during a lunch hour. Here, the series surely equals Hitchcock. **+10**

90% It might easily be said that *On Her Majesty's Secret Service* is just a little too good in places to be a 'proper' Bond film. Certainly, its visual gloss – courtesy of director of photography Michael Reed – isn't present in any of the other films, and the human story at its heart sits a little awkwardly with all that snobbery and violence. Lazenby acquits himself more than honourably (if only he'd done more). Oh, and did we mention that nasty little surprise ending?

CAST

George Lazenby James Bond
Diana Rigg Tracy **Telly Savalas** Blofeld **Gabriele Ferzetti** Draco
Ilse Steppat Irma Bunt **Lois Maxwell** Moneypenny
George Baker Sir Hilary Bray **Bernard Lee** 'M' **Bernard Horsfall** Campbell
Desmond LLewelyn 'Q' **Yuri Borienko** Grunther **Virginia North** Olympe
Geoffrey Cheshire Toussaint **Irvin Allen** Che Che **Terry Mountain** Raphael
James Bree Gumbold **John Gay** Hammond

The girls

Angela Scoular Ruby **Catherina von Schell** Nancy **Julie Ege** Scandinavian
Mona Chong Chinese **Sylvana Henriques** Jamaican **Dani Sheridan** American
Joanna Lumley English **Zara** Indian **Anoushka Hempel** Australian
Ingrit Back German **Helena Ronee** Israeli **Jenny Hanley** Irish

And

George Cooper Braun* **Les Crawford** Felsen*
John Creudson Draco's Helicopter Pilot* **Richard Graydon** Draco's Driver*
Reg Harding Blofeld's Driver* **Dudley Jones** Hall Porter*
Martin Leyder Chef du Jeu Hussier* **Bessie Love** American Guest*
Norman McGlen Janitor* **Bill Morgan** Klett* **Steve Plytas** Greek Tycoon*
Robert Rietty Chef du Jeu* **Elliott Sullivan** American Guest*
Joseph Vasa Piz Gloria Receptionist* **Brian Worth** Manuel*

SELECTED CREDITS

Assistant director **Frank Ernst** Camera operator **Alec Mills**
Stunt arranger **George Leech** Art director **Bob Laing**
Costume designer **Marjory Cornellus** Set decorator **Peter Lamont**
Stock car sequence director **Anthony Squire** Hairdresser **Eileen Warwick**
Make up **Paul Rabiger** & **Basil Newall** Wardrobe mistress **Jackie Cummins**
Main title designed by **Maurice Binder** Associate producer **Stanley Sopel**
Production supervisor **David Middlemas** Special effects **John Stears**
Editor & Second Unit director **John Glen** Director of photography **Michael Reed BSC**
Production designed by **Syd Cain GFAD**
Music composed, conducted and arranged by **John Barry** Lyrics by **Hal David**
Song 'We have all the time in the world' sung by **Louis Armstrong**
Song 'Do you know how Christmas Trees are grown?' sung by **Nina**
Additional dialogue **Simon Raven** Screenplay by **Richard Maibaum**
Produced by **Albert R. Broccoli** and **Harry Saltzman**
Directed by **Peter Hunt**

* unaccredited

You just killed James Bond: *Diamonds Are Forever*

1970: ever optimistic, Albert Broccoli and Harry Saltzman forwarded an advance for *Diamonds Are Forever* to George Lazenby. He sent it back. Plunged once more into searching for a new James Bond, Eon faced additional pressure from United Artists. Sliding box-office receipts threatened the very future of a franchise that, by the end of 1971, would have earned an estimated $500 million in all. To take Bond into the new decade, Eon's distributor would dictate a new leading man and a new approach. Never had more been at stake.

The play-safe philosophy that would dominate *Diamonds Are Forever* was evident in Richard Maibaum's first draft screenplay. *Goldfinger* had proved one of the most popular Bond films of the Sixties, and its enigmatic villain one of the best remembered characters in the series. Actor Gert Frobe remained on good terms with Eon (he had appeared in Broccoli's 1968 film *Chitty Chitty Bang Bang*) so it was decided to engineer a rematch of sorts. There was no way that Auric Goldfinger could have survived his high-altitude demise at the climax of the classic 1964 film, so Maibaum devised a new Goldfinger for Frobe to portray – the original character's twin brother, a Swedish shipping magnate armed with a huge laser mounted on a supertanker. The diamond smuggling central to Fleming's novel could, Maibaum decided, be woven into the screenplay as the means by which Goldfinger obtained the rare stones vital to his laser. When asked about the script in *Starlog* magazine in 1983, Maibaum remembered his original intentions clearly: 'This fellow is supposed to say to Bond at one point, "Oh, my brother Auric – mother always said he was a bit retarded." We were going to cast Gert Frobe again, but it didn't work out.'

Despite the fact that Blofeld (like Goldfinger's twin) didn't feature in Fleming's novel, it was decided to once more make SPECTRE's Number One the villain of the piece, and replace the supertanker with a diamond-encrusted laser-firing space satellite.

Maibaum incorporated a number of his producers' suggestions into his script, and devised a sequence reportedly inspired by one of Broccoli's dreams. Prior to a script conference, Broccoli imagined that he had visited his former boss Howard Hughes, only to discover an imposter sitting in the reclusive tycoon's place. This would mutate into the scene in which Bond discovers that Vegas billionaire Willard Whyte has been kidnapped and replaced by the parasitical Blofeld. Maibaum also took on board Saltzman's suggestion that much of the action could be set in the relatively inexpensive locations of Thailand and India, but later drafts would eschew jungle chases and tiger hunts to concentrate the action within the United States.

Maibaum originally intended to climax his script with vengeful Las Vegas big shots chasing Goldfinger across Lake Mead in everything from Chinese junks to Roman galleys. 'What I had was this fleet of boats in pursuit of Goldfinger,' he said, 'because he gave the city such a bad name. They wanted to do something patriotic to catch this terrible villain. I thought I had one of the best lines in the entire series when Bond, in the lead boat, broadcasts to the fleet, "Las Vegas expects every man to do his duty," a take-off of what Admiral Horatio Nelson said at Trafalgar. Just for the sake of the line, I was heartbroken when they rejected it.'

Danny Reisner, a UA vice-president, suggested that Broccoli and Saltzman should seek a new scriptwriter to redraft Maibaum's work. UA's David Picker nominated Tom Mankiewicz, the 28-year-old son of director Joseph. He'd previously co-authored the surfing drama *The Sweet Ride* (1968), starring Jacqueline Bisset, and adapted *Georgy Girl* as a short-lived Broadway musical. Picker had seen the show during its short run and been impressed by the script.

Mankiewicz was hired by Broccoli and Saltzman in autumn 1970, and began augmenting Maibaum's script. Key innovations included Blofeld's attempt to shake off 007 with numerous lookalikes, and the pre-credits sequence that saw Bond track his arch-nemesis down to South America, 'killing' him in a huge vat of

Thursday 12 August – on Connery's penultimate day of filming, Bond narrowly avoids a premature cremation at Slumber Inc.

boiling mud. Mankiewicz delivered his final draft in January 1971. Maibaum would later lament that his 'smash ending' had given way to 'an interminable thing on an oil rig'.

The revised first draft, undated but attributed solely to Mankiewicz, is almost exactly as per the finished film. It's scantly faithful to the novel, retaining only a few elements past its first 20 pages or so (Bond's original misson, the dentist scenes, Wint and Kidd, Tiffany, Shady Tree, the Las Vegas backdrop, the finale on board ship), bastardising others (the Acme Mud and Sulphur Bath, where Wint and Kidd murder a Mob traitor, perhaps becomes a backdrop for the teaser) and eliminating far more (the Spangled Mob, the book's main villains, and all their actual motivation). New are Blofeld, Plenty, Willard Whyte, the satellite-mounted laser – almost the entire thrust of the film's plot, in fact.

A few scenes in this screenplay are curtailed or omitted altogether in the finished print. Some blackly humourous dialogue was cut from scenes in Slumber Inc's Garden of Remembrance; as Bond passes Wint and Kidd, Kidd is arranging flowers in one of the niches. 'Mother loved azaleas, but they always made her sneeze . . .' remarks Wint. 'Now she can really enjoy them,' counters Kidd. Shortly after, Wint brains Bond with his mother's urn. 'Mother was always such a help . . .' he murmurs. Amusingly, the Whyte House casino scenes were intended to open with a cameo appearance by a named star playing themselves: 'Saxby spots well-known celebrity (à la Sammy Davis or Dean Martin) heading his way'. 'Hey, I just got a call from Mr. Whyte,' says Saxby, 'I understand you haven't signed your contract yet. What's the problem?' 'The money, if you can believe it,' moans the celeb. 'Considering your boss is a billionaire, for God's sake . . .' (In fact, Sammy Davis Jr did shoot the scene, which ended up on the fabled cutting room floor.) The script indicates that we should witness Shady Tree's assassination; bizarrely, Wint murders him with a real gun disguised as a water pistol ('Two was company, Mr. Wint.' 'Tree was a crowd, Mr. Kidd').

Absent from the finished print was a significant scene which makes sense of why Plenty is later found dead in Tiffany's pool, seeing as no connection is made between the two on screen. After Plenty has been thrown out of the window and Tiffany and Bond are making love, Plenty, soaking wet and wearing a pool cleaner's overalls, quietly re-enters the suite. 'She hears noises from the bedroom . . . moans of pleasure and the rustle of sheets. Her face falls, then sets in anger.' The girl then opens Tiffany's handbag and takes out a driver's licence, reads the address (120 Willowbrook Lane), replaces the licence, and sneaks back out.

The only other major alteration is to the very final sequence in which, on board ship, Wint and Kidd attempt to exact revenge on Bond and Tiffany. As scripted, the killers, disguised as waiters, bring a trolley of food to Bond and Tiffany's cabin, then send Bond to the ship's radio room where a message from Willard Whyte is apparently waiting for him. There, an operator assures Bond that no such message has been received. Meanwhile, Tiffany has been gagged and tied to her and Bond's bed; the killers have rigged up a 'sizzling pot of boiling oil, attached by rope' over the bed and then to the door handle. When Bond opens the door, the slack created will cause the boiling oil to pour over Tiffany. ('Perfect. It's Romeo and Juliet,' says Wint, closing the door. He sees Kidd start to cry. 'I just can't stand these unhappy endings,' wails Kidd.) Bond frees Tiffany after climbing through the cabin's porthole. Wint gets the boiling oil thrown in his face before being impaled on the sharp point of an ice sculpture on the trolley. Kidd dies in the same incendiary manner as he does in the finished version – in which, *à la From Russia With Love*'s Grant, Wint's lack of awareness regarding wines (and his pungent aftershave) gives away the assassins' plan to blow up Bond and Tiffany with a ticking 'Bombe Surprise'.

The relationship between Peter Hunt and his producers had soured during the arduous production of *On Her Majesty's Secret Service*, which was the last Bond film to benefit from his presence. Hopes of rekindling past glories may have motivated the appointment of Guy Hamilton to direct *Diamonds Are Forever* in autumn 1970. It would be the first of three consecutive Bond engagements.

The film's predominantly American supporting cast was headed by 30-year-old Jill St. John (born Jill Oppenheim), who was suggested to Eon by Sidney Korshak, a legal advisor enlisted by the company for the Las Vegas location shoot. St. John initially tested for the role of gold-digger Plenty O'Toole (Raquel Welch, Jane Fonda and Faye Dunaway had also been in the running), but Hamilton decided she would be better suited to play smuggler Tiffany Case.

Natalie Wood's younger sister Lana had earned notoriety following an appearance in *Playboy*, and soon after won the role of Plenty. Country and western singer Jimmy Dean played the drawling tycoon Willard Whyte; jazz musician Putter Smith appeared alongside Bruce Glover as effete homosexual assassins Kidd and Wint respectively. Blofeld now bore the 'remodelled' features of Charles Gray who, since appearing as the ill-fated Henderson in *You Only Live Twice*, had taken a

starring role in Hammer's *The Devil Rides Out* (1968) and featured in *Mosquito Squadron* (1968) and *Cromwell* (1970). Gray would skilfully reinvent Blofeld as an elegant British scoundrel, uttering venomous quips through a clenched cigarette-holder.

Bond's regular back-up were all contracted to appear, but the film nearly saw the introduction of a new Miss Moneypenny. 'When they asked about my availability for *Diamonds Are Forever*, my agent said that he wanted more money,' remembered Lois Maxwell, disgruntled because several days' work on each Bond picture disrupted her career. She was told that she would be replaced if she insisted on a pay rise. Undaunted, Maxwell dyed her hair black in order to win a role in the Agatha Christie thriller *Endless Night* (1971). 'I still had my black hair when, suddenly, the Bond people came through and said there had been such a furore because they were going to find a new Moneypenny that they wanted me to do it. I said "Great – but I have black hair." That's, I think, why they put me in the policewoman's uniform at Dover, because it was the only way they could get a hat on my head.'

'They were going to find a new Moneypenny'

The greatest challenge facing the production team and its distributor was filling the shoes of the absent George Lazenby, who was busy preparing his would-be comeback film *Universal Soldier* with director Cy Endfield. Roger Moore, then contracted to the lavish ITC series *The Persuaders!*, was again considered, but Broccoli and Saltzman tested numerous lesser-known hopefuls. They were most impressed with the 42-year-old American actor John Gavin, a former naval intelligence officer whose notable films included Douglas Sirk's *Imitation of Life* (1959), Alfred Hitchcock's *Psycho* and Stanley Kubrick/Anthony Mann's *Spartacus* (both 1960). Gavin's career was dominated by television work during the Sixties, but one curious exception had included a 007-type role in the French/Italian spy thriller *OSS 117 Double Agent* (1967), in which he starred alongside Curt Jurgens. After some promising screen tests, Gavin was given a holding contract to play James Bond in *Diamonds Are Forever*.

Nervous about the introduction of another new leading man after *On Her Majesty's Secret Service*, United Artists decided to make a last ditch attempt to lure Connery back. In February 1971, David Picker told Broccoli and Saltzman that he would authorise the payment of a huge salary. Associate producer Stanley Sopel was dispatched to meet the former Bond star at the Dorchester Hotel in London. Connery's films had met a mixed reception in recent years – neither *Shalako* (1968) nor *The Molly Maguires* (1970) had been financially successful – but he remained determined to develop his career in challenging new ways. Sopel did not, however, leave the meeting empty-handed – Connery sold him a second-hand Mercedes from a garage in which he had an interest.

Picker decided to tackle the recalcitrant star personally, and flew to London shortly after. He offered Connery a staggering $1,250,000 fee (payable in 18 weekly instalments) to appear as James Bond in *Diamonds Are Forever*. In addition, he promised a 12.5 per cent cut of the gross profits, and weekly compensation of $145,000 for every week the production

overran its agreed 18-week shooting schedule. Furthermore, Picker promised Connery that United Artists would bankroll two films of his choosing, in association with his own production company, Tantallon Films. He could choose to either star in or direct either.

The money alone was broadly in line with the $1.2 million and 30 per cent of net profits Connery reportedly received for *Shalako*, but the extra trimmings Picker offered made the deal far too good to refuse. 'I was really bribed back into it,' Connery cheerfully admitted. 'But it served my purpose.' (His purpose was an admirable one; in 1970, Connery had joined forces with industrialist Sir Iain Stewart and racing driver Jackie Stewart to found the Scottish International Educational Trust. Under the chairmanship of Sir Iain, vice-chancellor of Strathclyde University, the charity was committed to 'the advancement of education for the public benefit and the provision of facilities for recreational and other leisure time facilities.' Its biggest financial boost in its formative years came from Connery, who quietly donated every cent of his basic fee from *Diamonds Are Forever*.)

United Artists and Eon had bought the next best thing to a guarantee of improved box office returns, and Connery had been given the means to boost his charity's influence. Everyone was happy; even John Gavin was compensated with $50,000. (Gavin would continue acting, and made his Broadway debut in 1973. During the Reagan administration he served as US ambassador to Mexico.)

Backed by a $7,200,000 million budget, *Diamonds Are Forever* began shooting in Las Vegas on Monday 5 April 1971.

Connery flew to Vegas to join the shoot six days later, already talking excitedly of his plans to direct a new version of *Macbeth* as one of the two films accorded him under the terms of his deal with UA.

In February 1969, Connery had successfully sued French magazine *France Soir* over an August 1967 allegation that he was quitting the Bond films because he was no longer fit to play the part. In 1971, he would make little attempt to disguise the fact he had noticeably aged since *You Only Live Twice*, instead playing Mankiewicz's arch script to the hilt. He certainly seemed to be enjoying recreating 007 when questioned about the films' ongoing appeal at the end of April: 'There's the old escapism,' he admitted. 'It's set in exotic places. There are attractive birds, guns and humour. It doesn't make any great demands on anyone. Playing James Bond again is still enjoyable.'

The gruelling moon buggy scenes were shot in the Nevada desert during the first week of May; Hamilton also filmed in Oceanside, Palm Springs (which became Willard Whyte's luxury residence), Los Angeles' International hotel (which became became The Whyte House) and, most spectacularly, a semi-permanent oil rig off southern California, rented for $40,000 a day. 'We could have built a model in the studio,' claimed an unrepentant Harry Saltzman, 'but that wouldn't have been the same.' Unusually, foreign studio facilities were employed for the set piece car chase through Vegas' neon-lit streets, which was filmed across several nights on Universal Studios' north Hollywood backlot. Other locations included London, Dover, Southampton, Amsterdam and the South of France, where Bond's bikini-whipping interrogation of Marie was filmed.

Perhaps motivated by the incentive of Eady benefits, Eon centred shooting at Pinewood Studios from Monday 7 June. Ken Adam's sets dominated four stages, The Whyte House's impressive penthouse suite occupying A stage. Principal photography came to an end with Connery's filming of the coffin sequence at Slumber Inc on Friday 13 August – exactly on schedule. 'It can be done, you see,' Connery told *The Guardian*'s Tom Hutchinson, 'if there's money at stake. I'd been frigged about too much on other Bond pictures. There's so much bullshit that comes from bad decisions being made at the top . . .'

Although Paul McCartney was originally approached to compose the score for *Diamonds Are Forever*, in the end John Barry did the honours once more. His soundtrack included a lounge music parody that perfectly complemented the film's tacky Vegas backdrop. The theme tune was sung by *Goldfinger* veteran Shirley Bassey to the accompaniment of the wah-pedalled guitar sound prevalent at the time. Lyricist Don Black, who had previously worked on *Thunderball*, still cites the song as his favourite Bond theme: 'When I hear it today it does sound amazingly fresh . . . Shirley Bassey is so alive. She's almost salivating on the lyrics . . .'

In addition to producing the Bond title sequences, Maurice Binder's responsibilities also included overseeing the compilation of the film's trailers. For *Diamonds Are Forever*, Binder prepared an additional festive trailer, which opened with a reflection of Connery in a decoration hanging from a Christmas tree. As Connery turned to fire, the film's title emerged onto the screen and a female voice promised a special Christmas gift.

Older and greyer, but undeniably Bond. Sean Connery relaxes between takes in the Nevada desert

Diamonds Are Forever opened in America on 17 December 1971. In London, around 700 fans crowded around the Leicester Square Odeon for the British premiere on the 30th. It was a good omen. During the film's first week at the venue it grossed £35,000 – £13,500 more than the previous record. In its first 12 days, worldwide rentals amounted to $15,600,000. Overall US admissions of 26.5 million were a ten million improvement over *On Her Majesty's Secret Service*.

Connery's charisma had reversed Eon's fortunes and helped give the series a second wind. In terms of 'bums on seats', the film's performance in America would not be bettered by any other Bond until *GoldenEye* in 1995. A worldwide gross of $116,000,000, while only a slight improvement on *You Only Live Twice*, nevertheless signified that the decline in the series' popularity had been halted.

'Our timing was right,' a relieved Harry Saltzman told *The Observer*. 'Over the last few years the entertainment quotient has vanished from films. Take *One Day in the Life of Ivan Denisovich*. That's a marvellous film, but I came out shaking. How could you take your girlfriend to see that? I feel I owe you entertainment. I like people to laugh.'

'Predictably, *Diamonds Are Forever* is doing great business at the Leicester Square Odeon,' announced *7 Days* magazine on 12 January 1972. 'Who would not want to see a re-run of top-Sixties kitsch, with Connery instead of the ill-fated Lazenby back in the title role?

'Blofeld . . . is extremely unconvincing, and his tactics miserably incompetent. The plot is the old Edwardian stand-by, popularised by Sapper in *The Final Count*, "holding the world to ransom" via a laser-wielding satellite which consumes in its fiery rays the world's stock of guided missiles. None of the participants in the film can, visibly, lend themselves to this ludicrous fantasy for a second, so the charm of the action has to rest on by-play: fighting, fucking and gambling.'

Pauline Kael, writing in the *New Yorker* on 15 January, highlighted Bond's elevator struggle with smuggler Peter Franks as the point where *Diamonds Are Forever* lost its way: 'The Bond pictures depend on the comic pornography of brutality; the violence has to be witty. When people are just slugging each other, as in any movie fight, the point of the picture is blunted. This movie never recovers for long . . . The picture isn't bad; it's merely tired, and it's often noisy when it means to be exciting . . .

What's missing may be linked to the absence of Peter Hunt, who worked on the action sequences of all the earlier Bonds, and who directed the last one; perhaps it was he who gave the series its distinctive quality of aestheticized thrills. The daring seemed beautiful in the earlier films – precariousness glorified. This time, even when a sequence works (that is, both daring and funny), such as the car chase and the battle between Connery and the black and white Amazons [Bambi and Thumper], it lacks elegance and visual opulence; it looks like a sequence of the same kind in the Bond imitations. No doubt those of us who love the Bond pictures are spoiled, but really we've come to expect more than a comic car chase.'

Connery cashed his UA chips not with *Macbeth* (Roman Polanski was preparing his own version) but an uncompromising thriller based on John Hopkins' short-lived Royal Court play *This Story of Yours*. *The Offence* was directed by Sidney Lumet and

co-starred Ian Bannen and Trevor Howard. The film gave Connery one of his most compelling roles as a policeman who, during the course of the picture, emerges as a dangerous sadist. It proved unpalatable for audiences in 1972 and, by Connery's own saddened admission, 'died the death financially'.

Connery continued to take his career on an unorthodox path – his next film, *Zardoz*, a surreal science fantasy loosely based on *The Wizard of Oz*, also fared poorly – and remained steadfast in his insistence that he would never play 007 again. 'Of course the films will go on,' he predicted in 1971, 'but who'll play me I just don't know and can't guess.'

File: *Diamonds Are Forever*

Teaser Begins with two fast-cut scenes in which an unseen assailant accosts a Japanese and an Egyptian, demanding 'Where is Blofeld?' Cut to a beach, and Bond – for 'tis he – asks the same of a sunbathing strumpet, coming close to throttling her with the top of her own bikini lest she fail to divulge said information. So far, so good. And then into a sluggish sequence set in Blofeld's underground lair, where Bond's nemesis is transforming some hapless underling into his own spitting image. Bond kills the double, the 'real' Blofeld is revealed, Bond overcomes a couple of henchpersons and tips Blofeld into a broiling mud pit. For the audience, it's intended to function as a glorious reinstatement of Connery-Bond, avenging both Tracy and perhaps Lazenby-Bond's perceived failure, but the slovenly choreography and lethargic editing of the latter part undo any such ambition. Nice try, however. **8**

Titles Blofeld's cat, diamond choker around its neck, slips between various shadowed female body parts; hands cup gemstones. Literal and uninspired, it rather gives away the 'surprise' revelation that Blofeld's the villain, too. And, despite Ms Bassey's best efforts, the theme song's no 'Goldfinger' either. **3**

Bonkers plot Sent to investigate the possible stockpiling of diamonds – a practice that might cause widespread economic collapse – Bond uncovers a chain of smugglers leading to reclusive Las Vegas nabob Willard Whyte, whose empire has been commandeered by Blofeld. The diamonds power an immense laser beam which, mounted on a satellite and launched into space, will be used to precipitate an auction for world supremacy. Big on paper, but the connections between the various parties are hugely convoluted, and it strains credulity past breaking point that Bond's apparently unrelated mission should end up leading to the man with the cat. **5**

Locations Although the plot bears a satisfying sweep – the South African veldt, Red China, outer space – Bond spends the majority of the film tied to the mundane environs of Las Vegas. Still, the Amsterdam scenes are pretty, and we do get to see Bond chased across a mocked-up lunar surface. **6**

Gadgets Tiffany's closeted fingerprint scanner; Bond's peel-off fingertips; the electronic swipe cards inside the labs, which are way ahead of their time; Bond's piton gun; Willard Whyte's multimedia lavvy; Blofeld's voice synthesiser; the 'electro-magnetic RPM controller' Q uses to rig fruit machines; the spacebound laser beam itself; Blofeld's bathesub. No serious hardware – and no mad car! **3**

Girls Sunlounging Blofeld contact Marie. Moneypenny in customs uniform, still aching for a diamond ring (give it up, girl. Give it up). Wig-wearer Tiffany Case, who starts out a clever and dangerous professional criminal, but soon loses her bottle and begins to fret over her fate. She's vulgar ('Blow up your pants!'), self-absorbed, displays none of the class we've come to expect of a Bond girl and is reduced to weak-female gooning in the finale (she's incapable of firing a machine-gun: the recoil judders her backwards and – doh! – over the edge of the oil rig). Shady Tree's 'acorns'. Plenty, a one-dimensional gold-digger who gets an undeserved but chilling send-off. Gorilla girl Zamora. The quick-step and side-kicking Bambi and Thumper, who are much less gorgeous than we remember. **4**

Villains A fey and theatrical Blofeld who's happy to dress in drag, hates 'martial music' and takes no chances with his staff (a big sign inside his oil rig HQ reads 'IF IN DOUBT ASK'). An inveterate coward, he's having his getaway sub prepared long before the day is truly lost. He's fallen in with two-bit gangsters; only his two double-act pairings of henchpeople (Bambi and Thumper, Wint and Kidd) have any menace about them. The fragrant Wint and Kidd are funny, arch and dangerous – a sadistic Laurel and Hardy – and, by and large, their sexuality is presented in only a borderline offensive manner, especially for 1971 (Wint's obvious pleasure at having Bond crush his genitals with the Bombe Surprise is disappointing). **6**

Fights, chases, explosions A wonderfully barbaric set-to with the real Peter Franks confined to a steel mesh elevator. Bond's struggle with Bambi and Thumper begins superbly – Whyte's jailers move like panthers, and appear every bit as lethal – but once inside the pool, the girls present Bond no problem (how convenient). The moon/dune buggy chase is dreary, and the Las Vegas street sequence, with incompetent cops in pursuit of Bond (no clichés here, then) is plodding, conventional and nowhere near as good as it seems to think it is (it's not even got any music). And the showdown assault on the oil rig seems to be over before it begins. **4**

Dialogue and double entendres Bond, telling Felix he's hidden the diamonds inside Peter Franks' corpse: 'Alimentary, Doctor Leiter.' The 'Plenty O'Toole'/'Named after your father, no doubt' exchange. Bond congratulates one of Tiffany's hoods when after being thrown out of a high window, Plenty lands in water: 'Exceptionally fine shot.' 'I didn't know there was a pool down there,' drawls the thug. 'Right idea'/'wrong pussy' is up there with Goldfinger's 'Do you expect me to talk?' Blofeld's brushing aside of the threat posed by the submarines outside the Baja rig is brilliant: 'The Great Powers flexing their muscles like so many impotent beach boys.' **9**

Bond His reputation now precedes him – even a minor diamond racketeer is aware of covert agent James Bond – but the old feller still has what it takes ('Presumably I'm the condemned man and you're the hearty breakfast?' he enquires of a smouldering Tiffany). There's a moment sizzling with élan when, telling Tiffany that he's 'just popping upstairs for a moment', he walks across the balcony outside his hotel suite, stops, sniffs his carnation and begins rising upward – he's just strolled onto the top of the Whyte House's terrifyingly high outside elevator. But . . . having taken control of the crane which hoists Blofeld's bathesub, he chooses to toy with his arch enemy, bumping him to and fro and chortling merrily away to himself rather than confront him man-to-man as he would have done before. Consequently, we don't witness Blofeld actually get his come-uppance – and 'missing presumed dead' just isn't good enough. **6**

Plus/minus points Bond's entrapment within a blazing coffin is an all-time great moment, as is the 'wrong pussy' scene. But, tipping the scales in the other direction, the scene where the elephant plays the fruit machine and hits the jackpot is vile. Director Hamilton would clearly love to make the gaudy, neon-lit Las Vegas every bit as alien a locale as, say, Tokyo. The trouble is, it's all so achingly familiar from countless third-rate movies – and the association rubs off on this one, too. **-4**

48% A resolutely unspecial parade of mostly indifferent set pieces. Towards the end, Bond invokes a standby of Warner Bros' Loony Tunes cartoons – 'Good morning, gentlemen. The Acme pollution inspection' – which pretty much says it all. 'Oh my God, you just killed James Bond,' gasps Tiffany in her gee-whiz brogue early on. You're not far wrong, sweetheart.

CAST

Sean Connery James Bond
Jill St. John Tiffany Case **Charles Gray** Blofeld **Lana Wood** Plenty O'Toole
Jimmy Dean Willard Whyte **Bruce Cabot** Saxby **Putter Smith** Mr. Kidd
Bruce Glover Mr. Wint **Norman Burton** Leiter **Joseph Furst** Dr. Metz
Bernard Lee 'M' **Desmond LLewelyn** 'Q' **Leonard Barr** Shady Tree
Lois Maxwell Moneypenny **Margaret Lacey** Mrs. Whistler
Joe Robinson Peter Franks **David de Keyser** Doctor
Laurence Naismith Sir Donald Munger **David Bauer** Mr. Slumber
Sid Haig and **Marc Lawrence** Gangsters **John Abineri** Airline Representative*
Raymond Baker Helicopter Pilot* **Edward Bishop** Klaus Hergersheimer*
Nicky Blair Doorman (Tropicana)* **Larry Blake** Barker* **Ed Call** Maxie*
Constantin de Goguel Aide to Metz* **Gary Dubin** Boy*
Catherine Deeney Welfare Worker* **Clifford Earl** Immigration Officer
Mark Elwes Sir Donald's Male Secretary* **Brinsley Forde** Houseboy*
Donna Garratt Bambi* **David Healy** Vandenburg Launch Director*
Karl Held Agent* **Bill Hutchinson** Controller (Moon Crater)*
Janos Kurucz Aide to Metz* **Max Latimer** Blofeld's Double*
Frank Mann Guard (Moon Crater)* **Burt Metcalf** Maxwell* **Frank Olegario** Man in Fez*
Trina Parks Thumper* **Denise Perrier** Marie* **Shane Rimmer** Tom*
Henry Rowland Dentist* **Gordon Ruttan** Vandenburg Aide*
Michael Valente Gangster*

SELECTED CREDITS

Assistant directors **Jerome M Seigel** & **Derek Cracknell**
Continuity **Del Ross & Elaine Schreyeck** Camera operators **Bill Johnson** & **Bob Kindred**
Art directors **Bill Kenney** & **Jack Maxsted** Set decorators **John Austin** & **Peter Lamont**
Special effects **Whitney McMahon** & **Leslie Hillman**
Miss St. John's costumes by **Don Feld** Visual effects **Albert Whitlock** & **Wally Veevers**
Stunt arrangers **Paul Baxley** & **Bob Simmons**
Wardrobe supervisors **Ted Tetrick** & **Elsa Fennell**
Main titles designed by **Maurice Binder**
Production managers **Milton Feldman** & **Claude Hudson**
Editors **John W. Holmes** & **Bert Bates A.C.E.**
Production designed by **Ken Adam** Director of photography **Ted Moore B.S.C.**
Music composed, conducted and arranged by **John Barry** Lyrics by **Don Black**
Title song sung by **Shirley Bassey** Associate producer **Stanley Sopel**
Screenplay by **Richard Maibaum** & **Tom Mankiewicz**
Produced by **Albert R. Broccoli** & **Harry Saltzman** Directed by **Guy Hamilton**

* unaccredited

Are you 007?: *Live and Let Die*

1973: on Saturday 14 October, actor Roger Moore spent his 45th birthday far from his home town of London. On his second day of location filming for Guy Hamilton's *Live and Let Die*, the new James Bond was negotiating a mosquito-ridden swamp in Louisiana. While rehearsing the motor boat sequences central to the film, Moore had sustained a broken tooth and injured both his leg and his shoulder. The discomfort vied with his anxiety at stepping into the shoes of Sean Connery. 'I confessed to Guy that in reading the script I could only ever hear Sean's voice saying: "My name is James Bond"', revealed Moore in the book he later wrote about his experiences on the film. 'Guy said: "Look, Sean was Sean and you are you, and that is how it is going to be."'

Eon had begun its search for Connery's replacement in 1972, initially flirting with the idea of recruiting not from actors' agencies but the armed services. Advertisements were taken out in the 'situations vacant' columns of army journals, accompanied by the heading 'Are you 007?', before Equity reportedly stepped in and more conventional casting methods were adopted.

By June 1972, the quest had been narrowed down to a handful of hopefuls including Jeremy Brett and Julian Glover, who would later play villain Kristatos in *For Your Eyes Only*. Arguably the most intriguing candidate was the one who with least experience. Prior to appearing in no less than seven screen tests for *Live and Let Die*, Michael Billington had co-starred in Gerry Anderson's science fiction series *UFO* and popular BBC costume drama *The Onedin Line*. '[Billington] was a personal friend of Cubby Broccoli's,'

remembers his UFO co-star Ed Bishop, who himself had had minor roles in *You Only Live Twice* and *Diamonds Are Forever*. Billington never discovered why he wasn't awarded the role, but remained on good terms with Broccoli. He would later appear as quasi-Bond Sergei in *The Spy Who Loved Me*.

The possibility of casting Roger Moore had been dismissed by Saltzman and Broccoli both before and after his starring role as television's *The Saint*. When the actor was once again considered in 1972, Eon's hopes were dashed on learning that Moore was contracted to Lew Grade's ITC for a further season of *The Persuaders!* However, the pairing of Moore and Tony Curtis as crimebusting playboys failed to make the ratings when scheduled against *Mission: Impossible* in America, and Moore was released from his five-year contract. The timing was perfect: Moore's suave, self-deprecating screen persona was

May 1969 – former Bond Sean Connery meets Roger Moore at Les Ambassadeurs Club, off Park Lane. Following You Only Live Twice, Connery had been among those predicting that Moore would make an ideal Bond in accord with the self-parodying direction initiated by writer Tom Mankiewicz. In August 1972 Moore was offered a three-picture deal by United Artists and signed to play the character he jokingly called 'Jimmy Bond' in *Live And Let Die*, only the 12th significant film role of his career.

Mankiewicz's script added villain Kananga and his province of San Monique to Fleming's roster of characters, reducing Fleming villain Mr. Big to a mere cover for Mankiewicz's own bad guy. Fleming's plot – the smuggling of a pirate hoard to finance SMERSH operations – was made into a more mundane, drugs-related scenario. Three scenes would be dropped from this script. As Bond and Quarrel Junior fish for shark on the way to San Monique, Quarrel demonstrates the gas-pellet gun later used to despatch Kananga (an expansion of Bond's first encounter with Quarrel's father – 'His father and I locked horns with a Doctor named No several years ago' – was lost, too). Likewise cut was dialogue between Tee Hee and Kananga – wherein the latter threatens to have the former's other arm cut off and let him watch it being eaten by the crocodiles in the moat surrounding his home should Tee Hee so much as graze the skin of Tarot priestess Solitaire. Perhaps the single greatest loss was Bond's original opening scene, which was planned to continue on from the titles. In this, set in a lush private garden at night, Bond is handed a pair of contact lenses with secret documents etched into their surface in exchange for money by a older man. Hearing enemy agents approach, Bond helps the man over the garden's high wall – only to discover that it is in fact the side of a high building ('The MAN falls through the air with a scream . . .'). The scene then cuts to Bond's seduction of Italian agent Miss Caruso. Actor Michael Sheard, later famous as

tyrannical teacher Mr Bronson in BBC children's series *Grange Hill*, was cast as the hapless man, and two dummies made to perform the fall, but his scene was never filmed.

Guy Hamilton and production designer Syd Cain had undertaken their first recce for *Live and Let Die* as early as March, when they flew to Jamaica to identify suitable locations. Like *Diamonds Are Forever*, however, much of *Live and Let Die* would take place in the United States. The Dixieland funeral seen in the pre-credits sequence was shot in the French Quarter of New Orleans on Charter and Durmaine Streets. On Friday 13 October, Roger Moore began shooting the lengthy motor boat chase in a stifling bayou location some 30 miles away. Harry Saltzman accompanied the first unit from the beginning of the shoot, and kept Moore occupied in the evenings with hotly contested gin rummy games that usually left the star out of pocket. Albert Broccoli joined the unit on 20 October, but would keep a significantly lower profile than his partner throughout production.

By early November, Moore had overcome his leg injury only to succumb to a long-standing kidney stone complaint. Hamilton shot around his brief absence. The production was next joined by 21 year-old Jane Seymour; her role, that of the virginal Solitaire, had been planned for a black actress, but United Artists had insisted on a white leading lady. (Conversely, Mankiewicz's CIA agent, Rosie Carver, was written as 'a beautiful, dazed white girl'. The part went to black actress Gloria Hendry. Later, at Christmas 1973, while shooting *Gold* – directed by Peter Hunt – in Johannesburg, Moore went to see *Live and Let Die,* and discovered his love scenes with Hendry excised by the

South African censor.) Catherine Deneuve had been an early contender for Solitaire, but lost out to Seymour, whom Broccoli had spotted in *The Onedin Line*. She arrived with a note from Sir Richard Attenborough, who requested sympathetic treatment for his tired daughter-in-law: 'she may well need a shoulder to lean on'. Also present by this stage was Moore's old friend David Hedison, memorable as the mutating star of *The Fly* (1958), who had been contracted to play Felix Leiter. United Artists' David Picker kept a watchful eye on proceedings, and later returned to New York with a positive report.

The unit left for Jamaica on 29 November, in charter flights arranged at 24 hours' notice by Charles Russhon. Eon's long-standing 'technical advisor' also pulled the strings necessary to allow 14 firearms out of America and into Jamaica, and helped procure the then-revolutionary digital watch worn by 007. Filming in the Sans Souci Hotel in Ocho Rios commenced the first week of December. The 300-acre crocodile farm chosen as a key location was owned by mercurial stuntman Ross Kananga, whose surname had so impressed Tom Mankiewicz that he had already borrowed it for the film's main villain. The unit later shot coastal scenes at the Runaway Caves and the Green Grotto lake.

On 7 December the scene where Bond drives a double-decker bus through a low bridge, thus shearing off its top deck in spectacular style, was filmed at Montego Bay. Maurice Patchett, an instructor from London Transport's Chiswick bus depot, had already spent three months preparing for the stunt, which included providing Moore with, ahem, a crash course on the skid pan at Chiswick. As several hundred curious Jamaicans watched, Patchett took over from Moore as the bus headed for the bridge. The top deck had already been carefully separated and placed on rollers, enabling a relatively clean detachment when the bus ploughed into the bridge. 'I was not a bit scared,' said Patchett on his return to London. 'It sounded like a great lark to me . . . The funny thing was that I concentrated so hard on maintaining a precise 30 miles an hour that I forgot the bridge entirely. I was as surprised as anyone when I felt the bang.' Patchett was impressed at how quickly Moore took to HGV tuition. 'He'd make a good bus driver if he's ever short of a job.'

'If this doesn't work I'm finished . . .'

The Jamaican shoot came to an end shortly before Christmas. During the cast and crew's short break, a teaser trailer comprising highlights of the location photography was compiled for screening in Britain and America. In the last week of December, *Live and Let Die* moved into Pinewood Studios, where eight sound stages housed Syd Cain's 28 sets. Although Desmond Llewelyn was absent from the picture, both Bernard Lee and Lois Maxwell reprised their usual roles. Maxwell had been in Moore's class at RADA, and appeared alongside him in subsequent episodes of *Ivanhoe* and *The Saint*. Both Maxwell and Lee had guest-starred in different episodes of *The Persuaders!* Lee's presence had been made doubtful following the tragic death of his wife, Gladys Merredew, in a fire at their Kent home; Moore's friend Kenneth More had offered to play M on the condition that his fee was sent to Lee.

Lee's appearance was ultimately filmed on B stage, which was dressed as the interior

A Bond for the Seventies. Roger Moore would introduce his trademark cigar into his interpretation of 007

of 007's London pied à terre. Bond was interrupted seducing Miss Caruso with the aid of a watch that magnetically tugged down her zipper. Caruso was played by the voluptuous Madeline Smith, an actress Moore had recommended following her appearance in an episode of *The Persuaders!*

A largely American crew completed work on *Live And Let Die* in New York, where the Harlem scenes were filmed. When the film wrapped, Roger Moore left for California and the comfort of Albert Broccoli's Beverly Hills home. His film career thus far had seen only patchy success, and the premature cancellation of *The Persuaders!* had damaged his self-confidence. 'I realised three weeks before the opening: if this doesn't work I'm finished,' he later recalled. 'The cold wave came over me.'

Live and Let Die was the first Eon Bond film not to boast any musical input from John Barry. The title song was composed and performed by former Beatle Paul McCartney and his wife Linda. Commissioned before Tom Mankiewicz had completed his screenplay, Paul asked to be sent a copy of Fleming's novel. 'I read it and thought it was pretty good. That afternoon I wrote the song and went in the next week and did it . . . It was a job of work for me in a way because writing a song around a title like that's not the easiest thing going.' The thunderous result of McCartney's collaboration with producer George Martin (their first pairing since the *Abbey Road* sessions in 1969) was painted in broad rock and reggae strokes. 'Live And Let Die' hit the British charts in June 1973, reaching number 9; in America it peaked at number 2. It later became the first Bond theme to be nominated for an Academy Award.

Live and Let Die's British premiere took place at the Leicester Square Odeon on 4 July 1973; it would earn a respectable worldwide gross of $126,400,000 over the coming months. Although this was a handsome return on an estimated negative cost of $7 million, American admissions of 20.1 million placed the film behind all its Connery-starring forebears.

'What you will want to know is how Mr Moore's saintly feet fit into Sean Connery's discarded shoes,' predicted the *Evening News*' Felix Barker. 'Comfortably, I'd say, rather than impressively. For all his easy boyish charm he lacks the hard, sardonic quality of his predecessor . . . But I still think we shall grow to like the new incumbent well enough.'

The *New Statesman* was selective in its praise for the film: 'Guy Hamilton's *Live and Let Die* is, brutally, an ultra effort to get Roger Moore on to neighbourhood screens as a surrogate for Sean Connery, an attempt in which he succeeds . . . A stand-out performance is allowed to one Clifton James, hugely funny and accurate, as a Deep South Sheriff in a film bounding with blacks. Not the best of the Bonds, but I was shackled while I sat.'

'I confess that now and then I missed the handsome shark-mouth of Sean Connery,' admitted Dilys Powell in *The Sunday Times* on 8 July. 'But Mr Moore is all right. The throwaway lines are neatly thrown away. Marooned on a friable hummock in the middle of a crocodile pool he may betray no more than the faint disquiet of a man wondering if he has swallowed a bad oyster, but then who wants Olivier-type playing in a crocodile-pool? The elegance (for Mr Moore always looks a proper English gent) acquires a touch of irony; it will do.'

One of the film's most critical detractors was temporarily deposed scriptwriter Richard Maibaum: 'I didn't particularly like what they did to it. It was about nothing, a lousy cooking-some-dope-somewhere-in-the-jungle movie. That's not Bond at all. To process drugs in the middle of a jungle is not a Bond caper.'

File: *Live and Let Die*

Teaser Three killings: in New York, the British delegate to the United Nations is publicly murdered when his earpiece is strangely retuned; in New Orleans, a seconded British agent gets a switchblade in the gut while watching what he fails to realise is his own funeral procession; and in Caribbean island San Monique, another Brit succumbs to snakebite during a voodoo ceremony. No Bond, but the middle section might well be one of the most arresting openings of any action film; the sudden switch in tempo of the procession is sublimely, uh, executed. In fact, it's probably the most memorable aspect of the entire film. Inspired. **10**

Titles Blank-socketed skulls, firebrands and the usual shadow play. Menacing, dramatic – and cut well to Wings' stop/start theme. **7**

Bonkers plot Bond investigates three deaths linked to Kananga, an island dictator whose position is shored up by the application of *obeah* magic and fortune-telling. Kananga plans to flood the US with a billion dollars' worth of free heroin, driving established dealers out of business and doubling the number of addicts – whereupon he'll hike up the price of the reserves he's retained. It's all rather tawdry – no more than plain criminal – and hardly in the 00 section's league. **2**

Locations New York; New Orleans; San Monique; London; the Louisiana bayou. Oh, and down on a crocodile farm. It seems like Bond only ever goes transatlantic these days. Where's the sense of adventure? **2**

Gadgets The buzzing device that induces Dawes' 'brainstorm'; Bond's watch, which not only generates a hyper-intensive magnetic field powerful enough to

CAST

Roger Moore James Bond
Yaphet Kotto Kananga/Mr. Big   **Jane Seymour** Solitaire   **Clifton James** Sheriff Pepper
Julius W. Harris Tee Hee   **Geoffrey Holder** Baron Samedi   **David Hedison** Leiter
Gloria Hendry Rosie   **Bernard Lee** 'M'   **Lois Maxwell** Moneypenny
Tommy Lane Adam   **Earl Jolly Brown** Whisper   **Roy Stewart** Quarrel
Lon Satton Strutter   **Arnold Williams** Cab Driver 1   **Ruth Kempf** Mrs. Bell
Joie Chitwood Charlie   **Madeline Smith** Beautiful Girl   **Michael Ebbin** Dambala
Kubi Chaza Sales Girl   **B. J. Arnau** Singer   **Gabor Vernon** Hungarian Delegate*

SELECTED CREDITS

Continuity **Elaine Schreyeck**   Camera operator **Bob Kindred**
Wardrobe supervisor **Laurel Staffel**   Chief make-up **Paul Rabiger**
Hairdresser **Colin Jameson**
Assistant director **Alan Hopkins**   Art Director **Steven Hendrickson**
Camera operators **George Bouillet, Warren Rothenberger**
Shark scenes by **William Grefe**   Supervising art director **Syd Cain G.F.A.D**
Co-art directors **Bob Laing** & **Peter Lamont**
Special effects **Derek Meddings**
Optical effects **Charles Staffell**
Editors **Bert Bates, Raymond Poulton G.B.F.E.** & **John Shirley**
Stunts co-ordinated by **Bob Simmons**, **Joie Chitwood**, **Ross Kananga**,
Jerry Comeaux, Eddie Smith, Bill Bennet
Choreographer **Geoffrey Holder**   Costume designer **Julie Harris**
Casting director **Weston Drury Jnr**   Main title designed by **Maurice Binder**
Production supervisor **Claude Hudson**   Assistant director **Derek Cracknell**
Location Manager **Bernard Hanson**   Director of Photography **Ted Moore B.S.C.**
Title Song composed by **Paul and Linda McCartney** and
performed by **Paul McCartney and Wings**
Music Score by **George Martin**   Screenplay by **Tom Mankiewicz**
Produced by **Harry Saltzman** and **Albert R Broccoli**
Directed by **Guy Hamilton**

*unaccredited

deflect a bullet at long range, but will also rotate, becoming a miniature buzzsaw; the 'genuine Felix lighter'; a portable spy kit, which includes both a bug detector and a transmitter; cameras contained in the various scarecrows; the mike hidden in Samedi's flute. (Oh, and Bond's expresso maker. Which makes coffee. 'Is that all it does?' asks M, expecting more of a man so closely tied to Q's 'Special Ordnance Section.') Good toys, but this is a Q-free film – which we say is close to heresy. **6**

Girls Miss Caruso, the Italian agent who's undone by Bond's magnetism; Moneypenny, who covers up for Bond by covering up Miss Caruso, and who seems to now regard him with a big-sisterly amusement; Solitaire, an all-seeing Tarot reader to Kananga like both her mother and probably grandmother before her (and how old does that make him?); she loses her gift when she loses her cherry (bar that she picks up Gin Rummy quick, that's just about all we find out); the Oh Cult sales girl, who's got 'something in heads'; Rosie Carver, aka 'Mrs Bond' – a studiously bungling CIA *ingenue* whose loyalty is swayed by a few bloody feathers; the singer in the New Orleans Fillet of Soul, who shows more fire and va-voom than the rest put together. Three more crosses on the great Bond score card. **4**

Villains The little guy with the switchblade (a rare example of a Bond baddie who goes unpunished). Prosthetic wearer Tee Hee, who's amused by 'the least little thing', and gets to symbolically castrate Bond when he mangles his gun. Whisper (and guess how he gets his name). Adam, a bad MF on the water. Taxi driver Jim. Ol' Albert (he's a croc). Prime Minister Kananga, who talks the talk an' walks the walk disguised as Mr Big. The spirit world and its key emissary, the maybe-or-not immortal Baron Samedi. Plus, it seems, everyone of colour everywhere, bar token good guys Strutter and Quarrel, the only two blacks in this film not in Kananga's pocket. This film sends out a very clear message indeed – and it's none too palatable, either. **3**

Fights, chases, explosions The bus/motorcycle scenes are truly great, with a fantastic pay-off. The larking-about at the Bleeker flying school doesn't outstay its welcome, either – but the speedboat scenes are interminable, proof positive of the law of diminishing returns. Two good bangs (Billy-Bob's boat, when commandeered by Adam, and the heroin crops themselves). But scarcely a good grapple outside the Tee Hee scenes on the train (a blatant reprisal of the Grant/Orient Express scenes in *From Russia With Love*). **6**

Dialogue and double entendres Quoteworthy lines are few: 'Names is for tombstones, baby' (Mr Big); 'There's no sense in going off half-cocked, is there?' (Bond, about to give Solitaire Lovers' Lesson Number Three). Sadly, *Live and Let Die* continues to coarsen the Bond vocabulary – not only in Sheriff Pepper's cockamamie cussin', but also in the series' first use of a four-letter word (Mrs Bell's 'Holy shit'). **1**

Bond A sharp dresser – *viz* the black jacket and gloves he wears in New York – although his pale denim outfit seems a touch camp. Carries a gun well – watch his hands as he observes the ceremony in which Solitaire is prepared to be killed. A heartless weasel in bed, he goes to the trouble of rigging a Tarot deck to seduce Solitaire – but if that might be seen as a necessary evil in pursuit of his mission, his treatment of Rosie certainly isn't; when he pulls a gun on her, she protests that he wouldn't kill her – they've just made love. 'Well, I certainly wouldn't have done it before,' he sneers. Drinks bourbon and water, no ice. Enjoys a large cigar after a bath – and while hang-gliding, too. His caddishness does have its limits – he claims to be a 'gentleman' when he refuses to tell Kananga whether or not he's deflowered Solitaire. His kitchen displays a modernity at odds with the decor of the rest of his flat. Unlike earlier models, this Bond has class – in all senses. Unflappable. **9**

Plus/minus points No hat-tossing! Being largely a pastiche of another action sub-genre – blaxploitation film (*Shaft* et al) the film's 'unBondness' can be partly excused. Certain key moments are indisputably Bond in feel – the teaser, the Rosie sequences, the scene in which Mr Big reveals his true identity, Bond's escape from the crocodiles, the bit where Bond and Solitaire descend beneath the ground to uncover Kananga's underground base – and very good Bond at that. The final shot – the thought dead Samedi laughing at the audience – displays real chutzpah. **+10**

60% It's odd that *Live and Let Die* should feel so fresh when it goes to such lengths to duplicate *Dr. No*. Both are filmed in Jamaica; open with a Briton being killed by apparently innocuous passers-by; show Bond's apartment; have Bond menaced by a venomous creepy-crawly placed in his hotel room; have Bond and Quarrel sail out to the villain's domain under cover of night; have the villain keep islanders fearful by resurrecting mythological terrors with the aid of modern technology; include a bogus car driver in the pay of the baddy … The thinking is, presumably, that if these elements worked to introduce Connery-Bond, they'll usher in Moore-Bond equally well. But, brashly contemporary, it doesn't feel reheated – its down-to-earth villains and uncharacteristic soundtrack give it vitality and vigour. Moore is great, too.

Roger Moore and his wife Luisa on location in Jamaica for Live and Let Die. *Luisa took some of the photographs featured in her husband's subsequent memoirs of the shoot*

113

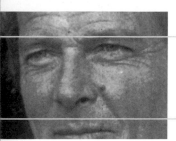

Lightly, lightly: *The Man With the Golden Gun*

1974: during production of *The Man With the Golden Gun*, Albert Broccoli defended the casting of Roger Moore to visiting interviewer Jean Rook. 'I thought we were scraping the bottom of the barrel,' he admitted. '[But] diet him and get rid of those damned [inquisitive] eyebrows and he's great. The greatest. Nearer what Fleming had in mind than Connery.' Broccoli continued to enthuse about *The Man With the Golden Gun*, boasting of a somersaulting car that would even top the stunts of *Live And Let Die*. He was less forthcoming when questioned about his partnership with Harry Saltzman. 'Relationships are strained,' he conceded after a long pause. 'Very strained.'

Saltzman had told Roger Moore of his intention to film *The Man With the Golden Gun* during the star's first week's work on *Live and Let Die*. Tom Mankiewicz's screenplay rejected much of Fleming's admittedly disappointing final novel in favour of a story that pitted 007 against an assassin whose skill and ruthlessness almost perfectly matched his own. Mankiewicz's work on the film came to a premature end following a reported disagreement with director Guy Hamilton. In an ironic reversal of the scripting circumstances behind *Diamonds Are Forever*, Richard Maibaum was invited to redraft Mankiewicz's work. Maibaum endured a reportedly fraught relationship with Saltzman, and was no fan of Moore's Bond, but he agreed to overhaul Mankiewicz's script, completing his first draft on 7 January 1974. His most prominent contribution was the grafting of the 'solex agitator' device and its attendant intrigue; the face-off between Bond and Scaramanga survived in the protracted climax, but only as an appendage to the struggle for this coveted McGuffin.

Two sequences would be lost to the draft of 7 January. The first was a comic scene at Hong Kong's airport in which Q attempts to persuade Bond to take a gadget-ridden camera to Thailand with him; one operates the camera's special functions – 'Gas ejection – instant solidification – liquid non-adhesion' – by selecting various shutter speeds. 'Most ingenious,' remarks Bond, 'But I'm sure there's one thing it can't do . . . Take a photograph.' 'There's no need to be facetious,' splutters Q. 'Actually you're right – but I'm working on it . . .' The closing duel was much longer: the pair taunt one another while cowering behind rocks and foliage – Bond calls Scaramanga 'chicken', Scaramanga calls Bond 'a limey punk' – and, before they enter Scaramanga's 'funhouse', Scaramanga attempts to outfox Bond by building a dummy of himself stuffed with seaweed. The villain wastes one golden bullet here – but is carrying another, despite his stated

A posed publicity still of Roger Moore as 007, taken
prior to The Man With the Golden Gun

certainty that he only needs one.

The role of Francisco Scaramanga went to no less than Ian Fleming's step-cousin and occasional golf partner, Christopher Lee. Best known for his numerous starring roles in horror films produced by Hammer, Lee's oft-reprised Dracula was considered definitive. (As struggling young actors, Lee and Moore had first met when both made fleeting appearances in the 1949 comedy *Trottie True*.) In a bid to challenge his typecasting, Lee had relished the role of Mycroft in Billy Wilder's *The Private Life of Sherlock Holmes* (1970); Scaramanga would represent another milestone. 'When I first read the script I visualised Scaramanga as a straight-down-the-middle heavy,' he told *The Times*' John Higgins. 'Scaramanga is not one of [Fleming's] most impressive murderers. Ian was already ill when when he wrote *Golden Gun* and I think he knew that the wells of his imagination were beginning to run a bit dry. So Guy and I, after a lot of talk, decided to make Scaramanga a little like Bond himself, a counter-Bond if you like, instead of the murderous, unappetising thug of the novel . . .'

Britt Ekland (now divorced from Peter Sellers) played Bond's dizzy sidekick Mary Goodnight; Swedish model Maud Adams was cast as Scaramanga's oppressed sexual accessory Andrea, and Parisian Hervé Villechaize played his vertically challenged manservant Nick Nack. (Villechaize would later find lasting fame playing a similar character in television series *Fantasy Island*.) Clifton James reprised his portrayal of JW Pepper from *Live and Let Die*; implausibly, Pepper and 007 are reunited when they collide while the off-duty redneck is holidaying in Thailand.

Scaramanga's golden gun remains one of the most memorable props in the Bond series. Comprised of an interlocking Waterman fountain pen, Colibri cigarette lighter, cigarette case and cufflink, in 1997 Eon insured the exhibited prop for £6,500.

Shooting began on 6 November 1974 at the part-submerged wreck of the *Queen Elizabeth* in Hong Kong harbour. (Moore was doubled, and wouldn't participate in location shooting in the area until the following spring.) Hamilton later took his crew to Macao and Thailand. The most spectacular scenery in the film was found in a cluster of tiny islands discovered by Broccoli, Hamilton and production designer Peter Murton near Phuket, off the Malay peninsula. One of the islands, Khow-Ping-Khan, became Scaramanga's remote hideaway.

Bond's crossing of a broken river bridge in a somersaulting car was the result of meticulous computer-calculated preparations undertaken by university students, who'd originally devised the stunt for an American Motors promotional tour. A Hornet X was specially modified for the stunt with customised suspension, a six-cylinder engine (specially installed to reduce the car's weight), centred steering and a fuel system designed to ensure that the car wouldn't stall 'mid flight'. Six cameras successfully captured stunt co-ordinator Jay Milligan's crossing on the first take.

In June, Roger Moore reported his discovery of a caveful of bats to Christopher Lee. 'I told him "Master, they are yours to command . . ." He knows he can't hit me until the film's finished.' Luckily, Lee was in good humour throughout the shoot: 'When we were out filming in Thailand . . . Guy kept on saying to Roger Moore and myself "Enjoy it, enjoy it! Lightly! Lightly!" And enjoy it I did.'

John Barry resumed scoring duties, and collaborated with lyricist Don Black on the theme tune. Lulu, whose *Boom Bang-A-Bang* had been joint winner in 1969's Eurovision Song Contest, had enjoyed a comeback in January 1974 with a spirited cover of David Bowie's *The Man Who Sold the World*. She followed it up with *The Man With the Golden Gun* in December, but the single failed to chart on either side of the Atlantic.

The Man With the Golden Gun received its world premiere at the Leicester Square Odeon on 18 December 1974. Initially impressive box-office returns would prove short-lived. In the United States, where the film opened on the 19th, audiences deserted Bond in droves; American attendances of 11.1 million would prove an all-time low for the entire series. A worldwide gross of $97.6 million against an estimated outlay of approximately $7 million hardly spelled financial ruin, but Eon's diminishing returns would demand a further rethink.

'Guy Hamilton's direction and the screenplay are comparatively placid and even monotone,' claimed *Variety*'s 'Murf'. 'At this rate, the tenth film might be phoned in . . . The comparatively sparse arrays of mechanical devices seem more a cost-cutting factor; as for maturity, either the relatively small number of juvenile double entendres, or the sense-numbing passage of more than a decade, or both, have rendered the character slightly stale.'

'There seems to have been hardly an attempt to interest us in characterisation,' said the *Sunday Telegraph*'s Tom Hutchinson, 'least of all with Roger Moore who plays agent 007 with [a] negative kind of smug rogueishness.'

Derek Malcolm's review in *The Guardian* was similarly typical of many appearing that December: 'Guy Hamilton . . . goes through his paces once again with admirable stoicism and occasional flair. But he can't disguise the fact that this script is just about the limpest of the lot...'

'That bugger's got half of what should all be mine'

'The sole inspiration is actually the casting of Christopher Lee,' claimed *Monthly Film Bulletin*. *The Times*' John Higgins had already given the actor's conbtribution to the film special mention: 'Lee plays the role lightly, urbanely, with a smile on the killer's face . . . he and the camera crew carry off the major honours of the movie.' The relatively smooth production of *The Man With the Golden Gun* in the Far East and Pinewood served as sharp contrast to the behind-the-scenes rumblings which finally erupted following its release. Harry Saltzman and Albert Broccoli had not seen eye-to-eye for some years. 'They're not exactly enamoured of each other,' said Sean Connery in 1971. 'Probably because they're both sitting on 50 million dollars or pounds and looking across the desk at each other and thinking: "That bugger's got half of what should all be mine."'

'We have different dispositions,' admitted Broccoli in 1973. 'But we never row in public. Let's put it this way, we are both difficult, rather than amicable.' Saltzman similarly made no secret of his frustrations with his partner: 'There are rows, very healthy rows. Movie making is a volatile business.'

Perhaps in an attempt to avoid confrontation, Saltzman and Broccoli had alternated production responsibilities on their latter Bonds: *Diamonds Are Forever* was largely overseen by Broccoli, *Live and Let Die* by Saltzman and *The Man With the Golden Gun* by Broccoli.

In an interview with *The Daily Mail* in 1973, Saltzman openly admitted that, with five Fleming Bond novels left to film, he had no intention of staying the distance. On 11 November the *Evening Standard* reported that he intended selling his 50 per cent interest in Danjaq – effectively a half ownership of the Bond film franchise – to Columbia Pictures. 'My battery of lawyers are currently having talks with their battery of lawyers,' he confirmed.

The bombshell came as news to Broccoli, who was reportedly under the impression that he had been in the running for Saltzman's stake. 'Broccoli says a divorce would require his approval,' claimed a *Variety* report of 19 December, 'beyond which he wouldn't comment.' Saltzman's actions raised serious implications for future Eon-produced Bond films: although Broccoli and Saltzman owned most of the Bond properties, their films had been financed by United Artists. The prospect of rival distributor Columbia assuming a 50 per cent stake in Danjaq's Bond licence cannot have been welcome.

It is likely that Saltzman's desicion to cut loose at this particular time was motivated by the need to raise capital. Of his recent extra-curricular ventures, *The Battle of Britain* (the 1969 film directed by Guy Hamilton and co-produced by Saltzman's old friend Benjamin Fisz) and *Toomorrow* (1972) had both lost money. By 1974, Saltzman's five-year ownership of The River Club on London's Embankment had

cost him an estimated £500,000.

An April 1978 report in *The Times* brought the true extent of his financial difficulties during this period to light. Saltzman was in court denying liability for a debt to an American legal company. Mr Justice O'Connor decided that Saltzman in fact owed the money, and revealed some of the circumstances that led to his earlier problems. The judge told the court that Saltzman and Broccoli had agreed to wind up Danjaq in 1972, but 'Mr Broccoli later refused to abide by that agreement.' He continued by revealing that Saltzman's subsequent attempt to have the company wound up by the Swiss courts proved unsuccessful, leaving his shareholding locked in the company indefinitely. 'In the autumn of 1972 [Saltzman's] position was desperate,' claimed Justice O'Connor. United Artists were quick to intervene between the 'desperate' Saltzman and Columbia. On 23 December 1975, UA chairman Arthur Krim announced that his company had made a successful bid and purchased Saltzman's share of Danjaq. Saltzman's speculated asking price was £20 million.

In June 1976, Saltzman made public his intention to purchase the then-dormant Shepperton Studios for £8 million. Although his bid for the 60-acre site was regarded sympathetically by the National Film Finance Corporation, recently introduced tax laws regarding resident foreigners made it impossible for him to stay in the UK, and the deal was scuppered. In 1980, Saltzman bought a controlling interest of theatre production company HM Tennent. Although Tennent staged some acclaimed productions under Saltzman's chairmanship, his plans to cross-finance between plays and films came to little. The company closed in 1991.

After *The Man With the Golden Gun*, Saltzman produced just two films: *Nijinsky* (1980), a challenging study of the complex relationship between the ballet dancer and his possessive mentor Diaghilev, and *Dom Za Vesanje* (*Time of the Gypsies*, 1989), a Romany coming-of-age drama that, it has been noted, was possibly the only film to require subtitles in every country in which it played.

Although comfortable from his substantial Bond earnings, Saltzman remained a frustrated film producer in his final years. His long-held dream to film *Tussy Is Me*, a portrait of Karl Marx's daughter Eleanor, would never be realised. Harry Saltzman died in his beloved Paris in September 1994.

File: *The Man With the Golden Gun*

Teaser In a garish shooting range beneath a distant island, international assassin Scaramanga – aka 'the man with the golden gun' – faces an unexpected challenge from gunman and Al Capone fan Rodney, who's been summoned by Scaramanga's dwarfish batman Nick Nack to try his luck against the killer for a sizeable bounty. Having tracked down his weapon at the heart of a maze, Scaramanga wins through with one shot – and celebrates by blowing the fingers off a life-size effigy of James Bond, the only man he considers his equal. Sinister and strange, the shooting gallery makes compelling use of optical illusion. Unusually, the teaser sets up the villain above the hero; this is not going to be the usual Bond fare ... **7**

Titles Thai girls ripple, reflected in water; hands caress the golden gun's barrel in a less-than-ambiguous manner. The most explicit sequence yet establishes a chain of sex, money and death – the girl, the gold, the gun – with admirable economy, albeit little subtlety; it builds to a shot of a naked girl flat on her back, stroking her own nipple. Too, too much. **6**

Bonkers plot Bond's mission to track down a missing solar power expert (who, in a blatant attempt to engineer the film's contemporary relevance, might alleviate the 'energy crisis') is curtailed when M receives one of Scaramanga's signature golden bullets; it has 007's number on it. Off his own bat, Bond hunts down Scaramanga, whose next target just happens to be that missing solar power expert. Bond becomes involved with his mistress, Andrea – whom, it transpires, had sent Bond the bullet; she wishes Bond to destroy her cruel lover. On behalf of the Chinese, Scaramanga has been sent after a 'solex agitator', a device which will give the Reds the boon of solar power. He swipes it himself, anticipating an auction for the solex, and retires to his private island, where the Chinese have kindly built a massive installation for the device. He and Bond are now set for a duel. Tortuous, over-involved, and riddled with lapses in logic – we can almost forgive the fact that Bond and Scaramanga just happen to be after the same man from the outset, and the fact that the Chinese can build the whole of the solex installation but not the agitator itself, but it seems absurd that neither the Chinese nor Hai Fat's organisation go after the traitorous Scaramanga (he *is* resident in their waters) – or even that Scaramanga, who charges (and gets) 'a million a shot', needs to bother himself with all this solar power malarkey in the first place (he goes to great pains to explain to Bond that 'Science was never my strong point' – that, bluntly, he doesn't have a clue what he's doing). Muddled, addle-headed bilge. **2**

Locations Scaramanga's extraordinary paradise island, somewhere in Red Chinese waters; London; the seamier bits of Beirut; Macau; Hong Kong; Bangkok, Thailand. Exotica *in extremis* (amusingly, even M berates Bond for dwelling in 'the world of Suzy Wong'). Shuttles the punter between points he'll never see. **8**

Gadgets Things have come to a pretty pass when the bad guys get all the fun: the golden gun itself, assembled from an ersatz cigarette case, lighter, cufflink and pen; the rifle Lazar customises for a three-fingered assassin, with its trigger housed in the butt; the solex agitator, a handy McGuffin which converts radiation from the sun into electricity; Scaramanga's car-cum-plane (which owes more, we venture, to *Chitty Chitty Bang Bang* than 'Mister Kiss Kiss Bang Bang'); and Scaramanga's 'sun gun'. Even the villain's house is basically a big toyshop – automated marionettes, bizarre funhouse gimmicks *et al*. All Bond calls upon is a fake nipple, the something a 'little kinky' he

March 1974 – Roger Moore introduces Britt Ekland, aka Mary Goodnight, to the press

barmaid in scanties at Macau's Bottoms Up club. Simpering ninny Mary Goodnight, whose two years' posting with Staff Intelligence appears to be a contradiction in terms; she may protest that 'killing a few hours as one of [Bond's] passing fancies' isn't her scene, but her 'hard-to-get act', by her own admission, is as brief as her bikini. She can't even control her backside, nearly causing Bond to come a cropper (no, really). Oriental skinny-dipper Chew Mee. Hip's be-gymsliped nieces Cha and Nara, who beat up an entire karate school between them. **7**

Villains Hai Fat and his various lackeys pale in comparison to Francisco Scaramanga, the best-characterised Bond villain yet. Beyond his biography (born in a circus; father a ringmaster, possibly Cuban; mother an English snake charmer; traumatised by a childhood incident involving an elephant; a trick shot artist at ten, a rear gunner at 15, becomes a KGB assassin after the war; goes freelance in the late Fifties) Scaramanga's sexuality is fascinating: he has a third nipple, legendarily a sign of invulnerability and great sexual prowess; like a bullfighter, he makes love before killing, believing it'll improve his eye; and he caresses Andrea with his gun, surely a particularly twisted example of transference. Likes tabasco sauce, gold jewellery, and a girl in a bikini ('no concealed weapons'). He's eager to please, believes he and Bond to be the same ('We are the best'). Has a perverse love/hate relationship with malevolent, impish, French-speaking butler-chef Nick Nack, who will inherit Scaramanga's wealth if he can find someone able to outgun Scaramanga (who, in turn, relishes the arrangement, which keeps him on his guard at all times). Revealingly, Scaramanga claims to be an artist; killing Bond in a duel will be his masterpiece. He's a vain, deluded, cold, obsessive egomaniac; if, as we are invited to speculate, he really is Bond's shadow, what does that tell us about Bond? **10**

Fights, chases, explosions The boat and car chases merely reprise sequences in both *Live and Let Die* and *Diamonds Are Forever*; again, they're way too long, and spoiled by the ugly presence of a loudmouthed American. The almost mute karate school scenes are blisteringly well-staged, however, as is the three-against-one rough and tumble in Saida's dressing room (the thugs appear to

asks Q to whip up. Women's standard South East Asia dress includes a homing device hidden in a button on the back. **8**

Girls Tragic Andrea Anders, Scaramanga's mistress, who takes a pistol into the shower and sees Bond as her knight in shining armour. She's mistaken. Beirut belly dancer Saida, a Secret Service screw of long standing. A beat up Bond for no more than daring to kiss Saida's 'magnificent abdomen'. Odd). The immolation of Scaramanga's base is curiously unsatisfying, however well executed. **3**

Dialogue and double entendres The ribald theme song is one long stream of smut: 'He has a powerful weapon ... He comes just before the kill ... another poor victim/Has come to a glittering end' – and, outrageously, 'His eye may be on you or me/Who will he bang?/We shall see'. Bond to M: 'who'd pay a million dollars to kill me?' M to Bond: 'Jealous husbands, outraged chefs, humiliated tailors ... the list is endless.' 'I've lost my charm!' wails Saida, noticing that the golden bullet she keeps in her navel is missing. 'Not from where I'm standing,' counters Bond rakishly. Bond, with Lazar in his sights: 'I am now aiming precisely at your groin. So speak or forever hold your piece.' The barbed duologue between Bond and Scaramanga is outstanding: after Scaramanga has claimed that they are the same ('ours is the loneliest profession'), Bond retaliates: 'There's a useful four-letter word, and you're full of it. When I kill it's on the specific orders of my government, and those I kill are themselves killers.' 'You get as much fulfilment out of killing as I do, so why don't you admit it?' counters his adversary. 'I admit killing you would be a pleasure,' returns Bond. Later, Bond's epitaph for Scaramanga – 'Flat on his *coup de grâce*' – is rightly delivered coldly, without relish. Minus one point for the coarse Pepperisms only. **9**

Bond See above. He still enjoys a good cigar, and prefers Dom Perignon '62 above the '64 offered. The safari suit's a little unfortunate, though. His cruel treatment of Andrea – when he slaps her, he slaps her hard – is a throwback to the harsh Bond of *Dr. No* and *From Russia With Love*. **7**

Plus/minus points Despite gorgeous location photography, inspired staging (Gibson's assassination outside the Bottoms Up club, the scene in which Bond seduces Andrea while Goodnight is locked in a wardrobe, the Secret Service base inside the scuppered *Queen Elizabeth*, Nick Nack disguised as a demon in Hai Fat's garden) and clever quotation from sources as varied as *Enter the Dragon*, *Westworld* and *The Lady From Shanghai* – *The Man With the Golden Gun* is shot in the foot by its nebulous, nonsensical storyline. The dubbing of a comic

sound effect over the hyped-up 360º mid-air roll executed by Bond in a car is simply crass. **-10**

57% What went wrong? For the first two-thirds of its length, *The Man With the Golden Gun* is a great James Bond film – fast, funny, clever, opulent. And then the cracks in the artifice begin to show, and the whole falls apart with indignity. Christopher Lee and Roger Moore (both of whom are superb throughout, as is Maud Adams) do what they can with the film's largely risible climax, but the duel between Bond and Scaramanga is not enough of a challenge to either party – it should be an ordeal, not an amiable stroll – to function as a full conclusion. The tacked-on exploding base is no solution, either; it's patronising, desperate and utterly absurd. Oh, and Sheriff Pepper was bad enough once. Twice, he's an abomination.

CAST

Roger Moore James Bond
Christopher Lee Scaramanga   **Brltt Ekland** Goodnight   **Maud Adams** Andrea
Hervé Villechaize Nick Nack   **Clifton James** J. W. Pepper   **Richard Loo** Hai Fat
Soon Taik-Oh Hip   **Marc Lawrence** Rodney   **Bernard Lee** 'M'
Lois Maxwell Moneypenny   **Marne Maitland** Lazar   **Desmond LLewelyn** 'Q'
James Cossins Colthorpe   **Chan Yiu Lam** Chula   **Carmen Sautoy** Saida
Gerald James Frazier   **Michael Osborne** Naval Lieutenant
Michael Fleming Communications Officer

SELECTED CREDITS

Assistant director **Derek Cracknell**   Camera operator **Bob Kindred**
Continuity **Elaine Schreyeck**   Co-Art directors **Peter Lamont**, **John Graysmark**
Special effects **John Stears**   Miniatures **Derek Meddings**
Casting directors **Maude Spector, Weston Drury Jnr**   Wardrobe supervisor **Elsa Fennell**
Chief make-up **Paul Engelen**   Hairdresser **Mike Jones**
Production co-ordinator, Bangkok **Santa Pestonji**
Editors **John Shirley**, **Raymond Poulton G.B.F.E**   Stunt co-ordinator **W.J. Milligan Jnr**
Maintitle designed by **Maurice Binder**   Production supervisor **Claude Hudson**
Production designer **Peter Murton**
Directors of photography **Ted Moore B.S.C.**, **Oswald Morris B.S.C**
Music composed, conducted and arranged by **John Barry**
Title song sung by **Lulu**   Associate producer **Charles Orme**
Screenplay by **Richard Maibaum** and **Tom Mankiewicz**
Produced by **Albert R. Broccoli** and **Harry Saltzman**
Directed by **Guy Hamilton**

Keeping the British end up: *The Spy Who Loved Me*

1976: 'People keep asking me what it's like to be going solo,' said Albert Broccoli in the wake of Harry Saltzman's departure. 'Well, I always thought I was solo . . . I still control the Bond enterprise. Nobody gazumps me! United Artists put up 100 percent financing and that gives them the sole rights to distribute the films. My function is to deliver the films.' UA's response to the lacklustre performance of *The Man With the Golden Gun* had been to almost double that film's budget for its follow-up. With $13.5 million to spend, Broccoli would repay their confidence with the most audacious Bond yet.

On the posthumous instruction of Ian Fleming, *The Spy Who Loved Me* became the first Bond film to inherit nothing but its title from its literary antecedent. (The critical mauling that had greeted Fleming's 'experiment' with the Bond formula had also prompted him to request of his publishers that there be no reprints or paperback editions of the book following its original publication in 1962.)

Although the screenplay of *The Spy Who Loved Me* would be credited to Richard Maibaum and Christopher Wood, its roots lay in two different treatments of *Moonraker*. One had been authored by Cary Bates (a regular writer of *Superman* comic books in the Seventies), and the other was a joint effort between television producer Gerry Anderson and one of his most trusted scriptwriters/editors, Tony Barwick. Anderson recalls that he had been invited not only to write but produce *Moonraker* by Harry Saltzman in the early Seventies; Saltzman offered Anderson

$20,000 for his 70-page treatment, but Anderson declined. In *Gerry Anderson – The Authorised Biography*, he recalled why: 'I desperately wanted to produce this Bond picture myself . . . Had I accepted the $20,000 then Harry could have produced it himself, or handed it to another producer . . . I had hoped that Harry would eventually come back to me and I'd produce the picture, but sadly this was not to be.'

Anderson alleges that: 'In our treatment, we had an oil tanker which up-ended and fired atomic missiles. It was a secret missile launching pad. As it happened, some friends of mine were working on *The Spy Who Loved Me* and they let me sneak a look at the script. I thought it had similarities with our treatment so I started legal proceedings against Cubby Broccoli ... My lawyers weren't showbusiness lawyers, so I was really in a very weak position. I must confess I became very frightened, and after a few weeks decided

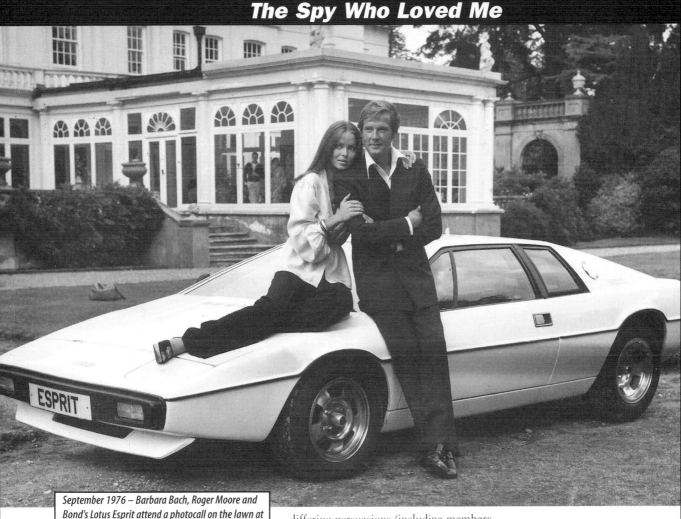

September 1976 – Barbara Bach, Roger Moore and Bond's Lotus Esprit attend a photocall on the lawn at Pinewood Studios. Nine Esprits would be used during the shooting of The Spy Who Loved Me

to drop the matter.' Anderson claims to have been offered £3,000, partly on the condition that he handed over the treatment and ensured any copies were destroyed. He agreed.

Other writers involved in cooking up a new story to fit Fleming's title included Ronald Hardy, Derek Marlowe, Sterling Silliphant, John Landis and Anthony Burgess. Richard Maibaum's first draft screenplay would incorporate a number of ideas from previous drafts (the huge submarine silo seen in the finished film was reportedly Burgess' inspiration), but this in turn proved untenable. Maibaum's script dealt with a group of terrorists of

differing persuasions (including members of the Red Brigade and the Black September organisation) mounting an attack on SPECTRE's headquarters. 'They level the place, kick Blofeld out, and take over,' Maibaum recalled. 'In the end, Bond comes in and asks, "All right, you're going to blow up the world. What do you want?" They reply, "We don't want anything. We just want to start over – the world is so lousy. We want to wipe it away and begin again. So there's no way we can be bribed." Rightly or wrongly, Cubby thought it was too political. So many young people in the world support these people that we would have had scrambled sympathies in the picture.'

The script department's musical chairs added to existing confusion over who was directing the picture – Guy Hamilton was originally contracted, but dropped out to pursue the opportunity to direct *Superman* (the job would eventually go to Richard Donner). He was replaced by *You Only Live Twice*'s Lewis Gilbert, who recommended Christopher Wood to redraft Maibaum's work. Writing as 'Timothy Lea', Wood had recently made a huge success of the saucy *Confessions . . .* books and ensuing film adaptations. From Maibaum's screenplay he retained the ship-swallowing supertanker (a possible development from the Anderson/Barwick script, but more likely a hangover from Maibaum's original draft of *Diamonds Are Forever*) and Jaws, the huge, steel-toothed thug who menaced Bond.

Wood's rewrite was accepted, but the final draft had yet to be written. In June 1976, two of Kevin McClory's film companies and Sean Connery (who in 1976 had begun collaborating with McClory and novelist Len Deighton on a new James Bond project) sought an injunction against *The Spy Who Loved Me*, and damages for alleged copyright infringement. Rather than face a potentially protracted legal battle, Broccoli instructed Wood to strip the shooting script of any references to SPECTRE. The McClory action was dropped, but preparations for a rival Bond film starring Connery continued.

'We've explored a certain lady who commands a $500,000 wage'

A fine cast, which included American actress Barbara Bach as Bond's sassy Russian ally, German star Curt Jurgens as the fanatical Stromberg (formerly Stavros, which was perhaps deemed too similar to Ernst Blofeld's middle name) and 7" 2' Richard Kiel as Jaws, was assembled. (Guy

Hamilton had earlier cast Green Cross Code Man Daivd Prowse in the part.) Former Bond hopeful Michael Billington took the brief role of KGB agent Sergei Barsov in the spectacular pre-credits sequence, and played 007 in the screen tests for auditioning actresses. Besides Kiel, the picture introduced a number of other regular and semi-regular characters: Geoffrey Keen's Minister of Defence, Walter Gotell's General Gogol and Eva Reuber-Staier's Rubelvitch.

Although Bach was awarded the most prominent female role in a Bond film since that given to Diana Rigg in *On Her Majesty's Secret Service*, she was nowhere near as well-known. 'I don't think there's any actress today that can support a picture box-office wise with the possible exception of Barbra Streisand,' Albert Broccoli told Open University researchers Tony Bennett and Janet Woollacott. 'But the price doesn't distinguish the girl in our film from the success of a Bond picture. I mean we've explored a certain lady in Hollywood who commands a $500,000 wage . . . and that blew her right out of the box for me because she'd contribute no more than Barbara Bach will.'

Bach, a former model and future wife of ex-Beatle Ringo Starr, told Bennett and Woollacott: '[Anya] meets up with Bond and it's only at the end of the film that there's any kind of attraction between the two of them . . . So it's quite different. Most of the girls in the Bond films have just been merely beautiful girls that, you know, have small parts that come and go. Anya stays from the beginning to the end.'

To accommodate Stromberg's enormous lair, the now-legendary '007 stage' was erected at Pinewood Studios. Working to a budget estimated at $1 million, production designer Ken Adam supervised construction from March 1976 onward. With a floor space of 374 by 160 feet, and a height of 53 feet, the finished facility – easily the largest sound stage in the world – also featured a huge water tank, itself the subject of some controversy. To create the submarine dock inside the supertanker *Liparus*, Eon planned to flood the tank with 1,200,000 gallons of water during the high summer of 1976 – a time of crippling drought and consequent water shortages. (It was claimed that the water was collected from a subterranean well conveniently situated beneath the stage itself.)

In a film where set pieces of an unprecedented magnitude jostled for attention, the ski-jumping parachute sequence at the beginning threw down an intimidating gauntlet. Second unit director John Glen filmed the jump off the 3,000-foot Asgard Peak in Canada's Baffin Island in July 1976. Stunt double Rick Sylvester received $30,000 for undertaking the jump, which was supervised and photographed by Willy Bogner Jr.

Principal photography began in August 1976. The initial five weeks' first unit photography were concentrated in Sardinia, and later Egypt. For the cliffside chase shot in Sardinia, Bond drove a specially modified Lotus Esprit (named 'Wet Nellie' in the script, although the line didn't make it to the screen). The amphibious craft was the result of a collaboration between Ken Adam and special effects supervisor Derek Meddings. (The underwater sequences were photographed by Lamar Boren in Nassau during October. Broccoli's stepson Michael G Wilson, who had briefly appeared in *Goldfinger* and was now a practising lawyer, supervised filming in the Bahamas.)

Gilbert and cinematographer Claude Renoir made optimum use of impressive Egyptian locations such as Cairo's spice market, the Gayer-Anderson Museum and the pyramids at Giza. For Bond and Anya's beautifully photographed cruise down the Nile, a felucca (a native Egyptian vessel) was borrowed. On location in Egypt, a sudden food shortage prompted Broccoli to don a chef's hat and personally cook, and serve, spaghetti for the 100-strong crew.

'I told him this was his finest hour,' recalled a tearful Lewis Gilbert at Broccoli's memorial service many years later, 'much more important than any script conference.'

Filming also took place at the Faslane submarine base on the Clyde; exterior shots of the supertanker were filmed in the Bay of Biscay, off France, Spain and Portugal. Following the conclusion of principal photography, Pinewood's 007 stage was formally opened by former Prime Minister Harold Wilson on 5 December. In attendance were Mr and Mrs Broccoli (who ceremonially broke a bottle of Champagne on the conning-tower of the USS *Wayne* submarine), Moore, Bach, Jurgens, Caroline Munro, John and Hayley Mills, Kenneth More, Donald Sinden and Richard Todd, plus 24 marching men from the Band of Royal Marines Commander in Chief Fleet.

Princess Anne attended the world premiere of *The Spy Who Loved Me* at the Leicester Square Odeon on 13 July 1977. An impressive upswing of *The Man With the Golden Gun*'s fortunes ensued; American admissions of 21 million and a worldwide gross of $185.4 million were later registered.

'It is the best Bond film so far,' enthused *The Sun*'s Chris Kenworthy on 7 July. 'The sexiest, the fastest-moving, and certainly the most witty.' *The Daily Mirror*'s Arthur Thirkell agreed: 'From the opening credits to the final fade-out kiss the latest James Bond epic is unqualified joy. This is cinema entertainment at its very best.'

'A case of licensed to overkill?' wondered *The Guardian*'s Tim Radford. 'It cost $13 million, lasts for two hours and five minutes, and the star of the show, yet again, is not Roger Moore, nor yet the very edible Barbara Bach, nor even the camp-amphibious Curt Jurgens as the super villain. It is the designer Ken Adam.'

The Spy Who Loved Me's critical success was bolstered by three near-misses at the 1977 Academy Awards. Ken Adam, Peter Lamont and Hugh Scaife shared a nomination for art direction, and American composer Marvin Hamlisch was nominated for a score that dabbled in the discotheque sound prevalent at the time. Hamlisch also shared a nomination with lyricist Carole Bayer Sager for best original song. Although the film failed to win any Oscars, its awe-inspiring sets and sophisticated theme tune, 'Nobody Does It Better', remain two of the best-remembered elements of the Bond series.

The premiere party for *The Spy Who Loved Me* was a lavish £143,000 affair hosted by Albert Broccoli at the Intercontinental Hotel in Park Lane. During the course of the evening, Broccoli discreetly broached the prospect of Moore's future participation in the Bond series – Moore's third Bond film was the last he was contractually obliged to appear in under the terms of his 1972 contract. Moore left his producer in no doubt over his eagerness to appear in the next instalment – *For Your Eyes Only*.

File: *The Spy Who Loved Me*

Teaser Beneath the sea, British nuclear submarine HMS *Ranger* vanishes after being attacked by an unseen foe. Soon after, KGB General Gogol learns that Russian nuclear sub *Potempkin* has suffered a similar fate. Gogol assigns his 'best agent', the gorgeous Triple X, to investigate the disappearance of the *Potempkin*; in London, M orders his 'best man' to pull out of his Austrian assignment to investigate the disappearance of the *Ranger*. In the Alps, Bond receives M's instruction but – thanks to a traitorous blonde – is waylaid by a posse of Russians on skis, including Triple X's lover Sergei, whom Bond kills in his flight. Bond escapes by skiing off the edge of an immense precipice, opening his Union Jack parachute while plummeting to the ground. Not only a thrilling prologue to the film proper, the teaser sets up the film's key subplot too, linking Bond and Triple X – through the killing of Sergei – long before their first meeting. The juxtaposition of M and Moneypenny with Gogol and secretary Rubelvitch is amusing, as is the unveiling of Triple X, whom we're initially invited to believe is hairy-chested Bond-lookalike Sergei. The ski jump stunt, of course, is outstanding. This has got it all. **10**

Titles Spotlit gymnasts turn slo-mo cartwheels, swing off gun barrels like the parallel bars. Bond appears, disarming five bare-breasted Cossack women in a line. Quite beautiful, if a little uneventful. **8**

Bonkers plot Shipping magnate Stromberg, obsessed with the undersea world, conceals hijacked nuclear subs inside a vast supertanker, planning to use their warheads to destroy both New York and Moscow (gambling that 'Inevitably, global destruction will follow'). He and his employees – all of whom appear to be guards clad in red uniforms – will then retire to a private undersea city. Bond and Triple X (actually Major Anya Amasova) are forced to co-operate in the search for the missing subs; when Anya learns that it was Bond who killed Sergei, she vows to kill him when their mission is complete. The first part of the plot is, of course, ludicrous: why can't Stromberg just bugger off to his submarine paradise, and leave the rest of us to our apparent decadence and corruption? Who's going to complain if he does – a few displaced turbot? How's he going to build his city – construction materials are going to be hard to come by in a post-apocalyptic wasteland, after all – and if he's built it already, why aren't we told? Like the *Liparus*, it doesn't hold water. And isn't there something rather familiar about all this? Something about a malevolent agency using a giant container to swallow up Russian and American rockets, playing each off against the other in a bid to bring about a thermonuclear holocaust? Perhaps Stromberg got the idea from certain events in Japan ten years previously ... The second plot strand is sheer melodrama, of course, but no less compelling for that. **4**

Locations Underwater; London; Moscow; Berngarten, the Austrian Alps; a Scottish naval base; somewhere off the coast of Sardinia; the Egyptian desert; Cairo; the Giza pyramids; the ruins at Karnak; somewhere up the Nile; Luxor; on the Rome-Sardinia express; in and around Sardinia. Bond certainly collects a few more stamps on his passport here. **9**

Gadgets Bond has a ticker-tape wristwatch, a ski-stick gun and a cigarette case-cum-microfilm reader. Anya hides cigarettes flavoured with stun gas in her garter. Q's field department is readying a decapitating tea-tray, a spring-mounted pouffe, a hookah-cum-machine gun and a camel saddle which conceals a sharp blade. Bond's car –

> *On the roof of Fekkesh's house in Cairo, Bond defends himself against Stromberg agent Sandor (Milton Reid)*

the best since *Goldfinger*'s DB5 – is a Lotus Special which not only ejects ground-to-air missiles, an oil slick, harpoons, black ink and mines, but also transforms into a two man-submarine (if that's not enough, Bond gets to whizz about on a jet-ski, too). The baddies employ a motorcycle sidecar which detaches to become a contact bomb, frogmen on *Thunderball*-like submersibles and the *Liparus*, a supertanker with modified bows which can swallow up unsuspecting submarines (and, in case of a hasty exit, can propel motorboats in collapsible casings from its sides). Stromberg's Atlantis HQ is pure science fiction. **9**

Girls The 'over-efficient' Moneypenny (who books separate hotel bedrooms for Bond and Anya, much to Bond's chagrin) and her cute Russian counterpart, Rubelvitch ('Rouble'-vitch, geddit?). KGB Major Anya Amasova, Bond's female alter-ego; she and Bond know of each other from the outset, right down to their drinks of choice. Acknowledging that each saves the other's life at least once, their one-upmanship throughout is funny and rewarding; it's a shame, therefore, that Anya is reduced to playing a damsel in distress in the last two reels. The Log Cabin Girl, who's metaphorically in bed with the Russians – and rather more literally with Bond. Stromberg's assistant, whose under-the-counter peddling of Bechmann and Markovitz's submarine tracking system causes not only Bond and Anya to finger Stromberg in the first place, but leads to her own demise (*à la* both Jaws and Helga in *You Only Live Twice*). Hosein's harem includes a little treasure of whom Bond announces his intention to 'delve deeply into'. Lamé-clad Felicca, who sets Bond up but gets accidentally shot in the back by a henchman while snuggling up to him (shades of Fiona in *Thunderball*). A receptionist with a plunging neckline at Bond's Sardinian hotel ('I have a message for you'/'I think you've just delivered it'). Stromberg aide Naomi, whom Bond first compares to a boat ('What a handsome craft. Such lovely lines') and later proves to be dangerous with a chopper (the lewd wink she gives Bond while trying to gun him down from the air is very cute). For Bond, another three bite the dust – as it were. **10**

Villains Karl Stromberg, 'one of the principal capitalist exploiters of the West' – an art-loving bloater apparently obsessed with the seven-tenths of the world undersea (a fascination actually expressed only in his Captain Nemo fancy of a submarine city and the fish head which symbolises his empire. Has webbed fingers, which is why he doesn't like to shake hands, but a mild physical deformity akin to a duck hardly explains his watery impulses). Ruthless by numbers, grandiose by rote – he even gets to say 'Good morning, Mr Bond. I've been expecting you' and a Blofeld-esque 'Goodbye, Mr Bond' within seconds of one another – and as mundane a megalomaniac as it's possible to get. Has in his pay an array of colourless incompetents – Felicca, Sandor, the *Liparus*' Blimpish captain – but only cartoonishly indestructible mute titan Jaws (about whom we learn nothing beyond his status as professional killer) presents our heroes any real challenge. **3**

Fights, chases, explosions An impressive rehash of the *On Her Majesty's Secret Service* ski scenes in the teaser; Bond's spat with the burly Sandor, and the cursory seeing-off he gives to Anya's heavies at the pyramids; yet another reworking of the *From Russia With Love* train scenes aboard the Rome-Sardinia express; an energetic dash along Sardinia's mountain coastline; and a glut of mayhem aboard the *Liparus* – stuntmen trampolene into shot hither and thither, Ken Adam craftsmanship gets scorched, and a job lot of Derek Meddings miniatures get comprehensively demolished – which tops even the excess of *You Only Live Twice*. And then two A-bombs go off. **8**

Dialogue and double entendres 'But, James – I need you,' wails the Log Cabin Girl as Our Man zips on a banana-yellow ski suit and prepares himself for action. 'So does England,' he declares deadpan, mock-heroic, setting precisely the distanced, ironic, don't-take-me-seriously tone of much of Bond's dialogue for the next few years. Long-term *Carry On* scripter Talbot Rothwell would have been proud of some of the more sniggerworthy asides herein (M's 'Tell him to pull out immediately', Bond's infamous 'Keeping the British end up, sir'). There are some subtleties, however: when Anya ups the bidding for the stolen microfilm, auctioneer Kalba tells Bond that, 'I think you will find the lady's figure hard to match.' **4**

Bond Adopts a naval commander's uniform again. Knows how to extract the warhead from an atomic bomb (amusingly, the procedure is rather like one of those games at church fêtes where one has to guide a loop around a twisty length of wire without touching it and making it buzz). When Anya notes that Bond was 'married only once. Wife killed', he cuts her dead: 'You've made your point.' 'You're sensitive, Mr Bond,' she remarks, perhaps a little bit incredulous. 'About certain things,' he replies. Of note is Bond's semi-apologetic justification to Anya for not recalling killing Sergei: 'When someone's behind you on skis at 40 miles an hour trying to put a bullet in your back, you don't always have time to remember a face.' Shoots an extra three bullets into Stromberg's dying body, which seems rather *Dr. No* excessive. **6**

Plus/minus points The naval scenes, all jargon and panic, are shot through with style and verisimilitude. Edward De Souza is wonderfully dry as the louche, Cambridge-educated Sheikh Hosein, and the additions to the series' supporting cast – General Gogol, particularly – are very welcome. The scenes where Bond is trapped on the *Liparus* ceiling rail, and where he and the *Wayne*'s captain wait to find out if they've successfully reprogrammed the warheads, are heart-in-the-mouth tense. But, again, the script's deficiencies outweigh much of the good. Even an otherwise innocuous scene – Bond's engineering of Jaws' demise by the application of an electromagnet to his metal gnashers – is undone when one merely enquires as to what an electromagnet is doing installed above a shark pool in the first place: what's it for, other than to provide an amusing hoist-by-his-own petard irony? **+2**

73% A slick and vacuous 'greatest hits' package. There's even one moment – Bond, having hijacked one of the Liparus' rail-cars, pulls up outside a vault where the prisoners are kept – which is identical to a scene in *You Only Live Twice*, right down to the look of the door and the very framing of the shot (given Ken Adam's design and Lewis Gilbert's direction, this surely can't be coincidence). It's a high-quality product, certainly, and the styling – particularly in Stromberg's luxurious living space – suggests that the series has found a Seventies idiom in which to rework its much-vaunted Sixties chic. But, despite a noble effort to give both Bond and 'the girl' a bigger stake in the narrative, too much of the whole feels soulless and empty.

CAST
Roger Moore James Bond
Barbara Bach Major Anya Amasova   **Curt Jurgens** Stromberg   **Richard Kiel** Jaws
Caroline Munro Naomi   **Walter Gotell** General Gogol
Geoffrey Keen Minister of Defence   **Bernard Lee** 'M'   **George Baker** Captain Benson
Michael Billington Sergei   **Olga Bisera** Felicca   **Desmond LLewelyn** 'Q'
Edward De Souza Sheikh Hosein   **Vernon Dobtcheff** Max Kalba
Valerie Leon Hotel Receptionist   **Lois Maxwell** Miss Moneypenny
Sydney Tafler *Liparus* Captain   **Nadim Sawalha** Fekkesh   **Sue Vanner** Log Cabin Girl
Eva Reuber-Staier Rubelvitch   **Robert Brown** Admiral Hargreaves
Marilyn Glasworthy Stromberg's Assistant
Milton Reid Sandor   **Cyril Shaps** Bechmann   **Milo Sperber** Markovitz
Albert Moses Barman   **Rafiq Anwar** Cairo Club Waiter
Shane Rimmer USS *Wayne* Captain   **Bryan Marshall** HMS Ranger Captain

SELECTED CREDITS
Ski sequence photographed and supervised by **Willy Bogner**
Art director **Peter Lamont**   Assistant art director **Ernie Archer**
Casting directors **Maude Spector**, **Weston Drury, Jnr**
Camera operator **Alec Mills**   Continuity **June Randall**
Make-up **Paul Engelen**   Hairdressing **Barbara Ritchie**
Fashion Consultant **Ronald Paterson**   Wardrobe supervisor **Rosemary Burrows**
Script editor **Vernon Harris**   Action arranger **Bob Simmons**
Ski Jump performed by **Rick Sylvester**   Special visual effects **Derek Meddings**
Special optical effects **Alan Maley**   Special effects (Studio) **John Evans**
Director of photography **Claude Renoir**   Editor **John Glen**
Main title designed by **Maurice Binder**   Production designed by **Ken Adam**
Music and theme song by **Marvin Hamlisch**
Theme Song 'Nobody Does It Better' performed by **Carly Simon**
Lyrics by **Carole Bayer Sager**   Associate producer **William P. Cartlidge**
Screenplay by **Christopher Wood** and **Richard Maibaum**
Produced by **Albert R. Broccoli**   Directed by **Lewis Gilbert**

Crazy when you think about it: *Moonraker*

1979: 'When I first directed films, I used to make an entire feature for less than the *Moonraker* telephone bill,' quipped director Lewis Gilbert. Heading a team which included many names familiar from *The Spy Who Loved Me*, Gilbert had been entrusted with its $30 million follow-up. The promised *For Your Eyes Only* had been sidelined in the wake of the science-fiction boom catalysed by *Star Wars* in 1977 and *Close Encounters of the Third Kind* in 1978. This time, Eon were sending Bond into space. The logistics beggared belief: 50 sets, 100 special effects technicians and five gondolas all went in to a film that would see the 'excess to success' formula through to its natural conclusion.

Ian Fleming's personal copy of *Moonraker* bears the inscription: 'This was written in January and February 1954 and published a year later. It is based on a film script I have had in my mind for many years . . .' *Moonraker*, one of Fleming's earliest Bond stories, would be the last of his full-length novels adapted for the cinema. Ironically, a book part-written with a film treatment in mind – legendary producer Alexander Korda (*Things To Come*, *The Four Feathers*, *The Third Man et al*) had turned Fleming's mind to such after expressing his enthusiasm for the novel *Live and Let Die*, and Fleming apparently wrote a full screenplay around the time of *Moonraker*'s publication in a bid to persuade Britain's Rank Organisation to purchase the rights – would translate to the screen with barely any recognisable elements intact, bar the name of its villain (the first, indeed, of the true Fleming megalomaniacs which the Bond films would lean so heavily upon) and a brief scene in which Bond and the heroine are trapped beneath a rocket readied to launch.

The film's basic story was by Tom Mankiewicz and Lewis Gilbert. Christopher Wood was commissioned to pen a screenplay that seemed to recycle a number of elements familiar from earlier adventures, most obviously Stromberg's hired killer Jaws, played once again by Richard Kiel. Sir Hugo Drax, the vengeful ex-Nazi of Fleming's novel, was reinvented as a despotic industrialist who plans to repopulate a decimated Earth with his largely Aryan master race. Whereas *The Spy*'s Stromberg had plotted a similar scheme from an underwater base, Drax's hideout would be a vast radar-cloaked space station.

James Mason was originally considered to play Drax, but the role went to prolific Parisian character actor Michael (aka Michel) Lonsdale. Highlights of Lonsdale's English-speaking work included Orson Welles' *The Trial* (1963) and a memorable co-starring role in *The Day of the Jackal* (1973). After *Moonraker*, he would feature in *Chariots of Fire* (1981), *The Name of the Rose* (1986) and *The Remains of the Day* (1993). Lois Chiles was cast as undercover CIA agent Holly Goodhead (the name was an invention of the scriptwriters, Fleming's *Moonraker* girl being undercover policewoman Gala Brand). A former model, Chiles had made her film debut in *The Way We Were* (1973), and had more recently been third-billed in the star-studded *Death On the Nile* (1978). In 1976, her agent had reportedly turned down the role of Anya in *The Spy Who Loved Me*, claiming she was unavailable. Chiles had in fact been stung by a critic who described her as 'no more than a table decoration' and taken time off to study acting in New York. In 1978, Gilbert found himself seated next to the actress on a flight to America. 'I told her we had actually thought of her for the last film,' he recalled, 'but we were told by her agent that she had retired.'

The 23-stone Richard Kiel had become something of a cult figure since his appearance in *The Spy Who Loved Me*; in *Moonraker* his character would be given the opportunity to turn over a new leaf and, towards the end of the film, recite his first line of dialogue (a rich 'Well, here's to us' as he shares a glass of champagne with tiny paramour Dolly while Drax's space station collapses around them). Although an extra line would be inserted to confirm that both Jaws and Dolly had touched down on Earth safely at the film's conclusion, Jaws would not reappear.

Desmond Llewelyn returned as Q, as did Lois Maxwell as Moneypenny. Maxwell's 22-year-old daughter Melinda appeared as an extra in the film, and stayed with the

Monday 7 August 1978 – a week before filming begins on Moonraker, Lois Chiles and Roger Moore meet the press in Paris. 'The most dangerous parts of a James Bond film are the love scenes,' Moore told reporters, perhaps mindful of the zero-gravity clinch that was in store

Broccoli family during shooting in Paris. Sadly, *Moonraker* would mark the end of Bernard Lee's 45-year film career. Already visibly frail, Lee would succumb to stomach cancer; he died in London's Royal Free Hospital on 16 January 1981. Although he made a notable contribution to such outstanding dramas as *The Third Man* (1949) and *The Blue Lamp* (1951), it is for his definitive M that he will be remembered.

As late as May 1978, the shooting script disclosed three sequences ultimately absent from the finished print, perhaps deemed too over-the-top even in as uncompromising an entertainment as Wood had forged. Jaws' first sight of Dolly (whose name is never actually given in the film's dialogue) was not noted as being accompanied by the *Love Story* theme eventually dubbed over it; instead, she was intended to introduce herself to him after pulling him free of the wreckage of the cable car: 'My name's Dolly.' 'Ga-ga, Gaga,' grunts the mute. Simultaneously, a caption beneath would read: 'Hello, Dolly.' More subtle, although no less of a send-up, was Drax's original reply to Bond's enquiry, 'What the hell are you up to here, Drax?', delivered after Bond has stumbled upon Drax's Brazilian launching site. 'It is a convention of the fiction beloved by parlour maids that the villain explains all before disposing of his victims,' avers the monomaniac. 'I do not intend to follow that precedent.' Funnier still was the planned identity of the 'problem' resident in Soviet General Gogol's bed: 'The camera pans to reveal a beautiful brunette in bed beside him, smoking a cigarette. We know her as Anya Amasova.'

'The Bonds are a bloody circus . . .'

A party aboard the Seine's *Ile de France* boat restaurant celebrated the commencement of principal photography on Monday 14 August 1978. One of the film's most spectacular locations was also one of the closest: Drax's palatial home was the 17th-century chateau of Vaux-le-Vicomte near Paris. In September, Gilbert started four weeks' location work in Venice. The canals hosted an absurd gondola chase, and the 16th-century Benedictine monastery of St Nicolo featured as the British Secret Service's Brazilian office. In January 1979, *Moonraker* moved to Rio de Janeiro, where the bustle of a specially staged carnival heightened the drama of the scenes in which Jaws stalks Bond's temporary assistant, Manuela. Shots used

in the cable car fight between Jaws and Bond were staged halfway up Sugar Loaf mountain. A motor boat chase, perhaps reminiscent of that suggested by Richard Maibaum in his first draft of *Diamonds Are Forever*, was filmed in Iguacu; from there, the ancient Mayan ruins of Tikal in Northern Guatemala served as the front for Drax's high-tech launching pad.

Punitive taxation laws introduced by James Callaghan's government had already sent Roger Moore into unwilling exile, and would force Eon to abandon Pinewood Studios for all but Derek Meddings' special effects unit. *Moonraker* was largely filmed in France, and would be billed as a co-production between Eon and Les Productions Artistes Associés. The film was co-ordinated from the Boulogne Studios near the Bois de Boulogne, a former Luftwaffe factory during the German occupation. While Boulogne hosted such scenes as Bond and Chang's virtual demolition of the Venini Glass museum, set construction was under way at the Epinay and Billancourt Studios north of Paris.

The three-tiered interior of Drax's opulent space station cost £250,000, and was built at Epinay. Some 220 technicians used 100 tons of metal, two tons of nails and 10,000 feet of wood on the enormous set. The exterior of the station was among the responsibilities of Meddings' model-makers at Pinewood's 007 stage. *Moonraker*'s pre-credits sequence was a mid-air struggle between Bond and Jaws originally devised by executive producer Michael G Wilson for *The Spy Who Loved Me*. 'We didn't use it . . . because we didn't know how to do it,' he said later. Wilson's notion was discussed with members of the US championship sky-diving team, whose master rigger designed a parachute which could fold to one inch thick and thus be concealed beneath a suit. A Panavision camera light enough to fit upon an operator's head was also developed. John Glen supervised the sequence: 'We were a small crew,' he told *Bondage* magazine. 'We had very cleverly designed parachutes with flat packs, and the wardrobe was specially designed with velcro sections so that when they'd finished doing their stunt they would just hand deploy and the chute would come out, having broken the velcro sections. It got very complex because when Bond is pushed out of the aeroplane, he is supposed to be without a parachute, but in fact [the stunt man] has a flat parachute and a reserve, so he had two parachutes. He then swoops down, dives on to a man who's in free fall, fights with him and steals his parachute and then puts it on, so he finishes up with three parachutes. The idea is crazy when you think about it . . .' The finished sequence was edited down from highlights of the five jumps performed during every day of shooting.

Principal photography came to an end in Paris on 27 February 1979. The rigours of the most gruelling Bond yet took their toll on the 51-year-old Moore, who had additionally undergone surgery following a recurrence of his kidney stone complaint. The 28-week schedule had allowed him a mere three days off. In 1984, he recounted a familiar occupational hazard: 'I did so many interviews on the Bond films; on *Moonraker* I did 388 – all of them as "in-depth, personal chats," which, of course was impossible. The Bonds are a bloody circus – they wheel 'em in and wheel 'em out.'

Such vital post-production elements as the film's theme song remained unrealised as late as May 1979. When young

singer/songwriter Kate Bush declined Eon's request to sing the John Barry/Hal David tune, Shirley Bassey stepped in to perform one of the most graceful opening signatures of the series.

The Duke of Edinburgh attended the premiere of *Moonraker* at the Leicester Square Odeon on Friday 26 June 1979. The film would benefit from the continuing vogue for glossy space fantasies, and unprecedented hype fuelled by a major marketing and merchandise campaign. Although *Moonraker*'s box-office run may not have exponentially reflected the hike in budget since *The Spy Who Loved Me*, the film nevertheless significantly bettered its predecessor. US admissions of 25.5 million nudged towards figures not enjoyed since *Diamonds Are Forever*, and a worldwide gross of $202.7 million would not be improved upon until *GoldenEye*'s triumphant performance in 1995.

Critical reaction was decidedly polarised; praised by the popular press, *Moonraker* suffered at the pens of more serious-minded critics. 'Producer Albert R Broccoli and director Lewis Gilbert seemed to be strapped for fresh thrills,' claimed *Variety*'s 'Har', 'falling back on formulas that worked in the past. As usual, however, they've come up with a wowser of an opening, but déjà vu sets in quickly after that as Roger Moore goes after a missing spaceship.'

The *New Statesman*'s John Coleman seemed unimpressed: '*Moonraker* . . . has tremendous space-shuttle hardware, a metal city in the heavens controlled by evil billionaire Drax (Michael Lonsdale, wasted for the umpteenth time), the inexplicably up-and-coming Lois Chiles as a CIA helpmeet to Roger Moore's

133

handsome Plastic Man 007, and a laugh or two more in Christopher Wood's script than the last one . . . brought the house down at a packed press show.'

'*Moonraker* is possibly the best novel from the initial quintet,' noted *The Guardian*, 'but this extravagant, imaginatively under-nourished film bears little resemblance to it . . . There's the usual stunning pre-credit sequence, after which everything else is a let-down: undertaker jokes, hot and cold running sexual innuendo, and yet another scrap on a cable-car. The chief innovation, and possible miscalculation, in producer Cubby Broccoli's artful package is having the villainous Jaws find true love with a myopic, homely blonde.'

Posters for *Moonraker* might have promised that 'Where other Bonds end . . . this one begins!', but 1979 would bring the most decadent era of Bond films to a close. Like *Diamonds Are Forever* before it, *For Your Eyes Only* would begin a new decade with an unequivocal dismissal of what had gone before.

File: *Moonraker*

Teaser A Boeing 747, transporting a Space Shuttle on piggyback from the US to the UK, is destroyed when two hijackers hidden within the shuttle itself launch it in mid-air. M calls upon Bond, who's on the 'last leg' of an African job. Cut to a private jet in flight. A (ho-hum) traitorous hostess holds Bond at gunpoint; both she and the pilot prepare to bale out. Bond struggles with the pilot; they fall out of the plane, only one parachute between them. In freefall, Bond wrestles with the pilot for the parachute; meanwhile, another figure launches himself from the

Richard Kiel, Lois Chiles, Roger Moore and Michael Lonsdale at Epinay Studios. Ken Adam's three-tiered space station was the biggest film set that had ever been constructed in France

plane – professional killer Jaws, who attempts to do for Bond. But Jaws' parachute fails, and he plunges into a circus tent far below. The kidnapping of the shuttle is tense and shocking, but the studiously spectacular antics ensuing – undoubtedly a consequence of the producers' misguided desire to outdo *The Spy Who Loved Me* – are lame, limp and realised without conviction. Moore's delivery of his few lines of dialogue is flat – a second-rate parody Bond – and Jaws' attempt to 'fly', flapping his arms to clowning circus music, is quite gruesome. **4**

Titles Parachuted women rain down in lines; nude tumblers vault the clouded moon. A flying Supergirl transforms into a jet plane, or something. The slowest-paced sequence yet, but irrefutably classy nonetheless. **6**

Bonkers plot The *Moonraker* shuttle's builder, industrialist Hugo Drax – a man obsessed with the conquest of space – has stolen the vehicle after one of his other six shuttles, of which the rest of the world knows nothing, develops a fault. In association with covert CIA agent Holly Goodhead, who has infiltrated Drax's operation, Bond discovers that Drax has sent a huge space station, concealed by means of a sophisticated radar jamming device, into orbit above the Earth. His six Moonrakers carry an élite of perfect physical specimens to the station. Once there, Drax plans to dump 50 globes containing a modified pollen lethal to all human life across the world; in time, the descendants of Drax's chosen few will repopulate the planet from scratch, reshaping it in Drax's image. It is, of course, *The Spy Who Loved Me* reprised, albeit largely without the *You Only Live Twice* bits; that said, it improves upon *The Spy* enormously. Given that Drax's ambitions are expanded on, the film makes good sense, in sharp contrast to *The Spy* (if, of course, one's prepared not to question too hard quite how Drax has managed to get his 'city in space' in the first place). The script does, quite cynically, give a curt but satisfactory answer to obvious questions raised as the plot progresses (the hijacking of the first Moonraker, the 'radar jamming', Bond and Holly being able to take the pilots' place in Moonraker 6). The arrival of the US Space Marines is, really, not much more ridiculous that the frogmen who parachute in to save the day in *Thunderball*, or the ninja army in *You Only Live Twice* (although they do seem to get to the station very quickly indeed, and it seems absurd

that they've been fully trained up and are readied for such an eventuality). Yes, it's outrageous, yes, it's bonkers – and yes, it's a proper story, too. **9**

Locations In the air, above the Yukon; London; in the air, somewhere else; in and around a grand French chateau in the middle of the Californian desert; the canals of Venice; Rio de Janeiro, Brazil; the Brazilian pampas; an ancient city in the South American jungle, somewhere around the upper reaches of the Amazoco; in outer space; Houston, Texas; the USSR. *Moonraker* wrings all it can from its settings and, noticeably, their surroundings – the chateau in the desert is a fabulous conceit, as is the use of the Rio carnival to obstruct Jaws' homicidal intentions, as is the ancient city concealing Drax's launching pad. **10**

Gadgets Bond carries: a dart-firing wristwatch which also hides an explosive wire and detonator; a cigarette case-cum-X-ray plate; and a lighter-cum-camera emblazoned '007'. He also uses both a motorised gondola-cum-hovercraft and a motorboat with a hang-glider attached; the latter carries mines and torpedoes (Drax's people have something similar). The CIA issue Holly with: a pen concealing a poison needle (later swiped by Bond); a dart-firing daily diary ('Fairly deadly diary,' smirks Bond, appealingly); a flamethrowing atomiser; and a handbag disclosing a radio transmitter. Q branch is testing exploding bolas, a sleeping gaucho dummy which springs open to reveal a machine-gun, and a laser weapon which both Drax and the US Space Marines have developed (the latter is less offensive when one considers that laser technology has been in use in the Bond universe for at last 15 years, since *Goldfinger*). Let's not even start on the space hardware. **8**

Girls A bog-standard femme fatale stewardess in the teaser. Corinne Dufour, 'a humble pilot' whose 'heart of gold' Bond exploits – something which leads to her be torn apart by Drax's dogs. Various of Drax's 'trainee astronauts', all of whom are perfect physical specimens with an aristocratic hauteur (watch how they look on placidly, with cold indifference, while Bond struggles with an anaconda). Holly Goodhead, a CIA agent whose cover story – that she's a doctor on loan from NASA – appears to be true; she knows her way around the technology, and is able to pilot a space shuttle, too. There's a certain one-upmanship shared between Holly and Bond reminiscent of that between 007 and Anya Amasova – minus, sadly, any real conflict, but their backchat is at least amusing ('If you're trying to be ingratiating, don't bother'). There's a very funny scene where Holly – who learned to fight at Vassar, the United States' first women-only college proper, devoted largely to the liberal arts – is allowed to beat up a few of Drax's technicians while Bond looks on, amused. Drax consorts the Countess Lubinski and Lady Victoria Devon (plus, later, a tweed-clad Mademoiselle and Signorina shooting grouse). A ravishing assistant at Venini Glass who, later, becomes a siren leading Bond to his doom in the jungle. Manuela, who works for Rio's Station VH and almost falls victim to Jaws, who's taken to impersonating Christopher Lee in Dracula mode. The Bond series only narrowly avoids its first topless shot in the Rio scenes; there's a sharp cut away from a shot of a reveller who's just about to whip off her silver bikini. Jaws' tiny, pigtailed object of desire. General Gogol's blonde 'problem'. The girls are all gorgeous, but only Corinne displays much real character; we're truly shocked to see her die. Yet again, Bond scores a treble. **6**

Villains Hugo Drax, a multi-millionaire whose vanity leads him to transplant a French chateau, brick-by-brick, to the Californian desert (he bought the Eiffel Tower as well, but was refused an export permit). 'What he doesn't own, he doesn't want,' we hear. Likes mixing with the cream of society – he's even played bridge with Britain's Minister of Defence. Plays a grand piano. Is able to control his Dobermans by the click of his fingers. Enjoys cucumber sandwiches – he tells Bond that afternoon tea is 'your country's one indisputable contribution to Western civilization' – and, like Goldfinger, affects a desire to play English country sports. Has a God complex ('my munificence is boundless', 'the ultimate dynasty which I alone have created'), but his perfect specimens are largely Aryan, and he's too keen on genocide to be interpreted as anything other than a space-age Hitler. Michael Lonsdale's performance is astonishingly controlled and precise: there's something really scary about the suppressed snigger in Drax's line, 'James Bond. You appear with the tedious inevitability – nnf – of an unloved season.' Elsewhere, Jaws reappears, as indestructible as ever (and now with a metal groin, which is quite disturbing seeing as he acquires a girlfriend half-way). His bathetic little

scenes with 'Dolly' are very sweet – his despairing search for her on the disintegrating space station is wonderful – but it's a shame they chickened out and let him survive (he was hardly going to turn up again, not now Dolly's turned him good). The wry little smile he and Bond share as they prepare for their set-to atop the cable car is inspired. Chang, Drax's first lieutenant, is no more interesting than any other henchman (the fact that both Bond and Drax pronounce his name 'Cha', however, is fascinating). **10**

Fights, chases, explosions Bond's fight with Chang, the latter in kendo gear, in the glass museum is pulled off with immense style (particularly the bit where Bond stops himself from throwing a dish valued at £1 million, whereupon Chang promptly shatters it). The moment in which an assassin rises out of a coffin aboard a motorboat-hearse are great, but the Venetian chase itself reprises *The Man With The Golden Gun* at best, degenerating into silly gooning (and Bond simply escapes Drax's hirelings by means of technology – not finishes them off, which is so wrong). The motorboat chase up the Amazoco is one-third of the length of the similar *Live and Let Die* sequence, and is consequently three times more effective (the explosions are A1, too). Sadly, the climax proves that laser beams are as nothing to good, old-fashioned lead ... **4**

Dialogue and double entendres Drax gives great quip: 'Look after Mr Bond. See that some harm comes to him,' and 'At least I shall have the pleasure of putting you out of my misery,' are, of course, two of the best lines in the entire series; 'You defy all my attempts to plan an amusing death for you,' comes close. Bond and Holly share some wry, acid dialogue ('Can you think of a reason why we can't have a drink afterwards?'/'Not immediately, but I'm sure I shall'). Bond's only really fine line comes after he and Holly have fallen free of the cable car, ripping his clothes in the process: 'Have you broken something?' asks Holly. 'Only my tailor's heart,' replies Bond. Surprisingly, there's not a great deal of innuendo, but the sheer magnificence of Q's final line more than makes up ('My God, what's Bond doing?' wails M as pictures of Bond and Holly making love in zero gravity are beamed direct to both Buckingham Palace and the White House. Replies Q, looking elsewhere, distracted: 'I think he's attempting re-entry, sir'). **10**

Bond Does remarkably little other than flit from location to location, breaking into somewhere to discover a label which will tell him where to go next. The fact that Holly is able to discover all this with far less hassle is quite galling – and if she weren't NASA-trained, Bond's entire enterprise would fall apart. But it's nice to see Bond do some proper spying again (safecracking in the chateau, searching the Venini Glass labs), however redundant he might be on the whole. **3**

Plus/minus points Points against: Bond's rippling wrinkles in the centrifuge scene (and that's just *Thunderball*'s 'traction machine' scene reworked); Bond chugging about St Mark's Square in his gondola-hovercraft, and the pigeon that does a double-take upon seeing him; the awful, awful back-projection in the cable car sequence. Points in favour: the grouse shooting scene ('You missed, Mr Bond.'/'Did I?'); the exquisite killing of Corinne; the hysterical scene where Bond drags M and the Minister of Defence into Drax's Venetian lab, only to discover it totally redecorated, even its dimensions changed; the menacing, blackly funny Rio scenes where Jaws' attempted killing of Manuela is halted by a conga; the fabulous 'siren-song' sequence; General Gogol's red pyjamas. It's fascinating to observe how *Moonraker* spoofs the two films responsible for its very existence: the 'alien music' from *Close Encounters of the Third Kind* is the code played on the keypad into the Venice lab, and *Star Wars* is perhaps suggested twice (Bond and Holly's first sight of the space station is akin to Luke, Hans and Obi-Wan's first sight of the Death Star, and Bond's shooting-down of Drax's globes is uncannily like Luke's climactic assault on the Death Star, right down to his turning off the automatic targetting and going to manual instead – using The Force, if you will). John Barry's space music is amazing – and we even get to hear '007' again. **+5**

75% Grudgingly, we'll give *Moonraker* the benefit of the doubt; it sets out to be an epic entertainment and, bar a couple of appalling lapses, succeeds. The Bonds are at their best when they pursue an uncompromising path right to the end of the line; this film does so, and in spades. The downside, however, is the increasing marginalisation of Bond himself, here little more than an irksome buffoon to the straight man, Drax.

CAST

Roger Moore James Bond

Lois Chiles Holly Goodhead   Michael Lonsdale Drax   Richard Kiel Jaws

Corinne Clery Corinne Dufour   Bernard Lee 'M'   Geoffrey Keen Frederick Gray

Desmond LLewelyn 'Q'   Lois Maxwell Moneypenny   Toshiro Suga Chang

Emily Bolton Manuela   Blanche Ravalec Dolly   Irka Bochenko Blonde Beauty

Michael Marshall Col. Scott   Leila Shenna Hostess, Private Jet

Anne Lonnberg Museum Guide   Jean Pierre Castaldi Pilot, Private Jet

Walter Gotell General Gogol   Douglas Lambert Mission Control Director

Arthur Howard Cavendish   Alfie Bass Consumptive Italian

Brian Keith U.S. Shuttle Captain   George Birt Captain, Boeing 747

Kim Fortune R.A.F. Officer   Lizzie Warville Russian Girl

Johnny Traber's Troupe Funambulists   Nicholas Arpez Drax's Boy

Guy Di Rigo Ambulanceman   Chris Dillinger Drax's Technician

Claude Carliez Gondolier   Georges Beller Drax's Technician

Denis Seurat Officer, Boeing 747   Chichinou Kaeppler Drax's Girl

Christina Hui Drax's Girl   Françoise Gayat Drax's Girl   Nicaise Jean Louis Drax's Girl

Catherine Serre Drax's Girl   Beatrice Libert Drax's Girl

SELECTED CREDITS

Camera operators **Alec Mills, Michel Deloire, Guy Delattre, John Morgan, James Devis**

Continuity **Elaine Schreyeck, Josie Fulford, Gladys Goldsmith**

Asst art directors **Marc Frederix, Jacques Duoy, Serge Duoy, Ernie Archer, John Fenner**

Special effects **John Evans, John Richardson, Rene Albouze,**

Serge Ponvianne, Charles Asscla

Wardrobe master **Jean Zay**   Wardrobe mistress **Colette Baudo**t

Make-up artists **Monique Archambault, Paul Engelen**

Hairdresser **Pierre Vade**   Costume designer **Jacques Fonteray**

Casting directors **Margot Capelier, Weston Drury**   Script editor **Vernon Harris**

Art directors **Max Duoy, Charles Bishop**

Action sequences arranged by **Bob Simmons**

Visual effects supervisor **Derek Meddings**   Visual effects art director **Peter Lamont**

Executive producer **Michael G. Wilson**   Director of photography **Jean Tournier**

Editor **John Glen**   Main title designed by **Maurice Binder**

Production designed by **Ken Adam**   Music by **John Barry**

Title song *Moonraker* performed by **Shirley Bassey**

Composed by **John Barry**, Lyrics by **Hal David**

Associate producer **William P. Cartlidge**

Screenplay by **Christopher Wood**

Produced by **Albert R. Broccoli**

Directed by **Lewis Gilbert**

We'll take ideas from anyone: *For Your Eyes Only*

1981: 'We decided the time had come to humanise Bond and make him less dependent on electronic hardware,' said Michael G Wilson in summing up *For Your Eyes Only*. 'If he's in a jam he has to rely more on his wits to get him out of trouble. It makes him much more interesting.' Albert Broccoli's stepson had been promoted to the rank of executive producer on *Moonraker*. His previous form – he'd been an electrical engineer before becoming a lawyer – had equipped him with valuable experience to steer the Bond films through the Eighties and beyond.

With no more full-length Bond novels to adapt, the title of Eon's latest film was taken from a collection of short stories written by Ian Fleming between 1958 and 1959. The screenplay was extrapolated from both the title story and one of its bedfellows, *Risico* (with a pinch of Fleming's *Live and Let Die* for good measure). Melina Havelock and Gonzales were drawn from *For Your Eyes Only*, in which one Judy Havelock murders von Hammerstein, the man who ordered her parents' assassination, with a bow and arrow while he is diving into a lake; Gonzales is one of von Hammerstein's hired hitmen. Bond meets Judy in woodland beside the lake, which would become a Spanish villa's swimming pool in the film. Mortal enemies Kristatos and Colombo (renamed Columbo) came from *Risico*, as did Kristatos' opium-impregnated rolls of newsprint, Lisl, the restaurant scene in which Colombo records Bond and Kristatos' conversation, and the fact that Bond is led to believe that

Colombo is the bad guy (it is, in fact, Kristatos). In addition, Richard Maibaum and Wilson introduced a *From Russia With Love*-style struggle for possession of the Polaris-baffling Automatic Targeting Attack Computer (ATAC).

In an interview with the *Sunday Express*, Wilson offered an insight into the scripting process of the modern Bond picture: 'We work out the outline of the story in committee,' he explained. 'There's Cubby, Richard [Maibaum] and myself and maybe a stuntman – we'll take ideas from anyone. Then we'll write a treatment, then the script itself . . .'

Since the expiry of Roger Moore's original contract with *The Spy Who Loved Me*, he had resisted Broccoli's attempts to tie him to a three-picture deal and had negotiated each subsequent film in turn. Earlier that year, Moore had twice spoofed his Bond persona by appearing in both an edition of *The Muppet Show* (in which, tuxedo-clad, he'd fend off Miss Piggy's efforts to seduce him) and, immediately afterwards, in Burt Reynolds vehicle *The Cannonball Run* (in which, again tuxedo-clad, he played a disturbed Jewish boy-turned-racing driver who believes himself to be one Roger Moore). In July, at a London press conference for wartime thriller *The Sea Wolves*, Moore had reportedly stated that he would not play Bond again. By August, Eon had yet to persuade Moore to return to the fold, and had already begun considering other alternatives. Michael Jayston, who had previously starred as a clandestine government agent in BBC television's 13-part espionage drama *Quiller* (1975), was allegedly high on the list of possible replacements while scripting was under way. (Jayston would eventually get to play Bond in a BBC radio adaptation of *You Only Live Twice* some ten years later.)

After over ten years' second unit and editing duties, John Glen was promoted to director. Early on, he devised a pre-credits sequence that would serve as an ideal introduction for the new Bond: 'There was some talk that that Roger wouldn't do *For Your Eyes Only*, so we had to be prepared – in case the negotiations broke down – to break in a new Bond. So the opening in the churchyard was my idea . . . to keep the continuity of character and reveal the new Bond in an exciting situation.' The script opens with Bond laying flowers on the grave of his murdered wife Tracy, before a helicopter unexpectedly arrives to take him to M's office. The vehicle is booby-trapped; its pilot is electrocuted and the craft falls under the remote control of a bald wheelchair-bound villain. Who strokes a white cat . . . 'As anxious as we were to mention who [the villain] was, we just let people use their imaginations and draw their own conclusions,' said Glen in 1981.

'I think it's a legal thing.' Had the scene been shot as originally scripted, 007's unseen captor would have greeted him over the helicopter intercom with the line, 'I thought we should celebrate the tenth anniversary of our last meeting', thus further reinforcing the sequence's links with *On Her Majesty's Secret Service*, already referred to in the inscription on Tracy's gravestone ('We have all the time in the World').

'We had to convince Roger to be more ruthless . . .'

In September, Broccoli and United Artists came to an agreement with Moore that would reportedly propel the star's earnings into the seven-figure bracket. Despite agreeing to appear in *For Your Eyes Only*, Moore was uneasy about the scene where Bond provided the nudge necessary to tip the evil Emile Locque's car over the edge of a cliff, killing him. 'We had to convince Roger to be more ruthless than, as an actor, he feels comfortable being,' said Wilson later. A jolting reminder of the brutality implicit in Connery and Lazenby's interpretations of Bond, the scene was emblematic of a marked shift in the tone of Moore's performance, remarkable for an actor whose take on Bond had seemed increasingly anodyne in recent films.

Broccoli for one was delighted that Moore had decided to make another film for him. The two had first met in a Curzon Street casino and, since working together on the Bond films, had developed a good-natured backgammon feud. 'There was one story published that I'd lost $260,000 to Roger,' said Broccoli. 'But it's not true. I don't mind being called a gambler, but I do mind people thinking the guy can beat me at backgammon.'

Roger Moore as Seymour Goldfarb Jr in the 1981 comedy The Cannonball Run. The actor spoofed his 007 image by playing a clothing tycoon who believed he was Roger Moore

French actress Carole Bouquet was cast as crossbow-wielding avenger Melina Havelock. Bouquet had made her film debut aged 19, as one of two actresses in the title role of Luis Buñel film *That Obscure Object of Desire* (1977). Soon after she had unsuccessfully auditioned for the role of Holly Goodhead in *Moonraker*. Following *For Your Eyes Only*, she modelled for Chanel No. 5 and remained busy in largely undistinguished French films. In 1989, she made a brief appearance in Francis Coppola's segment of the anthology *New York Stories*. Julian Glover was cast as villain Kristatos. Glover's career had taken in such diverse films as low-budget Hammer horror *Quatermass and the Pit* (1968) and the second *Star Wars* blockbuster *The Empire*

Strikes Back (1980). Following screen tests for Eon in 1972, he had been shortlisted as a possible new Bond in *Live And Let Die*. Chaim Topol played Kristatos' mortal enemy Columbo; best known for his portrayal of Tyve in the Oscar-nominated film of *Fiddler On The Roof* (1971), Topol had more recently played Dr Zarkov in Dino de Laurentiis' outlandish version of *Flash Gordon* (1980). Michael Gothard made a chilling impression as killer Locque, and Charles Dance – then early in his career – appeared as hitman Claus. Elsewhere, Cassandra Harris played Columbo's Scouse faux-Countess, Lisl Von Schlaf. Harris – born Sandra Waites in Australia – would marry West End actor and part-time labourer Pierce Brosnan at Kings Road Register Office on 27 December; of later significance, the couple lunched with Albert Broccoli during the *For Your Eyes Only* shoot.

Playboy magazine had enjoyed close links with Bond since Fleming's short story *The Hildebrand Rarity* had been published in the March 1960 issue. (The screen Bond is clearly a fan; in *On Her Majesty's Secret Service* he can be seen flicking through a copy, and in *Diamonds Are Forever* he is revealed to be a card-carrying *Playboy* Club member.) Late in 1980, *Playboy* continued the association by joining United Artists in sponsoring a 'Be a James Bond girl' competition, the first prize being a role in *For Your Eyes Only*. Although winner Robbin Young only fleetingly appeared as 'Girl in Flower Shop', *Playboy* readers would get to see considerably more of her.

Another *For Your Eyes Only* girl was 27-year-old 'Tula', a hostess on gameshow *3-2-1* who could be glimpsed in the swimming pool scenes. Her participation later attracted the wrong sort of publicity altogether when the press discovered that Tula (otherwise known as Caroline Cossey) had actually been born 'Barry', and had undergone sex-change surgery at the age of 17. 'They didn't know when they were filming,' she later admitted.

Filming began on 15 September 1980 at the Villa Sylva at Kanoni, in Corfu. During the five weeks the first unit spent on the Greek island, Moore suffered back problems and was forced to endure a diet of grilled fish in order to lower his cholestrol levels. ('What do I look for in a role? Not too much butter.' he later quipped.) There, the scenes where Gonzales' guards pursued Bond and Melina were filmed amidst tight, winding roads and hillside vineyards. In a brave revisionist move, Bond's Lotus Esprit is casually discarded courtesy of a built-in bomb activated by one of Gonzales' thugs, leaving 007 with no alternative but to call upon Melina's yellow Citroen 2CV. The sturdy vehicle took a spectacular pummelling in a chase which Remy Julienne supervised with a conspicuous disregard for local scenery.

Glen's team next moved to Kalambaka on the Greek mainland, where the film's climax was filmed at a high-perched monastery. Shooting was disrupted when neighbouring monks staged a demonstration againt Eon's presence, claiming that the sex and violence of the James Bond films offended the sanctity of the area. On 17 October the monks of Meteora closed their monasteries to visitors, and sent messages of protestation to the government and the Orthodox Church. At one point, they even hung their laundry out of their windows in the hope it would ruin the film crew's shots. Rick Sylvester, who had performed the spectacular ski/parachute jump at the beginning of *The Spy Who Loved Me*, doubled for Roger Moore during Bond's faltering ascent of the sheer face leading up to St Cyril's.

'I would have adored being M . . .'

At the end of 1980, the crew returned to Pinewood to shoot interior scenes. Ken Adam was busy on the film adaptation of Dennis Potter's *Pennies From Heaven*, so his former draughtsman and art director Peter Lamont took his place as production designer. The ailing Bernard Lee proved unable to shoot M's briefing of Bond; as a mark of respect to Lee, he was not immediately recast. In the film, M's scripted dialogue would be split between Q, Geoffrey Keen's Minister of Defence, but mainly taken by Tanner, played by James Villiers. In the Fleming novels, Bill Tanner is M's Chief of Staff; *For Your Eyes Only* would be Tanner's first appearance in the film series. In 1995, Villiers told interviewers Chris Howarth and Steve Lyons. 'Bernie Lee had had it really, bless his darling heart. Roger and Broccoli came to a play I was in at the time . . . They said they wanted me to be in the next Bond film – get down to Pinewood tomorrow, it's urgent because Bernie Lee can't do it, he's gone, finished. And he was dead in about a fortnight.

'So I did it, it was great fun. Had a glass of champagne and did the scene . . . the usual routine, very painless.' Villiers would be disappointed not to be called upon again: 'Basically I thought I was in, I thought I was going to be in the next one. I rang my agent and said, "Why aren't I playing M?" And he said, "Why did you think you were going to play M? There was never any question of you being a regular M – too young." M has got to be about seventy, I was in my early Fifties if that. I would have adored being M throughout . . .'

In January 1981 location shooting continued in Cortina d'Ampezzo, high in the Dolomite mountains of northern Italy. In a situation similar to that he'd encountered in Murren in 1968, John Glen was dismayed to discover that unusually mild conditions had left Cortina with very little snow. He duly had truckloads imported.

In February, on the final day of shooting the bobsleigh chase between Bond and various of Locque and Kriegler's goons in Cortina, tragedy struck. Twenty-three-year-old stuntman Paolo Rigon was killed when he became trapped underneath his bob. It was the first terminal injury incurred during the shooting of a Bond film.

'A scene which no-one really wanted to shoot . . .'

Al Giddings headed the underwater unit at the 007 stage tank, and in the Bahamas. In one memorable aquatic scrape, drawn from Fleming's *Live and Let Die*, Bond and Melina are tied to the back of Kristatos' boat and dragged across a shark-infested coral reef. '[The scene] has been in and out of Bond scripts for as long as I can remember,' John Glen told *Bondage* magazine in 1981. 'It's a scene which no-one really wanted to shoot, except for Cubby. The reason it was rejected by most directors was because it was such a complex sequence to shoot, with no guarantees that you were going to get it, because it was a mixture of underwater and above water. It involved four to five units shooting the material. It was very

difficult to to control . . . it was the highest [cost] of the Bahaman operation, running something like $2,700 per foot.'

The pre-credits sequence was retained with minor script amendments, even after it had become clear that Roger Moore would reprise the role of Bond. The cemetery where Bond lays the flowers on Tracy's grave was at Stoke Poges Church, near Pinewood. The helicopter was remote-control flown over East London's Becton Gas Works. The sequence would later attract unwelcome controversy . . .

Maurice Binder's title sequence was shot early in June 1981, and featured – for the first time – the theme tune's singer, Sheena Easton. Following her 'discovery' in BBC programme *The Big Time*, Easton had been offered an EMI contract in 1980. Her recording of the Bill Conti/Michael Leeson song would become a top ten hit on both sides of the Atlantic and earn an Oscar nomination. The naked silhouette in this latest Binder epic belonged to one Perri Small. When the model revealed her real name – Penelope Smallbone – to Albert Broccoli he became intrigued and noted its commercial potential. 'Maybe we should steal it,' he reportedly joked.

For Your Eyes Only opened at the Leicester Square Odeon on 24 June 1981 with a royal premiere attended by the Prince of Wales and his fiancée Lady Diana Spencer. Albert Broccoli, who stayed in London especially to attend, took the opportunity to celebrate the 20th anniversary of his first involvement with James Bond. Proceeds from the premiere went to the Royal Association for Disability and Rehabilitation. Several press commentators noted that, considering the premiere's beneficiary, *For Your Eyes Only*'s pre-credits action could have featured a less potentially insensitive portrayal of wheelchair users.

An impressive worldwide gross of $195,300,000 would greet the film's distribution, but US admissions of 19.8 million, a drop of almost six million since *Moonraker*, confirmed that the more realistic Bond films failed to excite as much interest in United Artists' biggest market.

For Your Eyes Only's theatrical poster featured an image of Roger Moore framed between a pair of slender, and bare, female legs. It was all a bit too racy for America's Boston *Globe* and Los Angeles *Times*, which cropped the picture just above the girl's knees. The *Pittsburgh Press* even replaced her bikini-covered bottom with a drawn-on pair of shorts. A number of ladies tried to benefit from the publicity generated by the controversy, but photographer Morgan Kane ended speculation over the legs' owners by telling *Time* magazine that they belonged to 22-year-old New York model Joyce Bartle. 'I was embarrased that I had to prove the legs were mine,' Joyce said. 'You know your own legs when you see them.'

'After the outer space exploits of *Moonraker* there was no choice but to bring Bond back down to earth,' said *Variety*'s 'Cart'. 'Entire film is probably the best directed on all levels since *On Her Majesty's Secret Service*, as John Glen, moving into the director's chair after a long service as second unit director and editor, displays a fine eye and as often as not keeps more than one thing happening in his shots.'

The Times' David Robinson found little to like in the film: 'There is no more pretence at probability, no attempt at sophistication in dialogue or character or relationships; not even any very great effort to make the stunt men look like their character doubles. Disbelief, it is clearly assumed, is rapturously and totally suspended.' *The Daily Telegraph* was similarly disparaging: 'Not much humour, and certainly no wit in a film that is always efficient but seldom, despite all the movement, really lively.'

The Glasgow Herald's Molly Plowright was brave enough to lend her support to the latest 007, even if she did bemoan the increasing prevalence of stunt doubles: 'Roger Moore is still around with close-ups and narrative links, as gentlemanly and debonair as ever. Indeed, I'm definitely beginning to prefer his 007 to the more lethal and ruthless one of his never-to-be-forgotten predecessor Sean Connery.'

As before, it seemed the hardest person to please was Richard Maibaum, who expressed frustration with the way Glen handled the romantic relationship between Melina and Bond: 'The whole idea was that the great lover James Bond couldn't get to first base with this woman because she's so obsessed with avenging her parents' death. Nothing was ever done with it . . .

'I think we blew an opportunity in *For Your Eyes Only* to go back to the *From Russia With Love*/*On Her Majesty's Secret Service* Bonds . . . we didn't have Sean to make it real.'

The long-standing debate between the relative virtues of Roger Moore and Sean Connery would soon cease to be academic. While Eon's thoughts turned to following up *For Your Eyes Only*, its original Bond was preparing to bring his self-imposed exile to an end.

File: *For Your Eyes Only*

Teaser Interrupting Bond's visit to wife Tracy's grave (and we're fascinated to note that Tracy is buried in suburban London – which she never visited – rather than her native Portugal), a bald, wheelchair-bound cat-lover – a former enemy of Bond's – fools Bond into entering a bogus Universal Exports helicopter. By remote control, the villain murders the pilot – one of his 'less useful people' – and seizes control of the chopper, winging it this way and that, Bond at his mercy. But Bond, in the back seat, makes his way around the outside and into the cockpit, where he severs the villain's control device. Gaining control ot the machine, he swoops down, catches the villain's wheelchair in the copter's runners and, despite desperate entreaties – 'We can do a deal! I'll buy you a delicatessen – in stainless steel!' – deposits the bad guy inside a giant gas chimney. A bizarre but extremely well-remembered comic-strip vignette utterly at odds with the film it precedes. And what the hell is this 'stainless steel' stuff about? (For legal reasons, we daren't suggest that the villain is Blofeld – who, of course, it isn't – but if it were, note how his method for destroying Bond mirrors almost exactly Bond's disposal of Blofeld in *Diamonds Are Forever:* rendered helpless inside a vehicle controlled by his nemesis, and buffetted to and fro. But it isn't Blofeld, anyway. Absolutely not. Oh no.) **9**

Titles A bare-shouldered Sheena Easton trills to a lift music backing; meniscii of bubbles burst behind. Oh look, here's a naked lady. And some fish. Isn't that nice? **3**

Bonkers plot In the Ionian Sea, the *St Georges,* a high-tech British electronic surveillance ship disguised as a Maltese fishing vessel, is sunk with all hands when it dredges up a mine. The ATAC system – a missile launching device – it was equipped with is downed with the boat; if the ATAC falls into enemy hands, Britain's entire Polaris fleet might be rendered useless, or worse. The British ask Havelock, a friendly marine archaeologist, to locate the wreck for them, but he and his wife are murdered before reporting back. Bond is dispatched to locate Havelock's assassin – who is promptly killed by Havelock's vengeful daughter, Melina. The whole is a plot devised by Kristatos, a drug smuggler and prominent member of the Corfu underworld who apparently uses Bond to locate the ATAC, which he plans to sell to the Russians. This rambling storyline features a nebulous menagerie of villains and loyalties; it's a little cloudy even once the identity of the bad guy has been made clear. And the fact that it's Bond who retrieves the ATAC is odd: Kristatos clearly has the technology to bring it up from the ocean floor, and certainly knows where it us, but whether or not he's able to actually disconnect it from the *St Georges* without triggering the self-destruct timer is never made entirely clear (does he have to wait for Bond to find it/disarm it? If so, why does he put so much effort into killing Bond beforehand?). And what are we to make of the giant spike mine seen in Kristatos' Albanian warehouse, identical to the one that sinks the *St Georges?* Was it Kristatos who sank the *St Georges* in the first place, or was it an accident? If the former, who told him about the ATAC? Not the Russians, 'cos General Gogol is clearly surprised to learn of the sinking. Oh, and what is Kristatos doing in Cortina? Hasn't he got more urgent business – which he could continue unmolested – in the Ionian? Or is he trying to entrap Bond and Melina? And so on ... That said, the story is fairly involving, but it's a shame that we get no demonstration of what the ATAC does; we're simply told what it may or may not do. So how are we supposed to care? Or is it just another silly Maibaum McGuffin? **5**

Locations London; the Ionian Sea, off the Albanian coast; Russia; near Madrid, Spain; Cortina, Northern Italy; Corfu; Albania; Greece. Pretty, rural, largely Mediterranean – just the sort of places for a cosy Saga cruise, in fact. Hardly the heady glamour of the jet set, is it now? **4**

Gadgets The bald guy's remote-control helicopter. The magical ATAC itself. The automated mirror concealed in Moneypenny's filing cabinet. Bond's Lotus, complete with a very drastic burglar deterrant. Q's latest toys include the Identigraph, a high-tech photofit machine, plus a hard plaster forearm and an umbrella which, when rained upon, snaps downward, its jagged spikes serrating the holder's neck. And, bar a few apparently real submersibles, that's it. The first film since *Dr. No* where Bond uses no real playthings in the field? **2**

Girls Rublevich (sic) returns, now clearly closer to employer General Gogol than is entirely proper in the workplace. Melina Havelock, a 2CV driver and practised

Another scene from The Cannonball Run, *released the same year as* For Eyes Only. *Goldfarb is ejected,* Goldfinger-*style, from the seat of his Aston Martin*

diver; she's half-Greek, and claims that 'Greek women, like Elektra, always avenge their loved ones'. Various bikini-clad lovelies lounging around Gonzales' poolside, whom the hitman throws wedges of banknotes. Sharon, Q's young tea-making assistant. Bumptious American teen Bibi Dahl, a figure-skating prodigy with an undiscerning eye which latches first on Bond and then on Aryan sharpshooter Eric Kriegler; she's not a virgin, is keen to indulge in a particular exercise which 'builds up muscle tone', and could 'eat [Bond] up alive!' A florist in Cortina. The 'Countess Lisl von Schlaf' (her name, given her Liverpool roots, we assume to be bogus) – a 'night person', said to be Austrian, and an 'expensive mistress' to boot. Melina is given a close look into the camera upon witnessing her parents' death, clearly signalling her intended significance, but ends up on the film's fringes, another 'bump' in the narrative, biding her time until she's given the choice to kill Kristatos (her clear intention is ultimately denied her, too). She doesn't even get to snog Bond until they go skinny-dipping in the final reel, either. Bibi is better-developed, albeit thoroughly irritating, but it's good to see Bond positively embarrassed by her mad pash for him ('You get your clothes on, and I'll buy you an ice cream'). He only actually seems comfortable with Lisl, who plays cards, is around his own age, and whose nightie slips as easily as her accent; she's the only of these we can be certain he sleeps with. Is Bond's libido beginning to fail him? Or is he just growing up? A reasonably sincere effort to give the Bond series less one-dimensional female characters; all three key women are at least interesting, but remain largely peripheral. **9**

Villains Ari Kristatos may be a Communist stooge, drug smuggler, killer and harbour (we understand) unseemly Humbert Humbert-style desires for his skating protégé, but he's still no more than a common crook whose King's Medal, we assume, was won under false pretences. Short-sighted thug Emile Leopold Locque is more of the same, although given that he escaped prison by strangling his psychiatrist we can assume that this near-mute henchman is at least pleasingly mad. It's he who pays off Spanish assassin Gonzales – although why he doesn't ask Gogol's agent, East German skiing/shooting champion Erich Kriegler ('doesn't smoke, he only eats health foods, he won't even talk to girls') to rub out Havelock for him we'll never know. Kriegler is, surely, the obvious choice – and doubtless would do it for KGB glory, not cash (he's also yet

another Grant-alike, right down to the cast-iron stomach muscles and high-cut trunks). **4**

Fights, chases, explosions Action sequences are to the point and mostly underlined by a clever little motif: the Spanish chase scene, already made amusing by Melina's hopeless 2CV, is interrupted by slow-moving traffic; the ski scenes are made more tense by Bond being set up to be shot when he gets caught up in a crowd going up to a ski-slope; points are scored when Bond puts each of his ice hockey-playing assailants away. The night-time raid on the Albanian warehouse is great, and the largely silent assault on remote monastery St Cyril's has something of the atmosphere of a World War II movie about it. **8**

Dialogue and double entendres The codewords Bond and Ferrera exchange ('The snow this year is better at Innsbruck'/"But not at St Moritz') owe more to John Le Carré than Ian Fleming. Bond seems to be getting positively philosophical in his old age, declaring sagely that 'The Chinese have a saying: "Before setting out on revenge, you first dig two graves"' – and, at the casino, 'Courage is no match for an empty shoe.' We don't hear a single sexual double entendre proper, but do laugh out loud at the scene in which Bond enters a confessional box in a Greek church and begins, 'Forgive me, father, for I have sinned' – whereupon Q is revealed in clerical robes on the other side of the partition: 'That's putting it mildly, 007 . . .' **4**

Bond Drinks ouzo, but finds a Cefalonian white robolo 'too scented for [his] palate', preferring a Theotaki aspro. Eats preveza prawns, savara salad and bourdetto (whatever they might be). He's genuinely desperate to avoid Lisl being killed, which perhaps explains his surprisingly callous and cold execution of Locque, kicking his teetering car off the brink of a cliff. Standing four-square in front of Locque's speeding car and firing through the windscreen is rock hard, too (although we're dismayed by Bond's clear lack of puff while running up stairs to outflank him). His wardrobe is nothing short of a disgrace, however (especially the bodywarmer and chunky Aran sweater he wears while climbing up to St Cyril's). **8**

Plus/minus points The synth-inflected score ranges between OTT *Godfather*-style histrionics (the killing of

Havelock), gruesome lurve muzak (the Bond/Lisl sex scene) and screeching horror movie pastiche (the scenes inside the submerged *St Georges*), befitting only a second-rate made for TV thriller. The 'tag' scene featuring That Bloody Woman seems at odds with the rest of the film, however brilliant John Wells' mute Denis might be (and the clichéd fog-bound Downing Street – straight out of Sherlock Holmes' London – betrays American influence, too). But the notion that Havelock's parrot might give away the villains' lair is pleasing, and Bond's ultimate ordeal – climbing up the sheer face leading up to St Cyril's, his progress hindered by a sadistic heavy – is nothing short of stunning. The actual climax – Bond hurls the ATAC into the air, lets it smash on rocks below, turns to General Gogol and says: 'That's detente, comrade. You don't have it, I don't have it' – is about as perfect an ending for an espionage thriller as could be devised. **+7**

61% Low-key, subdued and cold, *For Your Eyes Only* catches fire infrequently; it'd like to be *From Russia With Love*, but in its eagerness to be unlike *Moonraker* forgets that *From Russia* wasn't all hard-nosed and dour – that that had had its exotic moments, too. A case of throwing out the baby with the bathwater, perhaps?

CAST

Roger Moore James Bond
Carole Bouquet Melina   **Topol** Columbo   **Lynn-Holly Johnson** Bibi
Julian Glover Kristatos   **Cassandra Harris** Lisl   **Jill Bennett** Brink
Michael Gothard Locque   **John Wyman** Kriegler   **Jack Hedley** Havelock
Lois Maxwell Moneypenny   **Desmond LLewelyn** Q
Geoffrey Keen Minister of Defence   **Walter Gotell** General Gogol
James Villiers Tanner   **John Moreno** Ferrara   **Charles Dance** Claus
Paul Angelis Karageorge   **Toby Robins** Iona Havelock   **Jack Klaff** Apostis
Alkis Kritikos Santos   **Stag Theodore** Nikos   **Stefan Kalipha** Gonzales
Graham Crowden First Sea Lord   **Noel Johnson** Vice Admiral
William Hoyland McGregor   **Paul Brooke** Bunky   **Eva Reuber-Staier** Rublevich [sic]
Fred Bryant Vicar   **Robbin Young** Girl in Flower Shop   **Graham Hawks** Mantis Man
and **Janet Brown** as The Prime Minister
John Wells as Denis

SELECTED CREDITS

Casting by **Maude Spector**, **Deborah McWilliams**
Costume designer **Elizabeth Waller**   Wardrobe master **Tiny Nicholls**
Wardrobe for Miss Bouquet and Miss Harris by **Raemonde Rahvis**, London
Ski suits by **Bogner**   Assistant art director **Ernie Archer**
Make-up **George Frost**, **Eric Allwright**   Hairdressers **Stephanie Kaye**, **Marsha Lewis**
Special effects **John Evans**   Skating scenes staged by **Brian Foley**
Production supervisor **Bob Simmonds**   Camera operator **Alec Mills**
Continuity **Elaine Schreyeck**   Action sequences arranged by **Bob Simmons**
Driving stunts arranged by **Remy Julienne**   Art director **John Fenner**
Editor **John Grover**   Visual effects supervisor **Derek Meddings**
Director of photography **Alan Hume**   Main title designed by **Maurice Binder**
Production designed by **Peter Lamont**   Music by **Bill Conti**
Title song performed by **Sheena Easton**, Music by **Bill Conti**, Lyrics by **Michael Leeson**
Associate producer **Tom Pevsner**   Executive producer **Michael G. Wilson**
Screenplay by **Richard Maibaum** and **Michael G. Wilson**
Produced by **Albert R. Broccoli**   Directed by **John Glen**

Amiably fatigued: *Octopussy*

1982: on the evening of 29 March, Roger Moore took the stage at the Motion Picture Academy to announce the latest recipient of the Irving G Thalberg Award. In his acceptance speech, Albert Broccoli would describe his award 'for continued production excellence' as the 'highest point of my career'. He mentioned former colleagues Irving Allen, Harry Saltzman and Arthur Krim, before thanking the Academy for 'allowing a farm boy from Long Island to realise this dream.' Pre-production on *Octopussy*, Eon's 13th James Bond film, was well under way. But the first of several potential crises was already threatening to eclipse Broccoli's ongoing achievement ...

Upon its 1980 release, United Artists' *Heaven's Gate* earned a lasting reputation as one of the costliest disasters in cinematic history. As a genre, the Western was dealt a blow from which it never fully recovered; as a studio, United Artists was crippled by the poor return on its $40 million investment. United Artists' possible demise would have had serious implications for Eon; fortunately, MGM acquired the struggling UA in May 1981. MGM chairman Kirk Kerkorian – an airline mogul and Las Vegas hotelier – was keen to revitalise the flagging fortunes of the newly merged companies and saw film production as a viable avenue. The James Bond series would be a reliable mainstay as the decade progressed.

Octopussy was officially announced by Steven Bach, UA's global production head, and Albert Broccoli in April 1982. 'Bond is in progression in terms of what the pictures make,' said UA president Norbert Auerbach, who later confirmed that the organisation had authorised a basic outlay of $25 million. 'We have no problem accommodating that kind of budget . It's always a risk, but it's a risk we're willing to take . . . [Broccoli is] an extremely responsible producer who would love to bring them in at 15 or 20 or 12 or whatever because he knows the less the picture costs the more money he and we will make.'

With the support of the stabilised MGM/UA confirmed, Broccoli prepared to begin a new round of negotiations with Roger Moore. Auerbach had been confident that Moore would sign on the dotted line ('You don't run away from success') but Broccoli initially found persuading his star difficult. Auditions with possible replacements were once more undertaken (American actor James Brolin was, at one stage, considered a likely 007) before Moore successfully negotiated a seven-figure salary of $4 million plus a percentage of profits. 'I always say I don't want to do another Bond film just before we start negotiating my fee for the next one,' Moore later claimed. 'It's part of the poker game I play with Cubby Broccoli . . .'

As well as growing concerns about his age, the 54-year-old Moore also expressed frustrations that echoed those of his most famous predecessor: 'The real drawback to acting Bond is that it's not acting. You are just a comic-strip hero, the central figure around which the action and the gadgets revolve. Bond is exactly the same in the last scene as he is in the first. I'm not saying I'm the world's greatest actor, far from it, but I do enjoy acting.'

Following reassurance that he was home and dry with his distributor and his star, Broccoli's anxiety over his third challenge would not dissipate so quickly. After a protracted development stretching back to 1976, Kevin McClory had finally succeeded in mounting the first 'rogue' Bond film since *Casino Royale* – and persuaded Sean Connery to reprise the role he'd once claimed he'd left behind for good. Principal photography on McClory's new version of the *Thunderball* story, *Never Say Never Again*, would overlap with filming on *Octopussy*. Two Bond films, and two James Bonds, were going head-to-head. If Broccoli harboured any serious concerns over whether his film would come off worse, he kept them to himself.

Although its title came from an Ian Fleming short story posthumousy published in book form in 1966, *Octopussy*'s screenplay referred to events in the original text in a historical context only, as part of a told tale in which Bond permits Octopussy's gold-thieving father, Major Dexter-Smythe, a noble demise. The only other obvious Fleming input to the story comes during the scene in which

Bond inflates the London auction price of a Fabergé egg versus associates of the KGB, a scene drawn from the *Octopussy* collection's *The Property of a Lady* (the title – part of the auction catalogue – is ostentatiously positioned within the screenplay, too). The first draft of *Octopussy* was delivered shortly after the release of *For Your Eyes Only* and written by Bond newcomer George MacDonald Fraser. Best-known as the author responsible for the seven *Flashman* novels, Fraser had also contributed screenplays to such films as Richard Lester's *The Three Musketeers* (1974) and Guy Hamilton's *Force Ten From Navarone* (1978). Fraser's *Octopussy* script, written in association with John Glen and Albert Broccoli, was later squeezed out when Richard Maibaum and Michael G. Wilson collaborated on two treatments that were ultimately developed into a finished screenplay.

'None of that space colony crap . . .'

'We're sticking to the format that we've come back to, using more or less *From Russia With Love* for style,' Glen told *Starlog* magazine. 'We're staying with that straight-down-the-line narrative. We are not cheating. We will not press a button and have a miracle happen. Bond will have to do it for real, and he might have to suffer.'

'There's none of that space colony crap like they had in *Moonraker*,' concurred a more succint Richard Maibaum, who added: '*Octopussy* owes very little to the book and it's the least gadgety of any of the films . . . It's nothing like anything ever written by Ian Fleming.' Glen's enthusiasm for the Fleming texts and Maibaum's apparent dismissal of their influence on the latest project may go some way towards explaining the disparity of direction represented in different elements of the finished film.

'Just a comic strip hero . . .'

The deadly octopus of Fleming's short story had been replaced by the seductive head of a gang of sometimes-criminal Amazons. Albert Broccoli cast Maud Adams in the title role after a chance reunion with the Swedish actress on a plane flight. Adams' career had benefited from her appearance in *The Man With the Golden Gun*, and she'd gone on to make notable appearances in *Rollerball*, *Killer Force* (both 1975) and *Playing For Time* (1980). Her co-starring credit in *Octopussy* distinguished her as the only actress to feature so prominently in two Bond films. French actor Louis Jourdan could already boast of over 40 years' film experience before he was cast as Kamal Khan. His notable American films had included *Three Coins in the Fountain* (1954), *Gigi* (1958) and *The VIPs* (1963). His performance in the title role of BBC television's *Dracula* (1977), an acclaimed and faithful adaptation directed by Philip Saville, was one of the highlights of his career. Swedish actress and athlete Kristina Wayborn first came to Broccoli's attention playing Greta Garbo in a television biography. As Magda, she eagerly performed some of the character's less dangerous stunts herself. Davis Cup tennis star Vijay Amitraj played Bond's Indian ally Vijay, and Michaela Clavell, daughter of Shogun novelist James, played Miss Moneypenny's glamorous young assistant Penelope Smallbone. (One of the Bond series' legendary out-takes features Lois Maxwell introducing Roger Moore to the secretary

as 'Miss Smallbush'.) Never to reappear, the character shared her name with the model who appeared in Maurice Binder's *For You Eyes Only* title sequence.

Following an inauspicious screen debut in the little-seen Hammer support feature *Slave Girls* (1967), Steven Berkoff had worked steadily in films from Kubrick's *A Clockwork Orange* (1971) onwards. Although frequently expressing contempt for the medium and its hangers-on, Berkoff saw his film work as a lucrative sideline to his innovative stage work. The founder of the acclaimed London Theatre Group, Berkoff continues to essay numerous villains in films of variable quality. He can be seen in *Beverly Hills Cop* (1984), *Rambo* (1985) and *Fair Game* (1995). His crazed General Orlov in *Octopussy* was one of the highlights of the picture, and the first in a number of similarly fanatical Soviet renegades to appear in the Bond series thereon.

Shooting began with the second unit photography of Bond's mid-flight struggle with Kamil Khan's henchman Gobinda outside Khan's plane. Stuntman Jake Lombard (doubling for Roger Moore) and sequence supervisor BJ Worth (doubling for Kabir Bedi) had previously appeared in *Moonraker*, where they had taken part in the memorable pre-credits sequence. Only master shots were completed during this initial shoot – back projection close-ups of Moore and Bedi were completed at Pinewood during the last ten days of studio photography in 1983.

First unit photography began at Checkpoint Charlie in Berlin on Tuesday 10 August. The first scene in the can was M's briefing of 007 – Robert Brown replaced the late Bernard Lee as Bond's superior. (Brown and Moore had first worked together over 20 years before, when Brown had played Squire Gurth to Moore's Ivanhoe.)

On Monday 16 August shooting began at Pinewood. British locations included the Nene Valley steam railway in Peterborough, where the international array of privately owned locomotives helped disguise the Cambridgeshire location with little more than a lick of paint. The nearby Wansford Junction doubled as Karl Marx Stadt. At RAF Upper Heyford near Oxford, exterior shots of Octopussy's circus tents and animals were filmed; the base was also dressed as the USAF base at Feldstadt, West German,y that 007 gatecrashes in his rush to defuse Orlov's atomic bomb.

The lengthy pre-credits sequence, in which an undercover Bond is discovered at a South American military base and makes his escape from heat-seeking missiles aboard a one-man jet, was filmed at RAF Northolt, 15 miles west of London. Such a jet had originally been scripted to appear in an early draft of *Moonraker*, and used by Bond as a means of escaping Drax's headquarters. The Bede jet used in *Octopussy* was one of only two in existence, and named Acrostar. Its owner, pilot 'Corkey' Fornof, flew the plane on Roger Moore's behalf.

On 12 September, location photography began at Udaipur – 'City of Sunrise' – in Rajestan, India. The majestic Lake Palace Hotel, on Lake Pichola, was used as Octopussy's island retreat. The distinctive three-wheeled taxis seen in a chase sequence were replicated at Pinewood, where production designer Peter Lamont oversaw construction of six identical, and expendable, vehicles. For Lamont, the construction of Octopussy's ornate

At RAF Upper Heyford near Oxford, Roger Moore appears at a photocall with some of the girls from Octopussy's International Circus. Mary Stavin (left) was a former Miss World; Carolyn Seaward (right) had been a runner-up

ceremonial barge was the greatest challenge, and the result of cannibalising two dilapidated barges the production team discovered at Bombay. Stifling heat added to Roger Moore's ordeal – on occasions, a clean white shirt was required from shot to shot – and a stomach infection that stayed with the actor on his return to England added to his discomfort.

Following completion of the Indian shoot, filming continued at Pinewood until 24 December. The expansive 007 stage was put to use as the courtyard of Kamal's palace. Following a Christmas break, Moore returned on 3 January 1983. Towards the end of the studio shoot, he would reportedly meet Sean Connery (who was shooting *Never Say Never Again* at Elstree) for dinner – evidence that a personal rivalry between the two Bonds was mere speculation on the part of an over-imaginative press. Moore completed *Octopussy* on 21 January.

Composer John Barry asked Tim Rice, who had written the lyrics for such stage phenomena as *Jesus Christ Superstar* and *Evita*, to collaborate on the film's theme. Working to a stipulation that Barry's music should not be accompanied by a song actually entitled 'Octopussy', Rice composed 'All Time High', and suggested Elaine Page as vocalist. Shirley Bassey was later considered, but the song was finally offered to Nashville-born Rita Coolidge. The theme would reach number 75 in the British chart, and number 36 in America. 'I don't think the record would have been any bigger had anyone else done it, or any smaller,' reflects Rice, who is the owner of an award commemorating the tune's one million radio plays. The song was immortalised on certain film posters, proclaiming *Octopussy* as 'James Bond's All Time High!'

'Autumnal, mellow, clubbable . . .'

The Prince and Princess of Wales attended the premiere of *Octopussy* at the Leicester Square Odeon on 6 June 1983; the film earned a record-breaking £426,773 at the box office in its first five weeks of release. A diminished worldwide gross of $183,700,000 failed to reflect the American audiences' appreciative response: approximate US admissions of 25.5 million – equal to those of *Moonraker* – were the joint highest enjoyed by Moore's Bond.

'It's part parody and part travesty, and it's amiably fatigued,' claimed a disapproving Pauline Kael in the New York *Times*, in response to the film's American release on 10 June. 'It's not the latest-model Cadillac; it's a beat-up old Cadillac, kept running with junkyard parts . . . The director, John Glen, seems to lose track of the story, and

neither he nor the writers appear to have thought out the women's roles.'

'Later in the year Sean Connery steps into the hand-made shoes in *Never Say Never Again*,' anticipated the *Glasgow Herald*'s Lindsay Mackie. 'Maybe Connery will bring his sense of menace to the screen, but Moore is playing it autumnal, mellow, clubbable.'

Following *Octopussy*'s lucrative release, Eon's thoughts turned not to its immediate follow-up, but its immediate competition. *Never Say Never Again* was in the can, and awaiting a Warner Bros release. 'We have the established Bond,' asserted a cool Michael G. Wilson. 'They have to establish theirs.'

File: *Octopussy*

Teaser Discounting the almost suffocating smugness of the final line – Bond, in a tiny mini-jet, taxis into a remote petrol station and demands 'Fill her up' – then this is very, very good indeed. Set in an un-named South American republic – given the producers' propensity for quietly skimming the Zeitgeist, dare we suggest that it's intended to be Argentina, in 1982 a target for proletarian opprobrium following the Falklands/Malvinas dispute – Bond disguises himself as one Colonel Toro and breaks into a military airbase, intending to detonate a bomb. He's captured, but escapes both with the aid of a sultry lovely and inside a miniature aircraft; fired on by heat-seeking missiles, he pilots the jet back through the complex and uses the missiles to destroy the base itself. We cannot, however, fail to record the unfortunate fact that Bond's mini-jet is disguised as a horse's arse. No, really. **8**

Titles A Bond silhouette flings nude women about would-be balletically. Bored and aloof blue-lit girls pose, their curves like mountain ranges, while a stylised neon Bond stencil glides over their bodies. Nothing special. **4**

Bonkers plot In East Berlin, 009 is mortally wounded by a knife-throwing circus performer, but crosses the border and dies in the West, an immensely valuable Fabergé egg on his person. Bond is sent on the trail of the egg, which – like other art treasures – has been smuggled out of Russia at the bidding of one General Orlov, a fanatical near-Blimpish malcontent dismayed by his fellow Soviets' lack of crusading zeal. The treasures are being laundered by exiled Afghan prince Kamal Khan with the aid of the reclusive Octopussy and her sisterhood of drop-outs, some of whom are involved in a travelling circus used to smuggle the goods. But Khan is helping Orlov to detonate an atomic bomb inside an American airbase in West Germany, using a performance by Octopussy's circus as cover; Orlov intends that this supposed 'nuclear accident' will force the Americans out of Europe, enabling the Red Army to trample all over the continent. To confuse matters further, Octopussy is the daughter of a man whom Bond had encountered many years before; she, it transpires, knows nothing of the bomb plot. There are several stories here, some better than others. The Orlov strand is satisfyingly megalomanic, even if his methodology seems a little awry; can he guarantee US withdrawal from Europe following the 'disaster', for example? (This could easily be fixed, perhaps by a pre-credits scene in which Bond helps avert a genuine accident, and leading to a Brussels scene in which the US are told that should any such near-catastrophe occur again, they'll be forced out of the continent.) As it is, it seems almost wishful thinking on Orlov's part. Still, he is mad. So that's all right, then. There are real problems elsewhere: why the fake eggs if Orlov can supply real treasures such as the Romanoff star? Where does Orlov's nuclear bomb come from? What, precisely, is the nature of his agreement with Khan? Does Khan share Orlov's desires, or is he motivated purely by money? Is Octopussy smuggling the jewellery into the West knowingly (she claims not to know anything of it to Bond, but later appears to be fully aware of what's going on)? Is Octopussy to go unpunished simply because the bad guy double-crosses her? Octopussy's core story, however grandiose – it is indeed a Bond-style plot – gets bogged down in nebulous intrigue; too much cloak and dagger, way too little down-the-line exposition. (While writing this book, someone asked us what Octopussy was actually about. We were stumped.) **3**

Locations A South American airbase; East Berlin; West Berlin; London; Moscow; around and above a water-edged Indian city (Udaipur?); rail sidings near Karl Marx Stadt, East Germany; a circus at an airbase in Feldstadt, West Germany. There's plenty to see, and the Indian sequences are largely beautiful – but are hampered by sudden night-to-day jumps and, later, parts of the outside of Kamal's palace being clearly built in studio. **5**

Gadgets Bond's bomb-in-a-briefcase; a horsebox concealing a miniature plane; a supercharged Indian three-wheeled cab; a fake crocodile suit-cum-sub, which conjures up images of *Goldfinger*'s teaser. Q department turn up an ascending Indian rope trick, a spiked door, a homing device inside a Fabergé egg which enables Bond to track the egg's progress via a high-tech wristwatch, and a fountain pen which releases a flow of acid (Bond's subsequent remark regurgitates the 'poison pen' gag poured scorn upon in *Casino Royale*). The Thugs' lethal steel yo-yo is probably the scariest weapon ever seen in the series. **6**

Girls Pre-credits flirt Bianca, whom Bond promises to see in Miami. Penelope Smallbone, Moneypenny's 'new assistant'. Rublevitch makes her last appearance in the series, whispering messages in Orlov's ear. Pickpocket and gymnast Magda – 'Now there's a lady' – who, in bed, tells Bond that she needs 'refilling' (she appears to be Kamal's consort for a while, but reverts to being just another one of Octopussy's girls in the finale). A suggestive Assistant Manager at Bond's Indian hotel. And Octopussy herself, a jewel-smuggler who's diversified into 'shipping, hotels, carnivals and circuses' and who lives with her 'girls' in a floating palace. In Sri Lanka, Bond allowed her father, a gold thief and leading expert on octopi, to commit suicide rather than face a court-martial, for which she is grateful; now, Octopussy sees herself and Bond as 'two of a kind', for no readily explicable reason. She even offers him a job. Her girls, some of whom wear red uniforms, include Gwendoline and Midge; all are international waifs and strays. Bond pulls only Magda and Octopussy. **7**

Villains Col. Toro and cohorts. Mischka and Grischka, two identical knife-throwing twins who appear to be part of Octopussy's circus, but act on Khan and Orlov's instructions. The shaven-headed General Orlov, a strutting, gesturing, posturing and pompous Communist zealot delighted/disgusted by the political progress made by

Roger Moore as a disguised Bond, between takes on 007's attempt to locate and disarm Orlov's hidden bomb

a tiny moment where – for a fraction of a second – it seems as though the car isn't going to start. In that moment, Louis Jourdan's reaction is sublime. Kamal's lieutenant is the blunderbuss-wielding Gobinda (similarly, there's a very funny scene right at the end where Kamal orders Gobinda to go outside his in-flight plane and deal with Bond, who's hanging off the wing. 'Out there?' asks Gobinda, eyes wide as if to say 'Are you mad?'). Mufti and his hired Thugs. Oh, and Octopussy, sort-of- maybe (see Bonkers plot above). **5**

Fights, chases, explosions The South American airbase explosion is truly enormous, but later sequences – the tussle between Bond, Gobinda and one of the twins on the roof of Octopussy's train, and the climactic struggle on the wing of Kamal's jet – seem rather old hat. The car running on rails is outrageous – and all the better for it, too. **5**

Dialogue and double entendres Moneypenny to Penelope, when Bond offers the latter a bouquet of flowers: 'Take it, dear. That's all you'll ever get from him.' Kamal 'suggests a trade. The egg for your life'; replies Bond, 'I'd heard the price of eggs was going up, but isn't that a little high?' A bedraggled Bond, hauled up aboard a tourist ferry having just escaped Kamal's 'hunt', is asked by a sightseer 'Are you with our group?' 'No, I'm with the economy tour,' he replies. Q, waiting on the river's edge for Bond: '007 on an island populated exclusively by women? We won't see him 'til dawn.' And Bond to Q, inside a balloon: 'I trust you can handle this contraption, Q?' 'It goes by hot air,' announces Q proudly. 'Oh, then you can,' smirks Bond. (The latter may be forced and completely pointless, but it is nothing less than brilliant.) **5**

Bond Ends up in traction. Wears a creeping caterpillar across his top lip as part of his Colonel Toro disguise. Knows a lot about Fabergé eggs. Plays backgammon (and the way in which he announces his double six without even looking at the die to confirm is very, very cool). He does, however, demonstrate a patronising and imperialist streak: 'Keep you in curry for a few weeks, won't it?' he says while tipping an Indian cashier. His reaction upon being served 'stuffed sheep's head' is wrong; a gourmand like Bond should relish the prospect, not flinch in disgust. Appears to have a sixth sense for danger; as the Thugs

pressure groups such as CND ('The West is decadent and divided. It has no stomach to risk our atomic reprisals. All through Europe daily demonstrations demand their unilateral nuclear disarmament . . .'). Ends up shot in the back by Gogol's troops while trying to flee to the West, believing that he will go down as 'a hero of the Soviet Union'. Kamal, formerly an Afghan prince, now a seller of goods of dubious provenance. Hunts, plays 'Polo, cricket, tennis' and cheats at backgammon ('It's all in the wrist'), 'lives like a Maharajah', owns a Rolls and a private jet. Knows a great deal about truth-begetting drugs. When he and Gobinda get into their car, ready to drive away from the base they've left a ticking atomic bomb inside, there's silently sneak up on Octopussy's island, he wakes, dresses and stands by the window. 'Something wrong?' asks Octopussy. 'Not really. Just a feeling,' he replies. **4**

Plus/minus points The Soviet war room is an art direction triumph; high, clinically white and featuring a vast map of the world with key areas coloured blood red towards which the huge conference table revolves in its entirety (and note how Orlov's address, once the lights are dimmed, becomes like something out of *Dr. Strangelove, Or...*). Steven Berkoff is superbly disassociated and manic as Orlov, both in his scenes with Walter Gotell's General Gogol (now a sage conciliator) and Moore. Again, the film's not entirely original: the spider webs Bond blunders into are out of *Raiders of the Lost Ark*, the scene where oil from the yo-yo drips onto Bond's face, alerting him to the fact that an assassin lies above his and Octopussy's bed, is much like the death of Aki in *You Only Live Twice*, the face-hugging octopus shares that habit with Ridley Scott's *Alien*, and Bond's trick of tilting a car onto two wheels was first seen in *Diamonds Are Forever*. Things we loathe: a snake charmer playing Monty Norman's James Bond theme; a camel doing a single take; the fakir's crudely subtitled outburst 'GET OFF MY BED'; Bond creating a stampede by flinging rupees in the air, thus escaping Gobinda (which is nothing short of contemptible); Bond using a video camera to zoom in upon a technician's heaving cleavage ('I haven't time for these adolescent antics,' says Q. We wholeheartedly agree); Bond telling a wild tiger to 'Si-it!' (a reference to the septuagenarian star of BBC television's *Training Dogs the Woodhouse Way*); Bond's Tarzan howl; Q's Union Jack balloon. Oh, and there's a really strange moment following the killing of Vijay by yo-yo: Q tells Bond that 'He was alive when I found him.' Are we supposed to infer that cuddly old Q could bring himself to put Vijay out of his misery? **-9**

43% Like the Fabergé eggs so key to its narrative, *Octopussy* is gilded in glitter and tinsel – but, unlike those treasures, reveals only a gapingly hollow interior. It's not quite as shallow as it appears – the Orlov storyline is immensely striking, as is the clever and tense black farce of the scenes in which Bond, dressed as a clown, attempts to stop the bomb in the circus from going off – but great moments do not make this largely indifferent and sometimes very bad film whole.

CAST

Roger Moore James Bond
Maud Adams Octopussy **Louis Jourdan** Kamal **Kristina Wayborn** Magda
Kabir Bedi Gobinda **Steven Berkoff** Orlov **David Meyer** Twin One
Anthony Meyer Twin Two **Desmond Llewelyn** 'Q' **Robert Brown** 'M'
Lois Maxwell Miss Moneypenny **Michaela Clavell** Penelope Smallbone
Walter Gotell Gogol **Vijay Amitraj** Vijay **Albert Moses** Sadruddin
Geoffrey Keen Minister of Defence **Douglas Wilmer** Fanning **Andy Bradford** 009
Philip Voss Auctioneer **Bruce Boa** U.S. General **Richard Parmentier** U.S. Aide
Paul Hardwick Soviet Chairman **Suzanne Jerome** Gwendoline
Cherry Gillespie Midge **Dermot Crowley** Kamp **Peter Porteous** Lenkin
Eva Reuber-Staier Rublevitch **Jeremy Bullock** Smithers **Tina Hudson** Bianca
William Derrick Thug with Yo-yo **Stuart Saunders** Major Clive
Patrick Barr British Ambassador **Gabor Vernon** Borchoi **Hugo Bower** Karl
Ken Norris Colonel Toro **Tony Arjuna** Mufti **Gertan Klauber** Bubi
Brenda Cowling Schatzl **David Grahame** Petrol Pump Attendant
Brian Coburn South American V.I.P. **Michael Halphie** South American Officer
Roberto Germains Ringmaster **Richard Graydon** Francisco the Fearless
Gary Russell Youth in Sports Car*.

SELECTED CREDITS

Costume supervisor **Tiny Nicholls**
Assistant art directors **Ernie Archer**, **Jim Morahan**, **Fred Hole**
Special effects supervisor **John Richardson** Camera operator **Alec Mills**
Continuity **Elaine Schreyeck** Action sequences arranged by **Bob Simmons**
Driving stunts arranged by **Remy Julienne** Art director **John Fenner**
Make-up supervisor **George Frost** Hairdressing supervisor **Christopher Taylor**
Supervising editor **John Grover** Costumes designed by **Emma Porteous**
Casting by **Debbie McWilliams** Director of photography **Alan Hume**
Main title designed by **Maurice Binder** Production designed by **Peter Lamont**
Music composed and conducted by **John Barry**
The Song 'All Time High' performed by **Rita Coolidge**
Music by **John Barry** Lyrics by **Tim Rice**
Associate producer **Tom Pevsner** Executive producer **Michael G. Wilson**
Screen story and screenplay by **George MacDonald Fraser** and
Richard Maibaum & **Michael G. Wilson**
Produced by **Albert R. Broccoli** Directed by **John Glen**

*unaccredited

Legally bona fide: *Never Say Never Again*

1976: The ten-year exclusion period agreed between Kevin McClory and Eon had elapsed, and the Irish producer was once more free to exploit his rights in *Thunderball*. In the peaceful seclusion of County Louth in Eire, McClory had quietly united novelist Len Deighton with none other than Sean Connery, and the three collaborated on a new screenplay with a familiar title – *James Bond of the Secret Service*. Connery approached the script as simply 'an exercise', little imagining that a lengthy train of events had been set in motion – a train of events that would culminate in an astonishing comeback for the actor who had pledged to 'never again' play Bond ...

Brimming with confidence in the screenplay, Kevin McClory placed a full-page advertisement in the 12 May 1976 edition of *Variety*, announcing *James Bond of the Secret Service*, a Paradise Films production (McClory owned a plantation on Paradise Island in Nassau). Shooting was anticipated to commence in the Bahamas in February 1977. Rumours began to circulate: although no announcement had been made concerning a lead actor, or indeed any other casting or technical details, industry pundits tipped Orson Welles to play Blofeld, Trevor Howard to play M, and Richard Attenborough to direct. The title of the Connery/Deighton/McClory screenplay

'Anybody who proceeds does so at legal peril ...'

was later identified as *Warhead*. As far as can be established, Blofeld's *Warhead* caper would have been one of

SPECTRE's most imaginative to date. Working from an undersea base named Aquapolis, the SPECTRE chief would have enforced an order to stem the pollution of the world's oceans by assassinating the politicians he held responsible. SPECTRE's systematic scuppering of planes and boats in the Bermuda Triangle would have netted three nuclear devices, each placed inside specially primed mechanical sharks. Co-ordinated from a base inside the Statue of Liberty, the sharks would first have targeted New York (via the sewers) and then the Antarctic ice cap (thus flooding the planet) if Blofeld's bid for world domination – Operation Hammerhead – met with resistance.

The first indication that the rapidly snowballing project – a serious rival to Eon's forthcoming *The Spy Who Loved Me* (with which it shared, entirely coincidentally, plot elements such as a villain with an underground base and the hijacking of nuclear weapons) – would meet obstruction came in the 30 June edition of *Variety*. In a curt response to a second McClory advertisement, United Artists chairman Arthur Krim laid down the law: 'Danjaq and United Artists are entitled, through the rights granted by Ian Fleming and the Fleming estate, to the exclusive use in the future of the "James Bond – 007" character, except for "Thunderball". The exception as to "Thunderball" is strictly limited to the use of the character in remakes of (films of) the story of "Thunderball", with the right to use the name of the character in the advertising and exploitation of any films of "Thunderball", without the right to use "Thunderball", "James Bond" or "007" in the title, and does not extend one whit beyond this. Accordingly, except as stated above, no person, corporation or entity other than Danjaq and United Artists can use, or grant rights to use, the character "James Bond – 007" in any film which goes beyond the story of "Thunderball", and anybody who proceeds on any other premise does so at legal peril."

Albert Broccoli, United Artists and The Fleming Trust instigated a legal battle to obstruct the progress of the Paradise Films project. Wary of the delicate situation surrounding *Warhead*, Connery remained largely tight-lipped about its development over the coming years.

The laboured progress of *Warhead* continued throughout the remainder of the Seventies. It emerged that McClory had apparently asked Connery to direct the film; incredibly, it also appeared that McClory's potential backers Paramount had requested that Connery be asked to star as Bond. Following much reflection on the possibility, Connery had tacitly agreed.

'Good to see you Mr Bond,' says Algeron the armourer. 'Now you're on this I hope we're going to have some gratuitous sex and violence.'

Paramount were reportedly on the verge of making a 'colossal offer' when *Warhead* seemed to finally run aground. 'I am now awaiting the outcome of the legal problems,' Connery told the 17 December edition of the *Sunday Mirror* in 1978. 'Before I put my nose into anything, I want to know it is legally bona fide.'

By 1980, Connery seemed to have resigned himself to the fact that the legal obstacles were insurmountable. 'When I first worked on the script with Len I had no thought of actually being in the film,' he told the *Sunday Express*' Roderick Mann. 'It wasn't until my wife Micheline suggested it would be fun to try it again that I agreed. But clearly it's not on the cards now.'

McClory had argued that he had collaborated with Fleming on three treatments with Ian Fleming – *Bond in the Bahamas, Latitude 78 West* and *James Bond of the Secret Service*. How, he reportedly asked, could he be tied to a remake of *Thunderball* – a film that had yet to be produced at the time of his Eon settlement?

A breakthrough came in summer 1981 when McClory's pitch came to the attention of Jack Schwartzman, the former executive vice-president of Lorimar Pictures. Schwartzman, an independent producer whose background lay in tax and entertainment law, phoned Connery. 'I discussed the project with Sean and got his understanding that if I could put the elements together, he would be interested in playing Bond again.' Schwartzman struck a deal with McClory for the rights to film a new version of the *Thunderball* story ('I deliberately did not purchase the *Warhead* script,' he said. 'At the time I made my deal, it was the subject of litigation and I didn't want to be tarred with the same brush . . .') and the potential Bond picture fell under the auspices of Taliafilm – the company headed by Francis Coppola's sister Talia Shire Schwartzman.

In a 1981 interview with *Starburst* magazine, Connery seemed flattered when told that John Glen would have welcomed the opportunity to direct Connery in an instalment of the Eon series. He nevertheless reacted cautiously to the prospect of appearing in a new Bond film: 'I wouldn't certainly get my feet wet in that direction again unless I could do it my way.'

When Schwartzman succeeded in disentangling the red tape surrounding Talia's Bond picture he sought a signature from Connery. The star later explained his stipulations to Marjorie Bilbow: 'Primarily the first one was that one was indemnified against any of these law suits that were flying around, and then certainly on the creative side I wanted to be totally protected and I wanted the best cast possible. So I had script approval as well and casting approval, director approval and lighting cameraman . . .' Schwartzman agreed, and reportedly offered Connery a $3 million salary and a percentage of profits. The title of Connery's comeback – which some critics suggested might provide his career with a boost following a recent spate of box-office disappointments – was prompted by Micheline: *Never Say Never Again*.

Working alongside executive producer McClory, Schwartzman commissioned Julien Plowden to write a screenplay carefully tailored around the remake rights available to them. A second screenplay was written by Lorenzo Semple Jr. Semple's previous credits had included episodes of the *Batman* television series, the spy spoof *Fathom* (1967), *Papillon* (1973) and *Flash Gordon* (1980). His script would make an amusing virtue of Bond's advancing years (Connery would have turned 52 by the time filming began).

Philadelphia-born director Irvin Kershner, fresh from a resounding success with *Star Wars* sequel *The Empire Strikes Back* (1980), was asked to meet with Connery and Schwartzman. Kershner, whose previous form (which included Connery's 1966 comedy *A Fine Madness* and the 1978 thriller *The Eyes of Laura Mars*) suggested his skill at characterisation may be in tune with Connery's goals for the film, agreed to direct. 'I went back and re-read Ian Fleming,' he remembered, recounting his preparation. 'I also looked at some of the old films . . . and I realised which ones I liked and which were not up to par – and then I decided to forget I had ever seen any of them. So as far as I am concerned, there was never a Bond picture before. I'm not trying to copy anything.'

Impressed by his compelling lead in the Oscar-winning *Mephisto* (1981), Connery expressed an interest in casting Austrian actor Klaus Maria Brandauer as SPECTRE Number One Largo (renamed Maximilian this time round). 'Klaus Maria Brandauer . . . is unquestionably one of the best actors in Europe if not the world,' said Connery in the film's publicity notes. 'Another of our villains is Max Von Sydow, another very fine actor . . .' Sydow, best-known for his starring role in Ingmar Bergman's 1957 masterpiece *The Seventh Seal*, was approached to play Blofeld, in the character's first legitimate screen appearance since *Diamonds Are Forever*.

Former model and *Playboy* cover girl Barbara Carrera became a full-time actress in 1976 and subsequently appeared in such films as *The Island of Dr Moreau* (1977) and *I, the Jury* (1982). Kershner persuaded her to accept the role of SPECTRE Number Twelve, assassin Fatima Blush (the name was inherited from an early *Thunderball* treatment) before the script had even been completed. To play Domino (surname now Petachi) Micheline Connery suggested Kim Basinger following an encounter with the blonde actress at London's Grosvenor House Hotel.

Basinger, then embarking on a film career that would bring her great recognition during the Eighties, had previously worked mainly in American televison. Felix Leiter was played by black actor Bernie Casey, a former American football player who had made his film debut in *Guns of the Magnificent Seven* (1969) and more recently appeared in Burt Reynolds thriller *Sharky's Machine* (1981). During production, Casey recalled a revealing conversation with Connery: 'He said Felix Leiter has been in all the Bond films he's made, and I said "Really? Which one is he – I don't remember him" . . . He explained that since Felix Leiter is not memorable, let's make him black, and at least that will make him more noticeable and therefore more memorable . . . It changes nothing in the texture of the story. I think it's a nice move.'

Never Say Never Again ushered in an entirely new set of Secret Service office staff – Edward Fox as M (a distinguished stage actor and major star since 1973's *The Day of the Jackal*, Fox was a self-confessed Fleming fan who claimed to have read all the original Bond novels), Alec McCowen as Q/Algernon and Pamela Salem as a hopelessly infatuated Miss Moneypenny. Other notable cast members included Prunella Gee, who had unsuccessfully auditioned for *The Spy Who Loved Me*, as masseuse Patricia Fearing, and television comedian Rowan Atkinson in an early film role as bumbling FO official Nigel Small-Fawcett. Credited only as 'Lady in Bahamas', former Hammer starlet Valerie Leon earned a special distinction – that of appearing in three Bond films as three different, albeit minor, characters. The achievement was made all the more notable by the fact that the three films – *Casino Royale, The Spy Who Loved Me* and *Never Say Never Again* – were

Executive producer Kevin McClory (left) and producer Jack Schwartzman on location in Nassau. Schwartzman later admitted that he had underestimated the scale of Never Say Never Again – he funded the cost of the film's over-runs out of his own pocket

each produced by different companies.

Schwartzman secured a $34 million budget from distributor Warner Bros and shooting began in Nizza, on the French Riviera, on 27 September 1982. Connery held reservations about Semple's script and ongoing revisions were made; together with Kershner he added material himself, but the most significant doctoring was undertaken by television sit-com writers Dick Clement and Ian La Frenais. Connery had requested their input personally, and was especially pleased by the humour they injected into the script. (To his later annoyance, a restriction imposed by the Writers' Guild of America precluded their receiving a credit on the finished film.) Clement and La Frenais later confessed that the 'fill this beaker'/'from here?' gag between Bond and a petite nurse was recycled from their prison sitcom *Porridge*. The largely British crew were based in

Nice, and spent nearly two months in the South of France. Filming took place inside the casino at Monte Carlo, and the Villa Rothschild at Saint-Jean-Cap-Ferrat doubled as Largo's exotic North African home Palmyra. In mid-November 1982 they moved to Nassau in the Bahamas, where filming was at one point concentrated around the *Thunderball* location of Clifton Pier. *Thunderball*'s Ricou Browning had already spent some weeks preparing underwater photography, and would later continue his work in Florida. Connery spent several days filming underwater sequences, although much of the material is apparently absent from the finished print. Bond's simulated rescue of a kidnapped hostage at the beginning of the film was filmed on the Nassau mainland.

By the time the unit had reached the Bahamas the atmosphere had become strained. 'Myself and the assistant director [David Tomblin] produced that picture,' a disgruntled Connery would later claim.

His frustrations were shared by Kershner: 'Jack [Schwartzman] was a very good businessman, but he didn't have the experience of a film producer. He and I had divergent views of what the film should be. I tried to maintain what I could of my vision, but you can only do so much when the studio sides with the producer, whether he's right or wrong.

'The best part was working with Sean and with Klaus. Klaus is a great, great actor and I really wanted a bad guy who was not a usual bad guy with a patch over the eye and a leer. Of course, working with Sean was just a pleasure. But the film was not a happy film – in fact it was a very unhappy film for most of the people working on it. It was disorganised – totally disorganised. Everyone suffered as a result. And, of course, we always had the problem that I [had to] shoot a film that did not impinge on the images or the rights of *Thunderball* the film. I had to stay with the book, but the book was not do-able as a film!'

Towards the end of the schedule in 1983, interiors were filmed at Elstree Studios in Borehamwood, Hertfordshire. Three months of construction work resulted in the expansive 'Well of Allah' underwater cavern and exotic temple seen in the film's climax. British locations included Luton Hoo, which became the palatial Shrublands health farm, and Waddesdon Manor.

Principal photography was completed, over schedule and over budget, by spring 1983, although minor additional photography was undertaken during the summer. The score – later criticised as anachronistic and misjudged – was written by Oscar-winning *Thomas Crown Affair* composer Michel Legrand. Schwartzman had originally wanted James Horner to compose the film's musicc, but had been over-ruled.

Whether the delay that bumped the film from a summer to a winter release was down to legal or logistic reasons is unknown, but it is likely that both *Octopussy* and *Never Say Never Again* benefited from the breathing space between them. Unprecedented anticipation for a Bond film built up the American premiere of *Never Say Never Again* on 7 October 1983. The film's opening weekend reaped almost $9 million, a significant improvement on *Octopussy*'s $8 million. In London, the film premiered at the Warner West End on Wednesday 14 December 1983. Special guest Prince Andrew rubbed shoulders with Kershner, McClory, Sean Connery and brother Neil, as well as former Bond girl Barbara Bach and her husband Ringo Starr. *Octopussy*'s six-month lead may have been a contributory factor in *Never Say Never Again*'s significantly weaker worldwide grosses: US domestic rentals of $28,200,000 – compared to *Octopussy*'s $34,031,196 would nevertheless not be bettered in that key market until *GoldenEye* in 1995.

'Unapologetic about the unlikeable facets of 007 . . .'

'As opulently mounted as the mainline series entries . . . [*Never Say Never Again*] marks something of a retreat from the far-fetched technology of many of the later Bonds in favor [sic] of intrigue and romance,' remarked *Variety*'s 'Cart'. 'What clicks best in the film is the casting. A recurrent problem in some recent Bonds has been a confusion and softening of the villainy, as well as a reluctance to make the femmes real real bad girls. In this line, Klaus Maria Brandauer . . . makes one of the best Bond opponents since very early in the series.'

The British press welcomed Connery back with open arms: 'He is unapologetic about the unlikeable facets of 007,' noted David Castel in the *Sunday Telegraph*. 'In other hands these have been allowed to soften in ingratiating flippant comedy. It's the first time in a decade that the Bond films have had a new feel and a new look.' *The Guardian*'s Derek Malcolm enjoyed 'the undeniable pleasure in watching Connery traverse the part again, effortlessly suggesting both the arrogance the part needs and the sly humour without which it could so easily become unbearable.'

American critic Roger Ebert best summed up the euphoria felt by enthusiasts who flocked to the second Bond film released during 1983: 'There was never a Beatles reunion. Bob Dylan and Joan Baez don't appear on the same stage anymore. But here, by God, is Sean Connery as Sir James Bond. Good work, 007.'

If anything can be read into Connery's ensuing lay-off – his cameo in *Highlander* would not be seen until 1986 – then the strain of shooting *Never Say Never Again* clearly took its toll. McClory's sporadic *Variety* advertisements are indicative of his continued desire to pursue his stake in the James Bond franchise (most recently, in 1996, he advertised his intention to mount a Bond film entitled *Warhead 2000AD*) but nothing has yet materialised. For Connery, it seems that *Never Say Never Again* really was the final encore. He is now more commonly associated with rumours of a Bond comeback as a villain, rather than the hero that made him famous. 'They've considered me a villain ever since I stopped doing them,' he joked in 1995. 'I'm too old to play Bond. I don't think I would play a villain, unless it was a really marvellous part . . . and $7 million.'

File: *Never Say Never Again*

Teaser In lush foreign climes, Bond storms a rural villa where swarthy no-goods hold a brunette beauty hostage. Having punched, shot, kicked, jumped and swung his way to her bedside, he's in the process of untying her when she stabs him in the chest. Rest easy, however; it's all part of a Secret Service training exercise. Although not a teaser *per se* – the film's opening credits run over the action, and halt before the sequence is over – it's enough of a mini-movie in spirit to qualify with honours. It posits Bond as a one-man army, albeit one who, patently, has not been keeping up with the changing world scene, having failed to learn any lessons from the notorious Patty Hearst debacle of 1974, in which a kidnappee fell spectacularly in with the aims of her kidnappers. Cleverly implicit, therefore, is the question: where's he been for the last ten years or so? Inspired in content, but marred by the inapt, inept and insipid theme song dubbed over most of it. **8**

Titles Row upon row of crude cut-out '007' motifs disappear as the camera zooms into the opening sequence proper above. Anonymous. **0**

Bonkers plot By hooking an army captain on heroin and implanting a fake cornea into his eye, SPECTRE succeed in acquiring the warheads inside two Cruise missiles; one is placed beneath the White House, and the other is to be buried in a subterranean river beneath the oil fields of the Middle East. Blofeld demands a sum equivalent to 25 percent of NATO members' annual oil purchases, threatening to detonate the two devices should he not receive the ransom within one week. A stray book of matches leads Bond to Nassau resident billionaire Maximilian Largo, who is revealed to be the SPECTRE agent managing the whole operation. Although it does plug *Thunderball*'s key problem – that the over-riding threat is neutered by the British Government's intention to pay up – by extending those menaced directly to encompass the whole of NATO, *Never Say Never*'s storyline opens up further gaping holes: the story of the Washington bomb, for example, is related entirely at second-hand, and we're not told how SPECTRE pull off this considerable feat at all. The 'tears of Allah' pendant, disclosing the eventual location of the second bomb, is a terribly convenient way for Bond to save the day – is it an ancient artefact that tells Largo of the existence of the well in the first place (unlikely, given that we're told it's pretty much worthless), or does he have it made up (even more unlikely. What is it, an *aide-memoire*)? And why give it to Domino? Whatever, it's a plot device straight out of the Ark (that is, of course, *Raiders of the Lost Ark* …) **7**

Locations A villa, somewhere, maybe South America; Secret Service HQ, somewhere, maybe London; health spa Shrublands, somewhere in rural England; SPECTRE HQ, somewhere, maybe a continental city (Paris?); an American air base, somewhere in England; in and around Nassau, the Bahamas; the Riviera, somewhere in the South of France; Largo's retreat somewhere off the coast of North Africa; ancient underground caverns not very far away from Middle Eastern oil fields. Director Irvin Kershner shows no particular interest in any of these climes, conspicuously avoiding any show of local colour. The picture simply moves from anonymous tourist trap to anonymous tourist trap; perhaps this, more than almost any other characteristic, differentiates *Never Say Never* most from every film in the Eon series. The geography's screwy, too. A shame. **1**

Gadgets Blofeld has an *objet d'art* skull concealing a TV camera. The corneal recognition system used to commence the warhead arming process at the airbase is

way ahead of its time (albeit ridiculously impractical, the 'logic' being that the US President has to fly to England if he wants to start a nuclear war). Fatima deposits cute little radio-controlled bombs all over the place, and uses an electronic attractor to signal a shark to eat Bond. Q, aka Algernon, is a oikish, troglodytic sinusitis sufferer: he gives Bond a Union Jack pen which fires an exploding nib, and something that 'looks like a watch, but it's really a laser'. Largo's game, Domination (basically Battleships through Risk) causes its players unspecified, possibly fatal, pain. The American XT-7Bs, platform versions of *Thunderball*'s jet packs. All a bit token, and none come across as especially thought through. **5**

Girls The 'hostage'. Miss Moneypenny is a smart brunette with a prim dicky-bow, and although wide-eyed, naive and perhaps a little bit dumb ('Ooh … do be careful,' she says, clasping her hands together when Bond tells her that he has to 'eliminate all free radicals') she's rather more forward than we've come to expect ('You should be in bed,' Bond tells her late at night. 'James, we *both* should be,' she replies). A cute little nurse at Shrublands who wants Bond to fill her beaker. The endlessly fascinating Fatima Blush is SPECTRE's Number Twelve, and she's a cruel, vain, sexually voracious and quite demented killer

Kim Basinger, as Domino, in conference with director Irvin Kershner. The actress would later star in 9½ Weeks and My Stepmother Is An Alien

(watch her reaction in the casino scene after Largo gives her another chance to kill Bond; like a smitten young bride she skips downstairs, letting her hair down and humming gaily). Has a pet python which she wraps round her neck and kisses, and keeps a syringeful of heroin in the garter she wears, *Carry On/St Trinian's* style, beneath a nurse's uniform. She water-skis, scuba-dives and shows a penchant for dangerous driving. Like a black widow, Fatima demonstrates a desire to consume (or worse) her mate after coupling ('Spread your legs,' she tells Bond when she finally has him at gunpoint. 'You're quite a man...But I am a superior woman. Guess where you get the first one ...'). She dresses like Cruella de Vil and the last sign of her passing, like the Wicked Witch of the West, is a pair of smoking, teetering heels and naught else. White-coated and dyed-blonde physiotherapist Patricia Fearing, despite being aware of Bond's 'reputation', offers him after-hours service on a plate. The 'Lady in Bahamas' who, in a good-natured little gag, reels in Bond. Nicole, a French agent numbered 326, who does little other than get drowned by Fatima. And high-kicking, legwarmer-clad *Fame*-type Domino Petachi, who seems terribly amused to discover that she's been indecently assaulted by a man posing as her masseur, and ends up stripped to her scanties and auctioned off to swarthy Arabs *à la* wartime comic strip heroine *Jane*. Domino may be a little underdeveloped (as it were), but Bond's tally here hits a magnificent four (Patricia, the Lady in Bahamas, Fatima and Domino). **10**

Villains Blofeld, now a dapper and seemingly benign old gent with a tidy beard and a taste not for clinical, high-tech decor but elegant chintz. SPECTRE Number One, the Bucharest-born Maximilian Largo, is an industrialist worth $2.482 billion, a philanthropist with an interest in orphans, an amateur marine archaeologist with 'the biggest boat in the Caribbean', a helicopter pilot, a muzak-loving voyeur who builds two-way mirrors in gyms, and a computer games designer, too. 'He's certifiable,' Bond tells Domino – and, by God, he's right: Klaus Maria Brandauer's Largo is a manically determined, pathologically venomous pop-eyed loon prone to chilling mood swings. When Domino casually asks 'What if I leave you?' he bursts out laughing, mugs to the camera, baldly, states 'Then I cut your throat' – and smiles again. When he finds out that Domino might do just that, he smashes up the ship's gym

with a fire axe; later, he forces himself upon her, kissing her like a headbutt (and when their lips disentangle, his drool hangs between them). A very scary man indeed. His henchmen include man-mountain Lippe, whom dumb-bells bounce off. **10**

Fights, chases, explosions Bond's punch-up at Shrublands with Largo's thug Lippe passes through a roomful of TV viewers cheering on some sports event, none of whom notice the real action going on behind. Not a very action-packed film by Bond standards – the tremendous teaser, a motorcycle chase and a (very good) stunt on horseback notwithstanding – and the final tussle underwater between Bond and Largo is all rather timid. **8**

Dialogue and double entendres 'Oh! You're Mr Bond,' exclaims physio Pat. 'I believe I'm having you in half an hour.' 'Shplendid [sic]!' replies Bond, effortlessly roguish. 'Your room or mine?' The film displays a certain wry, revisionist cynicism – 'Apart from those present in this room, the information resides only with the CIA and British Intelligence,' M tells a gung-ho US military bigwig. 'Wonderful!' snarls the latter, sarcastically. 'That means by now it's all over the Kremlin!' – and Small-Fawcett's assessment of Largo effectively parodies the imperialist streak still germane to the Bond series nearly two decades on from the death of Churchill: 'he's charming ... I mean, *foreign*, but charming nonetheless.' And many more: 'Do I look like the sort of man who'd make trouble?'/'Frankly, yes – and you'll jeopardise the tourist trade if you start going around killing people ...';'I've made you all wet!'/'Yes, but my Martini's still dry ...';'You know that making love to Fatima was the greatest pleasure of your life'/'Well, there *was* this girl in Philadelphia ...' Best of all is Q/Algy's glorious metatextual eulogy for Connery-Bond: 'Good to see you, Mr Bond. Things have been awfully dull round 'ere. Bureaucrats running the 'ole place, everything done by the book, can't make a decision unless the computer gives you the go-ahead ... Now you're on this, I hope we're going to have some gratuitous sex and violence.' **10**

Bond Always has a Martini at five. Packs a suitcase stuffed with goodies – 'Beluga caviare, quail's eggs, vodka, *foie gras* – Strasbourg' – in case of emergencies at Shrublands. His urine has an acid effect. Dances an excellent tango with Domino, and gives away an amazing $267,000 for the pleasure (we only hope she was worth it). Begins the film marginalised and ends it claiming to be retired – M fearing for the security of the free world unless he returns to the Service. That's the way to do it. Minus one point for winking to camera. **9**

Plus/minus points Edward Fox makes a brilliantly stuffy, silly-arse stuffed shirt M – a long way away from Fleming's admirable Admiral, but valid and funny nonetheless. Clever cross-cutting in the scene where Fatima attempts to blow up Bond in his bed makes for a memorable set piece. The scene in which Bond persuades a terrified bouncer that the cigar case he has been forced to hold is a bomb that will go off should the bouncer make any lateral movement is uproarious. Sadly, Rowan Atkinson helps muff the film's final moments with his cretinous and deeply unfunny Small-Fawcett. The last line should be a triumphant, punch-your-arm-in-the-air moment, but it's just plain cheesy. **+6**

74% The most American-influenced of all Bond films – revealed in its clear lack of interest in travelogue, its quietly savage depiction of Britons as insignificant buffoons, the classless psychopath it takes for its villain – *Never Say Never Again* might be an extravagant way to cock a snoot, but succeeds in making great mileage out of Bond himself (something which, at the time, the Eon series was finding increasingly hard). Although it's dated surprisingly badly (Domino's legwarmers, the Domination game), it's a different enough take on sibling *Thunderball* to more than justify its existence. A minor triumph.

CAST

Sean Connery James Bond
Klaus Maria Brandauer Largo   **Max Von Sydow** Blofeld   **Barbara Carrera** Fatima
Kim Basinger Domino   **Bernie Casey** Leiter   **Alec McCowen** 'Q' Algy
Edward Fox 'M'   **Pamela Salem** Miss Moneypenny   **Rowan Atkinson** Small-Fawcett
Valerie Leon Lady in Bahamas   **Milow Kirek** Kovacs   **Pat Roach** Lippe
Anthony Sharp Lord Ambrose   **Prunella Gee** Patricia   **Gavan O'Herlihy** Jack Petachi
Ronald Pickup Elliott   **Robert Rietty**, **Guido Adorni** Italian Ministers
Vincent Marzello Culpepper   **Christopher Reich** Number 5
Billy J. Mitchell Captain Pederson   **Manning Redwood** General Miller
Anthony Van Laast Kurt   **Saskia Cohen Tanugi** Nicole
Sylvia Marriott French Minister   **Dan Mearden** Bouncer at Casino
Michael Medwin Doctor at Shrublands   **Lucy Hornak** Nurse at Shrublands
Derek Deadman Porter at Shrublands   **Joanna Dickens** Cook at Shrublands
Tony Aileff Auctioneer   **Paul Tucker** Ship's Steward   **Brenda Kempner** Masseuse
Jill Meagher Receptionist at Health Spa   **John Stephen Hill** Communications Officer
Wendy Leech Girl Hostage   **Roy Bowe** Ship's Captain

SELECTED CREDITS

Underwater sequence directed by **Ricou Browning**   Costume designer **Charles Knode**
Casting **Maggie Cartier**, **Mike Fenton** & **Jane Feinberg** (U.S.)
Supervisor of special visual effects **David Dryer**   Special effects supervisor **Ian Wingrove**
Supervising art director **Leslie Dilley**   Production manager U.K. **John Davis**
Title song sung by **Lani Hall**   Trumpet solo by **Herb Alpert**
Camera operators **Chic Waterson**, **Wally Byatt**   Chief make-up artist **Robin Grantham**
Make-up and hairdresser to Mr Connery **Ilona Herman**   Chief hairdresser **Stephanie Kaye**
Wardrobe supervisor **Ron Beck**   Stunt co-ordinator **Vic Armstrong**
Motorcycle stunts by **Mike Runyard**   Title 'Never Say Never Again' by **Micheline Connery**
Furs & leathers especially designed for Barbara Carrera by **Fendi**
Music by **Michel Legrand**   Lyrics by **Alan** & **Marilyn Bergman**
Supervising film editor **Robert Lawrence**
Production designers **Philip Harrison**, **Stephen Grimes**
Director of photography **Douglas Slocombe B.S.C**
Associate producer **Michael Dryhurst**   Executive producer **Kevin McClory**
Based on an original story by **Kevin McClory**, **Jack Whittingham** & **Ian Fleming**
Screenplay by **Lorenzo Semple, Jr**   Produced by **Jack Schwartzman**
Directed by **Irvin Kershner**

Ready to retire:
A View To a Kill

1983: on 13 December, the day before the British premiere of *Never Say Never Again*, newspaper reports confirmed that Roger Moore had been contracted for another Bond film. The success of *Octopussy* may have been an influence in Eon's decision to persuade the publicly recalcitrant Moore to sign on the dotted line once again. Privately, however, Moore had reportedly reached a new understanding with Albert Broccoli: *From A View To a Kill* would mark his final appearance in his most famous role. In America, the so-called 'battle of the Bonds' had already shown a strong public endorsement of Roger Moore's portrayal. 'That's life isn't it,' director John Glen later observed. 'You don't know you've succeeded until you're ready to retire.'

The self-effacing Moore deflected enquiries over his latest salary and percentage with characteristic humour. 'I'm playing James Bond again because I feel sorry for Cubby,' he joked. 'He'll have a terrible job finding anybody else who will work as cheap as I do.' Moore's later reflections on his long-running portrayal of Bond perhaps betrayed a hint of resignation. 'You develop a persona that audiences accept. James Bond – when you play something that long, you really don't have to learn it. You know the character, you know how

'The very last ones left from the crew of Dr. No . . .'

he's going to react, what he's going to say, what his thoughts are . . . Having established the way you're going to be, you have to stick with it.'

John Glen had originally expressed an interest in working with George MacDonald Fraser once more, but he laid the groundwork for the screenplay that took its name from Ian Fleming's 1960 short story with Richard Maibaum, Michael G Wilson and Albert Broccoli. They decided on the destruction of Silicon Valley as a suitably dramatic premise, and Maibuam and Wilson collaborated on a first draft. Their original idea, to have ruthless tycoon Max Zorin manipulate Halley's Comet into crashing into the area, was soon dropped as the script began to take shape early in 1984.

The actors considered by Eon for recent Bond villains had included Lee Van Cleef and Rutger Hauer – a star of similar, if not greater, stature was chosen to play Max Zorin. Christopher Walken had began his career as an adult film actor in *Me and My Brother* (1968), appeared alongside Sean Connery in *The Anderson Tapes* (1971) and won his greatest acclaim in *The Deer*

Roger Moore, Fiona Fullerton, Tanya Roberts, Alison Doody and Christopher Walken gather around Albert Broccoli to celebrate the re-opening of Pinewood's 007 stage

Hunter (1978), for which he was awarded a Best Supporting Actor Oscar. Subsequent films had included *Heaven's Gate* (1980) and *Pennies From Heaven* (1982).

Tanya Roberts had joined the cast of television detective series *Charlie's Angels* in 1980; Broccoli had seen her in the 1982 film *The Beastmaster* and asked her to audition for the role of Stacey Sutton, the geologist and heiress who becomes Bond's ally in San Francisco. Following her starring role in 1984's *Sheena Queen of the Jungle* Roberts joined the cast of the

renamed *A View To A Kill*. Zorin's mercenary assassin May Day was played by model and disco diva Grace Jones, whose Amazonian physique had first brought her to Eon's attention when she played villainess Zula in *Conan the Destroyer* (1984). Former *Avengers* star Patrick Macnee would politely decline Jones' offer to show him a slice of modern night-life while he was filming his role of thoroughbred expert and undercover chauffeur Sir Godfrey Tibbett. He had been suggested by Roger Moore (Macnee had played Dr Watson to Moore's Great Detective in the 1976 TV movie *Sherlock Holmes in New York*). Moore's recommendation was passed to Albert Broccoli for final approval. 'I wasn't sure how Cubby would react,' remembered Macnee in his autobiography *Blind In One Ear*, 'since I had once berated him for stealing Honor Blackman away from *The Avengers* to play Pussy Galore in *Goldfinger*.' There were evidently no hard feelings.

'That wasn't Bond, those weren't Bond films . . .'

After over 20 years of loyal secretarial service, and a unique claim to have featured in every Eon Bond film, Lois Maxwell appeared as Miss Moneypenny for the last time. She later recalled a touching conversation with her producer that highlighted the remarkable achievement: 'The phone rang and it was Cubby. And he said, "Lois, how are you?" and I said "I'm fine" and so on. And he said, "Do you realise that you and I are the very last ones left from the crew of *Dr. No*? There's just you and I." And I hadn't realised that. And we talked about all our friends who had gone, with great affection. At the end of the conversation he said, "Lois, take very good care of yourself will you," and I promised I would . . .' Broccoli denied Maxwell's request that her character be killed off, and the stalwart secretary was last seen sobbing into a handkerchief, Bond missing presumed dead. Some years later, the original Moneypenny was seen to hand in her resignation to M (played by Terence Connolly) when Maxwell starred in a droll television commercial for the Brook Street Employment Agency.

A major production crisis occurred before the cameras even rolled: the 007 stage at Pinewood was almost entirely destroyed by fire during a blaze that took an hour and-a-half to bring under control on 27 June 1984 – just two weeks before it was due to host shooting on the lavish Ridley Scott film *Legend*. The facility was rapidly rebuilt in time for *A View To a Kill*, and officially reopened on 7 January 1985. At the suggestion of Cyril Howard, Pinewood's managing director, renamed the 'Albert R Broccoli 007 Stage' in honour of a producer who had stayed loyal to the studio for so long.

Two sequences in the script never made the finished print. The first was a slight but amusing scene in which, following his unsuccessful pursuit of May Day in Paris, Bond is seen being released from the cells of a Parisian police station. At the front desk, an aggrieved sergeant (actor Albert Simons was cast) gives back to Bond the possessions obviously confiscated from him earlier – a watch with a garotting wire, a pen which causes paper to combust, and a lighter concealing a miniature oxy-acetelene torch which singes the sergeant's eyebrows. More substantive was the loss of a long sequence in which Q sets his 'snooper' device to eavesdrop on conversations inside Zorin's pumping station; the snooper sees off guard dogs by spraying a foul-smelling liquid over them. When it gets stuck, Q tells Bond that one should 'never desert a fellow agent in the field . . .'

Backed by an estimated budget of $30 million, *A View To a Kill* commenced second unit filming in July 1984. Roger Moore began work on principal photography at Pinewood on 1 August. British locations included Royal Ascot racecourse, a waterlogged quarry in

Wraysbury near Staines and the Amberley Chalk Pits Museum in West Sussex. Macnee recalled that Bond and Tibbett's exploration of the warehouse hidden beneath Zorin's stables was filmed in an eerie automated Renault production plant.

Foreign location work took John Glen's crew to Iceland for the pre-credits sequence and, more prominently, France for memorable sequences including the Eiffel Tower chase between Bond and May Day. For May Day's spectacular evasion of 007, BJ Worth doubled Grace Jones during the parachute jump from the Tower. A number of falls were undertaken to distil a smooth result. Zorin's chateau was Chantilly, a sprawling 18th-century estate.

Approximately a third of the schedule was spent in San Francisco, where the Golden Gate Bridge provided a spectacular backdrop to the film's climax wherein Zorin and Bond, decamped from the former's blimp, struggle atop its highest rafters. *A View To a Kill* wrapped at the 007 stage, where Peter Lamont had constructed the impressively devastated interior of the Zorin mine, in January 1985. Over a hundred stuntmen, an unprecedented figure for a Bond film, had been used throughout. Roger Moore's tenure as James Bond was over.

Reflecting on *A View To a Kill* in 1996, he revealed reservations that may have dampened any feelings of regret: 'I was horrified on the last Bond I did,' he admitted. 'Whole slews of sequences where Christopher Walken was machine-gunning hundreds of people. I said "That wasn't Bond, those weren't Bond films." It stopped being what they were about. You didn't dwell on the blood and the brains spewing all over the place.'

Composer John Barry approached a pop group to collaborate with him on the theme tune. Duran Duran, whose impressive record sales and 'New Romantic' image had brought them recognition on both sides of the Atlantic in the early Eighties, recorded 'A View To a Kill'. On its release in May 1985, the single became the first Bond theme to go to number one in the American Billboard chart. In Britain, it reached number two, accompanied by an inventively edited video that spliced the individual group members into the sequence where Bond pursues May Day through the infrastructure of the Eiffel Tower.

One of the more unusual post-production tasks was the preparation of an on-screen disclaimer distancing the fictional Zorin from any living person or organisation,which ran prior to the film itself. According to a New York *Times* report of 17 May 1985, a memo circulated to MGM/UA employees had advised of the existence of company called 'Zoran', whose activities were 'far removed from fantasy technology or world domination'. The company was Zoran Ladicorbic Limited, run by a fashion designer called Zoran. The newspaper's Janet Maslin decided to ask David Englander, Zoran's counsel, whether he believed the Bond villain had been modelled on the designer. 'It's too soon to say,' Englander jokingly responded. 'I'll have to check with my client as to his extra-curricular activities.'

A View To a Kill opened in America on 24 May 1985. The Prince and Princess of Wales attended the British premiere at the Leicester Square Odeon on Wednesday 12 June. In its first seven days at the venue the film accrued £117,642. Overall US admissions to the film were estimated at 16.6 million – a significant dip from the

25.5 million enjoyed by *Octopussy*. A worldwide gross of $152,400,00 was similarly indicative of the film's downsized appeal.

'Basic problem is on the script level,' claimed *Variety*'s 'Jagr', 'with the intricate plot never offering the mindless menace necessary to propel the plot. First third of the pic is devoted to introduction of characters in a horse-fixing subplot that has no real bearing on the main action . . . Director John Glen . . . has not found the right balance between action and humor [sic] to make the production dangerous fun.'

'On leaving France for San Francisco, the film sighs and dies,' wrote the *Financial Times*' Nigel Andrews. 'Tanya Roberts is the vaporous female interest. Moore masquerades boldly but none too persuasively as a *Financial Times* journalist . . . and the movie only screeches into top gear again with a fight involving hero, villain and an exploding dirigible high above the Golden Gate Bridge. The Bond series must learn some new tricks or trumps if it isn't to become, after 14 outings to date, all formula and no content.'

In the months following the release of *A View To a Kill*, diminished box office returns suggested the formula that had seen Eon through the Seventies and early Eighties may have run its course. Roger Moore's departure offered the opportunity for a timely rethink.

Disco diva, model and actress Grace Jones played Zorin's statuesque henchwoman May Day

File *A View To a Kill*

Teaser On an icy Siberian shore, Bond recovers a microchip from the body of the earlier-felled 003, fending off a party of Russian militiamen in his flight back to a British submarine disguised as an ice floe and helmed by blonde compatriot Kimberley Jones. Although the action sequences break no new ground (we've seen similar in *On Her Majesty's Secret Service*, *The Spy Who Loved Me* and *For Your Eyes Only*) the location chosen is both arresting and well-photographed enough to distinguish itself. Sadly, the scenes are besmirched by the ill-advised use of The Beach Boys' 'California Girls' as an accompaniment to Bond's makeshift employment of a sno-cat's runner for a 'surfboard' – surely the most numbingly crass application of an extraneous pop culture reference in the series. Horrid. **3**

Titles A lowbrow Pirelli calendar/*Penthouse* sub-erotic effort which begins with a busty honey, nails coated in luminous paint, unzipping the front of her anorak to disclose Eon's '007' gun symbol plastered over her cleavage, and continues with shots of naked silhouettes on skis, a sniper rifle's crosshair sights (not what the film's title actually refers to), an ice sculpture melting and frequent cuts to a girl with *Dynasty*-style Big Hair and flames painted around her eyes. Simon Le Bon sings 'Dance into the fire' and – guess what? – a nude girl writhes around in a sheet of flame. And the guns held by the girls are all painted in shocking pinks *et al*, making them look like children's toys. A crude, silly and remarkably dated sequence lacking sense, sensuality, subtlety or even a semblance of style. **2**

Bonkers plot Industrialist Max Zorin assembles an international cartel of microchip manufacturers; Zorin intends to end American domination of the electronics industry by pumping sea water into a section of the San Andreas Fault and thus decimating Silicon Valley, US hub of that very industry. Bond is alerted to Zorin's intentions while investigating how the Russians have managed to duplicate a secret microchip resistant to damage caused by the magnetic pulse of an nuclear explosion; the technology has been leaked to the KGB following Zorin's purchase of the research company that developed the chip. For Zorin's 'Project Main Strike', read 'Operation Grand Slam'; we rate *Goldfinger*'s plot very highly, and here it is again. Consider: the villain is a European outsider who sometimes works in league with Communists; he plans to wipe out a massive American resource, thus increasing the value of his own stockpiled wealth; he conceals a model of the location of his target beneath a table, which he demonstrates to an assembled horde of possible conspirators (one of whom, upon demonstrating certain reservations, is discreetly executed); the villain owns a stud farm, and cheats at English country sports; Bond is run to ground and knocked unconscious by the villain's henchmen in woodland (here, an associate of Bond's has just been killed); the villain, who flees the scene of his undoing in his private aircraft, ends up falling to his death. It's a great, wild notion for a film, but it was done so much better before. Bond's linking to the main story is quite crude, and the sudden resurrection of the KGB sub-plot midway through downright baffling. Zorin's fascinating background – he's the product of Nazi genetic meddling – is thrown away, and the screenplay interprets the value of Silicon Valley painfully literally (microchips, after all, are not dug up out of the earth; you could be forgiven for thinking otherwise through watching this film). **6**

Locations Siberia, London, Ascot, Paris, rural France, but mostly San Francisco. The camera loiters only on tourist cliché – the first sight of London is denoted by a happy snapper's view of a Royal guardsman, the first of Paris by two holidaymakers photographing the Eiffel Tower, the first of San Francisco by the Golden Gate Bridge – and ventures no further into local colour (no bath-houses, no gay Mardi Gras). Zorin's mine is, at least, a new 'deadly environment' in which to place Bond, but it's no development on that seen on cinema screens in *Indiana Jones and the Temple of Doom* one summer earlier. Dull, dull, dull. **3**

Gadgets Bond uses: a thing that goes 'bing' to help trace 003's corpse; a submarine craft disguised as an ice floe; a pair of sunglasses with adjustable anti-glare filters; a roll-on device which reveals imprints on paper; a camera concealed in his signet ring; and two lock-cracking devices. Q demonstrates a radio-controlled prototype of a 'robot surveillance machine'. Zorin wins horse races by using a microchip implanted in his steed's flank; when the beast flags, he transmits a signal which releases steroids into the horses system. He's got an automated steeplechase course too (what for?) and an inflatable airship. Some big, extravagant ideas, but the Bond devices are simply procured, unquestioned, for whatever the occasion – a persistent weakness of the films, but especially noticeable here. **3**

Girls Kimberley Jones, with whom Bond spends five long days on the journey from Siberia to Alaska. Moneypenny, who Bond promises to buy dinner; she ends the film blubbing her eyes out, believing him dead. May Day, an outlandishly dressed, horse-taming, kickboxing American who, according to Q, 'must take a lot of vitamins', believes herself to be in love with Zorin and, needless to say, goes on top. Dominique *et ses papillons*, an Eiffel Tower cabaret act; Dominique persuades butterflies to flit about by whistling a soothing *chanson*. Zorin henchpersons Pan Ho, an Oriental firestarter, and the jodphur-clad Jenny Flex. Stacey Sutton, a broke geologist and oil heiress who happily tears up a cheque for $5 million. Keeps cats and canaries. (She is of no interest whatsoever.) And Pola Ivanova, a scuba-diving KGB agent who once posed as a dancer with the Bolshoi ballet so as to fulfil her orders to seduce Bond. The bubbles in the Nippon Relaxation Spa tickle her . . . Tchaikovsky, apparently. Bond has a high total (four), but Stacey and (especially) May Day are so woefully thrown away as to be insulting. Aren't women allowed character traits beyond simply being good or bad any more? Still, Pola's quite fun, even if her scenes have absolutely no bearing whatsoever to the plot. **5**

Villains The multi-lingual Max Zorin, described as a 'leading French industrialist' and 'staunch anti-Communist', and believed to have been born in Dresden and to have had fled to the West in the Sixties. He's actually the super-intelligent and completely psychotic product of Nazi experiments with steroids. Claims to be 'happiest in the saddle'. Kickboxes. Once a KGB agent. Gleefully machine-guns to death his own helpless and stricken workers when he floods his mine for no reason other than his own entertainment. But, given his background, has he no political motivation at all? Is it credible that all he wants to achieve is wealth? Ditto Dr. Carl Mortner, Zorin's 'breeding consultant' – actually Hans Glaub, a Nazi war criminal reponsible for testing steroids

on pregnant concentration camp internees, thus creating Zorin himself (which means that Zorin is not actually the perfect Aryan specimen he appears to be; his mother was probably a Jew). Other (largely nondescript) Zorin associates include a cartel of electronics tycoons, lieutenant Scarpine, corner-cutting geologist Conley and corrupt US state official Howe. **7**

Fights, chases, explosions May Day's leap off the top of the Eiffel Tower is a fine 'fuck me!' moment in best Bond tradition. Bond's pursuit of her thereafter is a well-mounted absurdity, his stolen car being sheared neatly in half and half again by other *rue*-users. Surely the Bond films can do better than enact live representations of Looney Tunes sight gags? What next, red throbbing lumps bursting from Bond's crown when he's thumped on the head? The steeplechase sequence is fresh, but marred by rotten back-projection (a recurrent feature of the Moore Bond films, far more so than his rarely-seen but much-remarked upon inquisitive eyebrow). The scrap in Stacey's house involving a Ming vase rehashes similar business in *Moonraker*. Similarly, the night-time car chase in which Bond and his gal are pursued across San Francisco by bumbling American cops brings back only painful memories of *Diamonds Are Forever*. Oh well. At least the mayhem in Zorin's flooded mine is convincingly messy. **4**

Dialogue and double entendres Horsewoman Jenny Flex: 'I love an early morning ride.' Counters Bond: 'I'm an early riser myself. . .' After Bond's nocturnal encounter with May Day, Zorin asks Bond whether or not he slept well; 'A little restless, but I got off eventually,' Bond replies. Having had a troublesome tycoon ejected from his airship, Zorin asks innocently: 'So, does anyone else want to drop out?' Following on from Blofeld's 'You only live twice, Mr Bond' and Melina Havelock's gratingly awkward 'For your eyes only, darling' comes the stiffest effort yet to wedge the film's title into its dialogue: as Zorin's airship passes over the Golden Gate Bridge, May Day remarks, 'Wow. What a view.' 'To a kill,' Zorin snaps. Ugh. **2**

Bond Drinks vodka, Bollinger '75 and Lafitte Rothschild (*soixante-neuf*, of course). Aliases include huntin', shootin' and fishin' buffoon James St. John-Smythe and *Financial Times* journalist James Stock. He appears to have learned a certain trick from *Live and Let Die*'s Kananga – that is, playing a tape recording of an innocuous conversation in a room he knows to be bugged, thus enabling him to go about covert business. Cooks *cordon bleu* – his *quiche des cabinet* goes down well with Stacey. He's gentlemanly (or paternal) enough to let Stacey sleep unmolested while he keeps armed watch over her; unfortunately, he falls asleep in his chair. Is awarded the Order of Lenin at the end. We hope he sends it back. **4**

Plus/minus points The idea that Bond can tell a US cop that his name is 'Bond, James Bond' and be met with the smart-alec response 'Well, I'm Dick Tracy and you're still under arrest' is abominable. Bond is a secret agent; third-rate policemen do not know who he is (okay, so that's a loaded interpretation of the line. Whatever, it's still a cheap, wise-arse crack that someone thinks is funny. It's not). And are we seriously expected to believe that the cops are unable to pursue Bond's frankly incongruous hijacked firetruck any further just because it's crossed a bridge? Don't they have police officers on the other side? And would the head of the KGB ever be found swapping hearty one-liners with his opposite number inside the very heart of the British Secret Service headquarters itself, as happens here? We think not. **-8**

31% Not even half-hearted, *A View To a Kill*'s very few good points – May Day's pleasingly bizarre assassination of Aubergine, the Eiffel Tower stunt, Patrick Macnee, Zorin's intriguing history – are little recompense for the dreary most part of this unimaginative and enfeebled plod through the Bond back catalogue.

CAST

Roger Moore James Bond

Christopher Walken Max Zorin   Tanya Roberts Stacey Sutton   Grace Jones May Day

Patrick Macnee Tibbett   Patrick Bauchau Scarpine   David Yip Chuck Lee

Fiona Fullerton Pola Ivanova   Manning Redwood Bob Conley

Alison Doody Jenny Flex   Willoughby Gray Dr. Carl Mortner

Desmond Llewelyn Q   Robert Brown M   Lois Maxwell Miss Moneypenny

Walter Gotell General Gogol   Geoffrey Keen Minister of Defence

Jean Rougerie Aubergine   Daniel Benzali Howe   Bogdan Kominowski Klotkoff

Papillon Soo Soo Pan Ho   Mary Stavin Kimberley Jones

Dominique Risbourg Butterfly Act Compere   Carole Ashby Whistling Girl

Anthony Chin Taiwanese Tycoon   Lucien Jerome Paris Taxi Driver

Joe Flood U.S. Police Captain   Gerard Buhr Auctioneer   Dolph Lundgren Venz

Tony Sibbald Mine Foreman   Bill Ackridge O'Rourke   Ron Tarr Guard I

Taylor McAuley Guard II   Peter Ensor Tycoon   Seva Novgoredtsev Helicopter Pilot

SELECTED CREDITS

Costume Supervisor **Tiny Nicholls**   Additional Wardrobe for Grace Jones **Azzedine Alaia**

Assistant Art Directors **James Morahan**, **Ted Ambrose**, **Michael Boone**

Ski Sequence Directed and Photographed by **Willy Bogner**

Special Effects Supervisor **John Richardson**   Production Supervisor **Anthony Waye**

Camera Operator **Michael Frift**   Continuity **June Randall**

Action Sequence Arranger **Martin Grace**   Driving Stunts Arranger **Remy Julienne**

Art Director **John Fenner**   Make-up Supervisor **George Frost**

Hairdressing Supervisor **Ramon Gow**   Editor **Peter Davies**

Costumes designed by **Emma Porteous**   Casting by **Debbie McWilliams**

Director of Photography **Alan Hume**   Main Title Designed by **Maurice Binder**

Production Designed by **Peter Lamont**   Music Composed and Conducted by **John Barry**

Title Song Performed by **Duran Duran**, Composed by **Duran Duran**

Associate Producer **Tom Pevsner**

Screenplay by **Richard Maibaum** and **Michael G. Wilson**

Produced by **Albert R. Broccoli** and **Michael G. Wilson**

Directed by **John Glen**

Paper thin:
The Living Daylights

1986: a new phase in the Eon saga began when producers and distributor agreed on a fresh face to play Bond. Roger Moore's replacement was to be Irish-born Pierce Brosnan, the 33-year-old star of NBC drama *Remington Steele*. Prior to achieving fame as the debonair television detective, Brosnan had accompanied his wife, actress Cassandra Harris, to location shooting for *For Your Eyes Only*, in which she'd appeared briefly as love interest Lisl. NBC had cancelled *Remington Steele*, and Brosnan was free to inherit Moore's legacy – or so he thought. In the midst of the publicity surrounding Brosnan's attachment to Bond, NBC decided to renew *Remington Steele*, requesting further instalments from production company Mary Tyler Moore Television. Brosnan was contractually obliged to the series and, in July 1986, watched his chance to play James Bond slip through his fingers. He was devastated. It was the new film's second false start.

Scriptwriters Richard Maibaum and Michael G. Wilson had chosen to follow-up *A View To a Kill* by turning the clock back. 'We decided it might be interesting to have a story about James Bond's first mission, and how he became the great 007,' recalled Maibaum. 'We wrote a treatment. I thought and Mike Wilson thought it was quite good. However, Mr Broccoli, who has an uncanny appreciation of what audiences want, among his other great talents, liked it but he said the audience wasn't interested in Bond as an amateur – as a man learning his trade . . . There was a lot of stuff in it that we regretted losing – the whole business about James Bond as a young naval officer, a wild one that couldn't be disciplined, who was reminded by his grandfather that the

family motto is "The World Is Not Enough" . . .'

The Living Daylights – a short James Bond story that made its debut in the first edition of the *Sunday Times Magazine* in February 1962 – would prove to be the last Ian Fleming title appropriated by Eon. After abandoning their earlier idea, Maibaum and Wilson extrapolated their screenplay from a relatively uneventful anecdote in which Bond is sent to secure the escape of a British agent from West Berlin by gunning down the unknown Russian sniper shadowing the escapee, ultimately revealed to be a beautiful blonde cellist. 'We had to take that and make a two-hour entertainment out of it,' remembered Maibaum. 'And that was quite a job.' Fleming's story was preserved, largely intact, in the opening 15 minutes of the film proper, before spiralling off into a fanciful saga of internecine KGB plot and counter-plot and illicit international arms dealing.

Maibaum and Wilson's second draft opened with Bond arriving at the Universal Exports building and, upon entering Moneypenny's office, poised to toss his hat onto the hatstand, observing that two other hats are already there. In M's office, he and the other two 00 agents are then briefed on the Gibraltar mission. The draft is written so that it is General Gogol, veteran of the previous five Bond adventures, who is being set up by Koskov as the deviser of the 'death to spies' policy; ultimately a new character, Pushkin, was created, with the transferred Gogol now making only a cameo appearance in the film's final scene. A hint of the earlier plan remains in the name given to Pushkin's woman – Rubavitch, very like Gogol's secretary Rublevitch. Originally, Bond and Kara escape the KGB man watching over Kara's apartment by stealing his car – and it is in this gadget-free vehicle that they are pursued to the Austrian border. When the car is written off on the frozen ice lake, they hijack a nearby 'ice yacht' in which they continue their flight. They vault a dam into trees and then take to Kara's cello case for the final leg.

Lost also was a lengthy sequence in Afghanistan. Having escaped the airbase with the aid of Kara's bra, and accompanied by Ranjit Khan (the name originally intended for Kamran Shah), Bond and Kara are taken to Landi-Kotal – 'the world's largest Thieves' Market' – in the Khyber Pass. At this stage, Bond and Kara are unaware that Ranjit leads the Mujaheddin resistance, and ask Ranjit to set up a meeting with their leader; alone in this enormous bazaar, Bond and Kara are pursued the two jailers from the airbase, who are acting on Colonel Feyador's instructions. Bond throws one into a huge colour-dying pit into which women are spinning yarn ('Better red than dead,' he quips), eventually losing the pair when he sets off his exploding key ring in a Chinese fireworks warehouse – whereupon he and Kara are intercepted by Ranjit's men. Likewise, Bond and Kara did not escape Koskov's plane by piloting a jeep out of the back, but here were intended to attempt to land on a US aircraft carrier in the Indian Ocean; the situation is complicated by the fact that the carrier threatens to shoot the plane down, and it is only upon receiving last-minute confirmation of Bond's credentials from M and Moneypenny in London that the carrier's captain relents and permits them to set down. (The plane slides off the end of the deck anyhow, and Bond and Kara only evade drowning by clinging onto the plane's torn cargo net.)

'We have to be aware of some social responsibility . . .'

With Brosnan out of the picture, the search for a new James Bond continued while the screenplay was being prepared; Sam Neill and unknown Australian actor Finlay Light were both subjects of speculative press reports. The debate was finally ended on 6 August 1986 when an actor few had thought to consider was announced as the new 007. Timothy Dalton was born in Colwyn Bay, Wales, on 21 March 1946. Trained at RADA, he joined the Birmingham Repertory Theatre in 1966. He made his film debut alongside Katharine Hepburn and Peter O'Toole in *The Lion in Winter* (1968), starred as

Eon introduced Timothy Dalton and Maryam d'Abo to the world's press in Vienna on the 5th October

Heathcliff in the 1970 version of *Wuthering Heights*, and played Prince Barin in the opulent *Flash Gordon* (1980). Dalton was best known for his television and stage work, and had earned a solid reputation with the Royal Shakespeare Company. He had made a bid for the role of 007 before: in 1968 he auditioned for *On Her Majesty's Secret Service*, and in 1982 had been approached by Broccoli and Wilson when the producers were looking for a new Bond for *Octopussy*. The acquaintance was next renewed in March 1986; Dalton was cast in *The Living Daylights* after reportedly screen testing scenes from *On Her Majesty's Secret Service*. Sean Connery, who in 1984 had become embroiled in a legal action against MGM/UA and Albert Broccoli over alleged non-payment of percentage profits and merchandise royalties, gave his thumbs up to the casting. 'I think they've made a very good choice. I haven't worked with Tim, but I know him and I think he will be good . . . I hope he's got a good lawyer and can stamp his personality against the hardware. I hope every success for him.'

Dalton's Bond would be promoted as virtually monogamous in the forthcoming film: 'It was not a conscious decision on my part to be post AIDS,' said Wilson, 'but I suppose we inevitably reflect current ideas. Of course, the Bonds are meant to be escapist, action-adventure films. But in its first five years of release, 300 million people will have watched this movie, and I think we have to be aware of some social responsibility.' This concern for Bond's health did not extend to his other major vice – Dalton's Bond, like Connery's and Lazenby's, would be seen cigarette in hand.

'It's very important to make the man believable so that you can stretch the fantasy,' said Dalton, outlining his philosophy towards the character. 'Whether people will like this kind of Bond is another question.'

Maryam d'Abo was cast as Czech cellist Kara Milovy, Bond's principal love – or rather, romantic – interest. In 1984 d'Abo had auditioned for the role of KGB agent Pola Ivanova in *A View To a Kill* (the part went to Fiona Fullerton); two years later she provided a glamorous foil to one of the actors screen testing for the role of James Bond. The actor, who has proved difficult to positively identify, was unsuccessful, but d'Abo was later invited to audition for the film by associate producer Barbara Broccoli (Albert's daughter). Following the release of *The Living Daylights* d'Abo posed for the September 1987 issue of *Playboy*, adorned with little more than a white cat and a cello. This much sought-after 'Women of 007' edition also features a naked d'Abo sprayed head to foot in gold in homage to *Goldfinger*.

Jeroen Krabbé, a hugely popular actor in his home country of Holland, played Communist bad boy Koskov. Screen hard man Joe Don Baker, noted both for his starring role in vigilante thriller *Walking Tall* (1973) and his portrayal of CIA agent Darius Jedburgh, a Knight Templar for the nuclear age, in Troy Kennedy Martin's epochal television thriller *Edge of Darkness* (1985), was cast as arms dealer Brad Whitaker; he would later switch sides to play CIA agent Jack Wade in *GoldenEye* and *Tomorrow Never Dies*. Welsh actor John Rhys-Davies played General Pushkin, Gogol's replacement, and Art Malik, who had featured in David Lean's *A Passage To India* (1984), was cast as Oxford-educated Afghan freedom fighter Kamran Shah.

Felix Leiter made his first appearance in an Eon Bond film since *Live and Let Die*, now a preppy all-American boy played by John Terry. Desmond LLewellyn, who hadn't missed an Eon Bond film since *Live and Let Die*, returned as Q, this time supplying Bond with a customised Aston Martin Volante. Caroline Bliss, an actress who had come to prominence playing Lady Diana Spencer in ABC's 1982 drama *Charles and Diana: A Royal Love Story*, stepped into Lois Maxwell's shoes as a younger, doe-eyed Miss Moneypenny.

Dalton had relatively little time to prepare before principal photography began at Pinewood on Monday 29 September 1986. There had been no opportunity to organise an introductory press conference until director John Glen took his unit to Vienna the following week. On Sunday 5 October, Dalton spoke to reporters the day before location shooting was scheduled to begin. 'I intend to approach this project with a sense of responsibility to the work of Ian Fleming,' he claimed, refuting a suggestion from one reporter that the part was 'paper thin'. Dalton described his Bond as a character 'living

on the edge.' Albert Broccoli endorsed 007's new, harder image: 'I don't want to deprecate Roger – we're very happy with what he's done – but you could say that Timothy will be carrying Sean's mantle. Tim's image is closer to Bond's that Roger's.'

Glen spent two weeks shooting in the Austrian capital, filming scenes at the Cape Deme, the Musikverein concert hall and the Reisenaad Big Wheel (immortalised in 1950's *The Third Man*) in the huge Prater amusement park. The unit next moved to Gibraltar to film the pre-credits sequence, in which Rock Gun on the island was dressed as the exterior of a secret radar installation. On Gibraltar, Dalton met a Royal Artillery Captain called James Bond and visiting press photographers were delighted at the opportunity for a picture of the two men together. Location filming later moved to Morocco, where scenes were filmed both in the casbah of Tangier and in a more generic expanse which stood in for Russian-occupied Afghanistan.

Studio filming was briefly interrupted when the Prince and Princess of Wales visited Pinewood on 11 December 1986. Diana cracked a sugar glass prop wine bottle over Charles' head, and the photographs made tabloid front pages the following day. Filming came to an end on 13 February 1987. Six days later Albert Broccoli was awarded an honorary OBE.

'Kinder, more human, charming and low-profile . . .'

For his final Bond score to date, John Barry recruited Norwegian pop trio a-ha to collaborate with him on *The Living Daylights*' theme tune. a-ha were then at the peak of their chart career, enjoying an almost unbroken string of top ten hits. Barry later described working with the group as being like 'playing ping pong with four balls' but the result of the uncomfortable collaboration was a single that reached number five in the British chart. The eagle-eyed can spot Barry making a brief cameo in the film as a conductor.

A distinctive promotional poster framed a dynamic Dalton within the trademark gun barrel. The poster's other focal point – a shapely girl in a sheer white dress – was Los Angeles model Kathy Stangel, who reportedly received $600 to pose for the picture. 'It was just another job,' she told the *Daily Mail*'s Baz Bamigboye. 'I posed with several different firearms and did all sorts of shots. But I didn't realise they had used me until I recognised my bottom all over Sunset Boulevard the other week.' An executive at MGM/UA told Bamigboye: 'People are supposed to think the girl is Maryam . . . I think that's Maryam's hair you can see.'

The Prince and Princess of Wales attended the premiere of *The Living Daylights* at Leicester Square Odeon on 29 June 1987. Encouraged by a recent increase in cinema attendance, MGM/UA struck 250 prints of the film in time for its general release on 10 July. The film opened in America on 31 July 1987. Although rising ticket prices ensured that *The Living Daylights'* American gross was higher than that of *A View To a Kill*, the film was seen by fewer people – an estimated 14.2 million (the lowest figure since *The Man With the Golden Gun*) in the US. Elsewhere, the film's success was unequivocal: a worldwide gross of $191,200,000 was a healthy return on an estimated negative production cost of $33 million. Curiously,

the film's Greek title translated as *Having the Finger On the Trigger* – in late 1961 Ian Fleming's working title for *The Living Daylights* had been *Trigger Finger*.

One of the most positive reviews came courtesy of Victoria Mather in the 30 June edition of *The Daily Telegraph*: 'All the traditional elements are in place and Dalton has restored a vital element to 007 – the very best of British, the amateur gentleman who is better than any professional. He is kinder, more human, charming and low- profile. For me he is Bond, James Bond.'

'You no longer expect more than you get, and by now are left noting only the fine tuning of the formula,' remarked *The Guardian*'s Derek Malcolm on 2 July. 'Dalton hasn't the natural authority of Connery nor the facile charm of Moore, but George Lazenby he is not. It's an able first go in the circumstances, though perhaps it could do with a bit more humour. The other main newcomer is Caroline Bliss as Miss Moneypenny, who looks as if she might prefer to be called Ms. And, of course, Maryam D'Abo as the one and only girlfriend in this episode – a Czech classical cellist who opens her legs for Dvorak rather quicker than for Bond.'

On the same day, the *Evening Standard*'s Alexander Walker raised the worrying prospect that Eon may have been misguided in their knee-jerk retraction from Roger Moore's style: 'Timothy Dalton looks poorly served by John Glen, once a tight editor and now a slack director, and doesn't begin to share the joke with the audience the way that the other Bonds did. He looks as if he takes it all for real and dislikes much of it . . . Cubby Broccoli and his associates should start the Think Tank going for the film after this, and decide what kind of Bond they want, for at the moment they haven't got one. And it's no good saying "give him time: you can't be Bond first time off." Connery was.'

File: *The Living Daylights*

Teaser Three 00 agents parachute into Gibraltar as part of an Admiralty exercise; their objective is to penetrate a radar installation before SAS men armed with paintball guns can 'kill' them. One is taken out of the game by the SAS, but the second is actually killed by an imposter. The third – Bond – pursues the murderous imposter, who attempts to flee in a jeep packed with explosives; Bond, the jeep and the imposter plunge over a rocky promontory, but Bond cheats death, parachuting onto the roof of a luxury yacht where a swimsuited lovely is complaining to a friend by mobile phone: 'If only I could find a real man …' Bond's identity remains disguised until after he's landed on Gibraltar, and our first sight of Dalton-Bond is nothing short of iconic, whipping his head around upon hearing another 00's dying scream. The key stunt is eye-popping but credible, and the pay-off – whereupon Dalton gets to utter Bond's immortal introduction – clever enough to raise a belly-laugh. A winner. **9**

Titles Maurice Binder's penchant for literalism here manifests itself in a shot of car headlights cut to Morten Harket's pidgin English wail: 'Comes the morning and the headlights fade away …' Beachwear-clad beauties don sunglasses, fire revolvers and pose inside tall champagne glasses. Snore. **3**

Bonkers plot Following the teaser – in which a bogus SAS man, actually an assassin, disturbs a set-up assault on a military installation – the story proper begins when a bogus assassin is herself set up to be assassinated by Bond during the course of the defection (later revealed to be bogus) of a KGB General. As a consequence of a bogus KGB 'death to spies' campaign, of which the bogus SAS man in the teaser was a part, the KGB General (who's since been snatched back by an assassin who bogusly poses as a milkman as part of a plan to set up a bogus gas explosion which will lead the bogus defector to be seized by a bogus medical team whom the British bogusly

believe to be KGB) attempts to set up Bond to assassinate another KGB General, who's uncovered certain of his (bogus) dealings. But Bond himself sets up a bogus assassination of this 'good' KGB General, thus fooling the 'bad' KGB General and his accomplice, a bogus American Major who's actually an arms dealer, into believing that the bad General won't be arrested by the good one. However, the bogus assassin set up at the outset, who's in love with the bad General, doesn't realise that she'd been set up in the first place, and sets up Bond – who's been bogusly claiming to be a friend of the bad General, and whom she now believes to be a KGB agent – to be kidnapped by the bad General, the bogus American Major and a freelance assassin who's been waging the bogus 'death to spies' campaign. And then they all fly to Afghanistan – bogusly posing as a medical mercy mission with the aid of a bogus human heart, but actually carrying a cache of diamonds bogusly disguised as an icepack around the aforementioned bogus internal organ – where somehow or other it all boils down to Bond having to destroy a planeload of heroin (not bogus, amazingly) lest the bad guys' unseen creditors get paid. 'Convoluted' isn't the word. **4**

Locations Gibraltar; Bratislava, Czechoslovakia; Austria; London; a secluded English estate; the Czech border; Tangier; Vienna; around and above a Russian airbase in Afghanistan. Given the storybookish, oddly dated feel of the European sequences, the leap to the squalor and strife of the final third jars. **8**

Gadgets Armament lovers will adore this film, which features: a huge, Walther-constructed assassin's rifle with laser sights which takes both soft-nosed and steel-tipped bullets; a laser-sighting shark barrel machine pistol; third generation 'starlight scopes'; and 'fire and forget' infantry mini-missiles with a range of five kilometres. The torpedo-shaped 'pig' is a scouring plug in the immense Trans-Siberian gas pipeline which British engineers have been working to modify 'for months', enabling it to carry a man. There's a revolving rake/metal detector at Blayden. Both Necros' personal stereo (the machine itself acts as a detonator, and the headphone cord is strong enough to act as a garotte) and his exploding milk bottles. In his gleaming new London workshop, Q (who is seen out of breath and popping pills) issues Bond with a whistle-activated key ring which not only emits stun gas but is packed full of plastic explosive (the keys open nine-tenths of the world's locks, too); Q has also been working on a missile-firing ghetto blaster, a sofa that swallows people and an updated Aston Martin with 'optional extras fitted' – a hubcap-mounted laser beam, port and starboard ground-to-ground missiles, a bulletproof rear window, outrigged skis, spiked gripping tyres and a rocket motor at the rear (this is, inevitably, the best vehicle since *The Spy Who Loved Me*'s Lotus). **9**

Girls Linda, whose cruising round Gibraltar yields only playboys and tennis pros. Stradivarius owner Kara Milovy who, in Bond's judgement, doesn't know 'one end of a rifle from the other'; all her life, she tells Bond, she has dreamed of going to the Viennese opera. Beats Bond with pillows, and calls him a horse's arse. Looks great in a nurse's uniform. Undergoes a bizarre and sudden metamorphosis from willowy, retiring cellist to rifle-waving, horse-riding hit 'n' run driver in the last half-hour (is this what finding out that your boyfriend's a traitorous, murderous embezzler does to a girl?). Rosika Miklos, a Trans-Siberian Pipeline operative who works covertly for the West, with the monumental cleavage she employs to hide her activities from her supervisor's eyes. We glimpse pictures of KGB assassins Natasha Zarky, a child impersonator who kills with 'exploding teddy bears', and Ula Yokhfov, who strangles with her thighs – just Bond's type, according to Miss Moneypenny, now a blonde,

myopic Barry Manilow fan who sighs longingly after Bond has slapped her bum. Pushkin popsy Rubavitch. Ava and Liz, Leiter's fetchers and carriers. Despite its reputation, *The Living Daylights* is nowhere near as progressive as it thinks it is – *viz* Moneypenny's longing sigh, Bond tearing Rubavitch's top off to distract a guard and Kamran's eyebrow-raised bafflement over 'Women!' **6**

Villains General Georgi Koskov, a clowning 'top KGB mastermind' who thinks caviare is 'peasant food'. Killer-for-hire Necros, a natural mimic who can burn his hand on a stove without flinching and who, with his blond looks, washboard stomach and swimming trunks is yet another Grant clone (is there a factory churning them out somewhere behind the Iron Curtain?). One-time mercenary Brad Whitaker, an arms dealer (and, allegedly, 'patron of the arts') who idolises 'great commanders' such as Caesar, Napoleon, Genghis Khan, Hitler and Cromwell, takes a $50 million down-payment from the Russians and has a Swiss bank account; he fancies himself an American Major, despite (or maybe because of) the fact that he was 'expelled from West Point for cheating'. Even though Whitaker's demise (crushed by a bust of Wellington, he meets his Waterloo) is pleasing, it's a shame that the bad guys don't meet with justice in a somewhat bigger way (Koskov is effectively led away in handcuffs, and 'Book 'em, Dano' is not a Bondian send-off by any stretch of the imagination). *The Living Daylights* falls very flat here, but that's not too surprising – the villains don't have a masterplan as such, and are simply looking to cover up their own criminal endeavours. **3**

Fights, chases, explosions Necros' assault on safe house Blayden is a gripping action set piece, although strangely reminiscent of the 'milkman' sequence which opens *Carry On Spying* (unintentionally so, we expect). Bond and Kara's flight for the Austrian border, evading police, roadblocks, sno-cats packed with Russian troops and even tanks – first in a gadget-heavy Aston Martin, next on a cello case – is good-natured and spectacular (with a charming pay-off, too). The Mujaheddin attack on the Russian airbase develops into nothing less than all-out war, with a rip-snorting, soaring finale (Bond's demolition of the bridge). **8**

29th June 1987 – at the premiere party for the Living Daylights Caroline Bliss left her Moneypenny image behind

Dialogue and double entendres Altogether now: 'Whoever she was, I must have scared *the living daylights* out of her ...' Pushkin is unimpressed by Whitaker's military idols: 'Butchers,' he scoffs, upon seeing the other's waxworks of Hitler et al. 'Surgeons,' corrects Whitaker. 'They cut away society's dead flesh ...' 'You should have bought lilies,' Bond, with murder in mind, tells the bouquet-carrying Pushkin – and Bond does get to later deliver Kara a crushingly funny put-down after he's beaten up the jailer at the Afghan airbase ('You were fantastic! We're free!' she pants. 'Kara,' he sighs, 'we're inside a Russian airbase in the middle of Afghanistan ...). It's all terribly stiff and po-faced and unmemorable otherwise (and where it isn't, derivative: 'We have an old saying too, Georgi – and you're full of it,' is straight out of *The Man With the Golden Gun*, for example). **3**

Bond Shrugs off the fact that his trousers catch fire in Gibraltar. Is 'bloody late' in Bratislava. Thinks Harrods foie gras is 'excellent', selects Bollinger RD over M's 'questionable' choice, and is back on the fags for the first time in years. Calls Kara's cello playing 'exquisite', but listens to light jazz on his car radio when he thinks she's asleep. Has a 'usual suite' at a grand hotel in Vienna. He's an old smoothie still, arranging for the ferris wheel to be stopped so he might take advantage of the confused Kara, and knows the word 'beautiful' in Afghan. But this is Bond presented as state assassin more than anything else: we see his mechanical preparations to eliminate a KGB sniper at the outset, and even witness the routine he adopts when about to execute a man (here Pushkin) face-to-face. We are, however, seriously concerned by his apparent loathing for both his boss and his job: 'Stuff my orders,' he tells Saunders. 'If he [M] fires me, I'll thank him for it.' **8**

Plus/minus points There's a wonderful, underplayed moment in the Vienna fairground where the owner of a shooting gallery is heard to refuse Bond any more prize-winning turns. The setting of a seduction scene aboard the very ferris wheel where Orson Welles' Harry Lime told Joseph Cotten's Holly Martins of war and peace and cuckoo clocks is brazen and audacious, but we love it nonetheless. The 'Smiert Spionem' card attached to a balloon which floats down to goad Bond following Saunders' death is quite macabre. The toe-curling 'all

CAST

Timothy Dalton James Bond
Maryam d'Abo Kara Milovy   **Jeroen Krabbé** General Georgi Koskov
Joe Don Baker Brad Whitaker   **John Rhys-Davies** General Leonid Pushkin
Art Malik Kamran Shah   **Andreas Wisniewski** Necros
Thomas Wheatley Saunders   **Desmond Llewelyn** Q   **Robert Brown** M
Geoffrey Keen Minister of Defence   **Walter Gotell** General Anatol Gogol
Caroline Bliss Miss Moneypenny   **John Terry** Felix Leiter   **Virginia Hey** Rubavitch
John Bowe Col. Feyador   **Julie T. Wallace** Rosika Miklos   **Kell Tyler** Linda
Catherine Rabett Liz   **Dulice Liecier** Ava   **Nadim Sawalha** Chief of Security Tangier
Alan Talbot Koskov's KGB Minder   **Carl Rigg** Imposter
Tony Cyrus Chief of Snow Leopard Brotherhood   **Atik Mohamed** Achmed
Michael Moor, Sumar Khan Kamran's Men   **Ken Sharrock** Jailer
Peter Porteous Gasworks Supervisor   **Anthony Carrick** Male Secretary Blayden
Frederick Warder 004   **Glyn Baker** 002   **Derek Hoxby** Sergeant Stagg
Bill Weston Butler Blayden   **Richard Cubison** Trade Centre Toastmaster
Heinz Winter Concierge, Vienna Hotel   **Leslie French** Lavatory Attendant

SELECTED CREDITS

Costume supervisor **Tiny Nicholls**   Military Dioramas **Little Lead Soldiers**
Production supervisor **Anthony Waye**   Camera Operator **Michael Frift**
Continuity **June Randall**   Art director **Terry Ackland-Snow**
Make-up supervisor **George Frost**   Hairdressing Supervisor **Ramon Gow**
Stunt supervisor **Paul Weston**   Driving stunts Arranger **Remy Julienne**
Aerial stunts arranger **B. J. Worth**   Editors **John Grover** and **Peter Davies**
Costumes designed by **Emma Porteous**   Casting by **Debbie McWilliams**
Special visual effects **John Richardson**   Director of photography **Alec Mills**
Main title designed by **Maurice Binder**   Production designed by **Peter Lamont**
Music composed and conducted by **John Barry**   'The Living Daylights' performed by **a-ha**
Composed by **Pal Waaktaar** and **John Barry**
'Where Has Every Body Gone?' and 'If There Was a Man' performed by **The Pretenders**
Music by **John Barry**, Lyrics by **Chrissie Hynde**
Associate producers **Tom Pevsner** and **Barbara Broccoli**
Screenplay by **Richard Maibaum** and **Michael G. Wilson**
Produced by **Albert R. Broccoli** and **Michael G. Wilson**   Directed by **John Glen**

together now' happy ending is enough to set one's teeth on edge, however. And the less said about that hopelessly wet and weedy theme song the better. **+7**

68% Not, perhaps, as drastic an overhaul as it seemed at the time, *The Living Daylights'* abiding characteristic today is surely its near-total humourlessness; worthy but dull, its hankering after inverted-commas 'realism' seems more than a little desperate. Dalton-Bond, although acquitting himself with some credit, is thoroughly wearing in his over-earnest manner, too. That given, its epic aspirations set it apart as the best Eon film of the Eighties by quite some way.

181

The dominion of the ordinary: *Licence To Kill*

1988: in February it was announced that the next James Bond film would not be shot at Pinewood, where Eon had produced all its Bond pictures bar *Moonraker*, but at the Churubusco Studios in Mexico City. *The Living Daylights* had previously occupied half of Pinewood's capacity, thus saving at least half the 500-strong workforce from likely redundancy. The news that *Licence Revoked*, the next film in Eon's Bond series, would be shooting elsewhere was met with disappointment. Eon's decision was influenced by a number of financial factors: in 1985 the British government's Films Act had abolished the Eady levy; foreign artists were now taxed at source and producers could no longer write off 100 per cent of their costs against tax. These considerations conspired with a weak dollar to lead Eon to the conclusion that filming in England may have added around ten per cent to production costs. And those costs were rising all the time. Albert Broccoli estimated that the entire budget of *Dr. No* would now fail to cover the price of striking sufficient prints of the 16th film in his series.

Eon had originally considered taking its next Bond production to China, and recces were conducted in November and December 1987. The idea was discarded (partly because, as director John Glen later remarked, the 1988 film *The Last Emperor* had blunted the country's novelty as a film location) and Douglas Noakes, the *Licence Revoked* accountant, suggested Mexico as an alternative. The eight stages at Churubusco offered Latin America's biggest film-making facility; in 1984 alone the studio had hosted *Dune*, *Romancing the Stone* and *Conan the Destroyer*. Use of Pinewood, it was decided, would be restricted to post-production and editing work only. 'I am sure Cubby is very upset about it,' said Jerry Juroe, Eon's head of marketing. 'All I can say is that 007 is still a British agent.'

A Writers' Guild of America dispute prevented Richard Maibaum taking an active role in the preparation of a screenplay. Instead, he collaborated with Michael G Wilson on an outline that Wilson alone developed into a finished script. The story was a brave departure from anything previously ventured: shortly after acting as best man at the wedding of

Felix Leiter, Bond discovers that Leiter's bride has been murdered and that his friend has been savaged by a shark. With grim determination, 007 launches a personal vendetta against Franz Sanchez, the sadistic drug baron responsible; his obsession sees him stripped of his licence to kill by a furious M. Although not based on an Ian Fleming story, Wilson and Maibaum injected their story with elements from *Live and Let Die* (when Bond finds the mauled Leiter his body is accompanied by a note that reads 'He disagreed with something that ate him'), but the springboard for the whole story had been the character of Milton Krest, a marine biologist associate of Sanchez's; the character had originally appeared in *The Hildebrand Rarity*.

Whereas Maibaum and Wilson had written *The Living Daylights* before knowing the idenrity of their new lead actor (relatively little last-minute work was done to tailor the script when a decision was made), *Licence Revoked* was prepared with Timothy Dalton's distinctive characterisation in mind. Dalton, however, later refuted the widely held suggestion that the screenplay was written specifically for him: 'I don't like the idea of anyone writing it for me, I really don't, and I don't think that's true because it would be very limiting. You should write a bloody good James Bond story and then I'll come along and do it, otherwise the film will be limited by what the writers think that I'm capable of, and not by what James Bond is capable of. What may have been meant was that my approach to the film is the only approach that I could have: one that is closer to the earlier films . . .'

John Glen, commissioned to direct his fifth

'This is the make-or-break one . . .'

consecutive Bond film, harboured concerns as the shooting date approached. 'I think, financially, this is the make-or-break one,' he claimed. 'The producers are finding it more and more difficult to get their money back. [*The Living Daylights*] itself cost $33 million and promotion and advertising another $36 million but, with interest charges building every week, it's a struggle to keep profits in front of the race.'

Timothy Dalton with two of his Licence To Kill co-stars: Talisa Soto (left) and Caroline Bliss

The role of Bond's resourceful CIA sidekick Pam Bouvier was given to Carey Lowell, a New York-born former model who had most recently appeared in the 1988 comedy *Me and Him*. The film's bizarre subject (a talking penis) meant that distributor Columbia was still debating its British and American release as *Licence Revoked* went into production. Lowell went on to co-star in the poorly received *The Guardian* (1990) and made brief appearances in *Sleepless in Seattle* (1990), *Leaving Las Vegas* (1995) and *Fierce Creatures* (1996). Once a professional opera singer and a semi-regular character in the *Hill Street Blues* television series, Robert Davi, playing coca nabob Sanchez, had recently completed work on *Die Hard* (1988), a successful example of the violent action films that vied for the attention of the Bond films' traditional box-office constituency. He was cast in *Licence Revoked* after a suggestion by Richard Maibaum.

Sanchez's mistress, Lupe Lamora, was played by Talisa Soto. The former Miss Galaxy's feature film experience had been limited to an appearance in Paul Morrissey's *Spike of Bensonhurst* (1988); to many viewers she would have been more familiar from her role in the promotional video for Nick Kamen's successful 1986 single *Each Time You Break My Heart*. Anthony Zerbe was best known for his extensive television and stage work, but had appeared in such notable films as *Papillon* (1973) and *Rooster Cogburn* (1975) before being cast as Milton Krest. David Hedison earned the distinction of being the only actor to play Felix Leiter twice when he reprised the role he had last played in *Live and Let Die*. Since appearing in Roger Moore's Bond debut, Hedison had worked alongside his friend in *North Sea Hijack* (1980) and *The Naked*

Face (1985). Robert Brown's M and Caroline Bliss' Moneypenny (both making their final Bond appearances) were seen relatively briefly, but Desmond Llewelyn was awarded the biggest role of his film career when, following a tip-off from an anxious Moneypenny, Q uses his leave to unofficially assist Bond as a field operative. Llewelyn's scenes supplied a sombre film with its only real light relief (his appearance drew an enthusiastic cheer at the London press screening) and he enjoyed himself enormously. 'That was marvellous,' he later recalled. 'I was on location in Mexico and for the first time in my life I made some real money out of a Bond film.'

An international crew principally comprised of Mexican and British technicians occupied seven stages at Churubusco at various points during the making of *Licence Revoked*. Shooting commenced on Monday 18 July 1988; location photography would generally concentrate in nearby areas such as Durango, Vera Cruz and Temoaya. The extensive Isthmus City casino scenes were filmed at the Casino Espagnol, in reality a restaurant and social club for Spanish nationals (gambling is outlawed in Mexico).

In August, the crew shot material in Key West, a cluster of islands off the coast of Florida. It was here that the pre-credits capture of Sanchez was largely filmed using an aerial unit based at Sugarloaf Key Airport, and co-ordinated by 'Corkey' Fornof – the Acrostar pilot from *Octopussy*. Key West had once been the home of author Ernest Hemingway; Bond hands M his weapon at Hemingway House with the words 'a farewell to arms'.

Underwater photography was conducted off the Isla Mujeres near Cancun. The astonishing truck chase leading to Bond's final confrontation with Sanchez was supervised by Remy Julienne (who had acted as vehicle stunt co-ordinator on all the Glen-directed Bonds) and filmed on desert roads near Mexicali over seven arduous weeks.

Towards the end of the shoot, a week was spent filming the interiors of Sanchez's house at a luxurious Acapulco residence belonging to a friend of Albert Broccoli's. The drawbacks of basing the production in Mexico had now become apparent: the intense heat had caused technical problems with the equipment, and reportedly so overwhelmed the 81-year-old Broccoli that he had been forced to return to Los Angeles. Additionally, language barriers and local union restrictions had made co-ordinating the 200-strong crew difficult. Timothy Dalton confessed to being homesick, claiming at one point that he missed 'a decent pint of bitter'.

The film wrapped, on schedule, on Friday 18 November. Crucially, however, associate producer Tom Pevsner later estimated that the film would have been completed even sooner had it been shot at Pinewood.

It wasn't until posters and other promotional material bearing the title *Licence Revoked* had been printed that title of the film was changed to *Licence To Kill*. The official explanation was that *Licence Revoked* would prove too difficult to translate in foreign territories – others noted that a high proportion of audience members at American test screenings had reportedly not understood the meaning of the word 'Revoked'. Another unprecedented change in the credits occurred at the close of the film, when a

'Appreciably more violent than any Bond . . .'

warning about the dangers of cigarette smoking was displayed midway between the cast and crew listings. The warning, John Glen claimed, came on the recommendation of Eon's lawyers, who noted that the film featured a genuine brand of cigarettes.

The score, which frequently revisited Monty Norman's original *Dr. No* theme, was the work of Michael Kamen. (The most inventive reprise occurred when, towards the end of the film, Sanchez fires a machine gun at the petrol tanker carrying Bond – the noise the bullets make as they ricochet off the vehicle recalls a snatch of Norman's signature.) An experienced producer and composer, Kamen had previously contributed to *Lethal Weapon* (1987), *Die Hard* (1988) and the acclaimed BBCdrama *Edge of Darkness* (1986). The opening theme was sung by Gladys Knight, and gave the veteran soul singer her first British top ten hit since 1977.

The more adult ethos prevalent in *Licence To Kill*, most obvious in the realistic violence that typified its action sequences, elicited stringent scrutiny from the British Board of Film Classification. Secretary James Ferman granted the film a 15 certificate – the highest ever accorded a Bond picture – only after requesting approximately 38 seconds of cuts. 'We thought the film was appreciably more violent than any Bond in the last 20 years,' he claimed, 'and is much darker than the films have ever been.' The bloody demise of Milton Krest was one scene that received special attention, and a number of shots of his swelling head were cut from the British print. 'Britain is only five per cent of the world market,' reacted John Glen, 'so, although it will cost us money, it won't be that substantial.' Three other versions of the film were distributed internationally: European audiences saw a less heavily edited version, and in America the 'Restricted' rated film saw fewer cuts still. Only in Japan, where the film's title translated as *The Cancelled Licence*, was it seen wholly uncut.

'Thick-eared action yarns we can get anywhere . . .'

The Prince and Princess of Wales were once more guests of honour at the Leicester Square Odeon premiere of *Licence To Kill* on Tuesday 13 June 1989. Alongside cast and crew-members from the film, former Bond stars Jane Seymour and Britt Ekland were also invited. Ominously, the British James Bond fan club magazine noted that, 'As usual the premiere attracted a large crowd outside the cinema, although it was noticeably smaller than [in] previous years', and lamented that ensuing media coverage was, with a few notable exceptions, 'scant'.

Licence To Kill opened in the United States on 14 July, and suffered from stiff competition that included *Lethal Weapon 2*, *Indiana Jones and the Last Crusade* (co-starring Sean Connery) and *Batman* – perhaps the most aggressively marketed film of the decade. 'The thinking behind bringing this film to Central America and having so many American actors in it is definitely to make the series more relevant to audiences in the United States,' explained Robert Davi prior to the release. '*Licence Revoked* is also going to be much tougher than the previous Bond films, and

that's something that will appeal to American audiences too.' Sadly, his prediction would prove amiss.

Estimated US box office admissions of 11.7 million placed *Licence To Kill* perilously close to the all-time low achieved by *The Man With the Golden Gun*. Its US gross of $34,667,015 didn't even cover an approximate negative production cost of $35 million. Worldwide, *Licence To Kill* grossed a total of $156,200,000 – a worryingly low figure by Bond standards, and a cause of serious concern to MGM/UA, to whom the 007 series had become a veritable cornerstone.

The reviews in the British press of 15 June were largely condemning: 'Grown up . . . is what *Licence To Kill* tries to be,' claimed Derek Malcolm in *Midweek*. 'But I have to say it doesn't succeed very well since the formula soon takes over again, and ultimately there are many more daft stunts than good lines. No, to be more grown up, the Bond movies would have to be written and directed better. And this one is very average in both departments . . .'

The Independent's Adam Mars-Jones suggested a new approach to revitalise the series: 'The health warning [during the credits] is the only clear sign of what the makers of the Bond series are constantly proclaiming – their desire to make the films more realistic and modern. In fact these ambitions are contradictory; the only way to boost plausibility is to abandon updating, and set the fantasy in period . . . All in all, the new James Bond is more like a low-tar cigarette than anything else – less stimulating that the throat-curdling gaspers of yesteryear, but still naggingly implicated in unhealthiness, a feeble bad habit without the kick of a vice.'

Nigel Andrews, writing in The *Financial Times*, was similarly disparaging: 'My view is that either 007 is a wisecracking, cuff-shooting Casanova of the Secret Service or he is any old spy. In *Licence To Kill* the dandyism has gone out of the series. Rather than raising the movie's temperature, the much-publicised (though hardly shocking) violence, demotes the film to the dominion of the ordinary. Thick-eared action yarns we can get anywhere, thank you very much.'

For the ardent Bond observer, attempting to unravel the tangled events of the next few years is a daunting task. The sporadic press reports of the period tell a convoluted story . . .

Albert Broccoli's reaction to the Bond series' perceived drop in popularity was dramatic: it was reported that Danjaq, the company he owned with his wife Dana and that in turn reportedly owned 50 per cent of the first nine Eon Bond films and 80 per cent of the remaining seven, was put up for sale. MGM/UA were initially interested, but baulked at the reported asking price $200 million. 'A properly placed British buyer would be in the best position to nurture the Bond material,' said Broccoli's spokesman Saul Cooper in August 1990.

Broccoli entrusted Eon with his daughter Barbara and stepson Michael G. Wilson, although Wilson later refuted reports that the company's commitment to producing the Bond pictures would be maintained as a condition of any sale. 'There is no clause that retains us,' he told *Variety* in August. 'Nothing is in negotiations now anyway. We had talks with UA. We're thinking about offering it to other people, and some of them are looking at it.'

Dalton and leading lady Carey Lowell at the West End premiere of Licence to Kill

Any potential sale, it was stressed, would not affect *Licence To Kill*'s follow-up. A new broom, however, seemed to be at work. According to a report in *The Sunday Times* of 12 August 1990, Broccoli had parted company with long-standing collaborators John Glen and Richard Maibaum. Spiros Skouras, who acted as agent for both men, would only say: 'They had many pictures together and worked together for a long, long time. It was a great thing for everyone involved.' Maibaum, for so long a crucial element of Eon's Bond series, died in 1991.

187

In 1990, the names that were allegedly approached to revitalise what *Variety* called the 'wilting Broccoli empire' included *Rambo* director Ted Kotcheff, and *Blues 'Brothers* director John Landis. *Variety* also reported that Broccoli had hired Alfonse M Ruggiero Jr, a television writer with credits on *Miami Vice* and *Airwolf*, to rewrite an original Michael G Wilson script, and had also approached *Razor's Edge* writer/director John Byrum and *Howard the Duck* writers Gloria and Willard Huyck. 'There is a desire to get some new people involved and get a fresh slant on the material,' claimed an MGM/UA spokesman, who accepted that the studio had little in the way of new releases except *Rocky V* and the forthcoming Bond picture. 'It's obvious that the series is a little tired.'

Other events overtook the development of the new picture. 'Basically,' Michael G. Wilson later told *Empire* magazine, 'the problems started when MGM/UA were taken over by Giancarlo Peretti, the Italian businessman.' In 1989 Kirk Kerkorian had sold the studio to Australian broadcaster Qintex who, in turn, were now negotiating to merge with Pathe Communications. Just days before the anticipated merge date of 23 October 1990, it was reported that Danjaq had filed suit against MGM/UA and Pathe in an attempt to block an international TV licensing agreement of the films in the Bond back catalogue. It was alleged that the distributor had reached agreement with French, Spanish, Italian, South Korean and Japanese territories without first consulting Danjaq. Quoted in *Variety*, Danjaq's attorney Howard King claimed that the deals were 'improvident in a number of respects. Their most obnoxious aspect is the length of the terms at ridiculously low rates . . .' The suit claimed that Pathe was intending

to sell the TV distribution rights overseas in an effort to raise funds for its acquisition of MGM/UA. King continued: 'If these deals take effect we're going to be foreclosed for the remainder of this century from exploiting the Bond films in the major foreign television markets, which are the next frontier for exploiting the value of these works.'

In 1996, Broccoli's friend and legal advisor Norman Tyre recalled the fighting spirit that typified the producer's defiant attitude in the midst of his failing heath: 'He was confronted with a choice; accepting a subordinated position for future Bonds, or facing a nasty drawn-out lawsuit . . . he was informed crystally clear, that the chances of success in the lawsuit were less than 50 per cent, and that the cost of litigation would be between three and four million dollars. I asked him for his decision. Without a moment's hesitation he announced loudly and clearly "Let's go for it!", so typical of our Cubby.'

By 1992, fresh stories were emerging of Broccoli's difficulties. Amongst these, were a *Variety* article reporting rumours that MGM/Pathe was looking for a new James Bond. The new chairman of the organisation variously referred to as MGM/Pathe and MGM/UA was Frank Manusco – he had hired John Calley (who, as a Warner Bros executive had been amongst those overseeing the production of *Never Say Never Again*) to become president of United Artists and revitalise the subsidiary. Calley's ideas included a relaunched Bond – and he reportedly presented Broccoli with a shortlist of potential lead actors that included Pierce Brosnan, Ralph Fiennes, Hugh Grant and Liam Neeson. Broccoli remained adamant that Dalton would reappear.

Danjaq's protracted legal dispute finally came to a satisfactory conclusion. 'We had to fight our way through that, which took three years,' Wilson told *Empire*, 'until finally Peretti was pushed out, clearing the decks for us to go forward again. It's really been a problem for MGM.'

'The court case was generally solved earlier this year,' Timothy Dalton told Ivor Davies in the 6 August 1993 edition of *The Daily Mail*. 'And now we have a writer – Michael France who wrote Sylvester Stallone's newest hit *Cliffhanger* – who is going to come up with a story. When we've all agreed on that, he'll write the script, and then we'll look for a director. I would think the earliest we'll start will be next January or February.'

File: *Licence To Kill*

Teaser A Drug Enforcement Administration helicopter stalls Felix Leiter, who's on the way to his wedding, to apprise him of the fact that Sanchez, a wanted drug baron whom Leiter has been studying for some time, has made a rare visit outside his safe haven of Isthmus City to retrieve his errant mistress from the nearby Cray Key. James Bond, Leiter's best man, merrily joins in the pursuit of Sanchez, ultimately securing his capture by hooking Sanchez' plane to the 'copter. Bond and Leiter then parachute down to the church, just in time. Although Leiter's wedding is an elaborate conceit – the gimmick underlined by a visual gag in which Bond and Leiter's parachutes are compared to bridal trains – it has an air of Bondian excess enough to win out over the perhaps unspecial main action. **7**

Titles Overwrought nonsense with cameras and girls. **3**

Bonkers plot Bribing DEA agent Killifer, Sanchez escapes a police convoy and has his goons disturb Leiter's wedding night; Della is (probably) raped and killed, Leiter fed to a shark and horribly maimed. Discovering their bodies, Bond breaks into a coastal warehouse belonging to a Sanchez cohort and, bent on revenge, murders Killifer coldly.

Learning of Killifer's death, M – fearing that Bond's 'private vendetta ... could easily compromise Her Majesty's Government' – orders Bond on to an assignment in Istanbul. Bond instead resigns; M instantly withdraws Bond's licence to kill. Fleeing M's people, the fugitive Bond pursues Sanchez aided only by one of Leiter's informants. 'Drug baron', 'raped and killed', 'bent on revenge', 'private vendetta', 'Bond resigns'; do any of these phrases have any place whatsoever in a bonkers James Bond plot? They do not. A single point for Sanchez' stylish method of transporting cocaine (dissolving it in gasoline and having it ferried about in petrol tankers; the evidence can be destroyed with a single match if necessary). **1**

Locations In and around the Florida Keys; island Bimini; in and around Isthmus, South America. There's plenty of scope for sequences set in Hong Kong, from whence narcotics agents have been trailing Sanchez, posing as possible buyers. The opportunity is passed up. The least variety in environs since *Dr. No*. **2**

Gadgets The 'manta ray' cowl Bond cloaks himself with beneath the *Wavekrest* (and, as a rogue agent with no field support, how the hell does he rustle that one up?) Q – who poses as Bond's uncle – takes leave to bring Bond a battered suitcase containing 'everything for a man on holiday': an explosive alarm clock, 'Dentonite' toothpaste, a plastic explosive in a tube; a camera which takes '.220 high-velocity film'; an X-ray Polaroid camera with a laser beam in the flash; and a kit-part signature gun with an optical palm reader, enabling Bond alone to use it. Q later uses a two-way radio mic hidden in a broom. The villain's sole 'gadget' is a *You Only Live Twice*-style subterranean helipad. **6**

Girls Della, Felix's bride, who seems inappropriately keen on Bond. Occasional croupier Lupe Lamora, who watches Westerns, claims to love Bond 'sooo much', and cops off with El Presidente at the end. (The president, incidentally, is played by Pedro Amendariz Jr, son of the late *From Russia with Love* star.) Foul-mouthed Yank Pam Bouvier – one 'Shit!', one 'Bullshit!' – the last of Leiter's nine contacts to remain alive, is a CIA contract pilot and former army pilot who's been to 'the toughest hellholes in South America'. She's got a big gun when we first meet her, and remarks upon the relative lack of size of Bond's wee

Walther (a blatant cod-Freudian innuendo). Wears a bulletproof vest (handy when she's shot in the back), charges Bond $75,000 to fly him to Isthmus City, and gets her hair cut to pose as Bond's executive secretary, Miss – sorry, Ms – Kennedy. Keeps a pistol in her garter and has a velcro-detachable lower part of her evening dress to get to it. Hasn't smoked for five years before meeting Bond. A waitress at the Barrelhead Bar who calls Bond 'hon'. Moneypenny, who's 'worried sick' about Bond and persuades Q to join him in the field. Capital is made of Pam being made jealous of Bond's sleeping with Lupe, but it hardly seems in keeping with the feisty 'glam Ripley' established elsewhere. Lupe is a faithless gold-digger whose abilities extend no further than flicking through fashion mags and shuffling cards. We can't recall a principal Bond girl who appears to have less going on in her head, which is quite some achievement in itself. **4**

Villains Oh joy. *Live and Let Die*'s criminal fraternity without either ambition or glamour. Principal is pockmarked, pink-shirted paranoiac cocaine baron Franz Sanchez, who owns an 'invisible empire from Chile to Alaska', plus the Banco di Isthmus ('the world's largest private investment fund'), a casino, a corrupt President, Lupe, a large staff of hangers-on and – shades of Blofeld – a pet iguana with a diamond-studded choker which he keeps on his shoulder. He's wanted in the US on 139 felony counts – a total of 936 years in chokey. Auctions off his wares via corrupt tele-evangelist Joe Butcher at $22,000 per kilo. Bullwhips Lupe, has Lupe's lover's heart cut out and merrily watches Milton Krest pop like a balloon inside a decompression chamber. Gives an unintentionally hilarious masterclass in drug pushing to a table of corrupt Oriental businessmen ('Buy a mayor . . .'). Sanchez's main associates include: corrupt seaman Krest himself, a drunken pervert (he peeks through Lupe's windows at night); corrupt copper Killifer; probably corrupt Cuban-heeled sadist Dario, who's bad news (he 'used to be with the Contras 'til they kicked him out'); and germanely corrupt stiff-haired yuppie accountant Truman-Lodge, who talks exclusively in terms of demographic reports, 'aggressive marketing' and 'exclusive franchises'. Were Truman-Lodge acting for a world domineer like SPECTRE rather than a drug lord, he'd be very funny; despite the claims made elsewhere for Sanchez being 'plucked straight from the pages of today's news', it's actually Truman-Lodge

who articulates the late Eighties Zeitgeist in full. His demise is the subject of one of only two good one-liners; barks Sanchez, shooting Truman-Lodge full of lead, 'I guess it's time to start cutting overheads . . .' **3**

Fights, chases, explosions Bond's escape from the sea beneath the *Wavekrest* – pursued by homicidal frogmen, he fires a harpoon from beneath the water's surface into the body of a boat-plane skimming the water, which yanks him free of the killers, enabling him to use the body of the harpoon gun as a rudder to 'water-ski' to the wing of the boat-plane as it launches into the air, whereupon, in flight, he climbs into the plane and boots its occupants out – has the old magic in spades. It's used to great black comic effect later, where Krest's faltering explanation of this unlikely event only adds to Sanchez' suspicions of him ('he threw the pilots out and flew away'/'Like a leetle bird . . .'). The brawl at the sleazy Barrelhead Bar – which involves the ill-advised application of bottles, a pool cue and even a stuffed swordfish – is a classic of its type, and Sanchez' tank assault on the hideout of the Hong Kong narcotics operation a fabulous example of excessive force. The villain's exploding base (he has a drugs factory concealed beneath the outlandish 'Olympatec Meditation Institute') is a Bond staple we've not seen since *Moonraker* (and it's the most satisfying demolition in a while). The concluding set piece – the pursuit and destruction of four highly combustible petrol tankers amid precarious desert gullies – is simply awe-inspiring. **10**

Dialogue and double entendres M's outraged 'We're not a country club, 007!' upon being told of Bond's intention to resign. Lupe to Bond: 'Don't you men know any other way?' Bond to Lupe: 'It's Sanchez's way. You seem to like it.' After Krest has met his end in the decompression chamber, a Sanchez associate enquires after the thousands of dollars which are now coated in Krest's entrails. 'Launder it,' instructs Sanchez. Largely functional and witless. **2**

Bond Describes himself as a 'problem eliminator' and has 'big *cojones*', according to Sanchez. Will do 'anything for a woman with a knife'. In the *Wavekrest* cabin, he holds a knife to Lupe's throat and yanks her hair back hard. There is, we venture, a difference between a well-timed slap – which is, rightly or wrongly, a common currency shared by the sexes in action cinema – and sheer brutality. Which is what this is. Asks for a whole case of Bollinger RD to be sent up to his room, which is in keeping with the mindless excess he displays throughout. Moreover ... in *The Man With the Golden Gun*, Bond distinguishes himself from the villain by claiming that 'when I kill, it's on the specific orders of my government, and those I kill are themselves killers'; even as recently as *The Living Daylights*, Bond affirms to Saunders that 'I only kill professionals.' So who is this vengeance-fixated sociopath proclaiming himself to be James Bond? A man whose actions are not only not condoned by his government, but actually an embarrassment to them? A man who slaughters indiscriminately to satisfy his own bloodlust? Yes, Bond has always existed above conventional law – his very *raison d'être* is to go after those who cannot otherwise be touched – but not on a whim, not as self-appointed judge, jury and executioner. He certainly won't be forgiven for it, as he is here. Dalton is no better or worse than before, but not even Connery could have made the icy, disturbed individual presented here amount to anything more than a cruel imposter given someone else's name. Take away the number 007, it seems, and you've only half a man. This is not our hero. This is not James Bond. **O**

Plus/minus points M's introduction is clever – surrounded, Blofeld-style, by cats, he whirls round to reveal his true identity – but we find it very worrying that the only reason M's associates don't gun Bond down is because there are 'too many people' around. Conspiracy theory thriller, yes. Bond film, no. **-5**

33% Set in a *Miami Vice* world where gung-ho Americans spout lines such as, 'The DA's screaming to know what happened!', the misconceived *Licence To Kill* only jerks to life sporadically – in the 'waterskiing' scene, the Q sequences, when the villain's base blows up – when, in fact, it deigns to lower/raise itself to the level we expect from a Bond film. 'This is no place for you, Q,' snarls one-man army Bond, having just knocked the old duffer to the ground. He's right. This is not a James Bond picture; devoid of glamour, elegance, élan, it's a *Rambo*, a *Death Wish* – mean-spirited, second-division, conveyor-belt popcorn. It wasn't even made in Britain.

CAST

Timothy Dalton James Bond
Carey Lowell Pam Bouvier **Robert Davi** Franz Sanchez **Talisa Soto** Lupe Lamora
Anthony Zerbe Milton Krest **Frank McRae** Sharkey **Everett McGill** Killifer
Wayne Newton Professor Joe Butcher **Benicio Del Toro** Dario
Anthony Starke Truman-Lodge **Pedro Armendariz** President Hector Lopez
Desmond Llewelyn Q **David Hedison** Felix Leiter **Priscilla Barnes** Della Churchill
Robert Brown M **Caroline Bliss** Miss Moneypenny **Don Stroud** Heller
Grand L. Bush Hawkins **Cary-Hiroyuki Tagawa** Kwang **Alejandro Bracho** Perez
Guy De Saint Cyr Braun **Rafer Johnson** Mullens **Diana Lee** Hsu Loti
Christopher Neame Fallon **Jeannine Bisignano** Stripper **Claudio Brook** Montelongo
Cynthia Fallon Consuela **Enrique Novi** Rasmussen **Osami Kawawo** Oriental
George Belanger Doctor **Roger Kudney** Wavekrest Captain
Honorato Magaloni Chief Chemist **Jorge Russek** Pit Boss **Sergio Corona** Bellboy
Stuart Kwan Ninja **Jose Abdala** Tanker Driver **Teresa Blake** Ticket Agent
Samuel Benjamin Lancaster Della's Uncle **Juan Peleaz** Casino Manager
Mark Kelty Coast Guard Radio Operator **Umberto Elizondo** Hotel Assistant Manager
Fidel Carriga Sanchez's Driver **Edna Bolkan** Barrelhead Waitress
Edie Enderfield Clive **Jeff Moldervan, Carl Ciarfalio** Warehouse Guards

SELECTED CREDITS

Stunt Co-Ordinator **Paul Weston** Driving Stunts Arranger **Remy Julienne**
Aerial Stunt Arranger **'Corkey' Fornof** Camera Operator **Michael Frift**
Continuity **June Randall** Art Director **Michael Lamont**
Make-up Supervisors **George Frost**, **Naomi Dunne**
Hairdressing Supervisor **Tricia Cameron** Editor **John Grover**
Costume Designer **Jodie Tillen** Main Title Designed by **Maurice Binder**
Casting by **Jane Jenkins** and **Janet Hirshenson**
Original Score Composed and Conducted by **Michael Kamen**
Special Visual Effects **John Richardson** Director of Photography **Alec Mills**
Production Designed by **Peter Lamont**
Associate Producers **Tom Pevsner** and **Barbara Broccoli**
Written by **Michael G. Wilson** and **Richard Maibaum**
Produced by **Albert R. Broccoli** and **Michael G. Wilson**
Directed by **John Glen**

Corny lines included: *GoldenEye*

1994: confident that he had safeguarded the Bond franchise through one of the most precarious periods in its long history, Albert Broccoli took a back seat as Michael G. Wilson and Barbara Broccoli continued pre-production on the next film. A serious heart condition had left Cubby with another, more personal, battle to fight. On 12 April, Timothy Dalton made an announcement that disappointed those who had hoped the relaunched series would benefit from a familiar Bond. Dalton had reportedly signed a three-picture contract, but 'the delay since *Licence To Kill* had prompted a desire to move on. He would not, he had decided, appear in the follow-up. Although ten actors were tested, finding a replacement was relatively straightforward: Pierce Brosnan was offered the role of 007. This time, he was free to take it. 'There's a lot at stake,' he admitted during the filming of *GoldenEye* in 1995. 'Everybody wants to get this right, especially when you've been out of operation for six years. There's nothing like a bit of pressure . . .'

Following close consultation with Albert Broccoli, Michael G. Wilson and Barbara Broccoli, Michael France had begun scripting *GoldenEye*, an original story that took its name from that of Ian Fleming's Jamaican home, in May 1993. 'We didn't know it would be Pierce when we started,' he told *GoldenEye* magazine. 'It was sort of generally assumed that it would be Tim [Dalton] . . . I tried to write it with him in mind: a lot of physical action, some emotional intensity with [double agent] Trevelyan, and not a lot of humour.' A recce trip to Russia had inspired a scene (ultimately discarded) where Bond broke into the KGB headquarters in Moscow and Bond's reunion with Trevelyan amidst a dumping ground for Communist-era statues. 'I was told that there's a huge junkyard somewhere full of them . . . that's obviously an irresistible visual for Bond, and I wound up using it in the second draft.'

In 1994, France's material was reworked by British writer Jeffrey Caine. 'It was like detective puzzle stuff at the beginning,' Caine told *Sci-Fi Universe* magazine. 'I argued that what Bond typically did was to throw himself into a dangerous situation and see what happened, rather than cerebrally follow a trail of clues. We put in a whole new first act and I said that what we needed to do was to show

Trevelyan/006 and Bond in action in the beginning, to establish who they were. And then cut from titles to where Bond is now, and something has to happen which puts him on the trail of Trevelyan without knowing it's Trevelyan.' Next aboard was Kevin Wade, whose contribution to the screenplay included reportedly loaning his surname to Bond's CIA liaison. In September, *Real Men Don't Eat Quiche* author Bruce Feirstein – a friend of Barbara Broccoli and her husband Fred Zollo – was invited to contribute an additional polish. Caine and Feirstein would share on-screen credit for the screenplay; France would be credited for the story.

Eon's long search for a director resulted in the appointment of Martin Campbell. Born in New Zealand, Campbell had relocated to Britain in 1966 and directed his first film, *The Sex Thief*, in 1973. In the following year he directed *Eskimo Nell*, an amusing and incisive satire on the very sex films it is sometimes mistaken as being an example of. Experience of a more valuable nature was gained when Campbell directed episodes of filmed television series such as *The Professionals*, *Shoestring* and *Minder*. The apocalyptic BBC drama *Edge of Darkness* (1986) catalysed his career, and he soon graduated to Hollywood and such films as *Criminal Law* (1989), *Defenseless*(1992) and *No Escape* (1994). 'I'm good at action,' he once modestly claimed.

Pierce Brosnan was told he had finally won the role of James Bond on Tuesday 1 June. Like his two predecessors, he was reportedly offered an initial three-picture contract. 'To be honest there was never anybody else in the frame,' Campbell told *What's On In London*. 'I saw some people just in case, but I think Pierce is actually

much better now than he would have been then. I saw the [1986] screen tests and he looked unbelievably young.' Brosnan's 91-episode run in *Remington Steele* had come to an end in 1987, the same year he appeared alongside Michael Caine in *The Fourth Protocol*. Shortly after, Brosnan's wife Cassandra developed cancer, and he devoted himself to caring for her. She died in 1991. Cassandra's death had a profound effect on Brosnan, and he worked little in the ensuing years. Prior to being cast in *GoldenEye* he had featured in *Mister Johnson* (1991), *The Lawnmower Man* (1992) and *Mrs Doubtfire* (1993). A bearded Brosnan (he was preparing to film a TV adaptation of *Robinson Crusoe*) was introduced to the press at the Regent Hotel in London on Wednesday 8 June. He outlined his philosophy towards Bond: 'I would like to see what is beneath the surface of this man, what drives him on, what makes him a killer. I think we will peel back the onion skin, as it were.'

'I would like to see what is beneath the surface of this man'

Campbell was enthusiastic about a screenplay that embraced many of the best-loved motifs and situations from the classic Bond pictures: 'When you're given the job your first instinct is to say "Oh, I'll rewrite this whole thing and do it differently," and then you think, "Hold on, this series has been going for 33 years and it's been a huge success. People will expect certain things." So I went back and watched all the films, and realised that those elements, corny lines included, are absolutely terrific. I certainly wouldn't want to tamper with a lot of that.'

There was, however, one exception to his presentation of Bond's traditionally dapper image. 'I don't give a damn about everyone's perception of the character. I think smoking causes cancer therefore he doesn't smoke.'

Ironically, considering that Eon had chosen to establish a foreign production base for

'Boyish charms I might actually have succumbed to . . .'

Licence Revoked, *GoldenEye* could not find studio space at Pinewood. In the 18 months leading up to the application, the facility had staged *Mary Reilly*, *First Knight*, *Interview With the Vampire* and *Hackers*. The lavish Gerry Anderson series *Space Precinct* (directors for which included John Glen) was in residency, and managing director Steve Jaggs reported that his order book was full. Forced to find an alternative, Eon happened upon a disused Rolls-Royce factory at Leavesden Aerodrome, near Watford in Hertfordshire. The buildings on the 150-acre site, which was closed in 1993, were adapted for use as a huge, and exclusive, six-stage studio from June 1994 onwards.

By 21 November, the screenplay would be broadly identical to that eventually filmed, except in a few places. Still extant at this stage was Bond's assault on the guardhouse which leads to the dam over the Arkhangel Chemical Weapons Facility; in five planned shots, a black-clad figure would be seen to eliminate two chess-playing sentries prior to running across the top of the dam and jumping off. M's widely noted spiel in which she puts Bond down as 'a sexist, misogynist dinosaur' bore a different emphasis entirely; here, she would go on to describe him as 'a relic of the Cold War . . . Whose boyish charms I might actually have succumbed to ten years ago'. Wisely, any concomitant 'did-

they-or-didn't they?' debate, which might have perhaps entirely undermined the credibility of the Bond/M relationship, would be averted in the finished version ('whose boyish charms, although wasted on me . . .'). CIA contact Jack Wade's gardening obsession – only obliquely referred to in the finished version – was played up a great deal, too. Outside Zukovsky's lair, Bond and Wade were to have passed by an informal arms bazaar – an illicit car boot sale for automatic weaponry – and, inside, Zukovsky would first be seen dismissing an arms merchant whose wares he deduces to be counterfeit.

The cast of *GoldenEye* were unveiled to the press at 'Eon Studios' on Sunday 22 January 1995. Bond's treacherous colleague Alec Trevelyan, the former 006, was to be played by Sean Bean. The Sheffield-born actor was best known to television audiences as Lieutenant Sharpe in the feature-length adaptations of Bernard Cornwell's historical adventures. Bean had co-starred in Derek Jarman's controversial biopic *Caravaggio* (1986) and had more recently appeared in mainstream films such as thriller *Patriot Games* (1992).

Izabella Scorupco would play computer programmer Natalya Simonova. Born in Bialystok, Poland, in 1970, Scorupco suffered a poverty-stricken childhood before emigrating to Stockholm with her mother in 1978. The film *No One Can Love Like Us* (1987) turned her into a star, and she consolidated the success with three hit singles and a successful album, *Iza*. Scorupco later relocated to Milan for a brief time, and soon made the front cover of Italian *Vogue*. *GoldenEye* marked her debut in an English-language film. Dutch former model Famke Janssen was cast as Fiona Volpe-esque assassin Xenia Onatopp, the most prominent role yet in a career that had included parts in *Fathers and Sons* (1992) and *Lord of Illusions* (1995). Eon had requested to see footage featuring Janssen in the latter film while it was still in production, and asked her to appear in screen tests for *GoldenEye* soon after.

Joe Don Baker was cast as brash American liaison Wade – a very different role from the arms dealer he had played in *The Living Daylights*. Baker had previously worked with Campbell on *Edge of Darkness* and *Criminal Law*. Former *Comic Strip* company member Robbie Coltrane had realigned his career with his compelling portrayal of a cynical criminal psychologist in television drama *Cracker*. Cast in *GoldenEye* as Russian gangster Valentin Zukovsky, Coltrane was so enamoured of his character that he reportedly requested that Zukovsky be left alive in the final screenplay, hopeful he might get the opportunity to reprise the role.

Distinguished stage and screen actress Dame Judi Dench replaced Robert Brown as M; her casting reflected the fact the latest head of MI5 was a woman. The lady in question, the little-seen Ms Stella Rimmington, declined to comment on the film, but then Prime Minister John Major would remark on the resemblance between the Secret Service chief and Dame Judi. 'They certainly look very similar', he said.

Thirty-three-year-old Samantha Bond, an actress acclaimed for her work with the Royal Shakespeare Company and the National Theatre, replaced her friend Caroline Bliss as Miss Moneypenny. 'On screen, at least, Moneypenny in this film is a slightly more together person,' she claimed, 'It's a more even relationship between her and James Bond.' In her

Pierce Brosnan is unveiled as the new James Bond on 8 June 1994

belief, Moneypenny and Bond had never actually been lovers: 'I think she's far too canny for that. However attractive James may be, you'd no more want to get involved with him than drink ink. He is still, I'm afraid, one of those men. But how many "new men" do you really know?' One familiar face among the MI6 staff was that of the redoubtable Q, played once again by Desmond LLewellyn. The 81 year-old actor's 15th Bond appearance would prove relatively low-key compared to the prominent role he had played in *Licence To Kill*, but *GoldenEye*'s repackaging of familiar Bond elements and situations would have been unthinkable without Q's traditionally acerbic briefing. 'I'm an old-age pensioner now and, thanks to Q, I'm earning some money,' he said after completing his one and-a-half days' filming. 'I don't regret it at all. I've had fun on every single Bond film I've done.'

Backed with a reported budget of $50 million – a comparatively modest sum in relation to the money spent on similar action films such as *True Lies* (1994) – filming had begun on Monday 16 January.

At Leavesden's 'Eon studios' 007 was reunited with a familiar accessory

Brosnan, who had bought all the Ian Fleming Bond novels in 1986 when he was initially preparing for the role, kept a copy of *Goldfinger* with him at Leavesden. 'Just for the significance of it,' he explained. 'As a boy in 1964, just over from Ireland, *Goldfinger* was the first film I ever saw and that was the touchstone. Little did I think I would be playing the role someday.'

In February, location shooting was undertaken in Monaco; exterior casino shots were filmed at Monte Carlo, and the car chase between Bond's Aston Martin and Onatopp's Ferrari was filmed on mountain roads nearby. The yacht *Northern Cross* doubled for the *Manticore* during Bond's unsuccessful race to prevent Onatopp stealing the Tiger helicopter.

Bond's climactic struggle with Trevelyan was filmed at the Arecibo radar-radio telescope – the largest fixed radio telescope in the world. Michael France recalled that the location had been suggested by Michael G. Wilson: 'When we started talking about how to handle the climax and what we were going to do about making an antenna interesting, he dug out some photos of the [Arecibo] observatory.' The enormous structure is located nine miles south of Arecibo, on the northern coast of Puerto Rico. The location doubled for the Janus Syndicate headquarters in Cuba, and stuntmen Jamie Edgall and Sean McKay doubled for Pierce Brosnan and Sean Bean in the most dangerous sequences.

The opening shot of the pre-credits sequence was filmed at the Verzasca Dam in Locarno, southern Switzerland. For the 640-foot bungee jump that opened the sequence, stuntman Wayne Michaels doubled Brosnan. Michaels then valiantly performed a shorter jump to help

Campbell achieve the close-ups he required. The Russian nerve gas plant that it is 006 and 007's mission to sabotage was constructed at Leavesden; the airfield's runway was used as the launching point for Bond's motorbike-to-aeroplane escape.

Second unit director Ian Sharp spent just over a week in St Petersburg (the former Leningrad) to capture footage that was later matched to a backlot dressed by production designer Peter Lamont. The scene where Jack Wade meets Bond at St Petersburg airport was actually filmed at a suitably freezing Epsom race course in April. Other more immediate locations included the Nene Valley steam railway in Peterborough, previously the site of extensive filming during the production of *Octopussy*.

On 1 June, a year to the day since Brosnan won the role, he was greeted on the St Petersburg backlot by Roger Moore. The former 007, who was at Leavesden to visit his son Christian (working as a third assistant director) and co-producer Michael G. Wilson, initially joked that he been asked to take over! The final sequence filmed by Campbell was the St Petersburg tank chase, mounted under the scrutiny of stunt co-ordinator Simon Crane. As a stuntman, Crane had previously doubled Timothy Dalton in *Licence To Kill* and Brosnan in *The Fourth Protocol*. Principal photography came to an end on Tuesday 6 June.

The extensive model work, which was employed alongside the less traditional post-production art of digital imaging, was supervised by Derek Meddings. A long-standing contributor to Eon's Bond series, Meddings had first contributed to *Live and Let Die* and shared a 1979 Oscar nomination for visual effects in *Moonraker*. 'I don't want my work

repaired by a computer,' he said proudly. 'There's got to be a human element.' Shortly after his work on *GoldenEye* was complete, Meddings succumbed to cancer. The film would be dedicated to his memory.

The responsibility for *GoldenEye*'s music was segregated: John Altman and David Arch were credited with symphonic music (which included the rousing new interpretation of the Bond theme that graced the trailer) and Parisian Eric Serra, best known for his regular collaboration with director Luc Besson, composed the synthesiser tracks. The title music was produced by Nellee Hooper (who had previously overseen recordings by such artists as Bjork and Madonna), written by Bono and The Edge (respectively vocalist and guitarist from Irish supergroup U2), and performed by Tina Turner. She first heard the song when Bono and The Edge sent her a home demo: 'It was extremely rough,' she remarks, recalling her initial reluctance to commit to the recording. 'I learned the lyrics and then Nellee rang me from London and he said "I've put down a track – I just want to make sure it's in the right key." I heard the track and I knew immediately: it's good.' When released as a single in November 1995, *GoldenEye* reached number ten in the British chart.

Maurice Binder, who had either designed or indirectly influenced every Eon title sequence from *Dr. No* to *Licence To Kill*, had died early in 1991. The astonishing titles for *GoldenEye*, both a homage to and development of Binder's style, were designed and directed by Daniel Kleinman. With a background as a commercial artist and illustrator, Kleinman made his directing debut with the promotional video for Heaven 17's 1983 hit *Crushed By the Wheels of Industry*. He went on to direct over one hundred videos, and later television commercials, gaining a reputation for his pioneering use of effects devices such as Paintbox and HARRY. Prior to *GoldenEye*, Kleinman had directed the BBC comedies *Smashie and Nicey – the End of an Era* with Harry Enfield and Paul Whitehouse, and *How To Be a Little Sod* with Rik Mayall.

On 17 November 1995 the film opened in America, where it catalysed a major resurgence in the popularity of James Bond. The Prince of Wales, by now separated from his wife, attended the British premiere of *GoldenEye* at the Leicester Square Odeon. According to subsequent press reports he enjoyed the film so much he could be heard to enthusiastically cheer during key moments. The film opened in London on 22 November, and commenced general release from the 24th.

The final US admission figures were an estimated 29 million – a patronage unrivalled by any Bond picture since *You Only Live Twice*. As of May 1996, *GoldenEye*'s estimated US gross had reached $106,429,941; the worldwide gross totalled an impressive $350,731,227. True to the promise at the end credits of *Licence To Kill*, James Bond had returned.

'This is the best Bond movie since *On Her Majesty's Secret Service*,' declared Kim Newman in *Empire* magazine. His review followed an enthusiastic consensus among Fleet Street critics: 'Bond is back at his best' proclaimed Alexander Walker in the *Evening Standard* of 9 November. 'The film is located precisely on the cusp between fantasy and near reality. For the first time in a Bond film there is even something that could be called emotion. The packed preview audience fell silent,

listening to the feelings in the scene where Bond finds his secret service comrade, 006, is a Guy Burgess-like traitor. Since when did feelings count in Bond adventures? Here they do in a script that makes friendship betrayed the mainspring of its action, not simply ladies seduced and bedded or assassins tricked and treated to their own medicine.'

'Brosnan shares none of Connery's virtues,' remarked Tom Shone in *The Sunday Times* on 19 November, 'but has also been careful to avoid Moore's vices. It doesn't give him much room for manoeuvre, but then manoeuvring in tight corners is the one thing Brosnan is quite good at . . . It's the sort of skill that comes in handy amid the swift, crisply defined action sequences of the film – by far the best since *The Spy Who Loved Me*. The director, Martin Campbell, comes to Bond from such dull blockish thrillers as *Criminal Law*, *Defenseless* and *No Escape*; but he has also served a stint on the television series *Homicide: Life on the Street*, whose fast, fleeting style has helped toughen *GoldenEye* into an impressively urgent film.'

Even hardened Bond cynic Derek Malcolm accorded *GoldenEye* the mantle 'film of the week' in *The Guardian* on 23 November: 'No one could say that the plot wasn't forged out of conventional Bond material. Nor that the fantasy hasn't a tinge of realism to give an edge to its absurdity. That's the strength of the movie. It gives its audiences what they've always wanted, while obliquely suggesting that Ian Fleming's hero is a bit of a cad by modern standards . . . If *Four Weddings and a Funeral* suggested Britain could still make highly commercial films, *GoldenEye* proves the point.'

On 27 June 1996, Albert Romolo Broccoli – known to one and all as Cubby – passed away. He was 87. While never well enough to visit the set of *GoldenEye*, Broccoli had followed the film's progress closely, and died content in the knowledge that his legacy was safe, and successful, in the hands of his family. At a moving memorial held at the Leicester Square Odeon on Sunday 17 November, Roger Moore, Timothy Dalton and Pierce Brosnan joined Bond luminaries past and present in paying tribute to their paternal producer. 'I wanted *GoldenEye* to be great for him, and only him,' said an emotional Brosnan during his speech, 'and I want the next one to be great for him, and him only. I missed him in *GoldenEye* . . . and I will miss him throughout the making of number 18.'

File: *GoldenEye*

Teaser A black-clad figure makes an impossible bungee jump from the crest of an impossibly high dam. Bond (for 'tls he) is then able to break into the toilets of a Soviet chemical weapons dump; further inside, he encounters fellow agent 006, Alec Trevelyan. In the heart of a nerve gas store, they set detonators to blow the facility up, but are captured by troops belonging to one General Ouromov. 006 is shot in the head, but Bond escapes outside; he runs towards a light aircraft which is taxiing off a mountainside runway, but falls off the plane with the pilot. The aircraft trundles on regardless. As Ouromov's soldiers watch, disbelieving, Bond seizes a motorbike and makes for the end of the runway. First the plane, then the bike roar over a sheer face, plunging into a chasm. Incredibly, Bond freefalls into the plane, wrestles with the controls, pulls it out of its terminal dive and soars over the weapons store as the charges he'd set explode. Mission accomplished. A jaw-dropping spectacle book-ended by two of the finest stunts in the series (better, even, than *The Spy Who Loved Me*'s pre-credits, and giving *Goldfinger*'s a run for its money). Disbelief well and truly suspended; if he'd pulled a bird too, we'd have fainted. **10**

Titles A fabulous, ever-changing vista of images with genuine pretensions to surrealism (Magritte-esque raining Walthers), hefty symbolism (women pound colossal sickles with hammers, crawl out of collapsing Soviet statues like maggots out of rotten meat) and relevance to the film, both in specific ideas (a twin-headed woman with a cigar in one mouth and a retractable gun in the other, suggesting two- faced Roman god Janus, the villain's pseudonym) and in a broader sense (the titles are intended to depict the nine-year gap between the teaser and the main film, during which the USSR as was falls). Its tightly-clothed figures are innately more erotic than Binder's writhing spot-the-nipple nudes of later years, too; that this sequence bears such scrutiny tells a tale in itself. **10**

Bonkers plot Nine years later, Bond witnesses the hijack of a revolutionary new French helicopter, able to function regardless of all electronic interference, by a killer with links to a St Petersburg criminal syndicate, Janus. The helicopter is next observed flying over a secret Space Weapons Research Centre in Russia; the copter's hijackers – assassin Xenia Onatopp and the renegade General Ouromov – steal a secret device, the GoldenEye, which controls one of two spacebound nuclear devices – the detonation of which creates a radiation surge which destroys anything with an electrical circuit on the Earth immediately below. One is set off, destroying the centre; the villains flee. Bond goes after the Janus syndicate, discovering its head to be none other than his embittered former comrade Alec Trevelyan; desiring revenge upon the British, whom he holds responsible for the deaths of his Cossack-descended father and mother, Trevelyan plans to detonate the second device over London immediately after electronically raiding its banks, giving himself 'more money than God' and precipitating 'a worldwide financial meltdown'. Although the villain's plan has a satisfying grandiosity, it's lost in a welter of cross-motivation and unexplained (or inexplicable) connections. Was 006's 'death' in fact a staged defection? If not, how did he survive (a) a bullet in the head, (b) the exploding Arkhangel store, and (c) the nerve gas undoubtedly released in the course of the explosion? At what point did he learn the truth of his lineage? When did Ouromov inform Trevelyan of the existence of the GoldenEye – before or after the Arkhangel incident? Or did Trevelyan know about it already and seek out Ouromov beforehand?

If so, why does it take nine years to steal the GoldenEye? Are they waiting for someone to invent the Tiger helicopter? Why does Alec want to seize all that money? If he's motivated only by revenge against the British, why precipitate a 'worldwide financial meltdown' by erasing every electronic record in the City of London? (In such a circumstance, the money he's earned will surely become useless.) If he's motivated by revenge against Bond, why does he claim that he 'thought of asking [Bond] to join my little scheme'? Was that before or after Bond adjusted the timers on the Arkhangel detonators? The radar dish is in Communist Cuba – is Castro in league with Trevelyan? Why are there vast vats of (a) fuel and (b) liquid nitrogen stored beneath the dish? What are they for, if not – surely not! – simply to enable Bond to break in and blow the villain's base sky-high? Touches all the right bases, but fails to follow its machinations through, opening up new and superfluous holes at almost every turn. Oh dear. **5**

Locations The Arkhangel dump, Soviet Russia; in and around Monte Carlo; Severnaya, northern Russia; London; outer space; St Petersburg; a Caribbean island; Cuba. A Bond film actually shot in the streets of the (former) Evil Empire? Whatever next? **8**

Gadgets Nine years ago, Bond possessed bungee rope, a piton/laser gun and a digital lock-cracking device. In Monte Carlo, he calls upon both a digital camera and an Aston Martin DB5, now registered as BMT 214A (two digits from the *Goldfinger/Thunderball* machine), with a compartment for Bollinger and an instantaneous colour fax connected to Moneypenny's database installed inside. Later, he drives a (German) BMW with 'all points radar' (the only device we see him use in the field), plus stinger missiles concealed beneath the headlights, a self-destruct system and a parachute at the rear. Q department is testing a rocket-firing leg cast, an ejecting chair, a false telephone kiosk with a deadly airbag inside, and a silver tea tray which acts as an X-ray document scanner. Bond is issued with a leather belt with a 75 feet long high tensile wire built into the buckle, a class 4 grenade with a four-second fuse built into a pen; he also employs magnetic mines and a watch that expels a laser beam (the latter is the subject of one of the film's many casual subversions of established Bond practice, in which the villain asks after Q

when seizing the device from Bond). The pen (and Boris' nervous clicking of it) is used to clever effect, creating probably the picture's most tense moment. **9**

Girls Neurotic MI6 assessor Caroline, who castigates Bond for showing off the size of his ... ego. Fast Georgian native and ex-Soviet fighter pilot Xenia Onatopp who smokes huge cigars, likes her vodka Martini 'straight up, vis a tvist', and appears to be capable of reaching orgasm only when killing people. The best villainess since Fatima Blush, she purrs, she scowls – and is cursorily despatched, the film's most arresting character thrown away glibly with a crack about 'a good squeeze'. Theatre-goer Moneypenny, whom Bond has never seen after hours, has 'a gentleman' on the go and suggests that Bond's behaviour might be construed as sexual harrassment. Level Two computer programmer Natalya Fyodorovna Simonova, who wears a cosy cardigan, spouts the jargon of armchair therapy [see *Dialogue* below] and tastes like strawberries, according to the villain. Zukovsky's mistress, would-be country singer Irina, and the trio backing her. Xenia alone stands out among this anodyne bunch – and she, amazingly, doesn't have sex with Bond (well, not technically). **7**

Villains Scar-faced former 006 Alec Trevelyan lives on a train (*à la You Only Live Twice*'s Tiger Tanaka), is literate enough to model himself after a two-faced Roman god, and has treacherous Lienz Cossack blood. Claims that half of everything is luck (the other half is fate), was the first arms dealer to re-stock the Iraqis after the Gulf War, and forces himself on Natalya. A potentially fascinating character undone by over or under-exposition [see *Bonkers plot* above], he's assisted by Xenia, by hip-flask swigging General Arkady Grigorovich Ouromov, and by geek Boris. **6**

Fights, chases, explosions The teaser, the destruction of Severnaya, Bond's breaking out of the Military Intelligence building, the St Petersburg tank chase ... all are phenomenal, and all would be diminished were it not for the picture's relentless bang-bang-bang editing style (which also helps to disguise sometimes-iffy modelwork). The 'big finale' really is quite pedestrian, nonetheless. **8**

Dialogue and double entendres *GoldenEye* makes great play of subverting Bond cliché: 'Come out with your hands above your heads'/'How original'; 'another stiff-assed Brit with your secret codes and your passwords'; 'What? No small talk? No ... chit-chat? That's the trouble with the world today – no-one takes the time to do a really sinister interrogation any more. It's a lost art ... ' We love Trevelyan's description of Bond's funeral: 'a small memorial service with only Moneypenny and a few tearful restaurateurs in attendance.' Bond, observing Zenia depart with an Admiral: 'I like a woman who enjoys pulling rank.' And let's not forget Boris' coarse password, KNOCKERS, as exposited to Natalya ('They're right in front of you, and can open very large doors'). But although some of the dialogue is simply overdone ('I might as well ask you if all the vodka Martinis ever silence the screams of all the men you've killed, or if you find forgiveness in the arms of all those willing women for the dead ones you failed to protect'), Natalya's 'boys with toys' line is nothing short of disastrous, as is her later outburst to Bond on a lurid Bounty bar beach: 'You think I'm impressed? All of you with your guns, your killing, your death?' Her claim that what keeps Bond alive is what keeps him alone is simply paying lip service to the character's supposed 'deep problems'. But the remainder of the film, quite rightly, stems from the assumption that Bond is a fixed point in an unchanging world; that to do what he does, he must remain innately superficial. A noble effort compromised by being pushed too damn hard on occasion. **8**

Bond Makes his most patronising comment since Goldfinger's 'run along – man talk' to Caroline ('What's that, dear?'). Claims that 'Enjoy it while it lasts' are 'the very words' he lives by. His suspicions of Xenia are sparked by his observation that her Ferrari has false numberplates. Notes that 'a licence to kill is also a certificate to die'. His waist size is 34. In a previous mission, he shot one-time KGB man Valentin Dimitreyevech Zukovsky in the knee and stole both his car and his girl. Uses a Walther PPK, 7.65mm. Displays visible terror when he thinks that Zukovsky might actually shoot him in the groin. His parents died in a climbing accident. Is utterly bamboozled by Natalya's operation of Internet technology. His two finest moments in the film are non-verbal: in the tank, he glances over his shoulder to glimpse the devastation he's wreaked, adjusts his tie, and guns the vehicle on; and,

while fixing detonators to the radar dish's fuel canisters, he flicks his head almost imperceptibly, as if irritated by a bee, when bullets buzz the wall just inches from his head. Yes. **9**

Plus/minus points Tanner's description of M as 'the evil queen of numbers', and the magnificent M/Bond scene proper, which is worth the price of admission alone. Not sure about the wishy-washy closing sequence, though. **+9**

81% 'Bond. Only Bond,' gasps the villain, half admiring, as Our Man prepares to derail a speeding train with a tank. *GoldenEye* is a restatement, not a reinvention, and only seems to go awry in trying too hard (probing the psyches of both Bond and the villain is probably not a good idea). In concluding that Bond is necessarily stuck in the past – 'a relic of the Cold War' – *GoldenEye*, perversely, gives him a future at last.

Beat the boat and save the lion: *Tomorrow Never Dies*

1996: 'The next films will be equally as important and as challenging,' said Pierce Brosnan, reflecting on the success of *GoldenEye*. 'They'll have to risk it and push the character into areas where we reveal more about Bond. It has to be done, otherwise I'll just be repeating the same performance. There are many shades to look at and, without peeking too much behind the curtain, we'll have to work to maintain the Bond enigma.'

The origins of 'Bond 18', as *Tomorrow Never Dies* was known during its pre-production, reportedly lay in a treatment by novelist Donald Westlake that was prepared – and discarded – before the release of *GoldenEye* in 1995. By 1996, Bruce Feirstein was developing a new story initially inspired by Britain's imminent hand-over of Hong Kong to China.

Martin Campbell was reportedly approached to helm the picture, but declined the opportunity. 'Martin just didn't want to do two Bond films in a row,' explained his agent Martha Luttrell. By September, MGM/UA and Eon had agreed on a director. Roger Spottiswoode was born in Britain in 1947 and, after serving an apprenticeship in television production, first came to notoriety when he edited three Sam Peckinpah films in three consecutive years: *Straw Dogs* (1971), *The Getaway* (1972) and *Pat Garett and Billy the Kid* (1973). Spottiswoode made his directorial debut with the Canadian stalk and slash horror *Terror Train* in 1980, and went on to lens such diverse pictures as *Air America* (1990), *Stop! Or My Mom Will Shoot!* (1992) and *Under Fire* (1993). He earned greatest acclaim for the television dramas *And the Band Played On* (1993) and *Hiroshima* (1995). Persistent press reports of friction between Spottiswoode and his cast during the shooting of *Tomorrow Never Dies* would be dismissed by Pierce Brosnan as 'absolute rubbish'. Spottiswoode himself described directing the Bond film as 'a vacation. It's something entertaining, enjoyable, and fun.'

One of Spottiswoode's earliest tasks was to oversee a reworking of Feirstein's script. Seven Hollywood scriptwriters were reportedly flown to London for a brainstorming session at the Athenaeum Hotel. 'I would describe it as fun,' remarked Robert Collector, one of the writers invited. 'No one was paid, and it was made clear to everyone that no writing was to be done. It was a free weekend in London.' One of the seven, former *Star Trek* writer and director Nicholas Meyer, was asked to contribute to the Bond script on the strength of his ideas. At various junctures, the script was also re-written by David Campbell Wilson and Daniel Petrie

Jr. Petrie had made a huge impact with the Eddie Murphy vehicle *Beverly Hills Cop* in 1984, and gone on to script the Spottiswoode-directed films *Shoot To Kill* (1988) and *Turner and Hooch* (1989). Amid continued speculation over Bond 18's protracted development Feirstein was recalled to adapt Petrie's screenplay into a shooting script with little over a week to spare before principal photography began.

Eon's 18th Bond story focussed on communist China for the first time in the series' history, and pitted 007 against an unusual adversary – megalomaniac media baron Elliot Carver. Operating from a technologically advanced stealth ship, Carver schemes to increase the global circulation of his 100 million-selling newspaper *Tomorrow* and boost the ratings across his extensive satellite television enterprise. Carver's audacious bid for communication supremacy involves nothing less than engineering World War III and offering his subscribers a ringside seat. In his attempts to locate and prevent Carver, Bond becomes implicated with his former lover Paris – now Carver's wife – and collaborates with resourceful Chinese agent Wai Lin. 'Carver hooks into the fear that people have about the consolidation of power among the few,' Michael G Wilson told *USA Today*. 'And we do nothing to allay those fears,' he laughed.

A more confident Pierce Brosnan ('The part is mine, the shoes fit,') was joined by a cast that was assembled from late 1996 onwards. As had been the case with *GoldenEye*, Sir Anthony Hopkins was strongly mooted to play the film's villain. After reportedly expressing an initial interest in Bond 18, he turned the opportunity down. In February 1997, talks between Eon and Jonathan Pryce resulted in the actor being cast as Elliot Carver.

Recent highlights of Pryce's distinguished career had included a co-starring role as Juan Peron in Alan Parker's *Evita* (1996) and a Cannes award for best actor following his leading role in acclaimed biopic *Carrington* (1995). For his stage work, Pryce had won both Olivier and Tony Awards for his starring role in Broadway's *Miss Saigon*.

'There's a style of fighting that we're used to . . .'

Hong Kong chopsocky star and former Miss Malaysia Michelle Yeoh was awarded the role of Wai Lin – an agent of the People's External Security Force in Beijing – in late 1996. 'She plays a kind of female Bond,' revealed Brosnan while publicising his film *Dante's Peak*. 'She's his Chinese counterpart.' Yeoh's character, referred to as Lin Pao in early drafts of the screenplay, would demand much of the 33-year-old actress' renowned martial arts abilities. During filming, Yeoh was frustrated that insurance restrictions prevented her from performing more of her own stunts. She was eventually joined by her team of 'boys': 'We will have six of them and a stunt co-ordinator from Hong Kong,' she anticipated. 'There's a style of fighting that we're used to and it's a lot easier when you work with people you're used to . . . So it's very good that MGM and Eon have realised this and [second unit director] Vic Armstrong has agreed that I work with people I've worked with before.'

Carver's wife Paris was played by Teri Hatcher, the co-star of ABC television's *Lois and Clark: The New Adventures of Superman*. Hatcher was the subject of much gossip column speculation during her stay. 'She finished *Superman* on Monday, flew to Britain on Tuesday and was on the set on Wednesday,' Brosnan told *The Sun*'s Andy Coulson. 'We got our own chemistry going and it's great on film. That's the most important thing.' Although Hatcher was pregnant during shooting, reports from the set confirmed that her figure was trim enough to pass muster during her character's romantic clinch with Bond.

Twenty-three-year-old Cecilia Thomsen, the girlfriend of rock star Bryan Adams, made her film debut as Scandinavian university lecturer Professor Inga Bergstrom. 'Some girls will say I have all the luck,' she remarked, 'but doing the bedroom scenes actually became embarrassing. I don't mind walking around naked at home, but I did feel uncomfortable taking my clothes off in front of the film crew.' Pierce Brosnan 'thoroughly enjoyed the morning we spent in bed together. It was her first movie role but she is a natural.'

The actors playing Bond's back-up – Dame Judi Dench, Samantha Bond, Joe Don Baker and Desmond LLewellyn – all reprised their *GoldenEye* roles. Dench and Bond appeared with another *Tomorrow Never Dies* actor, Eoin McCarthy, in *Amy's View* at the National Theatre throughout the summer of 1997.

'More action. Better girls. Faster cars . . .'

Since *GoldenEye,* the studio space rented by Eon at Leavesden had been purchased by a Malaysian consortium called Third Millennium. The renamed Millennium Studios had in turn been block-booked by George Lucas' Jak Productions and transformed into a base from which he would mount his long-awaited trilogy of

Star Wars prequels. The 400,000 square feet still available were insufficient for Eon's needs so, as the start date for Bond 18 loomed, Eon searched for an alternative. A disused grocery distribution warehouse in nearby Frogmore, St Albans, was customised in much the same way that Leavesden had been before and similarly dubbed 'Eon Studios'. Pinewood's 007 stage was booked to house the interior of Carver's stealth ship, and principal photography on Frogmore's stages and backlot was scheduled to begin on Tuesday 1 April 1997.

The first sequence actually filmed was the pre-credits prologue, which was shot from 18 January 1997 in the French Pyrenees. 'The most difficult task, by far, is being original,' said Vic Armstrong, supervising filming at one of Europe's only operational high-altitude airfields. 'We haven't gone for a big stunt at the beginning of the film like they usually do in the Bond films because there is such an expectation that it might not come up to scratch.' The sequence, featuring Bond's theft of a jet fighter in Afghanistan, was complete by February.

In March, the second unit filmed night-time scenes in Portsmouth, which was reportedly doubling for a location in the South China Sea. HMS *Westminster* and the naval establishment HMS *Dryad* were used; actor Bruce Alexander played the captain of the fictional HMS *Chester*.

Filming began at Eon Studios on 1 April. The 200-strong first unit was due to spend three weeks shooting in Vietnam from 1 May, but Eon's plans were scuppered when the country's government had a change of heart. 'They just found us a bit too ambitious for what's still a rather sketchy infrastructure,' explained Eon spokesman

Gordon Arnell. Other reports suggested that Vietnam's Ministry of Culture had consented to the presence of the Bond location unit, but Ho Chi Minh City's People's Committee had raised an objection to the series' supposed negative depiction of communism. A Vietnamese culture ministry spokesman explained that permission had been refused for 'many complicated reasons'.

During the first two weeks of May, British locations included RAF Lakenheath and the American air base at Mildenhall, Cambridgeshire, which doubled for Okinawa, Japan, during Bond's encounter with Jack Wade. Later in the month, it was reported that Pierce Brosnan and Teri Hatcher had filmed scenes at Stoke Poges Golf Club, the location for 007's famous confrontation with Auric Goldfinger. Different units simultaneously shot footage at foreign locations such as Mexico, Hamburg and Florida during the six month schedule.

The Vietnam shoot was hastily rearranged to take place in Thailand, and on 15 May a press conference was held in Bangkok. Brosnan's first words gave some idea of the strain imposed by the 104-degree Fahrenheit heat: 'Water, water. Hot, hot, hot, hot . . .' The two-week stint in Thailand included a daring stunt where Bond and Wai Lin leap a hovering helicopter on a motorbike that resumes its journey across Vietnamese rooftops. According to Michael G. Wilson, the filming in Thailand alone would cost an estimated $4 million. Production designer Allan Cameron ensured the scenes doubling for Ho Chi Minh City (the former Saigon) were matched by the carefully prepared backlot at Frogmore.

Back in Britain, a chase involving Bond's

remote-controlled BMW 750 (courtesy of Q) was filmed at a car park in Brent Cross. The location was doubling for Hamburg, where other parts of the sequence had already been filmed. One concerned member of the public, unaware that the ensuing devastation was for the benefit of Vic Armstrong's cameras, called the London Fire Brigade. Another headache occurred when, on 17 July, Pierce Brosnan was reportedly injured during the filming of a carefully choreographed fight. One of his opponent's helmets hit his face, and Brosnan sustained an injury that required eight stitches. 'It's a pain, literally,' said Brosnan while filming in Hamburg four days later, 'and it means only one side of my face can be shot until it heals.'

A strenuous, and at times controversial, shoot had come to an end by September. The scuttlebutt surrounding filming had ranged from serious speculation over labour relations, to more light-hearted criticisms of BMW's continuing product placement. (Sunday Times columnist Jeremy Clarkson was especially scathing: 'I thought [Bond] would have learnt his lesson after giving the hair dryer he drove in the last film away to a CIA agent.') Director Roger Spottiswoode said little throughout, perhaps preferring to focus on the job in hand: 'Bond is such an institution that everyone you know gives you ideas. More action. Better girls. Faster cars . . . But you have to be careful. One would not like to be known as the guy who ends the series.'

In June it was confirmed that American singer Sheryl Crow, who had achieved top ten British hits with All I Wanna Do and If It Makes You Happy in 1994 and 1996 respectively, had been commissioned to perform Tomorrow Never Dies' theme tune. David Arnold, who had previously won acclaim for his production collaborations with such artists as Bjork, had already been announced as the composer of the film's incidental music. (In October Arnold released *Shaken and Stirred*, an album of new interpretations of classic Bond themes. Collaborators included Jarvis Cocker, Chrissie Hynde and Iggy Pop.)

Rumours that Bond 18 would not be ready in time to meet its principal photography date had been circulating as early as January 1997. They had proved foundless. As post-production began, speculation mounted over whether *Tomorrow Never Dies* would meet its proposed release date. 'This film will be ready, and anyone who says it won't is either wrong or showing considerable bad faith,' reacted Guy Laurence, MGM/UA's executive vice-president of international distribution and marketing.

There was much at stake – some industry reports claimed that the budget had been as high as $100 million. MGM/UA's financial situation was described by *Variety* as 'tender' following another boardroom shuffle that had culminated in an acquisition by a group of investors that reportedly included Kirk Kerkorian and Frank Manusco. *Tomorrow Never Dies*, the studio's only scheduled release for Christmas 1997, was being regarded by some as the first test of the new regime. *Variety* correspondent Rex Weiner recalled the famous MGM logo in stressing the competition posed by James Cameron's lavish blockbuster *Titanic* – a film also due to open on *Tomorrow Never Dies*' projected American release date of 19 December. 'Bond must beat the boat and save the lion,' he claimed.

In Britain, audiences didn't have as long to wait. The London premiere of the film was scheduled for 12 December; during the summer a teaser trailer comprising a high-speed mix-and-match of footage provided a tantalising glimpse of the film's action highlights. The trailer culminated with Pierce Brosnan confidently striding towards camera and delivering a new twist on a line first uttered by Sean Connery some 35 years before. 'The name's Bond,' he asserted. 'You know the rest.'